The Changing Face of the "Native Speaker"

Trends in Applied Linguistics

Series edited by
Ulrike Jessner

Volume 31

The Changing Face of the "Native Speaker"

—

Perspectives from Multilingualism and Globalization

Edited by
Nikolay Slavkov, Sílvia Melo-Pfeifer,
Nadja Kerschhofer-Puhalo

ISBN 978-1-5015-2148-5
e-ISBN (PDF) 978-1-5015-1235-3
e-ISBN (EPUB) 978-1-5015-1210-0
ISSN 1868-6362

Library of Congress Control Number: 2021940954

Bibliographic information published by the Deutsche Nationalbibliothek
The Deutsche Nationalbibliothek lists this publication in the Deutsche Nationalbibliografie;
detailed bibliographic data are available on the Internet at http://dnb.dnb.de.

© 2023 Walter de Gruyter, Inc., Boston/Berlin
This volume is text- and page-identical with the hardback published in 2022.
Typesetting: Integra Software Services Pvt. Ltd.
Printing and binding: CPI books GmbH, Leck

www.degruyter.com

Contents

Nikolay Slavkov, Sílvia Melo-Pfeifer, Nadja Kerschhofer-Puhalo
Introduction: The changing face of the "native speaker" —— 1

Part one: Conceptual discussions

Jean-Marc Dewaele, Thomas H. Bak, Lourdes Ortega
Chapter 1
Why the mythical "native speaker" has mud on its face —— 25

Ulrike Jessner, Barbara Hofer, Emese Malzer-Papp
Chapter 2
The multilingual and multicompetent native speaker —— 47

Joan Pujolar
Chapter 3
New speakers: New linguistic subjects —— 71

Part two: Practices and representations

Jean-François de Pietro
Chapter 4
Is there a native speaker in the class? A didactic view of a problematic notion —— 103

Maria Zerva
Chapter 5
On the paradox of being native speakers of two "competing" languages: Turkish as the mother or the father tongue of Greek nationals —— 133

Olga Kagan, Miriam Minkov, Ekaterina Protassova, Mila Schwartz
Chapter 6
What kind of speakers are these? Placing heritage speakers of Russian on a continuum —— 155

Sofia Stratilaki-Klein
Chapter 7
The out-of-sight of "native speaker": A critical journey through models of social representations of plurilingual identities —— 179

Sílvia Melo-Pfeifer
Chapter 8
***Practice-proof concepts?* Rethinking linguistic borders and families in multilingual communication: Exploiting the relationship between intercomprehension and translanguaging —— 209**

Part three: **Policies and controversies**

Mariana Bono
Chapter 9
Provenance and possession: Rethinking the mother tongue —— 233

Nkonko M. Kamwangamalu
Chapter 10
The pluricentricity and ownership of English —— 253

Wendy D. Bokhorst-Heng, Kelle L. Marshall
Chapter 11
"I want to be bilingual!" Contested imaginings of bilingualism in New Brunswick, Canada —— 285

Nadja Kerschhofer-Puhalo, Nikolay Slavkov
Chapter 12
Questioning the questions: Institutional and individual perspectives on children's language repertoires —— 315

Jim Cummins
Afterword —— 347

Index —— 353

Nikolay Slavkov, Sílvia Melo-Pfeifer, Nadja Kerschhofer-Puhalo

Introduction: The changing face of the "native speaker"

Perspectives from multilingualism and globalization

1 The longstanding native speaker conundrum and the rationale behind this volume

Concepts used to approach and describe social and individual multilingualism are interpretative frameworks and constitutive of the reality they are intended to reflect. Because they have a biography, concepts cannot simply be considered part of a neutral apparatus of academic research or social structures. Assuming that concepts are not neutral leads us to believe that their use is not innocuous and that it induces a certain view of linguistic realities. We reflect on this by focusing specifically on the notion of *the native speaker* and by problematizing it, in terms of its conceptual underpinnings, the practices and discourses it promotes, the language policy perspectives it offers, and the political implications it may have. This volume is thus dedicated to a multifaceted and controversial concept, one that carries strong connotations related to monolingual proficiency and that induces a lot of questioning related to its (in)adequacy in the context of the "multilingual turn" (May 2014). The term *multilingualism*, as a known pre-globalization phenomenon but also a hyper-visible consequence of globalization, is used throughout this book as both *social* multilingualism, meaning the co-presence of different languages at the societal level as well as *individual* multilingualism, referring to individual linguistic repertoires, which have more recently been established as plurilingual competence and plurilingualism (Coste, Moore, and Zarate 1997, 2009; Moore, 2006, and subsequent work).

The question readers might be asking themselves is: Why another book about "the native speaker"? We would like to answer by drawing on Holliday's words:

> Although the native-non-native speaker division is well-established as a problem, as an ideology, native-speakerism has almost disappeared between the lines of our everyday professional lives. This is particularly damaging because issues may appear to have been solved when in fact they have not. (2015: 11)

Nikolay Slavkov, University of Ottawa, e-mail: nikolay.slavkov@uottawa.ca
Sílvia Melo-Pfeifer, University of Hamburg, e-mail: silvia.melo-pfeifer@uni-hamburg.de
Nadja Kerschhofer-Puhalo, University of Vienna, e-mail: nadja.kerschhofer@univie.ac.at

https://doi.org/10.1515/9781501512353-001

We believe that even though previous publications have consistently addressed the concept of the native speaker from various perspectives, its presence – sometimes tacit and other times overt – can be felt frequently on individual, professional, cultural, and societal levels. As such, the concept needs to be continually uncovered, discussed, and (re-)problematized. As we write this introduction in the summer of 2020, large-scale anti-racist protests are unfolding in the United States and around the world, and it is thus impossible to not draw parallels between the core focus of this book and long-standing questions of race, ethnicity, equality, and gender, to name just a few. Even though these complex issues have been known and discussed for many years, they persist and regularly cause outbursts of social debate that will invariably continue to occur for many more years to come. Similarly, the construct that we embark on will likely continue to generate debate in the future, bringing our thinking, practices, ideologies, pedagogies, and policies to a new level over and over again.

Our work and our decision to propose this volume have been informed by a number of previous calls for equity and inclusion in the language teaching and learning, teacher training, and language policy domains, amongst others. We are particularly influenced by scholars such as Vivian Cook (1991, 1999, see also Cook and Wei 2016) who criticised native-speaking norms as idealized, unattainable, irrelevant, and unfair and introduced the idea of *multicompetence*. We are also greatly influenced by Jim Cummins, one of the pioneers of a long-standing effort in Canada and around the world to support and increase linguistic equity and diversity in education. Cummins has long been exposing and opposing monolingual norms through seminal contributions such as the concepts of basic interpersonal communicative skills (BICS) and cognitive academic language proficiency (CALP) (Cummins 2008, 1981, 1979a), identity texts (Cummins and Early 2010), and linguistic interdependence (Cummins 1979b, 1991). A particularly apt recent example of his consistent program of countering monolingual norms is his critical characterization of Canadian bilingual education as "two solitudes" (Cummins 2007), the idea that English and French are continually treated as two separate monolingual goals and realities (see also Grosjean 1989, for the well-known appeal to scholars to recognize that a bilingual does not equal two monolinguals in one person).[1]

---

[1] Cummins' use of the term "two solitudes" draws on the quintessential Canadian novel by Hugh McLennan (1945) describing mid twentieth century Canadian society as two distinct dominant groups, English-speaking and French-speaking, who live side by side in the same country but are separated by a great linguistic and cultural divide and by a determination to not mix together and to continue on a path of unicultural and unilingual development in the foreseeable future. This has, of course, changed to a large degree over the years, but monolingual biases and orientations nonetheless remain strong in a country that is popularly portrayed as bilingual and multicultural.

Other scholars whose work has greatly influenced us in deciding to pursue this edited volume include Alan Davies (1991, 2003, 2013) who offered seminal advances in exposing and criticising the notion of the native speaker in applied linguistics, Ben Rampton (1990) who proposed alternative terminology (expertise, inheritance, and affiliation) to overcome the inaccuracies and inequities in the concept, and Thomas Paikeday (1985) who famously declared the native speaker as "dead". The question that remains – to use a phrase from the title of a film by Jim Jarmusch (2019) – is: What if "the dead don't die"?

In addition to the above authors, many others have, of course, contributed to a now significant body of critical literature and will be mentioned in the remaining sections of this introduction and the contributions included in the volume.

2 Being trapped by the very concepts and terms we denounce

The concept of a native speaker establishes conceptual connections with other terms, such as *mother tongue*, *first language*, and more generally with a monolingual perspective of language. What such terms have in common is that they are marked by a Western bias towards a nation-state organization of society that discursively constructs the inescapability of the "native speaker" both in social and scientific imagination. Thus, we are all more or less trapped by this notion on various levels. As Makoni and Pennycock (2007) and, more recently, Gramling (2016) recall, the native speaker is an invention parallel to other imagined and deeply entrenched notions such as "language" or "monolingualism". Holliday also explains that "native speaker" and "non-native speaker" are clearly constructed notions "because they are not self-evident on technical linguistic or even nationality grounds" (2015: 13) and should not be put into different speaker groups.

In the realm of the announced and praised "multilingual turn" in (language) education (Conteh and Meier 2014; May 2014), a call was made to rethink concepts whose continued circulation may internalise and reproduce inventions, such as "native speaker" (Ortega 2014) and "mother tongue" (Melo-Pfeifer 2018, 2019). This rethinking of the conceptual "business as usual" does not immediately imply a ban on the terms, reminding us that changing or eliminating the "monolingual habitus" (Gogolin 1994) that still pervades education and research is not an easy or trivial process. In fact, as Melo-Pfeifer (2019) concludes, some terms, such as "mother tongue", might still make sense from the perspective of speakers themselves and may have naturalised uses in their (professional) communities (e.g. the communities of current or future teachers). Furthermore, the term "mother tongue" has a strong affective resonance and speakers can feel empowered by associating themselves to a language, especially in a setting in which they are part of a minority or are minoritised. As "mother tongue" has so many different meanings, the criteria for determining it are themselves controversial, overlapping, or contradicting at times (Dabène 1994). Thus, a cautionary tale is called for when revisiting concepts apparently detached from the "multilingual turn" because individuals might want to be associated with a language or because alternatives can induce more misunderstandings than they can effectively solve. "L1", "mother tongue", "home language", "preferred language", and so on, may all face challenges related to technical accuracy, notions of status, prestige, and power, and the reality that they reflect or (re-)create. It may thus be necessary to take a careful and nuanced stance in revisiting the concepts when using a multilingual lens rather than dismantling them completely.

Related to the above ideas is De Pietro's claim (this volume) that the "native speaker" is entrenched in the social representations of what it means to speak a language, and, as a social representation, it is shared and shapes human relationships constitutive of reality. Furthermore, Péter Medgyes, a pioneer in the study of the differences between native and non-native language teachers, while admitting that "the dichotomy does not stand up to close scrutiny" concedes that "the majority of us still fall into either the native or non-native category" stressing that both have different characteristics, "different" used without value judgment (2017: IX). Medgyes further argues that acknowledging the differences may lead to the empowerment of the so-called non-native teacher (see also studies included in Copland, Garton, and Mann 2016; Cheung, Ben Said, and Park 2015; Martínez Agudo 2017). As Copland, Garton, and Mann put it (using a theoretically critical tone):

> (. . .) our classroom observations and the data from interviews with LETs [Local English Teachers] and NESTs [Native English Speaking Teachers] did not always chime with the positions in the academic literature, particularly those which argue from a theoretical position that the native speaker no longer exists, that 'native-speakerism' always works in favour of NESTs, or that the clash of educational cultures makes co-teaching a particularly challenging educational practice. (2016: 5)

The truth that has emerged over the course of several decades is that the native speaker has been commonly used as an abstract entity against which non-native speakers and teachers are compared in terms of linguistic proficiency, in rather qualitative terms, usually to the benefit of the former. Holliday coined the term "native-speakerism" (2005: 49) to refer to the widespread belief, in the field of English education, that "[n]ative speakers represent a 'Western culture' from which spring the ideals both of the language and of language teaching methodology." If we extend the term and its implications beyond the language teaching domain, it leads to the assumption that "the native speaker" represents some sort of moral, linguistic, or professional superiority.

To sum up, even though we might, as researchers, practitioners, and teacher trainers, see the concept of "native speaker" as blatantly outdated, it is still used partially because of the difficulties attached to avoiding it while criticizing it (Holliday 2015). As Medgyes concedes, other concepts "have not stood the test of time" (2013: 499). And more recently, Medgyes and Kiss contend:

> In an effort to replace the NEST/non-NEST nomenclature, several alternative labels have been recommended, but none of them are widely used in academic or classroom discourse (. . .); the two opposing terms "despite all their drawbacks, are the reality which cannot be simply 'magicked-away' (Pacek, 2005: 243)". It is a strange paradox that even the most vocal opponents are in the habit of using the NEST/non-NEST labels (. . .)"[2]
> (2020: 95)

So. . . the native speaker has a past and a present. Does it also have a future?

3 The native speaker: pride and prejudice?

As already established, while a number of researchers have pointed out that the "native speaker" concept is inadequate in many ways, it still enjoys a privileged status in various conceptual, methodological, and empirical research paradigms, in educational and institutional practices, and in social and political structures and discourses for some of the reasons described in the previous section. This is reminiscent of the well-known novel by Jane Austen, "Pride and Prejudice", where the author aptly describes inequitable and outdated traditions, laws, and practices related to gender, status, and wealth that were very difficult to shake off by the characters and by British society in general at that time. In a similar vein, countering Paikeday's (1985) claim that the native speaker is dead, Copland, Garton, and Mann declare that in fact "the concept of the native speaker is alive and kicking, although (. . .) what being a 'native speaker' entails is contextual and contested" (2016: 8). They claim that nowadays it is not being a native or a non-native speaker that has consequences in terms of getting a job or advancing in society, but rather ethnic, racial, and gender issues, as individual identities are multi-layered; they further argue that the

---

[2] For additional discussion, see also the contribution by Dewaele, Bak, and Ortega (this volume).

concept of native/non-native interacts intersectionally with other categories (see also Yazan and Lindhal 2020). As such, the "native speaker" label perhaps does have a future as long as we manage to disentangle it from various issues of discrimination. And this is indeed how native-speaker competence, as a theoretical construct, is intended to be used in the methodological framework of Chomskyan generative linguistics; that is, as an abstract scientific tool devoid of social connotations or biases. But more than just theoretical constructs, we need *theorethical* ones, a neologism merging "theoretic" and "ethical", meaning concepts that imply a positive, affirming, empowering, and celebratory attitude towards linguistic and cultural repertoires and experiences (Melo-Pfeifer and Chik 2020: 5).

On a practical, daily-life level, there are concrete challenges that the "native speaker" concept faces today. In a world of unprecedented mass (re)migrations, super-diversity, and continued globalization, the notion of a (single) native language simply does not apply or applies with a number of caveats to various populations. For example, children who are adopted internationally, immigrant families, Indigenous people exposed to increased contact with a majority or a national language, people who are educated in a language other than their original one, infants who have been exposed to regular input in two or more languages from birth, and people who intermarry across cultural and linguistic communities are just a few cases where the notion of a (single) "native" or "first" language fails to meet its fixed and presumably straightforward meaning. Such contexts are nowadays ubiquitous around the world and have drawn an increasing amount of interest, bringing to a new level our awareness of issues related to language repertoires (involving uneven proficiencies in different languages and different domains), literacy practices, and fluid/hybrid identities.

In an attempt to address contexts such as the ones mentioned above, recent thinking in bilingualism and multilingualism has advanced new theoretical frameworks and conceptualizations. We mentioned some of these earlier, but are repeating them here in the context of others, which may be overlapping, complementary, or even contradictory. They include translanguaging (Canagarajah 2013; García 2009; García and Wei 2014; Williams 1996), multicompetence (Cook 1991, 1999; Cook and Wei 2016), plurilingualism (Coste, Moore, and Zarate 1997, 2009), dominant language constellations and multilingualism as a new linguistic dispensation (Aronin and Singleton 2008, 2012; Aronin 2019), new speaker paradigms (O'Rourke and Ramallo 2011), and recognition of bilingual/multilingual first language acquisition involves more than a single language as "first" (De Houwer 2009), to name just a few.

We embrace the above frameworks as a whole because their composite elements generally acknowledge that the term "native" says too little about the linguistic skills of the speaker. At the same time, the native speaker doesn't need to be monolingual and this volume does not want to engage in any form of "de-competencing" the native speaker (see Gramling 2016: 52). The non-native speaker is, we could argue, also a native speaker in at least one language (see also the contribution by Jessner et al. in this volume). This is why associations such as "native speaker/monolingualism" and "non-native speaker/poor monolingual" have to be put into perspective, extending their narrow scope. In other words, the native speaker can be either monolingual or plurilingual, whilst the non-native is always plurilingual, meaning able to use different linguistic resources to co-construct meaning. Despite these differences, in what comes to be a rather unexplored domain in applied language studies, both natives and non-natives, monolinguals and plurilinguals can translanguage. That is, even what would be labeled a monolingual native speaker is able to engage in combined and articulated use of language(s) and other semiotic resources; this involves the composite nature of all languages as exemplified in the following statement by Derrida "We only ever speak one language. We never speak only one language" (Derrida 1998: 7; see also Yildiz 2012, regarding "the foreign in the mother tongue").

4 Aims and scope of the volume

As already indicated, the purpose of discussing the concept of "native speaker" in this volume is to unveil current misconceptions, trustful and distrustful assumptions, and the acceptability of related terms in our current linguistic dispensation marked by hyperdiversity of linguistic resources circulating in particular social contexts. We have convened a pool of both well-established and emerging scholars who come from various parts of the world and we have asked them to contribute conceptual-theoretical, methodological, and empirical studies from different contexts, thus addressing the problematic of the native speaker from multiple unique angles. We believe that this approach has a strong potential to advance the overall thinking in the field and ultimately produce a positive impact in our global world.

As we will see throughout the book, most of the authors chose to uncover implicit and explicit monolingual norms, which are rigid, static and often do not reflect (socio)linguistic realities highlighted by the use of the concept. Some of these authors claim that monolingual norms are ubiquitous in educational, organizational, and societal contexts around the world. The *ethos* of such contributions revolves around countering this and promoting bilingual and multilingual alternatives that are grounded in research, and are fluid, flexible, and relevant in an increasingly globalized world. Other contributions are more "native-speaker friendly" and acknowledge the usability or perhaps even inevitability of the term in research and in people's daily realities. Nonetheless, in addressing the question of whether the supremacy of the native speaker concept is appropriate given the diversity, fluidity, and dynamicity of today's global world, the contributions of the volume offer a resounding *No* as an answer. Taken together, these discussions constitute a new perspective, or the "changing face" of the native speaker, which represents the overarching core theme of the volume.

5 Organization of the volume

We have organised the twelve contributions of the book thematically into three sections. Section one focuses on conceptual-theoretical contributions, section two focuses on analyses of practices and representations, and section three focuses on policies and controversies. We must acknowledge that these thematic sections are far from clear-cut, are delineated along subjective lines, and often overlap. For instance, conceptual-theoretical contributions may also draw on policies and practices, while chapters dedicated to practices and representations may also involve conceptual-theoretical aspects, and so on. Nonetheless, we believe this organization will help the reader experience some common flavours that we felt "bind" the contributions within the three sections.

Section 1: Conceptual-theoretical discussions. This section includes 3 chapters addressing the concept of the "native speaker" from different but converging theoretical perspectives and signaling different aspects of the pervasiveness of native-speakerism. They all foreground the need to rethink the importance accorded to the native speaker in teaching and learning, in society, and in research. Some chapters revisit the history of the concept, discussing its foundations and (a)historicity, while others apply a multilingual lens to "decline it" in the plural form or suggest alternative concepts and terms.

In the inaugurating chapter of this section by Jean-Marc Dewaele, Thomas H. Bak and Lourdes Ortega called "Why the mythical 'native speaker' has mud on its face", the prejudices attached to the native speaker and the inequalities promoted by the dichotomy "native speaker/non-native speaker" (NS/NNS) are unveiled. After recounting the history of the concept "non-native" and commenting on its difficult and sometimes only approximate translation in other languages, the authors go on to recall the history of successive trials of substituting those concepts for less awkward ones. They propose substituting NS/NNS by L1/LX user and end their contribution by teasing the reader with the following question: "Will the new terminology and concept of L1/LX user take hold?"

In "The multilingual and multicompetent native speaker", Ulrike Jessner, Barbara Hofer and Emese Malzer-Papp explore different dimensions of the concept "native speaker" in general and "nativeness" more specifically, from a historical, political, linguistic, economic, and educational perspective. The authors adopt a dynamic and complex systems theory lens to challenge these concepts. They eloquently recall that the "native speaker" is a political, social, and linguistic construct as well as a trademark (similar to what in other literature may be called "commodification") in the field of English language teaching and learning, among others. The authors also acknowledge the still prevalent native speaker norms in educational institutions and expose two persistent myths in foreign language education: the teacher as a native speaker and the student as a future one. The chapter ends by highlighting the advantages of the multilingual speaker as a counterpart of the native speaker and by touching upon the emergence and use of another kind of nativeness: the "digital native".

In "New speakers: new linguistic subjects", Joan Pujolar analyzes the phenomenon of "new speakers" who have acquired a minority language through formal learning and are often contrasted with the community of "native speakers". New speakers seem at odds with received notions of belonging and identity. This becomes even more virulent with new speakers who can be constructed as racially different. Under the theoretical lens of studies on subjectivity, the author analyzes "linguistic mudes" of potential bilinguals who are making a claim for recognition as Catalan speakers in a field of tension between self- and other-categorization. The chapter provides a critical approach to the construction of language-based ethnicity and the specific affordances that language-based categorizations offer to subjectivity debates. The material shows that social classifications based on nationalist and colonialist understandings that co-naturalize language and culture are still prevalent, but are increasingly contested in late-modern societies by more fluent and hybrid identities of becoming.

Section 2: Practices and Representations. This section includes 5 chapters reporting on empirical studies or describing practices in formal educational and social contexts, where the representations related to the presence of "the native" are tacitly or implicitly felt and/or made salient in discourse and in praxis.

Jean-François de Pietro, in a chapter called "Is there a native speaker in the class? A didactic view of a problematic notion" acknowledges the role of social representations in the construction of linguistic facts and realities. He posits that even if the concept of a "native speaker" has a number of flaws, it is still largely entrenched in the social imagination. Adopting a (socio)didactic perspective, this contribution reveals how in school contexts the native speaker and, more visibly, the mother tongue are concepts enjoying consistent use in interaction. This is the case particularly in situations where efforts are made to construct a positive relationship with linguistic diversity in the classroom and in daily exolingual interactions. Thus, the author reminds us that if we take the specific perspective of the speakers, we have to recognise that the native speaker still exists. In this light, our question whether the "native speaker still makes sense", receives a conflicting answer: "yes, it does" and "no, it doesn't", depending on the circumstances.

In "On the paradox of being native speakers of two 'competing' languages: Turkish as the Mother or the Father Tongue of Greek nationals", Maria Zerva discusses the ideologies that bind the notion of "mother tongue" with the notion of "national identity". Taking a sociolinguistic stance, the author shows the dangers of naturalising the "mother tongue" as a sign of affiliation and loyalty to "national identity". Closely analysing the complex case of Turkish-speaking Orthodox Christian Greeks, Zerva decorticates the ambiguities and the love and hate relationships around the expressions "mother/father tongue" and "native speaker", showing that being or denying being called a native speaker of a so-called mother tongue can be a matter of personal choice rather than an external attribution.

"What kind of speakers are these? Placing heritage Russian speakers on a continuum" by Olga Kagan, Miriam Minkov, Ekaterina Protassova, and Mila Schwartz draws on data from four countries (Finland, Germany, Israel, and the United States) and focuses on Russian heritage speakers. The authors describe patterns of hybrid language use attested in all four populations studied and position the participants in a complex middle ground or a special 'no-man's zone'. This zone is in the midst of conflicting pressures and influences that come from various sources: a native speaker ideal, generally based on a monolingual norm of the Russian language coming from Russia as a perceived homeland and owner of the standard; the dominant language of the new host countries for the 1.5 or second-generation speakers originating from large waves of Russian immigrants; and the emerging idea of pluricentricity.

Sofia Stratilaki-Klein, in "The out-of-sight in plurilingual identities: A critical journey through models of social representations", analyzes how the school continues to reproduce injustice and inequality by engaging in teaching and learning of separated skills in different foreign languages, instead of acknowledging the benefits of plurilingualism. Adopting a conceptual framework intended to study social representations of plurilingual identities by immigrant children, she analyzes selected excerpts of interviews with children and parents living in France. Stratilaki-Klein offers the reader two discursive foci: an individual and a social one. The analysis reveals that some children and their parents have rather positive representations of plurilingualism, which differ from the negative discourse of certain actors in the education system. The study is a bold contribution to the increasing amount of literature indicating that despite changing demographics and sociolinguistic characteristics of student populations, the school is still encapsulated within a monolingual mindset.

In the last chapter of this section, called "Practice-proof concepts? Rethinking linguistic borders and families in multilingual communication: exploiting the relationship between intercomprehension and translanguaging", Sílvia Melo-Pfeifer sets out to expose the gap between theoretical conceptualisations (namely around "translanguaging") and speakers' discursive use of concepts. After discussing the notion of "translanguaging" and different positions in the research about its principles, the author analyzes multilingual chat room interactions where students use different romance languages. She makes the claim that, while speakers may engage in translanguaging in a situation that explicitly supports a multilingual communicative contract (although still monoglossic), native-speakerism is still visible in their use of dichotomies such as "native/non-native" and "mother tongue/ foreign language" as well as in the naming of languages, linguistic families and linguistic borders (see also Melo-Pfeifer and Araújo e Sá 2018). Thus, some notions associated with the "multilingual turn", such as "translanguaging", might seem to be "practice-proof concepts", or in other words theoretical concepts detached from speakers' realities and practices (an equivalent claim is made by Ortega 2014 while criticizing the use of the term "native speaker").

Section 3: Policies and controversies. This section is composed of 4 chapters analysing deeply ingrained policy issues that are not often brought to the foreground. The United States, Officially Bilingual Canada, Central Europe, and Africa are the geopolitical and sociolinguistic contexts of some post-colonial language-in-education concepts and policies covered by the authors contributing to the section. The four chapters reflect on and unanimously accept the need to rethink how ideas related to "native speaker", "mother tongue", or "bilingualism" shape national and educational policies and identities.

In "Provenance and Possession: Rethinking the Mother Tongue", Mariana Bono challenges the apparent innocuousness of the term "mother tongue", and reconsiders two connotations it carries (provenance and possession) as well as the burden they pose to a growing body of a diverse student population. As she poetically puts it, "[such students] bring to our campus and to our classrooms languages known or lost, remembered or forgotten, desired or rejected". Resorting to a diversity of perspectives on the "mother tongue", ranging from multilingual studies to linguistic anthropology, post-structural and postcolonial theory, Bono denounces and counters the dynamics of exclusion created and reinforced by the ideologies attached to the "native speaker" and the "mother tongue". The author demonstrates how these terms participate in the discursive construction of "the Other", thus becoming instruments of othering alongside gender, ethnic origin, and race in the reproduction of "glottopolitical hierarchies".

In his chapter on "The pluricentricity and ownership of English" Nkonko Kamwangamalu addresses Braj Kachru's "new Englishes" paradigm that proposes three concentric circles (the Inner, the Outer and the Expanding Circle) of English. This paradigm has been equated by some scholars with the trichotomy of English as a *native, a second, or a foreign* language. Kamwangamalu discusses the theoretical and functional usefulness of the distinction of native vs. non-native Englishes, which mirrors the traditional ENL/ESL dichotomy. Drawing on data from African Englishes, the author investigates some processes involved in the acculturation of English in both post-colonial and non-colonial contexts. He also presents lexical, syntactic and semantic features of marking ownership of English in African contexts. Such features include lexical transfer, internal lexical creativity, tag questions, and idiomatic expressions and are used by the author to contextualize the discussion of the acculturation and ownership of English in Outer Circle communities where English is spoken by some as first or only language. Favouring the notion of "English as a first language" as more appropriate than "English as a native language", the author argues that the English language has become pluricentric with centers not only in the Inner, but also in the Outer, and arguably the Expanding Circle.

"*I want to be bilingual!* Contested imaginings of bilingualism in New Brunswick, Canada" is a chapter by Wendy Bokhorst-Heng and Kelle L. Marshall that tackles language policies, language identity, and some of the various challenges of French immersion programming in Canada. It tells the story of a particular episode in the recent history of New Brunswick (ironically, the only officially bilingual province in Canada) where the provincial government decided to eliminate Early French Immersion in primary schools and introduce it at a later point in the curriculum. This caused various protests around the province and the authors traced the efforts of anglophone parents in the village of Sackville who chose to employ a curious ancient Acadian tradition (known as the *tintamarre*) to contest the government's new policy. Essentially, these parents demanded that their children receive the opportunity to be educated primarily not in their native language (English), but in French, from an early point in their lives. This exposes a curious Canadian paradox: when it comes to official languages, the right to early education in the native language is guaranteed by federal and provincial legislation, but the right to (early) bilingual education is not, and sometimes parents have to fight for access to this "privilege".

"Questioning the Questions: Institutional and Individual Perspectives on Child Language Repertoires", by Nadja Kerschhofer-Puhalo and Nikolay Slavkov, is a contribution that draws on data from two studies, one in Austria and one in

Canada. The Canadian study explores the methodological and ideological positioning of language background questions included in primary school registration forms. The Austrian study focuses on plurilingual self-portraits and on interviews with school children who describe their language repertoires in words and images. Rather than offering a comparison between the two countries, the authors draw on the data as a conceptual springboard for a discussion of two different perspectives on individual language repertoires. One is top-down, rigid, and linear: preconceived notions about children's language repertoires ensuing from educational administrations' questionnaires. The other is bottom-up, non-linear, heterogenous, and continuously re-negotiated: children's own perceptions. The chapter demonstrates how notions such as "mother tongue", "first" or "native" language that are seemingly straightforward and fixed under the first perspective become fuzzy, fluid, and complex under the second (see also Jim Cummins' afterward to this volume).

6 Editors' personal and professional positionalities

All three editors have experiences and observations in crossing borders (real and metaphorical), which is important in explaining how they came together to co-edit a volume about "the native speaker". Positionality refers to the placement of researchers in relation to the objects they investigate, in this case, the concept of "the native speaker". It has to be acknowledged that this positionality also influences how we see the theme and how our understanding and outlook of the concept may be biased. That is why, for the sake of transparency, we decided to include a section in this introduction where we present some aspects of our own personal experiences, identities and positionalities as researchers.

Nikolay Slavkov is originally from Bulgaria but left his home country in his early twenties. After living, studying, and working in various other countries, including the United States, China, and Ethiopia, he now calls Canada home. Issues of global migration and the related diversity of linguistic experiences are known to him firsthand, as they are known to millions of other people who have moved around due to globalization. The concept of a native speaker has fascinated him for a long time. As a teenager in Bulgaria, he used to listen casually to British tourists who came to the ski slopes of the Rila Mountains and, as an English language learner at that point, he tried to strike conversations with them and impersonate their accents. Later on, as an undergraduate exchange student in the United States, he jokingly competed with other international students about who had more authentic American pronunciation (i.e. "no foreign accent") and asked American students (native speakers) to act as judges. He lost that contest to a close friend (an international student from Estonia) and is now quite happy with his non-native English pronunciation. In retrospect, he realizes how long it took him to revoke the universally accorded privileged status of native-speakerism and to build an identity as a competent multilingual speaker; that is, to use the term proposed by Vivian Cook, Nikolay likes to think of himself as a multicompetent individual who does not want or try to assimilate into a largely unattainable norm or target either linguistically or socially. Nikolay has also become gradually aware of the inadequacy of the term "native speaker" in the course of his life because English, his non-native language, eventually became his strongest tool of written expression while other languages in his repertoire, including his "native" Bulgarian, have remained far less developed and underused in this respect, even though he has maintained a Bulgarian identity and has transmitted this language to his children.

Nikolay Slavkov's research in applied linguistics became influenced by the notion of a native speaker through his work with children who are bilingual from birth (Slavkov 2015). Bilingual first language acquisition (BFLA) is a term popularized by De Houwer (1990, 2009) that Nikolay embraces as it contributes to the now wide recognition that a BFLA child has two first or two native languages, even though one or both of them may not conform to a monolingual native speaking norm. His recent work on language ideology and language policy amounts to a series of studies investigating how bilingual or multilingual children's repertoires are captured (or not) through language background questionnaires included in school registration forms across Canada (2016, 2018, 2020). This work exposes native-speaker-oriented biases and ideologies embedded in seemingly innocuous administrative artifacts such as the simple question of "What is your child's first language?" or "What is your child's home language?". Such questions are essentially posed to parents or guardians upon registering their children for primary school in Canada, and as such both the practical and ideological scope of language background profiling is significant. This work was inspired by a personal experience with the primary school system where Nikolay saw his trilingual daughter's repertoire repeatedly misrepresented in the school's registration database, a "technical error" that he believes is systematic and symptomatic of native-speaking ideological biases coupled with technological, spatial, and terminological constraints.

Sílvia Melo-Pfeifer, a Portuguese living and working in Germany, has been observing how passing or not passing for a native speaker is, in different settings, experienced by herself as a kind of micro-aggression, undermining different aspects of her identity, or as an explanation of what it means to be plurilingual. In different papers with an auto-ethnographic stance (e.g. Melo-Pfeifer 2017), she revealed how "authentic" is constantly attached to her personality as a teacher at a higher education institution in Germany and how this has made her reflect on what that adjective might mean. Authenticity was sometimes defined by her students as "not even trying to pass for a native", which is "not really negative" (meaning, "well, it might be somehow negative"). And then, there is always the name, this kind of hybrid German-whatever... In different contexts, professional, social, and familial, being constantly corrected in cases where the form becomes more salient than the content, is also a daily experience of what it means not to be a native speaker for Sílvia, that is, not to be able to pass for one. But also passing for a native speaker, a Portuguese native, might come with signs of micro-aggression, as soon as aspects related to migrant and economic status, hierarchy, and (lack of) German language skills are brought to the interaction arena.

In her scholarly work, Sílvia Melo-Pfeifer argues that just as "mother tongue", also the "native speaker" has defenders and detractors. She acknowledges that the "explanatory adequacy" of "native speaker" and the proprieties attached to this particular concept sometimes justify certain positionalities in her research (Flores and Melo-Pfeifer 2014; Melo-Pfeifer 2017; Yanaprasart and Melo-Pfeifer 2019). Following Flores and Melo-Pfeifer's reasoning, comparing the "native" child to the "non-native" (child growing up bilingually or acquiring the majority language) might be advantageous for the non-native, serving as an "argument" that advocates for bilingual and multilingual education, for breaking the prejudice against "unbalanced bilingualism", and for deconstructing negative stereotypes. Furthermore, when analysing how students assessed her teaching, Sílvia came to notice that they were keen to accept her multilingual teaching approaches and practices and learn from her despite her "non-native" status (that is, having an accent and making mistakes in the language of instruction). This led her to believe that perhaps it is not the concept *per se* that is problematic, but the misusages attached to it (reminiscent of Copland, Garton, and Mann's 2016 claim mentioned earlier in this introduction). Aware of Holliday's critical observation, Sílvia acknowledges that she may be domesticating the problem by constructing the dichotomy of native and non-native speakers as harmless and useful, "as long as [the terms] are employed carefully and objectively" (Holliday 2015: 17). She believes that such a positionality is a much needed critical stance in research and should be reflected upon. She is trying to do it here, in public!

Nadja Kerschhofer-Puhalo was born in Vienna and raised in a multilingual and translocal family dispersed in such distant parts of the world as Austria, Egypt, Croatia, Lebanon, France or Australia. She grew up in Austria in a time when a multilingual family situation was seen as literally strange, exceptional or exotic. When people ask her where she comes from, she prefers to answer "from Vienna", always waiting for the next question: "But where do you *really* come from?" While German is her "first language", it is not her "mother tongue". The women in her family, who had enjoyed their education in French schools in the Middle East (where "native languages" were forbidden), were practising what we today would call translanguaging, but what was for them every-day practice: hopping and switching between different "languages", voices and accents, as they changed topic or interaction partners, creating by their voices, stories and daily routines a heterotopic space of their own, inspired by linguistic, ethnic, cultural and religious diversity experienced in their youth in Cairo, Alexandria or Beirut. In this "language and diversity hub" her interest for comparing words, accents and whole systems of communicative resources grew even further as she studied modern and classical languages. Studying Linguistics, Oriental Philology, and Teaching German as a Second Language in Vienna and Berlin she engaged in the study of all language-related matters, beyond the local towards more global and universal aspects; the idea of common underlying principles of human language was particularly fascinating to her. As a teacher of German and adult basic education, she encountered the many facets of second language acquisition and linguistic diversity, but also the learners' struggles for agency, participation and acceptance in their new lives after migration.

Nadja Kerschhofer-Puhalo's current research interests focus on multilingualism and multiliteracies, combining her scientific work in second language acquisition and literacy studies with experiences in pedagogical contexts and teacher education. Since 2013, Nadja has been leader of the Literacies and Multilingualism research group at the University of Vienna and is engaged in several projects on literacy, multilingualism, and identity. Combining linguistic and pedagogical approaches, she investigates the many facets of plurilingual children's reading and writing acquisition in contexts of migration, multilingualism, and multimedia use. In a participatory research design and inspired by the New Literacy Studies, she collaborates with teachers and students in primary and secondary schools as well as with institutions of adult education and in-service-teacher training. The project *My Literacies* investigated primary school children's language and literacy practices in school and in out-of-school contexts (Kerschhofer-Puhalo, Schreger, and Mayer 2020). The project *Views in*2 Literacies* encouraged young people and adults to share their stories about language learning and literacy acquisition on a participatory web-platform. All projects are inspired by principles of participatory research and citizen science and encourage participants to express their views and perspectives. Working with students of diverse linguistic, ethnic or national origins, Nadja observed how strongly the learners' self-concepts and personal feelings of affiliation and loyalty to "native" or family languages and majority languages, of success or deficiency are influenced by current debates on migration and education, and on language and social diversity (Kerschhofer-Puhalo and Mayer 2020). To further develop inclusive practices of research in plurilingual literacy education, she follows the general motto: There is not an "either-or" and the "in-between" or "mixed" is not a problem; moreover, reconsidering our own positionality in research is a must and combining different voices and perspectives is always an asset.

7 Intended audience

This book will interest researchers, teacher educators, and (graduate) students who wish to expand their knowledge in current, critical issues in multilingualism, new methodologies, and re-conceptualizations of traditional terms and views in the fields of applied linguistics, language education, and language policy. In addition, the book will be of interest to policymakers, language assessment professionals and organizations, as well as migration and (re)settlement agencies and services. In challenging the well-established notion of a native speaker, the book also has strong social implications that may be of interest to various activists, politicians, and members of the general public who are interested in critical social change, migration, racism, and discrimination, and other equity issues related to language and belonging.

As editors, we believe that the scope, the multiple contexts and perspectives, and geographic diversity covered by this edited volume will be beneficial for applied linguists and educators, and will also have positive social impacts on an international scale. We hope that the breadth and depth of the volume will offer readers new knowledge and appeal to multiple audiences.

References

Aronin, Larissa & David Singleton. 2008. Multilingualism as a new linguistic dispensation. *International Journal of Multilingualism* 5(1), 1–16.
Aronin, Larissa & David Singleton. 2012. *Multilingualism*. Amsterdam and Philadelphia: John Benjamins.
Aronin, Larissa. 2019. Dominant language constellation as a method of research. In Eva Vetter & Ulrike Jessner (eds.), *International research on multilingualism breaking with the monolingual perspective*, 13–26. Cham: Springer.
Canagarajah, Suresh. A. 2013. *Translingual Practice: Global Englishes and cosmopolitan relations*. New York: Routledge.
Cheung, Yin L., Selim Ben Said & Kwanghyun Park (eds.), 2015. *Advances and current trends in language teacher identity research*. London: Routledge.
Conteh, Jean & Gabriela Meier (eds.), 2014. *The multilingual turn in language education. Opportunities and challenges*. Bristol: Multilingual Matters.

Cook, Vivian. J. 1991. The poverty-of-the-stimulus argument and multicompetence. *Second Language Research* 7(2), 103–117.
Cook, Vivian. J. 1999. Going beyond the native speaker in language teaching. *TESOL Quarterly* 33, 185–209.
Cook, Vivian J. & Li Wei (eds.), 2016. *The Cambridge handbook of linguistic multi-competence.* Cambridge: Cambridge University Press.
Copland, Fiona, Steve Mann & Sue Garton. 2016. Introduction: positions, experiences and reflections on the native speaker issue. In Copland, Fiona, Sue Garton & Steve Mann (eds.), *LETs and NESTs: Voices, Views and Vignettes*, 5–19. British Council.
Copland, Fiona, Sue Garton & Steve Mann (eds.), 2016. *LETs and NESTs: Voices, Views and Vignettes.* British Council. https://www.teachingenglish.org.uk/sites/teacheng/files/pub_BC_Book_VVV_online_screen_res_FINAL.pdf (accessed 25 May 2021).
Coste, Daniel, Danièle Moore & Geneviève Zarate. 1997. *Compétence plurilingue et pluriculturelle. Vers un cadre européen commun de référence pour l'enseignement et l'apprentissage des langues vivantes: Études préparatoires.* Strasbourg: Éditions du Conseil de l'Europe.
Coste, Daniel, Danièle Moore & Geneviève Zarate. 2009. *Plurilingual and pluricultural competence.* Strasbourg: Council of Europe. Retrieved from https://rm.coe.int/090000168069d29c
Cummins, James. 1979a. Cognitive/academic language proficiency, linguistic interdependence, the optimum age question and some other matters. *Working Papers on Bilingualism* 19, 121–129.
Cummins, James. 1979b. Linguistic interdependence and the educational development of bilingual children. *Review of Educational Research* 49(2), 222–251. https://doi.org/10.3102/00346543049002222
Cummins, James. 1981. The role of primary language development in promoting educational success for language minority students. In California State Department of Education (ed.), *Schooling and language minority students: A theoretical framework*, 3–49. Los Angeles: National Dissemination and Assessment Center.
Cummins, James. 1991. Interdependence of first-and second-language proficiency in bilingual children. In Ellen Bialystok (ed.), Language processing in bilingual children, 70–89. Cambridge: Cambridge University Press. doi:10.1017/CBO9780511620652.006.
Cummins, James. 2007. Rethinking monolingual instructional strategies in multilingual classrooms. *The Canadian Journal of Applied Linguistics* 10(2), 221–240.
Cummins, James 2008. BICS and CALP: Empirical and theoretical status of the distinction. In Nancy H.Hornberger (ed.), *Encyclopedia of language and education*, 71–83. Boston, MA: Springer. https://doi.org/10.1007/978-0-387-30424-3_36 (accessed 25 may 2021).
Cummins, James & Margaret Early. 2010. *Identity texts: The collaborative creation of power in multilingual schools*. Trentham Books Ltd. Westview House 734 London Road, Oakhill, Stoke-on-Trent, Staffordshire, ST4 5NP, UK.
Dabène, Louise. 1994. *Repères sociolinguistiques pour l'enseignement des langues.* Paris: Hachette.
Davies, Alan. 1991. *The Native Speaker in Applied Linguistics.* Edinburgh: Edinburgh University Press.
Davies, Alan. 2004. The Native Speaker in Applied Linguistics. In Alan Davies & Catherine Elder (eds.), *The Handbook of Applied Linguistics*, 431–450. Oxford: Blackwell.
Davies, Alan. 2013. *Native speakers and native users: Loss and gain.* Cambridge: Cambridge University Press. doi:10.1017/CBO9781139022316

De Houwer, Annick. 1990. *The Acquisition of two languages from birth: A case study*. Cambridge: Cambridge University Press. doi:10.1017/CBO9780511519789.

De Houwer, Annick. 2009. *Bilingual First Language Acquisition*. Tonawanda, NY: Multilingual Matters.

Derrida, Jacques. 1998. *Monolingualism of the Other; or, The Prosthesis of Origins*. Stanford University Press: Stanford, California.

Flores, Cristina & Sílvia Melo-Pfeifer. 2014. O conceito 'Língua de Herança' na perspetiva da Linguística e da Didática de Línguas: considerações pluridisciplinares em torno do perfil linguístico das crianças lusodescendentes na Alemanha. *Domínios de Lingu@gem* 28(3), 16–45. Número especial "Migração, linguagem e subjetividade" [The concept 'Heritage Language' from the perspective of Linguistics and Language Didactics: multidisciplinary considerations around the linguistic profile of Lusodescendant children in Germany]. URL http://www.seer.ufu.br/index.php/dominiosdelinguagem.

García, Ofelia. 2009. *Bilingual education in the 21st century: A global perspective*. Chichester: Wiley-Blackwell.

García, Ofelia & Li Wei. 2014. *Translanguaging: Language, bilingualism and education*. New York: Palgrave Macmillan.

Gogolin, Ingrid. 1994. *Der monolinguale Habitus der multilingualen Schule*. Münster: Waxmann.

Gramling, David. 2016. *The invention of monolingualism*. London: Bloomsbury Academic.

Grosjean, François. 1989. Neurolinguists, beware! The bilingual is not two monolinguals in one person. *Brain and language 36*(1), 3–15.

Holliday, Adrian. 2005. *The struggle to teach English as an international language*. Oxford: Oxford University Press.

Holliday, Adrian. 2015. Native-speakerism: Taking the concept forward and achieving cultural belief. In Adrian Holliday, Pamela Aboshiha & Anne Swan (eds.), *(En)Countering Native-speakerism. Global Perspectives*, 11–25. Hampshire: Palgrave Macmillan.

Kerschhofer-Puhalo, Nadja, Christian Schreger & Werner Mayer. 2020. My Literacies. Insights into children's extracurricular literacy experiences. *Proceedings of the 3rd International Conference Literacy and Contemporary Society: Identities, Texts, Institutions*, Nicosia. Cyprus, 674–686. http://www.pi.ac.cy/pi/files/epimorfosi/synedria/literacy/2019/3rd_Lit_Con_Proceedings.pdf (accessed 25 May 2021)

Kerschhofer-Puhalo, Nadja & Werner Mayer (2020), Pluriliterale Identitäten und Selbstkonzepte von Grundschulkindern im Spannungsfeld zwischen Schule, Familie und Communities [Pluriliteral identities and self-concepts of primary school children between school, family and communities]. In Mirjam Egli Cuenat, Manno, Giuseppe and Desgrippes, Magalie (eds.), *Mehrschriftlichkeit und Mehrsprachenerwerb im schulischen und ausserschulischen Umfeld • Plurilittératie et apprentissages plurilingues à l'intérieur et hors du contexte scolair* [Pluriliteracies and multilingual language acquisition in school and out-of-school contexts] (Special Issue *VALS-ASLA Bulletin Suisse de Linguistique Appliquée*) 259–277.

MacLennan, Hugh. 1945. *Two Solitudes*. Macmillan of Canada.

Makoni, Sinfree & Alastair Pennycook. 2007. *Disinventing and reconstituting languages*. Clevedon: Multilingual Matters.

Martínez Agudo, Juan de Dios (ed.). 2017. *Native and non-native teachers in English language classrooms. Professional challenges and teacher education*. Berlin: De Gruyter.

May, Stephen (ed.). 2014. *The multilingual turn: Implications for SLA, TESOL and bilingual education*, 1–6. New York: Routledge.

Medgyes, Péter. 2017. Foreword. In Juan de Dios Martínez Agudo (ed.), *Native and non-native teachers in English language classrooms. Professional challenges and teacher education*, X–XI. Berlin: De Gruyter.

Medgyes, Péter. 2013. Native Speaker. In Michael Byram & Adelheid Hu (eds.), *Routledge Encyclopedia of Language Teaching and Learning*, 497–500. London: Routledge.

Medgyes, Péter. & Tamas Kiss. 2020. Quality assurance and the expatriate native speaker teacher. In Juan de Dios Martínez Agudo (ed.), *Quality in TESOL and teacher education. From a results culture towards a quality culture*, 94–102. London: Routledge.

Melo-Pfeifer, Sílvia. 2018. The multilingual turn in language education: facts and fallacies. In Andreas Bonnet & Peter Siemund (eds.), *Foreign Language Education in Multilingual Classrooms*, 191–212. New York, Amsterdam: Benjamins.

Melo-Pfeifer, Sílvia. 2019. Business as usual? (Re)conceptualizations and the multilingual turn in education. The case of mother tongue. In Eva Vetter & Ulrike Jessner (eds.), *International Research on Multilingualism: Breaking with the Monolingual Perspective*, 27–41. Cham: Springer.

Melo-Pfeifer, Sílvia. 2017. « *Es ist nicht wirklich negativ, sondern eher authentisch* »: l'authenticité plurilingue du professeur universitaire « non-natif ». Une étude de cas de la perception des étudiants à l'Université de Hambourg. *VALS-ASLA Bulletin Suisse de Linguistique Appliquée* 106, 99–119 (ISSN 1023-2044).

Melo-Pfeifer, Sílvia & Maria Helena Araújo e Sá (2018). Multilingual interaction in chat rooms: translanguaging to learn and learning to translanguage. *International Journal of Bilingual Education and Bilingualism* 21(7), 867–880. DOI: https://doi.org/10.1080/13670050.2018.1452895.

Melo-Pfeifer, Sílvia & Alice Chik. 2020. Multimodal linguistic biographies of prospective foreign language teachers in Germany: reconstructing beliefs about languages and multilingual language learning in initial teacher education. *International Journal of Multilingualism*. publ. Online https://doi.org/10.1080/14790718.2020.1753748

Moore, Danièle. 2006. *Plurilinguismes et école*. Paris: Didier.

O'Rourke, Bernadette & Fernando F. Ramallo. 2011. The native-non-native dichotomy in minority language contexts: Comparisons between Irish and Galician. *Language Problems and Language Planning* 35(2), 139–159.

Ortega, Lourdes. 2014. Ways forward for a bi/multilingual turn in SLA. In Stephen May (ed.), *The Multilingual turn. Implications for SLA, TESOL and bilingual education*, 32–53. New York & London: Routledge.

Pacek, Dorota. 2005. Personality, not nationality: Foreign students' perceptions of a non-native lecturer of English at a British University. In Enric Llurda (ed.), Non-native language teachers: Perceptions, challenges and contributions to the profession, 343–362. New York: Springer.

Paikeday, Thomas. M. 1985. *The native speaker is dead!* Toronto: Paikeday Press.

Rampton, Ben. 1990. Displacing the 'native speaker': expertise, affiliation, and inheritance. *ELT Journal* 44, 97–101.

Slavkov, Nikolay. 2020. Language Background Profiling at Canadian Elementary Schools and Dominant Language Constellations. In Larissa Aronin & Joseph Lo Bianco (eds.), *Dominant language constellations*, 117–138. New York: Springer.

Slavkov, Nikolay. 2018. What is your 'first' language in bilingual Canada? A study of language background profiling at publicly-funded elementary schools across three provinces. *International Journal of Bilingual Education and Bilingualism* 21(1), 20–37.

Slavkov, Nikolay. 2016. In search of the right questions: Language background profiling at Ontario public schools, *Canadian Journal of Applied Linguistics 19*(1), 22–45.
Slavkov, Nikolay. 2015. Language attrition and reactivation in the context of bilingual first language acquisition. *International Journal of Bilingualism and Bilingual Education 18*(2), 715–734. doi: 10.1080/13670050.2014.941785
Swan, Anne, Pamela Aboshiha & Adrian Holliday (eds.), 2015. *(En)Countering Native-speakerism. Global Perspectives*. Hampshire: Palgrave Macmillan.
Williams, Cen. 1996. Secondary education: Teaching in the bilingual situation. In Cen Williams, Gwyn Lewis & Colin Baker (eds.), *The Language Policy: Taking Stock*. Llangefni (Wales): CAI.
Yanaprasart, Patchareerat & Sílvia Melo-Pfeifer. 2019. Students' perceptions of authenticity of plurilingual non-native teachers in multilingual Higher Education settings: an explorative and comparative case study of Geneva and Hamburg. *European Journal of Higher Education* 9 (3), 327–342. DOI:10.1080/21568235.2019.159774.
Yazan, Bedrettin & Kristen Lindhal (eds.), 2020. *Language teacher identity in TESOL. Teacher education and practice as identity work*. London: Routledge.
Yildiz, Yasemin. 2012. *Beyond the mother tongue: The postmonolingual condition*. New York: Fordham University Press.

Part one: **Conceptual discussions**

Jean-Marc Dewaele, Thomas H. Bak, Lourdes Ortega
Chapter 1
Why the mythical "native speaker" has mud on its face

Abstract: The terms "native speaker" (NS) and "non-native speaker" (NNS) continue to be widely used in applied linguistics and foreign language learning and teaching despite a growing wave of criticism about the difficulty in defining them accurately, the (neo)racist ideology they reflect and the deficit view they perpetuate among foreign language learners and teachers. These issues are explored in more detail, focusing on the history of the terms NS/NNS and their enduring perverse social consequences. We consider alternative views and explain the reasoning behind the development of a new terminology: "L1 user versus LX user" (Dewaele 2018). We conclude that the field needs to abandon the toxic terms "NS/NNS" and adopt neutral terms that emphasise the equal status of first and foreign language users – which can often be the same person.

Keywords: L1/LX user, deficit view, (neo)racist ideology, native-speakerism, multilingualism

1 Introduction

The terms "native speaker" (NS) and its nemesis, the "non-native speaker" (NNS), continue to be widely used despite increasing criticism in the last forty years about the lack of clarity of their meaning, the insurmountable difficulty in defining them, the ideology they reflect and the deficit view they perpetuate about foreign language users (Holliday 2015). We will argue that continued use of NS/NNS is an obstacle in the pursuit of equality and equity in education and research. It is fundamentally unjust to judge a person's linguistic competence solely on the fact that they were born into the language. Most people would agree that those born without a silver spoon should not suffer from social discrimination, yet there is much less support for those who want a job in language teaching and were not born with a silver tongue. In other words, linguistic discrimination is still rife.

Jean-Marc Dewaele, Birkbeck University of London, e-mail: j.dewaele@bbk.ac.uk
Thomas H. Bak, University of Edinburgh, e-mail: thomas.bak@ed.ac.uk
Lourdes Ortega, Georgetown University, e-mail: Lourdes.Ortega@georgetown.edu

The obstacle for research is both ethical and substantive: not only does the NS/NNS dichotomy render the majority of speakers in the world deficient but also, as we will explain later, there is no empirical backing to the myth that being born into a language grants fixed psycholinguistic privileges to its users.

In this chapter we explore these issues in more detail, discussing the history of the terms and their enduring social consequences. We consider alternative views and propose new, improved terminology. We conclude that the terms NS/NNS need to be urgently relegated to the vocabulary bin of history, where they can rot in the company of banned racial slurs and homophobic insults.

2 A historical overview of the "native speaker" (NS) concept

In her comprehensive review of the "emergence of the English native speaker" Stephanie Hackert dates the first attested use of the term *"native speaker"* to a lecture given at the Columbia College in New York in November 1858 by a New England philologist, businessman, lawyer and politician George P March (Hackert 2012:63). March's speech advocates the establishment of an English *"native philology"* and extolls the virtues of *"home-born English"* as the expression of *"the domesticity of Saxon life"* and *"the nutriment drawn from the maternal breast"*, contrasting it with austere Latin of the *"severe Romans"*. Hackert interprets the speech as an expression of the ideology of "Anglo-Saxonism": Anglo-Saxon superiority over the Roman world. Emerging for the first time in the 16th Century in the context of reformation and giving ideological support for the break with Rome, it re-appeared in the USA of the "Great Migration", a country feeling threatened by a large number of non-English speaking (and often Catholic) immigrants. Thus, from the very beginning, the notion of the NS has been carrying with it ideas of superiority and exclusion.

However, the subsequent popularity of the term "NS" was not only due to British imperial power and American economic and technological dominance. It seemed to combine Herder's notion of the authenticity of "Volksstimme" ("voice of the people"), popularised in England through romantic poets Coleridge and Wordsworth (see Hackert 2012: 161), with practical considerations, such as the choice of the most appropriate language teachers. In 1836, the East India College at Haileybury discussed critically the merits of employment of a *"Native Persian"* as its Persian teacher, balancing the *"utmost purity and correctness"* of his language with a considerably different use of Persian as a lingua franca by the *"Natives of India"* (Fisher 2012: 345).

The popularity of the term "NS" might have been further strengthened by a shift in Western education from the classical languages of Greek and Latin (for which no "NSs" existed) to modern ones and by the parallel emphasis on spoken rather than on written word. It has been reinforced by Chomsky's influential concept of an *"ideal speaker-listener, in a completely homogeneous speech community, who knows its language perfectly"* (Chomsky 1965).

However, by the late 20th Century, the term "NS" also had its outspoken critics. Halliday (1968) noted that "A speaker who is made ashamed of his own language habits suffers a basic injury as a human being: to make anyone, especially a child, feel so ashamed is as indefensible as to make him feel ashamed of the color of his skin" (p. 165). Another famous linguist, Ferguson (1983) added that "The whole mystique of the native speaker and the mother tongue should probably be quietly dropped from the linguist's set of professional myths about language" (p. vii). This push to reject the use of NS led to some premature rejoicing. Paikeday (1985) proclaimed the end of the NS myth by entitling his book *The Native Speaker is Dead*:

> I am convinced that "native speaker" in the sense of the sole arbiter of grammaticality or one whose intuitions of a proprietary nature about his or her mother tongue and which are shared only by others of his own tribe is a myth propagated by linguists, that the true meaning of the lexeme "native speaker" is a proficient user of a specified language, and that this meaning satisfies all contexts in which linguists, anthropologists, psychologists, educators, and others use it, except when it directly refers to the speaker's mother tongue or first-acquired language without any assumptions about the speaker's linguistic competence.
>
> (p. 87)

Unfortunately, the NS myth turned out to be much more resilient, and more pernicious, than anyone could have guessed at the time. Rampton (1990) argued that the efforts to drop or modify the terms ended up "testifying indirectly to their power" (p. 97) and that alterations needed to be more than merely cosmetic. He listed the following five properties for the myth behind the "NS" label:

1. A particular language is inherited, either through genetic endowment or through birth into the social group stereotypically associated with it.
2. Inheriting a language means being able to speak it well.
3. People either are or are not native/mother-tongue speakers.
4. Being a native speaker involves the comprehensive grasp of a language.
5. Just as people are usually citizens of one country, people are native speakers of one mother tongue. (p. 97)

Interestingly, although most languages have a term for a person who has learned a language from birth, the origin of such terms and their connotations vary significantly and the English notion of a "NS" does not translate particularly well into other languages. Some languages have a term similarly derived from the word for "being born", e.g. the Russian term "родной язык", related to the verb "родить" ("to give birth", or, in reflexive form, "to be born") and the noun "родина" (motherland). Similar forms exist in Bulgarian ("роден език"), Czech, "rodný jazyk" and Lithuanian ("gimtoi kalba").

However, even if the etymology is similar, the use might be divergent: in Russia, "родной язык" might well be used to refer to the language of the original ethnic group (where it is different from Russian), even in people who are not fluent in it, as Russian is their dominant language in most contexts.

Interestingly, a similar situation can be observed in parts of Africa. Lüpke (2016) describes a case of a West-African girl Emily, taken into foster care at the age of 5 years by a related family, but speaking a different language from that of her parents (the topic of "native language" and adoption will be discussed in more detail later in this section). Asked about "her language" Emily might well refer to Pepel, the language of her father although her dominant language at the moment is Gujaher, the language of her new foster family. Should she return to her original family, the dominance of Pepel is likely to be re-established. It would be tempting to classify Pepel, according to contemporary English terminology, as her "heritage language", but Lüpke would argue that terms such as "native" or "heritage" language are not useful to describe the fluid multilingual reality of West Africa (see also Kagan, Minkov, Protassova and Schwartz, this volume).

What seems to be the most common term, across the world as well as across different language families, is the notion of "mother language": from French "langue maternelle" and German "Muttersprache", through Turkish "ana dili" and most of the languages of India (Indo-European as well as Dravidian), to Chinese "母语("mǔ yǔ"), with the notable exception of Polish, which speaks of "język ojczysty", related to "ojciec" ("father") and "ojczyzna" ("fatherland"). In some languages, terms derived from "native" and "mother language" co-exist, as in Spanish "hablante nativo" and "lengua materna.", or in Bulgarian "роден език" and "матерен език".

Few languages have words which are not derived from either "birth/being born" or "mother/father." Dutch and Afrikaans have the terms "thuistaal" and "huistaal", respectively, for the language spoken at home. Croatian has, along the word "mother tongue" ("jezik materinski"), the notion of "izvorni govornik," loosely translated as "authentic speaker," from the word "izvor" "source," hence a speaker close to the source. In Greek, although the commonly used term is "μητρική γλώσσα" (mother tongue), there exists also the notion of "φυσικοί ομιλητές," "natural" speakers (a term related to but distinct from "native"). However, both these terms are used much less frequently than "mother language" and might sound to some speakers as artificial.

The idea of a "first language", frequently expressed by linguists as L1 (and discussed in more detail later, in the context of "L1 user"), seems to be less frequent in colloquial languages, although it does appear in the German word "Erstsprache" (first language), alongside "Muttersprache" (mother language), "Familiensprache" (family language) and "Herkunftssprache" (language of origin) or in French "première langue", as distinct from "langue maternelle" or "natale".

Given the difficulty of translating the English word "native speaker" into other languages, some of them resort to a direct borrowing. In Poland, it is not unusual to find advertisements for language teachers using the English term, also in connection with languages other than English (e.g. "Hiszpański Native Speaker," "Spanish native speaker"). The term became polonised by applying to it Polish inflectional rules with different degrees of phonological and orthographic assimilation ("native speakerzy" or even "natywi", e.g. in "mamy natywów" "we have native speakers").

Apart from the difficulty of translating it into other languages, one of the biggest problems of the concept of the "native speaker" is its static determinism. It treats language as something acquired in the first years of life and from then on unchanged and unchangeable. Accordingly, it does not take into account shifts in language dominance which have been shown to be possible at any point during the lifespan (see also Jessner, Hofer and Malzer-Papp, this volume). For example, international adoption happens as early as 3 months or as late as 11 years of age. These young children quickly forget their first language and switch over to the language of the new country and family (Nicoladis and Grabois 2002). Even though they may retain subtle traces of the first language (e.g. Choi, Broersma, and Cutler 2017; Montrul 2011), as adults they cannot remember it and instead speak their family language: which language should they be considered "native speakers" of? Language shift can also happen to older children and adults be it through education, emigration, work, leisure or marriage (see also Kerschhoffer-Puhalo and Slavkov, this volume). Indeed, significant shifts in language use by individuals can still occur rather late in life, e.g. after retirement, even without any change in place of residence. A study examining the use of English and Gaelic across the lifespan in the Inner and Outer Hebrides, Scotland (de Bruin et al. 2016) demonstrated that the pattern of language use can change significantly after retirement, once the work pressure of speaking English is removed from Gaelic speakers. Were they "NSs" of Gaelic, a language they spoke as first at home, but could not use for much of their life, at school (at the time of their childhood, the whole schooling was conducted in English only) or at work? Or of English, a language they started learning only at school, but in which they were fully proficient and which became dominant for many in their later life. Or were they "NSs" of both?

As the de Bruin et al. (2016) study illustrates, the notion of a "NS" can be particularly problematic in the context of minority languages, where often the language spoken at home is different from that of schooling. This is an issue that has been addressed by Pujolar and O'Rourke's work on "new speakers" of regional minority languages in Europe. These new speakers learnt their language through schooling and typically sound different from those who grew up with the language from birth (O'Rourke and Pujolar 2021; Pujolar, this volume). The new speakers' deviation from the native norm raises issues in the community about their identity, authenticity, linguistic ownership and pluricentricity (see also Kamwangamalu, this volume).

The notion of a single native language, determined entirely by the earliest experiences, is also not supported by neurology and neuroscience. Although patients with brain diseases affecting language, such as stroke or dementia, can revert to the almost exclusive use of their first language through their disease (Vega-Mendoza et al. 2019), such a pattern is by no means universal, and the "native tongue" might be in fact more affected than the languages learned subsequently (Aglioti et al. 1996; Mehmedbegovic and Bak 2017). Indeed, the descriptions of aphasia (language disorder caused by a brain injury or disease) contrast "Ribot's law", a selective preservation of the first "native" language, with Pitre's law, where *recovery comes first and most completely in the language most used just before the injury, whether or not it is the patient's mother tongue* (for a brief but informative overview, see Pearce 2005).

All these issues have been widely recognised and, as Rampton (1990) pointed out, all the properties of an imaginary "NS" have been strongly contested, "Yet despite the criticisms, the terms NS and mother tongue remain in circulation, continuously insinuating their assumptions" (p. 98). More than ten years on, Davies (2003) lamented the fact that in applied linguistic and foreign language learning and teaching circles the term "NS" remained a common-sense reference point, despite the difficulty of deciding who can and who cannot claim this status. He pointed to potentially racist uses of the term, as it can be used to deliberately exclude speakers of certain varieties of a language or highly proficient NNS.

3 Native-speakerism and its ideological roots

The racist and discriminatory work of the terms NS and NNS that Davies (2003) lamented is particularly ominous and enduring for teachers who are "non-native" speakers of the language they teach, and the problem is persistent. As Llurda (2009) pointed out, around the turn of the century applied linguists have "finally come to grips with the idea that non-native speakers may be as good teachers as natives, and that good language teaching requires a good command of the language plus the right amount of training and ability to teach a language" (p. 46). He noticed that researchers tried to eliminate the discrimination between NS and NNS language teachers by minimizing any perceived differences between them and by "vindicating the role of the non-native speaker as a rightful language teacher" (p. 43). Yet, after years of relentless criticism of the concept of the NS, nothing much had changed: "The native speaker is under attack but I would dare say it still is in a pretty good shape" (p. 48). Thus, much as claims about the death of the NS, or its imminent decline and fall, which as we have already pointed out have been made since the 1980s without ousting the label, Llurda argued that the proclamation of the end of the NS expressed authors' wishful thinking that was countered by the stark reality.

Mahboob (2004) considered the case of English Second Language (ESL) teaching in the United States. How could cherished American values of equality be violated in the field of ESL by treating NNS teachers of English as unwanted step-children? Part of the problem, according to Mahboob (2004), was that programme administrators do not want NNS in the belief that students do not want them. He referred to a study by Cook (1999, 2000) showing that young ESL students in the UK, Belgium and Poland did not have a clear preference for NS teachers. The often repeated claim that learners prefer teachers who are NS was disproven in Dewaele, Mercer, Talbot and von Blanckenburg (2020). The authors developed a design to measure implicit bias against NNS teachers in judgements of teaching competence. Participants were close to 300 Austrian and German pre-service EFL teachers who had German as an L1. They watched an identical 5-minute video of a teacher in front of an EFL classroom and rated her on four dimensions (language, teaching, assessment, communication) through Likert scales. A final item asked how much they would love to have this person as an English teacher (again measured with a Likert scale). It was followed by an open question on the reasons why. Half of the participants were told that the teacher was a NS, the other half that she was a NNS. The judgments were found to be similar in both conditions. Teaching skill turned out to be the strongest predictor of loving the teacher, followed by language skill. Analysis of the qualitative data showed that very few participants mentioned the words NS/NNS. The evidence suggests that there was minimal bias against NNS teachers in this population of learners of English. In other words, while it may be true that, in some contexts, some students have internalized the ideology of NS superiority and project it onto their ideas of who is a good language teacher, it is not the case that all students fall prey to such an ideology, and many look for other attributes in their teachers when they judge good language teaching.

Holliday (2005) introduced the term "native-speakerism" to describe an ideology "that upholds the idea that so-called 'native speakers' are the best models and teachers of English because they represent a 'Western culture' from which spring the ideals both of English and of the methodology for teaching it" (p. 6). In further research, Holliday and Aboshiha (2009) observed that there is a deep and sustained prejudice against NNS teachers which is "connected to an inherent racism within the fabric of Western society" (p. 669). The prejudice is not recognised because the terms NS and NNS appear neutral, which allows a denial of their ideological underpinnings. The authors attributed this to the dominant modernist research paradigm and its perceptions of objectivity and accountability. A second element is the apparently neutral description of individualist versus collectivist cultures, which "are in fact underpinned by cultural prejudice" (p. 669). The authors argued that the adoption of a postmodern qualitative research methodology could allow researchers to circumvent the ideological problems linked to the concepts of NS and NNS and "engage with the subjectivities of the unspoken discourses of TESOL professionalism" (p. 669).

Holliday (2015) described "native-speakerism" as a "wide-spread cultural disbelief – a disbelief in the cultural contribution of teachers who have been labelled 'non-native speakers'" (p. 11). He also lamented the fact that native-speakerism has a wide-ranging negative impact on how teachers are perceived by colleagues and students. Holliday added that it falsely positions NS teachers as culturally superior and NNS as inferior, which leads to discriminatory employment practices. The NNS teachers are not the only ones to suffer from such a distinction, the NS teachers suffer too as they are commodified, i.e. reduced to a list of marketable attributes, which typically do not include their hard-earned professionalism and training. Leonard's (2019) study added fresh evidence that native-speakerism leads to discrimination. In her qualitative study of four EFL teachers from Vietnam and China, she found that NS networks in participants' institutions exerted power to reinforce the ideal of NS teachers – often using the presence of NS as a marketing tool- and to restrict the agency of the NNS teachers. Learners felt that only NS teachers had instinctive, innate knowledge of English, yet they preferred the clearer explanations of the NNS teachers. One participant reported that he felt marginalised and treated unfairly after discovering that his NS colleagues in a Vietnamese school earned three times as much as him despite the fact that he did the same job equally well.

Kumaravadivelu (2016), in a passionate piece in *TESOL Quarterly*, argued that 25 years of discussion on the inequity against NNS teachers in the field of TESOL "has not in any significant way altered the ground reality of NNS subordination" (p. 66). The NNS community is perceived as a subaltern community that is the victim of a hegemonic power structure. In order to break this choke-hold, he calls for the "decolonial option which demands result-oriented action, not just 'intellectual elaboration'" (p. 66). In other words, there is an urgent need for "a collective, concerted, and coordinated set of actions (. . .) to shake the foundation of the hegemonic power structure" (p. 66).

Lovrits and de Bres (2020) also showed that their four trainees on temporary contracts in a multilingual European Union institution regretted being pigeonholed as an 'NS' of English because it meant they spent a larger proportion of their time proofreading other people's English texts instead of doing more original work. As Holliday (2005, 2015) and Kumaravadivelu (2016) rightly diagnosed, at its roots the problem is symptomatic of a deeper clash within applied linguistics and foreign language learning and teaching between postpositivist or modernist and constructivist or postmodernist epistemologies. Scholars espousing the former epistemology see no place for ideologies in research and use the NS/NNS labels "as if their meanings were objective and neutral, denoting two natural categories of language users" (Ortega 2014: 36). When objectivity is taken as an ideal and neutrality as an attainable possibility in research, it is an uphill battle to confront the ideological content of the constructs, and the negative ideologies of language learning and language learners that they reproduce go unrecognized (Ortega 2019). It is unclear whether these broader epistemological tensions will ever resolve themselves. But we believe that a first step towards change is the creation of neutral terms that do not imply the domination of one group and the subordination of another.

4 Getting around the problematic NS/NNS terms

Holliday (2015) considered the "native-speakerist cultural disbelief" to be neoracist rather than simply racist because "race is not an explicit agenda in the minds of the people concerned" (p. 13). The term originates from Balibar and Wallerstein (1988) who pointed out that neoracism can take different forms and that it reflects rationalisation of exploitation, oppression and domination (p. 80). In the context of language teaching, native-speakerism is implicit and hidden behind "supposedly neutral and innocent talk of cultural difference" (Holliday: 13). Holliday pointed out that writing about the NS/NNS debate is difficult "because there is a necessity to use terms, 'non-native speaker' and 'native speaker', which should not be in use at all" (p. 12). A similar point had been made by Schmitz (2005) who wondered whether the terms NS/NNS represented a dangerous dichotomy before arguing that it was operational after all for the sake of comparisons. Both authors proposed solution was putting the terms 'NS' and 'NNS' between inverted commas "to signal 'so-called' and indicate a burden that has to be endured until the issue can be undone" (Holliday: 12).

Holliday's (2015) complaint about the lack of adequate terms to refer to NS and NNS was in fact not entirely justified because Cook (2002) had come up with a better term, replacing 'NNS' by 'L2 users', which he defined as "any person who uses another language than his or her first language (L1), that is to say, the one learnt first as a child" (p. 1). The notion of the L2 user is an important first step that can help dismantle native-speakerism. L2 users exploit the resources of the L2 for real-life purposes, which distinguishes them from L2 learners who acquire an L2 for later use. L2 users are thus legitimate users of an L2, irrespective of the level of mastery of the L2. Crucially, the term 'L2 users' allowed Cook to get rid of the deficit view, as they are "people who know more than one language without the overtones that cloud the words bilingual and learner" and who use the L2 minimally to maximally (Cook and Singleton 2014: 4). Cook (1999) had already downplayed the role of proficiency in the definition of the NS. For him an NS was a person who speaks "the language learnt first; the other characteristics are incidental, describing how well an individual uses the language" (p. 187). Cook (2005) pointed out that there is no more justification in considering a L2 user to be a perpetual L2 learner than claiming that an adult NS is an eternal L1 learner (see also Jessner, Hofer and Malzer-Papp, this volume and Stratilaki-Klein, this volume).

A second important step in Cook's (2002) argumentation was the notion of multicompetence, which comprised several stipulations laid out most recently by Murahata, Murahata and Cook (2016). Firstly, L2 users are multi-competent, in other words, users have other languages at their disposal and to focus solely on a single language would be reductionist. Indeed, "Multi-competence concerns the total system for all languages (L1, L2, Ln) in a single mind or community and their inter-relationships" (p. 38). Secondly, "Multi-competence does not depend on the monolingual native speaker" (p. 38), in other words, the L2 user systems should not be seen as "imperfect imitations of native speakers" (id). Thirdly, "Multi-competence affects the whole mind, i.e. all language and cognitive systems, rather than language alone" (p. 39). This point constituted an invitation to researchers of neighbouring disciplines to engage in inter-disciplinary research with applied linguists (Wei and Cook 2016). The notion of "multi-competence" is also in line with the concept of "plurilingualism" in which a person "lives" in two or more languages, none of which assume the position of a "main" or "dominant" one (Bak and Mehmedbegovic, in press).

Cook's (1999, 2002) substitution of the term 'L2 learner' and NNS by the term 'L2 user' in the early 2000s signalled the emergence of a broader and more inclusive view, as not everybody is a speaker, indeed, some are signers or readers or hearers. Cook thus offered the field a useful new concept, and a term that was untainted by negative ideological connotations or by the deficit view of bilingualism. The use of '2' in the term 'L2 user' remains problematic, however. In the field of Second Language Acquisition research, "second" covers all languages acquired after early childhood, regardless of actual numbers, sequence or contexts (Mitchell and Myles 1998). This could be confusing to other professional and scholarly audiences. For example, multilingualism researchers are by definition interested in more than two languages, and collapsing the third, fourth or fifth language of individuals under a single label "L2" is unhelpful because it lacks granularity. And many language teachers find it important to distinguish between foreign and second language contexts of learning, and for them 'second' is deeply different, rather than inclusive, of 'foreign.' Other scholarly voices have also objected against the adjective "second" because it carries a connotation of "secondary" languages as less natural and more detached from a speaker's identity, which may not be true in many cases (Valdés 2005). These shortcomings in the 'L2 user' label help perhaps explain why the term remains in low use. Ortega and Keck (2017) found that in a corpus of academic articles published between 2005 and 2015 across 11 key journals, comprising over 9 million words, the term 'L2 user' appeared only 1 per 10,000 words, whereas the use of the traditional 'L2 learner' label continued to be healthy and well, with an average of 11 occurrences per 10,000 words. The dichotomy of NS/NNS was ubiquitous, at 37 mentions per 10,000 words.

5 Substituting NS/NNS by L1/LX user

In their introductory chapter, Swan, Aboshiha and Holliday (2015: 1) call for an end to the "tyranny of native-speakerism" in worldwide English language teaching. They express a disbelief that despite the constant challenges and outpouring of critiques against native-speakerism, there hardly seems to have been any shift in the profession. The practice of putting the terms 'NS' and 'NNS' between inverted commas to signal 'so-called' (Holiday 2015) can only be a temporary measure. Cook's substitution of the term 'L2 learner' and NNS by the term 'L2 user' in the early 2000s is not without problems and it has not been taken up widely by researchers and teachers. The time has come to try to "undo" the issue by changing both the concept and the label, one more time. We do not think the notion of NS can be "bypassed" (Di Pietro, this volume).

Dewaele (2018) suggested replacing the dichotomy "NS/NNS" by L1 user/LX user. The label 'LX' refers to any new language acquired after the age at which the first language(s) was/were acquired, which for many language researchers is after the age of 3, to various levels of proficiency. Researchers could then switch between a global view on the multilinguals' LXs, or zoom in on the specifics of their L2, L3, L4, L5. We agree with Holliday (2015) that terms are needed to distinguish languages that were acquired very early and later in life. There is every reason to believe that L1(s) will share commonalities and that LX(s) will share their own unique commonalities. The crucial advantage of the labels "L1" and "LX", combined with the noun "user," is that it circumvents the negative ideological connotations that have become naturalized in the terms 'native' and 'second' in scholarly usage. These new labels do not imply inferiority or superiority and could refer to any number of L1s and LXs that were acquired to various degrees and potentially attrited. In other words, proficiency is not a defining characteristic. Being a L1 user usually means a high level of proficiency in this language, but it is not inherent in the label. Also, some LX users may in fact have higher proficiency in some domains than L1 users (Birdsong 2014). Moreover, Schmid (2011) has shown that an L1 can suffer from attrition. The gradual loss of L1 proficiency does not mean that that person suddenly ceases to be a L1 user. The process is gradual and there is huge inter-individual variation. Schmid (2020) used the metaphor of a computer virus to describe the effect of an LX on a L1 that starts by causing minute changes and can end up causing various malfunctions.

The absence of proficiency in the definition of language user means both L1 and LX users' competencies could be situated anywhere on the continuum between minimal and maximal, with no "full" competence implied as a benchmark or an end-point of language learning and no presupposition that a "perfect" command of a language is either unavoidable for L1 users or impossible for LX users. This is a crucial point because both monolingualism and bilingualism are best seen not as an all-or-nothing outcome but as gradient in nature (Luk 2015; Ortega 2019; Surrain and Luk 2017). All language learning results in gradient language competencies, regardless of starting age and whether one or more than one languages are involved (Ortega 2019). Moreover, variation in knowledge of the L1 can be important (Dąbrowska 2019). Some L1 users are highly literate while others can be illiterate; some may possess a very large vocabulary in some domains while others may have a much smaller one. Andringa (2014) found that when the variability of L1 abilities was included in his sample of 'NS,' many more of the 'NNS' in the same study were able to measure up to the standards of so-called native-like competence in a large battery of tests. Indeed, linguistic judges have also been found to have some difficulty in identifying fellow L1 users unerringly. Abrahamsson and Hyltenstam (2008) found that 10 Swedish L1 listeners who listened to 195 samples of Swedish LX users randomly mixed with 20 samples of a control group of Swedish L1 users did identify the LX users correctly but also mistook 2 Swedish

L1 users for being LX users. Hyltenstam, Bartning and Fant (2018) pointed out that the role of variation in language use among NS is downplayed by the defenders of the so-called standard language ideology for whom the standard language norm is reflected "in the researcher's metalinguistic knowledge and/or intuition about the standard language" (p. 6). They regret the downplaying of the variation in the L1 and the setting of a standard that is inadequate for L2 learners.

Dewaele (2018) thus argued that it would make more sense to talk about L1 users of a language (or multiple languages) rather than NS. An advantage would be that comparisons between L1 users and LX users would be a perfectly legitimate enterprise because none is assumed to have mythical full competence anyway. An added benefit is that 'NS' invokes the notion of someone who speaks an L1 purely, with no traces of other languages, that is, a monolingual (Ortega 2014). LX avoids this monolingual bias, because of course the L1 user (of one language) can be the same person who is an LX user (of other languages), that is, a multilingual user. Moreover, since multilinguals are L1 users as well as LX users, there never is a judgment about the person, only about the different languages in their repertoire. This is also an approach that allows researchers to move away from using monolingual controls by selecting other multilinguals who have the linguist's target language as an L1 or LX. Similarly, Cook and Singleton (2014) pointed out that since the monolingual NS is an abstraction it cannot act as a role model for L2/LX users.

6 Will the new terminology and concept of L1/LX user take hold?

Hyltenstam (2018) lauded the new dichotomy "L1-LX user", describing it as: "both well-conceived and reasonable *per se*" (p. 6) but expressed doubts whether it could change prevailing attitudes towards these groups. He noted that the substitution of emotion-laden words that have become 'impossible' by new terms is a well-known process but he seemed pessimistic about the chances of the L1/LX user dichotomy replacing NS/NNS:

> The future will decide whether this will happen to the native/non-native terminology, but in our view, we are not there yet. The use of this particular terminology is still the most common convention in second language research, and there is at present no widespread agreement on the substitute terms to use among the various suggested alternatives, should the prevailing terminology need to be abandoned. (p. 6)

Holliday (2015) agonised over the use of the term NS and NNS, putting them between inverted commas to signal his critical stance, and openly regretting the lack of an alternative to discuss the issue. Hyltenstam (2018) wondered whether the field would ever get rid of the terms NS/NNS which are so common and deeply ingrained. We strongly feel that combatting the NS/NNS dichotomy is **not** a battle against windmills and that the time is ripe for change.

We argue that the mere use of terminology with neoracist overtones that reflects an outdated view of language users' linguistic repertoire contributes directly to perpetuating a profound injustice. As it is impossible to neutralise the inherent negative ideological connotations of NS/NNS, the dichotomy should be jettisoned. The argument that nothing can be done because these terms represent a "most common convention" is a moot one. There are precedents for words that were gradually banned in interactions. Some emotion-laden words referring to race or sexual orientation have become taboo because they were deemed to be too offensive to be used in present times, even between inverted commas. Similarly, we argue that the terms NS/NNS and their specific conceptual representation have become equally toxic and should therefore be relegated to history's soundproof linguistic and conceptual bin. The observation that there is no widespread agreement on substitute terms for NS/NNS should not be an argument for inaction.

Cook (2002) made the first step, by substituting 'NNS' by 'L2 user' but keeping NS, though not necessarily a monolingual one (Murahata et al. 2016). The next step should be the substitution of 'NS' by 'L1 user,' terms that are perceived as interchangeable by many. We do feel that the new equitable understanding of the term L1 user amounts to re-positioning its meaning to some extent, in order to distance it from 'NS.' In other words, the two terms are not synonyms as they reflect very different ideological stances on the status of multilinguals' languages. The choice of the word 'use' is particularly relevant because it implies transience whereas 'NS' implies permanence. A person can use different languages like a cook uses different tools but the use of the tools does not define the essence of the cook. In this view, languages are communication tools – which can also be used to signal identity and belonging. Being a language **user** means the language is not a person's property. If nobody 'owns' the language, then there are no property rights and nobody can be denied the right to use it legitimately. This metaphor has its limits, as we do believe that languages acquired before a certain age have something in common that languages acquired in life later may lack. It is therefore useful to be able to distinguish L1(s) from LX(s).

The final step in the development of a new dichotomy is the substitution of Cook's 'L2 user' by 'LX user' in order to avoid any confusion about a language user's chronology of language acquisition (Dewaele 2018). The new dichotomy 'L1 user' versus 'LX user' allows a discussion of the issue of language status in multilinguals' repertoires in neutral terms as they are "equal and can be complementary" (p. 239). It acknowledges the fact that everybody can be a multicompetent user of multiple languages, acquired before and after early childhood to various levels of proficiency.

7 Conclusion

To conclude, after considering the literature on the debate on the NS/NNS, we realise that the metaphor in the title of the mythical NS having mud on its face is in fact only partially correct. Indeed, mud can be washed off whereas the ideological stain is indelible. How we name things and people matter, as they reflect how we see and value them. By using terms that reflect equality and equity, we signal that we want to see more equality and equity in society. Banning the use of derogatory terms is a crucial first step to end the hegemonic power structure that keeps NNS/LX users in a position of subordination (Kumaravadivelu 2016). The need to change terminologies reflects not just the "multilingual turn" in applied linguistics but also a desire to better align with societies around the world where multilingualism and multiculturalism have become established and accepted (Mehmedbegovic and Bak 2017) and where old-fashioned terms that reflect the preference for one group over another have no place.

The aim of the present contribution was obviously not to target monolingual L1 users – who may in fact be less "mono" than one might imagine if we think of the number of varieties, sociolects and dialects of their L1 that they may master to varying degrees combined with gradient LX competencies. The mud/stain is attached to the faceless monolingual habitus in education and research that seeks to discriminate against those considered linguistically impure and thus seek to perpetuate inequity surreptitiously.

Authors' Positionalities

Jean-Marc Dewaele grew up in Bruges, in Flanders where Dutch is the only official language. He used French with his family members and Dutch with everybody else. He quickly became aware that French was not appreciated by many of his Flemish friends because they considered it socially ostentatious. French used to be the language that the nobility and the bourgeoisie used among themselves, while Dutch was typically used with servants. There was ongoing resentment in the second part of the 20th century about Francophones having had condescending attitudes towards Dutch. He realised that languages can be (unwelcome) identity markers, and developed chameleon-like linguistic habits to fit in with both linguistic communities. He studied French and Spanish at the Flemish Vrije Universiteit Brussel (VUB) and had plenty of opportunities to observe the constant tensions between the Francophone majority and the Dutch-speaking minority in Brussels. The VUB was a Flemish beacon in a city that used to be Dutch-speaking before it was Frenchified in the 19th and early 20th centuries. Studying French at the VUB in the early 1980s was slightly incongruous, as the institution considered French to be language of the enemy and any use of French outside of the classroom attracted hostile glances from fellow students. Having obtained his PhD in French linguistics in 1993, Dewaele became a lecturer in the French department at Birkbeck, University of London. His complex Belgian bilingual identity was of little interest to the British, where he was considered a "Belgian" and instantly recognised as a foreign language user of English, a language he had started learning at school at age 14. Realising that his French-Dutch accent in English was a marker of his new migrant identity of which he was proud (Dewaele, 2016), and was not an obstacle for communication, he became interested in the debate about the "native" and the "non-native speaker".

Dewaele originally worked on the acquisition of French as a foreign language, adopting quantitative approaches. He was specifically interested in sociolinguistic, psycholinguistic and psychological aspects of second language acquisition (SLA). After moving to the department of applied linguistics in the mid-2000s, he became increasingly interested in sociopragmatics and in more general issues linked to the acquisition and use of multiple languages. Supervising 30 PhD students from all parts of the world opened up unexpected new horizons. Early collaborations with Aneta Pavlenko led to an enduring interest in interdisciplinary emotion research and in the process of acculturation of migrants. Visits to Japan and China raised his awareness about the oppressive native-speaker ideology in English Foreign Language teaching. In research with Peter MacIntyre that started in the early 2010s on learner emotions, they discovered that learners' realizations that they were unlikely to ever pass for a "native speaker" left them distraught, weighed on their enjoyment of foreign language classes, resulting in silence, unhappiness and weak performance. Influenced by Positive Psychology, they argued for a more positive approach in SLA, where the aim is to become fluent without having to sound like a "native speaker", and crucially, to be a happy learner and user of the target language.

Thomas H. Bak grew up in Cracow, Poland, as son of a Polish-speaking father and a German-speaking mother. However, advised by professionals, including psychologists, speech and language therapists and paediatricians (his mother was a paediatrician herself), his parents decided to speak to him only in Polish. At this time, it was feared that being raised with two languages would confuse a child and could even lead to schizophrenia.

Nevertheless, when having arguments, his parents switched usually to German to exclude him from the conversation, inspiring a lifelong linguistic curiosity and interest in language learning. But the associations with German were not only negative: his mother sang him dozens of songs in German, one of the most cherished memories of his childhood. Aged 17, he moved to Germany and completed the German A-level exam (Abitur). The only subject which caused him difficulties was English and his teacher advised him to choose a career which does not require speaking English.

Not heeding this advice, he went on to study medicine, developing a particular interest in language disorders and cross-cultural and cross-linguistic studies. From his electives in Turkey and Japan, through his doctorate on acute aphasia in Freiburg, Germany, to his clinical work in psychiatry and neurology in Berne, Switzerland, Berlin and Cambridge, UK, his research and clinical work has focused on language and its relationship with motor and cognitive functions.

His professional work merged even more with his personal interest in multilingualism and language learning after his move to the University of Edinburgh in 2006. His work has focused increasingly on the cognitive effects of multilingualism and language learning across the lifespan, in healthy ageing as well as in brain diseases such as stroke and dementia. A hallmark of his work is the wide variety of the studied populations, from the Western Isles of Scotland, through India to Singapore and from schoolchildren and young adults to healthy elderly and dementia patients. His work is highly interdisciplinary, including neurologists, psychiatrists, psychologists, linguists and neuroscientists, with a recent extension into sociolinguistics. Together with Dina Mehmedbegovic from University College London, Institute of Education, he developed the concept of "healthy linguistic diet" (Bak & Mehmedbegovic 2017).

In the years 2010–2018 he was the president of the World Federation of Neurology, Research Group on Aphasia, Dementia and Cognitive Disorders. Organising teaching courses in cognitive neurology and aphasiology in Latin America, Middle East and Asia allowed him not only to share his clinical and research experience with others but also to learn from them about diverse approaches to health and disease across different countries and cultures.

It is this diversity of populations, methods and theoretical approaches that characterises his position in the recent debates about the "bilingual advantage". In his publications he warns against simplistic yes-no dichotomies (Bak 2016) as well as against egocentric normative universalism, in which results from specific populations (often from researchers' own environment) are uncritically interpreted as reflecting universal rules (Bak & Alladi 2015, Bak 2016).

Lourdes Ortega grew up in southern Spain, seamlessly codeswitching between her mom's Andalucian and her dad's Castilian. During her college education in Cádiz, she also spent a year in München, speaking Hochdeutsch and being bewildered by Bavarian, all along while fleissigly translating the Ancient Greek classics into German for her German professors. In her free time, she would hang out with her best friends, who were from Thessaloniki and Crete. With a BA in Spanish Philology in hand, she emigrated to Greece and spent most of her 20s living and working in Athens as a teacher of Spanish and (most of the time) passing for a "native speaker" of the Thessalonikian variety she had learned first. Since 1993, Lourdes has lived in the United States. First, she was an international student in Hawai'i, apprenticing in second language acquisition (SLA) from the best mentors who soon became close friends: Mike Long, Craig Chaudron, and Dick Schmidt. Then she became a green card holder and a U.S. academic from abroad, surrounded by L1 English-speaking colleagues across three remarkably diverse departments and Ph.D. programs: Georgia State University, Northern Arizona University, and (back to) the University of Hawai'i. In the third life stage in the U.S., which extends to the present, she embraced her Americanized identity by obtaining dual citizenship, and she then moved in 2012 to Georgetown University, located in the Nation's capital. In hindsight, Lourdes knows she grew up deceptively monolingual and enjoying a truly rich linguistic environment that sharpened her multidialectal awareness. Quite remarkably, these experiences were also free from stigma, linguicism, or prescriptivism. From age 17 and onwards, as she boosted her English, then German, and then Greek, she felt a thrilling sense of unfinished knowledge that made the world tick faster. Being a "non-native speaker" was exciting, not oppressive! Moreover, she remembers only praise for her language learning efforts from "native speakers." These are all signs of harmonious bilingualism (De Houwer,

2015), and this is indeed how many elite multilinguals experience their family multidialectalism and their elective multilingualism. But in her adult years, Lourdes learned to also recognize and expect negative language ideologies. In Greece, she had some Mexican-Greek heritage students of Spanish in her classes, and she witnessed how the machinery of the language teaching profession (textbooks, exams, classroom interactions, implied messages) instilled linguistic insecurity in them for not being "native" enough. In both Greece and the U.S., she also learned to expect insidious microaggressions (Lui & Quezada, 2019) related to her Spanish from expats or visitors from Spain (often language teachers and/or fellow linguists!). To this day, she regularly receives backhanded compliments for her good Spanish – presumably despite being from the south – or, even worse, surprise-filled comments that her Andalucian accent is unperceivable – presumably questioning her linguistic authenticity. As a member of English-speaking academia, she has also learned to negotiate subtle indignities against her English. Her present language identity is thus a strong blend of a combative L2 user of English and an ally to speakers whose home languages or varieties are minoritized. She is adept at strategic essentialism (Spivak, 1993), playing the "native" and the "non-native" and the "multilingual" card as situations require! Most likely, these things help explain the intellectual and professional trajectory Lourdes took, from investigating instructional effectiveness during the late 1990s and 2000s to, by the mid-2000s, interrogating the ethical consequences of the dominant SLA research habitus in which she had been trained so well. Starting in the 2010s, she called for disciplinary action to overcome epistemic and ethical shortcomings by finding inspiration in bilingualism research and usage-based linguistics. The turning point of Brexit and the U.S. presidential election in 2016 brought an explicit discussion of social justice to her work. COVID-19 is helping her understand how several axes of social difference are powerful forces for learning a language, and how race matters in language learning (Rosa & Flores, 2017). She envisions a future for SLA when multilingual learning is investigated as gradient and probabilistic and when knowledge accounts for not only elite multilinguals but also marginalized and grassroots multilinguals. This is why in her personal and professional thinking the mythical "native speaker" must go!

References

Abrahamsson, Niclas & Kenneth Hyltenstam. 2008. The robustness of aptitude effects in near-native second language acquisition. *Studies in Second Language Acquisition* 30. 481–509.

Aglioti, Salvatore, Beltramello Alberto, Girardi Flavia & Franco Fabbro. 1996. Neurolinguistic and follow-up study of an unusual pattern of recovery from bilingual subcortical aphasia. *Brain* 119. 1551–1564.

Andringa, Sible. 2014. The use of native speaker norms in critical period hypothesis research. *Studies in Second Language Acquisition* 36. 565–596.

Bak, Thomas H. 2015. Beyond a simple yes or no. Cortex. 73, 332–333.

Bak, Thomas H. A brief linguistic autobiography. http://healthylinguisticdiet.com/multilingual-lives/

Bak, Thomas H. & Suvarna Alladi. 2016. Bilingualism, dementia and the tale of many variables: why we need to move beyond the Western World. Cortex 74. 315–317.

Bak, Thomas H., Dina Mehmedbegovic. 2017. Healthy linguistic diet: the value of linguistic diversity and language learning. *Journal of Languages, Society and Policy*. Published online 21 May 2017.

Bak, Thomas H. Cooking Pasta in La Paz: bilingualism, bias and the replication crisis. 2016. *Linguistic Approaches to Bilingualism* 6 (5). 699–717.

Bak, Thomas H. & Dina Mehmedbegovic-Smith. In press. The cognitive and psychological dimensions of plurilingualism, In Piccardo, E, Germain-Rutherford, A and Lawrence, G (eds.), *Handbook of Plurilingual Education*. Routledge, UK.

Balibar, Etienne & Immanuel Wallerstein. 1988. *Race, nation, classe: les identités ambiguës*. Paris: La Découverte.

Birdsong, David. 2014. Dominance and age in bilingualism. *Applied Linguistics* 35. 374–392.

Choi, Jiyoun, Mirjam Broersma & Anne Cutler. 2017. Early phonology revealed by international adoptees' birth language retention. *Proceedings of the National Academy of Sciences* 114 (28). 7307–7312.

Chomsky, Noam. 1965. *Aspects of the Theory of Syntax*. MIT Press: Cambridge, MA.

Cook, Vivian J. & David Singleton. 2014. *Key Topics in Second Language Acquisition*. Bristol: Multilingual Matters.

Cook, Vivian J. 1999. Going beyond the native speaker in language teaching. *TESOL Quarterly* 33. 185–209.

Cook, Vivian J. 2000. The author responds . . . *TESOL Quarterly* 34. 329–332.

Cook, Vivian J. 2002. (ed.) *Portraits of the L2 User*. Clevedon: Multilingual Matters.

Cook, Vivian J. 2005. Basing teaching on the L2 User. In Enric Llurda (ed.), *Non-Native Language Teachers*, 47–61. Boston, MA Springer.

Dąbrowska, Ewa. 2019. Experience, aptitude, and individual differences in linguistic attainment: A comparison of native and nonnative speakers. *Language Learning* 69(S1). 72–100.

Davies, Alan. 2003. *The Native Speaker: Myth and Reality*. Clevedon: Multilingual Matters.

De Bruin, Angela, Sergio Della Sala & Thomas H. Bak. 2016. The effects of language use on lexical processing in bilinguals. *Language, cognition and neuroscience* 31 (8). 967–974.

De Houwer, Annick. 2015. Harmonious bilingual development: Young families' well-being in language contact situations. International Journal of Bilingualism, 19 (2), 169–184.

Dewaele, Jean-Marc, Sarah Mercer, Kyle R. Talbot & Max von Blanckenburg. 2020. Are EFL pre-service teachers' judgment of teaching competence swayed by the belief that the EFL teacher is a L1 or LX user of English? *European Journal of Applied Linguistics* 8 (2). 1–24.

Dewaele, Jean-Marc. 2018. Why the dichotomy 'L1 Versus LX User' is better than 'Native Versus Non-native Speaker'. *Applied Linguistics* 39. 236–240.

Dewaele, Jean-Marc. 2016. Brussels-London: Crossing channels while juggling with social and cultural capital. In Zhu Hua & Adam Komisarof (eds.), *Crossing Boundaries and Weaving Intercultural Work, Life, and Scholarship in Globalizing Universities* (133–146). London: Routledge.

Ferguson, Charles Albert. 1983. Language planning and language change. In Juan Cobarrubias & Joshua Fishman (eds.), Progress in language planning, 157–179. Berlin: Mouton.

Fisher, Michael H. 2012. Teaching Persian as an Imperial Language in India and in England during the Late 18th and Early 19th Centuries. In B. Spooner & W. L. Hanaway (eds.),

Literacy in the Persianate world: writing and the social order (pp. 328–358). Philadelphia: University of Pennsylvania Press.

Hackert, Stephanie. 2012. The Emergence of the English Native Speaker: A Chapter in the Nineteenth-Century Linguistic Thought. De Gruyter-Mouton: Boston, Berlin.

Halliday, Michael Alexander Kirkwood. 1968. The users and uses of language. In Joshua Fishman (ed.), *Readings in the sociology of language*, 512–530. The Hague: Mouton.

Holliday, Adrian R. & Pamela Aboshiha. 2009. The denial of ideology in perceptions of 'Nonnative Speaker' teachers. *TESOL Quarterly* 43. 669–689.

Holliday, Adrian R. 2005. *The struggle to teach English as an international language*. Oxford: Oxford University Press.

Holliday, Adrian R. 2015. Native-speakerism: Taking the concept forward and achieving cultural belief. In Adrian Holliday, Pamela Aboshiha & Anne Swan (eds.), *(En)Countering Native-speakerism. Global Perspectives*, 11–25. Basingstoke: Basingstoke: Palgrave MacMillan.

Hyltenstam, Kenneth. 2018. Polyglotism. In Kenneth Hyltenstam, Inge Bartning, & Lars Fant (eds.), *High-Level Language Proficiency in Second Language and Multilingual Contexts*, 170–195. Cambridge: Cambridge University Press.

Kamhi-Stein, Lia D. 2016. The non-native English speaker teachers in TESOL movement. *ELT Journal* 70. 180–189.

Kumaravadivelu, B. 2016. The decolonial option in English teaching: Can the subaltern act? *TESOL Quarterly* 50. 66–85.

Leonard, Josephine. 2019. Beyond "(non) native-speakerism": Being or becoming a native-speaker teacher of English. *Applied Linguistics Review* 10 (4). 677–703.

Llurda, Enric. 2009. The decline and fall of the native speaker. In Li Wei & Vivian J. Cook (eds.), *Contemporary Applied Linguistics: Language Teaching and Learning*, Vol. 1, 37–53. Oxford: Continuum.

Lovrits, Veronika & Julia de Bres. 2020. Prestigious language, pigeonholed speakers: Stances towards the 'native English speaker' in a multilingual European institution. *Journal of Sociolinguistics* https://doi.org/10.1111/josl.12431

Lui, P. P.riscilla & Lucia Quezada. 2019. Associations between microaggression and adjustment outcomes: A meta-analytic and narrative review. Psychological Bulletin, 145(1), 45–78.

Luk, Gigi. 2015. Who are the bilinguals (and monolinguals)? *Bilingualism: Language and Cognition* 18. 35–36.

Lüpke, Friederike. 2016. Pure fiction – the interplay of indexical and essentialist language ideologies and heterogenous practices. A view from Agnack. In: *African Language Documentation: New data, methods and approaches*. Mandana Seyfeddinipur (ed), pp 8–39. http://nflrc.hawaii.edu/ldc/.

Mahboob, Ahmar. 2004. Demystifying the Native Speaker in TESOL. SPELT Journal 19. 1–14.

Mehmedbegovic, Dina & Thomas H. Bak. 2017. Towards an interdisciplinary lifetime approach to multilingualism: from implicit assumptions to current evidence. *European Journal of Language Policy* 9 (2). 149–167.

Mitchell, Rosamund & Florence Myles. 1998. *Second Language Learning Theories*. Cambridge: Cambridge University Press.

Montrul, Silvina A. 2011. First language retention and attrition in an adult Guatemalan adoptee. *Language, Interaction and Acquisition* 2 (2). 276–311.

Murahata, Goro, Yoshiko Murahata & Vivian J. Cook. 2016. Research questions and methodology of multi-competence. In Li Wei & Vivian J. Cook (eds.), *The Cambridge Handbook of Linguistic Multi-Competence*, 26–49. Cambridge: Cambridge University Press.

Nicoladis, Elena & Howard Grabois. 2002. Learning English and losing Chinese: A case study of a child adopted from China. *International Journal of Bilingualism* 6 (4). 441–454.

O'Rourke, Bernadette & Joan Pujolar. 2021. The debates on "new speakers" and "non-native" speakers as symptoms of late modern anxieties over linguistic ownership. In Nikolay Slavkov, (ed.), *The Changing Face of the "Native Speaker": Perspectives from Multilingualism and Globalization*. Berlin: De Gruyter.

Ortega, Lourdes & Casey Keck. 2017. *Is there a deficit framing of late-timed bilingualism in published research? An empirical look.* Paper presented at the International Symposium on Bilingualism, Limerick, Ireland. June 11–15, 2017.

Ortega, Lourdes. 2014. Ways forward for a bi/multilingual turn in SLA. In Stephen May (ed.), *The multilingual turn: Implications for SLA, TESOL, and bilingual education*, 32–53. New York: Routledge.

Ortega, Lourdes. 2019. SLA and the study of equitable multilingualism. *Modern Language Journal* 103 (S1). 23–38.

Paikeday, Thomas M. 1985. *The native speaker is dead!* Toronto: Paikeday Press.

Pearce, John M. S. 2005. A note on aphasia in bilingual patients: Ribot's and Pitre's Laws. *European Neurology* 54. 127–131.

Rampton, Ben. 1990. Displacing the 'native speaker': expertise, affiliation, and inheritance. *ELT Journal* 44. 97–101.

Rosa, Jonathan & Nelson Flores. 2017. Unsettling race and language: Toward a raciolinguistic perspective. Language in Society 46 (5). 621–647.

Schmid, Monika S. 2011. *First Language Attrition*. Cambridge: Cambridge University Press.

Schmid, Monika S. 2020. On attrition, spaceships and viruses. *Second Language Research* 36 (2). 199–202.

Schmitz, John Robert. 2005. On the notions 'native'/'nonnative': A dangerous dichotomy for world Englishes? *RASK – International journal of Language and Communication* 23. 3–26.

Spivak, Gayatri Chakravorty. 1993. Outside in the teaching machine. New York: Routledge & Kegan Paul.

Surrain, Sarah & Gigi Luk. 2017. Describing bilinguals: A systematic review of labels and descriptions used in the literature between 2005–2015. *Bilingualism: Language and Cognition* 22. 401–415

Valdés, Guadalupe. 2005. Bilingualism, heritage language learners, and SLA research: Opportunities lost or seized? *Modern Language Journal* 89. 410–426.

Vega-Mendoza, Mariana, Suvarna Alladi & Thomas H. Bak. 2019. Dementia and Multilingualism. In John W. Schwieter (ed.), *The Handbook of the Neuroscience of Multilingualism*, 608–624. Hoboken, N.J.: John Wiley.

Wei, Li & Vivian J. Cook (eds.), 2016. *The Cambridge Handbook of Linguistic Multi-competence*. Cambridge: Cambridge University Press.

Ulrike Jessner, Barbara Hofer, Emese Malzer-Papp
Chapter 2
The multilingual and multicompetent native speaker

Abstract: After three decades of research and debate about the "native speaker" and "native speakerism", the notion of "nativeness" is as topical as ever due to the changing paradigms of the multicultural and multilingual actualities of our globalized and digitalized world, which call for an urgent reconceptualisation of "nativeness". The present chapter explores aspects of the "native speaker" from a historical, political, linguistic, economic and educational perspective. We will focus on the concept's shortcomings when applied in multicultural and multilingual educational settings and offer a holistic and dynamic approach as a new matrix for its reconstruction. Our argumentation is theoretically embedded in a deeper comprehension of the dynamic and complex systems theory (Herdina and Jessner 2002) and its effects on the processes in the multilingual and multicompetent mind of a new generation of multilingual and multicompetent language users. We claim that in order to meet individual, educational, social, economic and political needs of coming generations we will have to develop a broader understanding of *nativeness* beyond old dichotomies. Such a line of argumentation is directed towards negotiation of identities and competences in volatile spaces such as diverse digital and online environments that eventually might mitigate the importance of *nativeness* in the traditional sense.

Keywords: nativeness, complex system theory, multilingual and multicompetent language user

1 Introduction

In 1983, Ferguson, the then director of the Centre for Applied Linguistics in Washington DC, challenged the hitherto largely undisputed status of the native speaker (NS) declaring that

---

Ulrike Jessner, University of Innsbruck and University of Pannonia, Veszprem,
e-mail: ulrike.jessner@uibk.ac.at
Barbara Hofer, University of Innsbruck, e-mail: hofbar@libero.it
Emese Malzer-Papp, University of Innsbruck, e-mail: emese.malzer-papp@uibk.ac.at

https://doi.org/10.1515/9781501512353-003

> Linguists ... have long given a special place to the native speaker as the only true and reliable source of language data . . . much of the world's verbal communication takes place by means of languages which are not the users' mother tongue, but their second, third or nth language, acquired one way or another and used when appropriate. This kind of language use merits the attention of linguists as much as do the more traditional objects of their research. (Ferguson 1983: vii in Davies 2013: 18)

Two years later, Paikeday (1985) launched his famous attack on the NS in *The native speaker is dead*. Paikeday's contention was that the native speaker "exists only as a figment of linguist's imagination" (25, in Jodai, Pirhadi and Taghavi 2014: 790), but not in real life. Many scholars have since raised their voice in support of these early critics (Cook 2003, Herdina and Jessner 2002, Holliday 2005, Garcia 2009), arguing that we do not need the "native speaker" as a norm and linking the native speaker model to political ideologies, social and 'linguistic imperialism' (Garcia and Wei 2014, Pennycook and Otsuji 2015). Almost 40 years on from the initial critical voices (Phillipson 1992), the theoretical debate about the native speaker is still unresolved, but it is as topical as ever. Concerns subsist particularly with regards to the use of the monolingual native speaker as the benchmark for bi- and multilinguals. In parallel to this, the realization is taking hold that the model of the native speaker as the ultimate goal of language learning needs to be replaced by the more realistic model of the multilingual user (cf. Cook 2002, Jessner 2008b).

As the aim of the chapter is to better illustrate the complexity of the debate, we will individually highlight different layers of the native speaker concept first, before offering the construct of multilingual proficiency in contrast to native speaker proficiency from a holistic perspective. Finally, we will highlight the challenges of the digital era in relation to the conceptualisation of the native speaker.

2 The native speaker as a political construct

When positioning the NS in a political, societal and economic context, we have to bear in mind that the notion and its connotations always depend on the historical background in which they are embedded. The native speaker debate in the US might have completely different implications than in England, France or in many Asian and African countries. This context sensitivity is aggravated by the fact that a considerable part of the available literature on this topic focuses exclusively on native speakers of English in Western and non-Western contexts (see for a review Calafato 2019). Nonetheless, the underlying ideological grounding might be comparable in many contexts. In the present chapter, we will briefly explore the historical mindset behind the native speaker myth from a political, ideological and ontological view, but will not go into historical differences inherent to individual systems since that would go beyond the scope of the present paper.

Wilhelm von Humboldt described language "as the spirit of a nation" (Sharifian and Jamarani 2017:16) in the 18th century, and in the late 19th century languages appeared on the political ideological level as bounded, rule-governed and pure systems. The idea of the nation state is premised on an ideology of unity, social cohesion, cultural and ethnic homogeneity and uniformity. Shohamy (2006) states that „[T]he formation of the nation-state is the key organizational principle underpinning the formation of linguistic and cultural homogeneity via the establishment of a common, usually single, hegemonic "national language" (29). In a similar line of argument, Makoni and Pennycook (2007) suggest that our "conception of language was originally constructed by states that wanted to consolidate political power, and in so doing established language academies, encouraged the preparation of grammars, dictionaries, and treatises to strengthen and standardize languages" (Garcia 2009: 23; see also Gogolin 1998: 80, 89).

The Western notion of nation as a historically constituted, political and stable entity, grounded on the idea of shared language, culture and identity, stands in opposition to more contemporary and less dogmatic conceptualisations of nations as communities. Community is then envisioned as based on shared space, and as accommodating different linguistic groups, a life-reality for multilingual communities in Africa, South Asia and many other parts of the world today (Canagarajah and Wurr 2011: 2). Sociolinguistic constellations of this type, wherein no common code is shared by all citizens, necessarily give rise to meaning-making practices that go beyond traditional monolingual forms of communication. The linguistic resources employed by speakers who operate in multilingual surroundings seldom belong to one particular language only, but rather include combinations of elements from multiple codes. Hybridization takes over from linguistic purity as speakers co-construct their own 'languaging' to serve the intended communicative purposes. In so doing, they set their own (functional and even temporary) norms and rules and deviate from the norm of the native speaker.

Importantly, as successful communication takes priority over accuracy, these deviations do not so much constitute a problem as a necessity for the negotiation of meaning. In addition, they are testimony to the speaker's resourcefulness.

Recent discussions of the NS as an idealized norm draw attention to the fact that in order to perpetuate the monolingual *status quo*, those in authority resort to language policies (LP) to organize, manage and manipulate language behaviours and to regulate language use in society. It is through language policies that decisions are made with regards to the preferred and legitimized languages and how they should be used, learned, taught and evaluated in a given context. Seen from this perspective, language policies are an influential tool that skilfully manipulate the "native speaker" image as a normative factor of hegemony structures. Operating on more or less hidden levels, they determine the legitimacy of certain languages and varieties and the illegitimacy of others, and they establish how languages are to be used, or not, with regards to grammar, pronunciation, lexicon, etc. (Shohamy 2006: 45). From the one-nation-one-language perspective, bi- and multilinguals are seen as a threat to the monolingual order because they violate and betray the very norms on which the nation state is premised (Shohamy 2006: 41).

3 The native speaker as a social construct

Having positioned the NS in a politico-historical context, it is easy to understand the social and cultural implications of the construct. The term "native" is a sociocultural attribute and implies properties related to birth and birthplace (see also Ortega in May 2014). Knowledge of the "native" language is a (supposed) prerogative acquired by birth. It indicates origin in an environment where a certain community speaks the "native language" as a first language. Native language ability is a product of social interaction and "affective tie" with a certain social and cultural group (cf. Pennycook 2012) and guarantees access to and affiliation with the group. In this context, language is a vehicle of emotional engagement with the social and cultural "we" in contrast to the cultural and linguistic "other". Those lacking the "fortunate position" (Matsuda 1999: 4) of nativeness are considered somewhat insufficient concerning their cultural and linguistic proficiency. Holliday calls this distrust towards non-natives "cultural disbelief" (Holliday 2015:11). According to Kramsch (1998) and Leung (2005), being a "native speaker" puts you into a privileged position as it includes "entitlement by birth, right acquired through education, and a prerogative membership in a speech community" (Kramsch 1998, Leung 2005 in Hua 2019:163). Therefore, Davies concludes that "the native speaker construct is a social concept, not a linguistic construct (Davies 1991 in Hall 2012: 11).

The NS is usually contrasted with the "non-native speaker" (NNS), a term which is considered negative. In a sociolinguistic context, *non-nativeness* is frequently associated with attributes such as insufficient and inferior in terms of linguistic competency and proficiency. According to stereotypical conceptions, this inferiority stems from the non-native speaker's lack of innate "instinctiveness" (Leonard 2019: 690) of competent language use. Such a mindframe completely ignores multilingual realities and settings as will be discussed in the section on the Dynamic Model of Multilingualism.

4 The native speaker as a linguistic construct

The validity of the "native speaker" as the privileged norm of a linguistic community has often been challenged. While many scholars call for a deconstruction of the notion (e.g. Hall 2012) as an "idealized and outdated myth" (Kramsch 1998), some sustain its legitimacy. Mack (1997), for instance, proposes to construe the monolingual native speaker as

> an individual who has been exposed to a specific language from infancy and who can function effectively in ONLY one language. (115, capitals in the original)

According to Mack (1997), the monolingual NS "has command of only one language. He/she cannot comfortably or fluently carry out tasks of language production or comprehension in more than one language" (115).

Davies (2003) intimates that NSs are widely taken to

> have a special control over a language, insider knowledge about 'their' language. They are the models we appeal to for the 'truth' about the language, they know what the language is ('Yes, you can say that'), and what the language isn't ('No, that's not English, Japanese, Swahili . . . '). They are the stakeholders of the language, they control its maintenance and shape its direction [. . .]. (1)

Referencing mainstream monolingual positions, Davies (2013) notes that the native speaker is generally delineated as somebody who
- acquires the L1 of which s/he is a native speaker in childhood
- has intuitions (in terms of acceptability and productiveness) about her/his idiolectal syntax and about those features of the standard language grammar which are distinct from her/his idiolectal syntax
- has a unique capacity to produce fluent spontaneous discourse, a huge memory stock of complete lexical items, and a wide range of communicative competence
- has a unique capacity to write creatively, including literature at all levels, from jokes to epics, metaphor to novels and/or
- has a unique capacity to interpret and translate into the L1 of which s/he is a native speaker (22).

The notion of the native speaker, it thus seems, is typically viewed as synonymous with being monolingual and having high levels of fluency and accuracy, both spoken and written. In other words, the monolingual NS is widely construed as *the* literate role model in possession of language in its "pure" form (Davies 2003: 1; little or no consideration, the reader will agree, is ever bestowed on illiterate native speakers). It is not surprising therefore that the designation *native speaker* has drawn criticism over the past years and decades.

5 Criticism of the native speaker norm

The one-sided focus on the monolingual native speaker and his/her (more or less) perfect command of L1 has been a major point of contention in SLA and multilingualism research in recent years and was first criticised by Grosjean (1985). Grosjean (1985) particularly objects to the assumption that bi- and multilinguals function in a monolingual, native-like way. He condemns the widespread appeal to the idealized monolingual native speaker, which, he says, results in a situation whereby bi- and multilinguals are treated as if they were several monolinguals in one person and which, in consequence, causes them to be evaluated against monolingual native speaker norms. Byram has gone so far as to speak of "linguistic schizophrenia" (cf. Byram 1990) when speakers and learners are forced to abandon "one language in order to blend into another linguistic environment" to be "accepted as a native speaker by other native speakers" (Byram: 1997:11). It is noted here that this monolingual bias also carries a marked judgmental undertone that leads to representations of bi- and multilinguals as inferior (see below).

Two additional arguments speak against the monolingual native speaker as the exemplary norm. First, monolingual native speakers are in a minority worldwide because there are more non-native speakers in the world today than (monolingual) native speakers (Edwards 1994, Jessner 2006). This begs the question of whether it is at all reasonable to hold on to an idealized abstraction of a speaker that does not fit with the majority of language users today. With Piller (2001) we should like to point out that the concept of the "native speaker", while having questionable explanatory value, seems to be "geared towards the exception rather than the norm" (112). Second, languages exhibit variability in the form of dialects, registers, styles, etc. How does one propose to account for this variability and, related to that, how does one account for inter-individual variability? How, indeed, can one establish what the idealized native speaker model must be if the native speakers of one and the same language all differ from each other with regards to their language use, and/or if native speakers of the same language adhere to different norms (such as in the case of pluricentric languages)? The answer might provide the notion of the "multilingual speaker" (as the counterpart of "native") who responding to her/his own norms escapes the imposition of restrictive monolingual standards.

6 The native speaker as a trademark

The contrasting terms "native" vs "non-native" originate from the field of English Language Teaching (Leonard 2019) and have turned into a popular label to differentiate between the NS as a proficient expert and the NNS as the less competent or deficient language user. Although the term is strongly associated with English teaching, it has found its way into other languages lacking a similar concept, such as German. The German synonym for *native speaker* is "mother tongue speaker" (MuttersprachlerIn), a term that does not seem as catchy as its English equivalent so that many give priority to the English word. The *native speaker* is a trademark and stands for cultural and linguistic proficiency and correctness, quality and professionalism.

However, the native speaker label is a controversial one. Especially in the case of English, the native speaker's claim of "ownership" (e.g. Medgyes in Agudo 2017, Hall 2012, Holliday 2005, Holliday 2015, Leonard 2019) of authentic language use is perceived to perpetuate "cultural chauvinism" (Holliday 2006). The critics of the concept argue that due to its internationality and large-scale distribution, English is the "property of all" (Leonard 2019: 678) and the communicative medium of many taught by many in multilingual settings (Cook 1991 in Hall 2012). The spectacular spread of English is due to its role as the language of wider communication as a result of British colonial power in the 19th century and the political and economic dominance of the US in the 20th century (Jessner 2006). The dominance of English as a *lingua franca* is also startling in Europe. It is spoken as a second language by 38% of the adults, and 94% of students learn English as a second language in educational institutions. (The Guardian, Monday 25th September 2017). All in all, it has become clear that English has become an important factor in the creation of multilingualism today (https://www.ethnologue.com/guides/most-spoken-languages).

The rapid spread of English in Europe, despite considerable competition from French or German, is indisputably due to the role of Great Britain and Ireland with their ca. 60 million users as the safeguards of standardized British English, the most esteemed form of the English language around the globe (Modiano 2017). In his article on the role of English in a post-Brexit European Union, Modiano contemplates how English will evolve in Europe when the British are no longer involved in determining or supporting language standards and their own idealized image of the English language. Who will "carry on the work of defending the structural integrity of British English in the face of competition from not only American English, but also from L2 users who increasingly utilize features indicative of discoursal nativization (Modiano 2017: 315)?" These considerations reflect the age-old debate on language standards and once again their empowerment of the native speaker norm.

But despite fierce criticism from the different disciplines, the native speaker concept, and especially its English embodiment, still prevails because it is a "powerful and lucrative asset" (Chowdbury and Le Ha 2014). The native English teacher is a top export. According to the data published on the homepage of the International TEFL Academy (https://www.internationalteflacademy.com/blog/), an estimated 250 000 native English speakers work abroad in more than 40 000 schools all over the world. 100 000 alone work in China. European cities like Prague, Madrid and Rome are home to 50–150 language institutes all of them marketing and exploiting the "native speaker concept" as a lucrative quality label.

A study conducted in 2011 revealed how job advertisements of these language institutions contribute to promoting the native speaker concept (Selvi 2011). A "plethora of web sites such as www.telf.com reveal that little has changed with many jobs calling for "native English applicants" (Hall 2012: 112). Interestingly enough, a look at the same search engine nine years later reveals that while the terminology has slightly changed, now decoupling the term from the prerogative of birth, the new wording brings about new problems. Many teaching institutions now look for the "native *level* English teacher". While the new term is an attempt to eliminate the ideological taint of the construct, the monolingual approach to an idealized proficiency norm remains, as there are no objective descriptors and markers to pin down the *native-like* proficiency levels of a language speaker.

Interestingly enough, while English language institutions capitalize on "native speakers", their German counterparts such as the *Goethe Institute* with language institutions in more than 90 countries around the world move beyond the NS as a benchmark for proficiency and professionalism. Their websites advertise for German language teachers with a focus on *pedagogical skills* and enthusiasm for *teaching* (https://www.goethe.de/de/spr/unt/adl.html).

7 The native speaker in education

Despite multicultural and multilingual classroom situations in our diverse and complex realities, the educational system in Austria and many other European countries still plays a central role in perpetuating the monolingual NS norm and *habitus* (Hofer and Jessner 2019; Shohamy 2006: 78). It is common practice in many schools around the world to treat learners "as potential approximations to native speakers and measure their achievements against those of monolinguals" (Andreou and Galantomos 2009: 200). With 'native-speakerism' being the pervasive ideology in language teaching and learning (Holliday 2006: 385), the question arises as to its effects on classroom practices and language learning. As Byram puts it, by referring to the native speaker as the norm we create "an impossible target and consequently inevitable failure" (Byram 1997: 11, Cook 1991, 1999; see also the discussion on multicompetence below).

The suggestion here as interpreted by the authors of this chapter is that such a native speaker orientation in educational institutions:

1) sends out the message that the native-speaker model is superior to that of the non-native-speaker, thus promoting a culture of 'native-speakerism' which highlights weaknesses and inadequacies, enforces adherence to standard rules and shows little tolerance for form deviations.
2) disadvantages those learners who may be motivated to learn and have high fluency but only low accuracy (in one or more languages) and are therefore penalized by the monolingually oriented system. This said, on the flip side high fluency might (despite low accuracy) also be seen as a better approximation to the native speaker.
3) does not value or encourage cross-language strategy deployment, creativity and risk-taking and as a result constitutes a hindrance to the development of an autonomous, self-reliant learning attitude.
4) discriminates against bi- and multilingual learners who do not typically have equal command of their languages and
5) discriminates against heritage and minority language learners whose dominant language is not the majority language but who are expected to perform in native-like ways in the majority language.

7.1 Teachers as native speakers

The NS approach in the context of teaching often leads to the misguided assumption that native speakers make better teachers than non-native speaker teachers. As Hall (2012) puts it, non-native language teachers also have to face a certain "hidden professional racism". Nativeness is automatically associated with high-level language skills and "instinctive" language proficiency. Thus, teachers who did not acquire their language skills from birth in a natural language environment are stigmatized as deficient language users and are often discriminated on the job market. For example, Spanish-English Dual Language

Immersion programs in the US suffer from an urgent language teacher shortage because US-born Spanish speakers are seen as linguistically inferior compared to their peers who were born in a Spanish-speaking country and gained their language competences there (Amanti 2019). However, as Pennycook points out, "proficiency comes from education and experience and not birth" (Pennycook 2012), and automatically empowering the hereditary speaker as proficient speaker is questionable. Language proficiency changes at different times in life and most native speakers are only proficient in some language domains. The preference for nativeness in language classes derives from the preconception that learning the language from a "native speaker" is more effective and the only way to acquire native-like language skills.

A study conducted by the DyME research group in Tyrolean (Austrian) kindergartens also substantiated this tendency. In the province of Tyrol 19,6 % of the children aged between 3 to 5 years attending kindergarten speak an L1 different from German (Statistik Austria 2018/19). However, due to Austrian educational policies, the main objective of kindergarten education is to equip children with German language skills necessary for school start, best mediated by Austrian native speakers. The study revealed that, despite the fact that a large number of children with an L1 different from German attend elementary educational institutions in Tyrol, less than 10% of the kindergarten caretakers have a multilingual background and can use the multilingual resources the children bring along, the focus being placed only on German (SPIEL Study report 2017).

In minority language contexts, the native speaker model takes on its own specific role. A good case in point is South Tyrol, offering an array of representations of the native speaker in a presumably multilingual society but monolingually oriented school system (see also Gogolin 1997). With regional autonomy and linguistic minority rights contributing to a strong monolingual (German) bias, the stance taken by a majority of political and educational stakeholders in South Tyrol is that multilingual education cannot guarantee attainment of high competence in L1 because the efforts that go into L2/Ln acquisition undermine young learners' development of L1.

The monolingual NS bias operates on two levels: on the one hand learners of an L2 are expected to attain high accuracy and near-native command in L2. On the other hand, the teacher (of both, L1 and L2) who is legally required to be a native speaker is widely seen as the (only) competent teacher to transmit the target language.

A recent survey among Italian native-speaker teachers and English native and non-native speaker teachers in South Tyrol has found a strong preference amongst the teaching profession for the native speaker model (Wieser 2019: 80). This was shown to be particularly the case among Italian teachers. The study revealed that two thirds of the teachers participating in the research were of the opinion that the native teacher is the best learning model for students. But how does the native speaker teacher fare? An important observation to make at this point is that NS teachers of L2 Italian, particularly if they come from the South of Italy, sometimes have poor command of the German language and/or are not always familiar with the local socio-linguistic and politico-historical context. At the same time, they may expect students to have a high proficiency in L2 Italian (simply because they are Italian citizens) when in reality learners do not always command the L2 at a sufficiently high level. The reasons for pupils' often poor mastery of L2 Italian are manifold and range from lack of motivation to inadequate teaching approaches (the focus in many L2 classrooms being on literature rather than language arts). Recommendations to the effect that L2 Italian ought to be taught as a foreign language rather than a second language has largely gone unheeded among the teaching profession. Indeed, in the L2 Italian classroom precedence is generally given to literature and the classics rather than to language use and communicative aspects, the argument being that German-speaking students in South Tyrol can be expected to have a sufficiently high level of proficiency in the national language to study the classics. In reality however, a sizable share of the student population only ever attains low levels of competency in L2 Italian.

7.2 Learners as future NS

Likewise, as already hinted at above, it is to be expected that learner behaviour and performance are evaluated differently depending on whether the set target norm is the monolingual native speaker or the functional multilingual user. The difference between the two concepts is that the former sees learners of languages as several monolinguals in one person while the latter focuses on "real-life use" (Jessner 2006: 10) irrespective of how "small or ineffective" (Cook 2002: 3) this use is. Jessner points out that using and learning can both form part of multilingual development, as in the case of migrant children who learn and use the new school language at the same time (Jessner 2006). Traditional foreign language teaching and learning methods are based on the idea that students should ideally, "get as close as possible to monolingual native speakers" (Cook 2002: 239). This approach ignores the fact that multiple language learning and use is a complex, non-linear process (Herdina and Jessner 2002, Jessner 2008a) that results from the dynamic interaction of the different languages in a multilingual's repertoire. These interactions produce different and partly completely new properties in language learning and use that are not measurable with monolingual standards. Thus "the multilingual speaker is a "unique but competent speaker-hearer" whose competences are not a sum of the "additive monolingualism of several languages" (Jessner 2016: 175). However, the image of the multilingual and multicompetent language user is flawed by many prejudices. Especially if this image is associated with migration and minority groups, multilinguals are seen as deficient language users who lack proficiency in all their languages. This especially applies to kindergarten and schoolchildren who are often classified and assessed based on their origin (Garcia 1984; Wenz and Hoenig 2020), appearance or name instead of on their competences. In a study about teacher's beliefs about multilingualism and the presence of heritage languages in the classroom, De Angelis (2011) found that most participants from Italy, Austria and Great Britain shared similar views and regarded the presence of heritage languages in the classroom as disadvantageous for the acquisition of the host language (De Angelis 2011: 229).

8 The multilingual speaker as counterpart of the native speaker

From the monolingual, fractional perspective described above, the ideal multilingual speaker is someone who has perfect and equal command of all his/her languages. He/she easily passes as a (monolingual) native speaker of the single languages (Piller 2001). Like his/her monolingual counterpart, he/she adheres to monolingual norms. That is to say, he/she does not mix the languages but keeps them apart and 'uncontaminated' in all situations, and is immune to interference effects, intrusions, lexical gaps, etc. In short, he/she behaves like the ideal speaker-listener envisaged by Chomsky (1965, see below).

The question is: how does this idealized speaker compare to the real multilingual? The fact of the matter is that the real multilingual speaker rarely has equal or near-native command of his/her languages. His/her understanding of language norms is different from that of the ideal monolingual NS, which is why he tends to deviate from these norms. He does not generally aim at accuracy or perfect mastery in individual languages, but instead,

1) has other uses for languages than the monolingual NS,
2) his/her knowledge of languages (whether first or additional languages) is typically not identical to that of the NS, and
3) his/her processing differs from that of the monolingual NS because the presence of multiple languages in the mind provides him with a different perspective on language, language choice and language use (Cook 2003, Herdina and Jessner 2002).

More recently, Canagarajah and Wurr (2011: 6) have characterized multilingual speakers as follows:
- multilingual speakers' languages are always in contact and influence and complement each other.
- multilingual speakers draw on all their languages for communication. They do not separate but intermesh their different codes. Their usage of language is heteroglossic rather than monoglossic.
- multilinguals have an integrated competence which is different in kind and degree from monolingual competence.
- multilinguals negotiate meaning *in situ*, as they cannot assume a common grammar or linguistic system when communicating with speakers of other languages.
- multilinguals' language practices are constantly renegotiated and reconstructed. Nothing is fixed and stable.

Recent research (Blackledge and Creese 2017, Canagarajah 2018, Garcia 2009, Kusters et al. 2017, Pennycook 2017) confirms that code-switching and translanguaging play a major role in contemporary multilingual communication with speakers drawing on their entire linguistic repertoires in order to find a common ground between their different languages and/or resources. In multilingual contexts, speakers cannot always assume a shared grammar (or language) so they rely on trans-lingual practices and strategies (Canagarajah and Wurr 2011: 2; Canagarajah 2018) which they use to overcome their language differences. These new practices are not necessarily seen as a "form of knowledge or cognitive competence, but a form of resourcefulness which empowers individuals to successfully navigate multi-lingual communicative situations" (Canagarajah and Wurr 2011: 2). Given that, according to monolingual criteria, the "native speaker" is the safeguard of perfect and uncontaminated language use, multilingual practices such as translanguaging, code-mixing or code-switching, in particular, are widely condemned as defective, and low attainment in the single languages is typically interpreted as proof of cognitive overload and linguistic inadequacy.

On a related note, it is important to bear in mind that, as multilingual users engage in communicative exchanges with (other) non-native speakers; they typically operate in spaces not shaped by the norm of the native speaker and, as a result, engage in situated practices that may be far removed from the model of the monolingual native speaker. In point of fact, for many multilingual speakers, the native speaker norm is probably neither a model they seek to emulate nor a realistic target to pursue.

What is more, multilinguals exhibit a so-called Dominant Language Constellation or DLC (Aronin and Singleton 2008), which is to say that the languages in their repertoire carry differential weight depending on their functional utility and perceived communicative needs (Herdina and Jessner 2002). Some of their languages occupy more central roles than others and are, by implication, more highly developed than more peripheral ones, which underscores the claim that multilinguals are fundamentally distinct from monolinguals because they have different proficiencies, different abilities and different needs (see also Aronin 2019).

9 The native speaker and the dynamic model of multilingualism

Since the *native speaker* concept has proved to be a flawed notion requiring revision, many scholars developed approaches to counter the problem. The strive to disentangle proficiency from "nativeness" has generated a number of more permeable terms and concepts such as 'proficient user' (Paikeday 1985), 'language expert' (Rampton 1990), L1 vs. LX user (Deweale 2018), 'functional nativeness" (Kachru 2004) or the "intercultural speaker" who mediates between different perspectives and cultures (Byram 1997: 48–53).

Cook (1999) irrevocably broke with the monolingual native speaker norm and introduced the term of the 'multicompetent user'; a concept that interconnects the different languages a person speaks, valuing language performance as a whole. The focus on the interdependence of the language systems of multilinguals and the dynamic processes between them serves as a starting point for more holistic approaches to multilingual language use. By applying Dynamic Systems Theory, Herdina and Jessner (2002) developed the Dynamic Model of Multilingualism (DMM). The DMM challenges the traditional values of linguistic theories (e.g. Chomskyan notions) and defines multilingual proficiency in contrast to "native speaker" proficiency as a holistic construct consisting of diverse components.

Jessner (2006, 2008 a,b, 2014) describes multilingual systems as the sum of language-specific and non-language-specific skills that emerge from processes such as language learning, language management and language maintenance, which are not available in monolingual systems. The interaction between the different language systems generates a number of emergent linguistic and cognitive abilities that have a positive influence on creativity, cognitive flexibility as well as communicative and problem-solving competences. Multiple language use also increases metalinguistic awareness, that is, the knowledge about languages, their conscious perception and the ability to see them as abstract constructs. All these skills and abilities inherent to multilingual experience can offer benefits concerning processes of language acquisition and language learning. With respect to language acquisition, learners can use meta- and cross-linguistic analysis drawing on their language knowledge and adapting and developing strategies that suit their needs.

Non-native language teachers being "proficient multilinguals by default" (Calafato 2019: 4) can profit from their better understanding of language structures and use this deeper understanding to explain to learners how the target language works (Riodan, 2018). Non-native language teachers can efficiently use their experience of having experimental knowledge gained through training and education (Calafato 2019). Ideally, they show a better understanding of multilingual competencies and their effects on learning processes. But in order to be able to use multilingual approaches in their classrooms, "teachers need a deeper understanding of cross-linguistic interaction and training in the use of similarities and differences across languages" (Jessner 2016: 174). As already discussed by Jessner in 1999 and also confirmed by several studies later on, among them Otwinowska's study about teachers' language awareness in Poland (2014), it is important that language teachers themselves are multilingual in order to be aware of the benefits and advantages of multilingualism in classroom situations.

The specific abilities and skills of non-native speakers and teachers described above *might* positively support their language learning and teaching activities depending on the circumstances. Since language systems function as complex and rather non-linear dynamic interacting systems (Herdina and Jessner 2002) and are subject to constant change, the high sensitivity to initial conditions plays a crucial role.

The dependence on initial conditions is used to refer to the unpredictability of the development of dynamic systems, where the interaction of multiple agents results in *new emergent qualities* that show properties that are different from any of the individual agents such as those assigned to the M-Factor in the DMM. One of the most crucial initial conditions in a multilingual system is linked to the linguistic environment of a child at birth, that is whether a child is born into a mono-, bi- or multilingual environment. Consequently, another example of initial conditions or states that can influence the trajectory of development are the language modes (Grosjean, 2001) multilingual students find themselves in in the learning environment. If in a monolingual classroom where the monolingual mode of the teacher favors monolingual students with the same linguistic background, the bi- and multilingual modes of children with a different linguistic mindset might influence students' linguistic behavior in the language of schooling and put them at a disadvantage.

Therefore, language learning and teaching set in monolingual native speaker ideologies considerably influences the development and behaviour of multilingual individuals. Negative attitudes towards multilingualism and multilingual practices in classroom situations impede multilingual children and teachers to reach their optimum in school performance and fully scoop the benefits of their linguistic and cognitive resources. Also, the assessment of multilinguals should be remodelled on an expert language user norm rather than the standard monolingual native speaker benchmark, which entails comparing learners to other, expert or successful, multilingual learners instead of native speakers, as suggested by Cook already more than twenty years ago (Cook 1991, 2012, De Angelis and Jessner 2012).

Such an approach is provided by approximative systems theory as discussed by Nemser (1971) and adopted in the DMM. Nemser (1971) "acknowledges the fact that learner systems are approximations of standardised conceptions of native-speaker systems. The fact that native-speaker systems are standardised does, however, indicate that native speakers themselves also only have at their disposal a partial or approximative system of LS_1. This appears particularly self-evident, when we consider the plethora of utility systems contained in any developed language system." (Herdina and Jessner 2002: 46).

From a more applied perspective, a multicompetence approach to language proficiency in multilingual education as discussed in links the DMM to the conceptualisation of Cook's multicompetence. Among the new features of multicompetence to be introduced as part of multilingual instead of monolingual traditional norms in (applied) linguistics is the native speaker concept, which needs reconsideration.

10 The legacy and future of the "native speaker"

As described in the previous paragraphs, the concept of the native speaker in language learning and teaching along monolingual paradigms is outdated and needs revision. While some scholars call for a complete deconstruction of the notion, others want to reconstruct it. Deconstruction would mean delegitimizing the notion as an artificial construct following ideological principles. But is nativeness *per se* not a legitimate concept? In its broadest sense, nativeness means everything we are exposed to in the early years of our lives (see also Melo-Pfeifer in Vetter and Jessner 2019). Being a native is not strictly related to a certain locality but can be any experience that forms and influences us from childhood on. In times of globalisation and powerful technological advancements, nativeness includes more than traditional forms of socialisation through language, culture and value systems. It also includes new technological environments and the early acquisition of skills necessary to navigate them.

From a DSCT point of view, as already pointed out, linguistic and nonlinguistic factors interact, with initial conditions playing a special role in the development of multilingual systems and multilingual proficiency. This applies to new developments in the use of languages and other semiotic signs for future communicative needs. The arrival of the digital era, to give an example, has considerably changed our social norms and has brought a new dimension into our thinking patterns. Having these changes in mind, Prensky (2001) revitalized the native speaker concept in a completely different, but for language learning and teaching very relevant context. He described his students as "native speakers" of the digital language of computers, video games and the Internet (Prensky 2001). In his seminal article *Digital Natives, Digital Immigrants* he ascribed "nativeness" to a whole generation that differs on the basis of their computer-based communication skills and not their language competences. "Digital natives" are those who have grown up using Information Communication Technology, and were born into a digital environment (Pasfield-Neofitou 2013). In the new online environment, traditional national, cultural and linguistic boundaries are blurred and competences such as computer knowledge, typing speed and understanding of "netspeak" gain more and more importance. Proficiency in this new context requires skills that are per se multilingual, transcultural and multimodal.

In his article *"Digital Natives" and "Native speakers"*, Pasfield-Neofitou (2013) examined the relevance of being "digital native" and "native speaker" in an online environment by analysing over two thousand intercultural communication instances online between Japanese and Australian participants. The results of the study show that computer-based communication competence "is more complex than being a native speaker or a digital native and requires not only linguistic and technical competence, but also the sensitivity to know how to combine these competences in a variety of situations with a variety of different interlocutors" (Pasefield-Neofitou 2013: 157). This sensitivity is an emergent new property as described in DSCT in the paragraph above that results from the interaction of several, in this case dissimilar systems: the linguistic, personal, technical and social ones. The more systems are involved (culture, social abilities etc.), the more complexity is generated. The interaction between the systems yields a number of new competences and qualities that shape the construct of nativeness in the sense of an early, formative experience in a new environment. Thus, if we opt for the reconstruction of the "native speaker" in the sense of DSCT, we also have to consider the new resources offered by "digital nativeness".

The *new native speaker* is a multilingual, transcultural and multicompetent language user who smartly combines technological competences with linguistic skills and cultural and social sensitiveness. His/her *nativeness* is not a static construct but is situationally negotiated and is strongly context-dependent. Stavans (Stavans in Breuer, Lindgren, Stavan and van Steendam 2021) showed in two small-scale exploratory studies on the use of emojis in multilingual contexts that there is for example an evolution "of a new notational encoding of a language repertoire, driven by a societally conceived practice." At the same time, the conclusions drawn from the study show how new concepts used by a generation of "digital natives" are measured and valued by traditional scientific norms such as the assumption that language has to be defined along the lines of complex grammatical structures (cf. Stavans, in press).

Educational systems of the future will therefore have to adapt to this fundamental change and adjust their learning and teaching environments to the needs and resources of a new generation of "native speakers" and "digital natives". This would help to avoid the scenario described by Prensky when "instructors who speak an outdated language (. . .) are struggling to teach a population that speaks an entirely new language" (Prensky 2001: 2). Nonetheless, it still needs to be explored how these new digital systems will affect communication of all kinds including multilingual systems, and how the new semiotic system will impact the complexity of multilingual learning and use.

Technology-based skills will presumably be just as or even more relevant than traditional linguistic resources. Identities and competences will be negotiated in volatile spaces such as diverse digital and online environments and the importance of nativeness will probably diminish or even disappear. Since the arrival of the digital era, language has already considerably changed and new forms of communication have developed, and this trend will continue. Language in the traditional sense will probably morph into a new communication tool adjusted to the requirements of digital technology. Language standards will probably pop up only punctually, when, for example, negotiating the language of voice-controlled intelligent personal assistants or artificial intelligence devices involved in communication such as robotic nurses. This transformation process can be only accommodated by holistic approaches to language and multilingualism that dynamically adapt to its complex interactions and allow new properties to emerge.

11 Conclusion

The above discussion shows that the *native speaker* concept as inherited from previous generations with its ideological implications will have to be revised. Scholarly efforts of the past decades to reconceptualise it and make it adaptable to the requirements of a globalised world with its multilingual and multicultural societies are steps into the right direction, however they do not go far enough. At its core, the "native speaker" still stands for a dichotomy between "we" and "them", monolingual vs. multilingual and proficient vs. deficient. Dichotomies (global vs. local, diversity vs. homogeneity etc.) might be symptomatic of our times but will become unsustainable in the twenty-first century where digital technologies will completely reshape our political, cultural, social, economic and educational environments. The term "digital natives" as introduced by Prensky (Prensky 2001) opens up a new dimension of the term and questions it as an absolute category. The new "nativeness" will have to focus on social identities of individuals that are shaped by "familiarity" with a certain environment or certain specialised skills and abilities rather than the innate affiliation with a group. Being a native speaker, native user etc. will need an understanding of nativeness that is based on a common and shared experience within a community or a certain group of people. Nativeness will become a dynamic and situationally defined concept that will be formed along specific skills and competences and the ability to efficiently combine them.

Authors' Positionalities

Ulrike Jessner Ever since I studied English and French at university to become a teacher of both languages I have been confronted with the ultimate goal of attaining native speaker level in both foreign languages. During my studies, I noticed that both languages also started showing influence on my native language German. But while I started reflecting on the dynamics of my multilingualism, on the institutional level the two subjects English and French were kept totally isolated from each other. At Graz University that even meant studying in two buildings far from each other, one of which was a beautiful villa formerly owned by the well-known scholar Hugo Schuchardt who we know had shown an early interest in the study of language contact.

In my research on multilingual learning and teaching the discussion of the native speaker norm has always played an essential part and I have become more and more aware of the complexity of the topic. In fact, political aspects of language have turned out to be most influential in the discussion of norms applied in differing contexts.

Whereas foreign language learners will keep on wishing to become native speakers in all their languages and often suffer from the comparison with the native speaker, in a natural or grassroots multilingual context speakers have learnt to balance their linguistic resources. That is why we as researchers in the field of Applied Linguistics need to continue putting more emphasis on the link between classroom teaching and natural learning phenomena like codeswitching.

Ulrike Jessner is Professor at the University of Innsbruck (Austria) and the University of Pannonia, Veszprem (Hungary) where she acts as founding member of the International

Doctoral School of Multilingualism. She has been engaged in the development of the research area of third language acquisition/multilingualism as a founding member and former president of the International Association of Multilingualism. She is founding editor of the *International Journal of Multilingualism* and the book series *Trends in Applied Linguistics* (Mouton de Gruyter). She also heads the DyME (Dynamics of multilingualism with English) research group.

Barbara Hofer Having grown up in a region where three language communities live side by side, Barbara Hofer came to experience linguistic inadequacy and feelings of non-belonging early on, the ideal of the native speaker haunting her much of her teenage years and beyond. Travelling on a train from Rome to Florence at the young age of 15, she was asked by fellow travellers "Ma voi lassu`cosa siete? Non siete ne tedeschi, ne italiani!" (But what are you up there? You're neither German nor Italian!). In upper secondary school she witnessed her late Italian teacher throw memorable tantrums in class which once had him cry out in rage "Odio questa lavagna perchè l'hanno fatta tedeschi!" (I hate this board because it was made by Germans!). More recently, aged 35, she was invited by friends of hers to spend time with them in Rome, "cosí impari l'italiano" (so you learn Italian). Not belonging to either, the native-speaker community of Italians, nor speaking proper German (because her native language is but a subordinate and purportedly underdeveloped variety spoken only in the Alpine region of South Tyrol) but rather failing to measure up to Standard German norms left her feeling that she did not really fit in anywhere. It was only as a mature student in one of Ulrike Jessner's seminars at Innsbruck University that she learned to adopt a multilingual perspective and became able to view her linguistic and cultural repertoire as something quite unique and valuable. In her current research, in which she investigates early multilingual competencies from a Dynamic Systems and Complexity perspective, she also critically analyses native speaker norm impositions calling for the replacement of the latter with multilingual targets.

Barbara Hofer is an English teacher and lecturer at the Free University of Bozen and a member of the DyME research team at Innsbruck University. Her research interests include multilingual learning and development, and multilingual awareness. Recent publications focus on early multi-competence, learner attitudes and multilingual assessment (*MSK MehrSprachigKompetent 9–12*, Hofer & Jessner 2019).

Emese Malzer-Papp was lucky enough to experience many facets of the (non) native speaker concept at a political, societal and private level. Born in Transylvania (Romania) to a Hungarian family she was a native speaker of Hungarian in a minority context. She became aware of the consequences of speaking the *wrong* language at a very early age when she was confronted with the majority language Romanian in kindergarten. This experience was a far-reaching one and strongly influenced her attitude to language and language learning.

Political engagement for the conservation of minority languages forced the family to leave the country and immigrate to Austria. At the age of 14 Malzer-Papp once again had to adapt to a new language environment by trying to measure up to the expectation of a German-speaking society. In order to actively take the challenge of being a non-native speaker of German, she decided to study Translation Sciences for English and Spanish with German as L1 at the University of Innsbruck. Her first application for admission was refused with the argument that she "was amputating her language flexibility necessary for an academic career by not being a native speaker of German". At her second attempt, however, she passed for a native speaker.

Since then her interest focuses on the sociolinguistic and psycholinguistic aspects of language learning and acquisition. Married to an Austrian she educates her children multilingually and observes closely the influence of language practices on identity and its societal repercussions. She is especially interested in the new forms of communication and how these will change the concept of language and communication in the future.

Emese Malzer-Papp is a language trainer for youngsters and adults and lecturer for Intercultural Communication at the University of Innsbruck. As a member of the DyME research team at Innsbruck University she focuses her research on language acquisition and development in early language learners as well as transformation of language in the digital era.

References

Amanti, Cathy. 2019. Is native-speakerism impacting the Dual Language Immersion teacher shortage? *Multilingua*. 38 (6). 675–686.
Andreou, Georgia & Ioannis Galantomos. 2009. The native speaker ideal in foreign language teaching. *Electronic Journal of Foreign Language Teaching* 6 (2). 200–208.
Aronin, Larissa. 2019. What is multilingualism? In David Singleton & Larissa Aronin (eds.), *Twelve lectures in multilingualism*, 3–34. Bristol: Multilingual Matters.
Aronin, Larissa & David Singleton. 2008. Multilingualism as a new linguistic dispensation. *International Journal of Multilingualism* 1. 1–16
Blackledge, Andrian & Angela Creese. 2010. *Multilingualism. A critical perspective*. London, New York: Continuum International Publishing Group.
Byram, Michael. 1990. *Language learners' perceptions of a foreign culture the teacher's role*. Washington, D.C: ERIC Clearinghouse. https://eric.ed.gov/?id=ED324961
Byram, Michael. 1997. *Teaching and assessing intercultural communicative competence*. Cleveldon: Multilingual Matters.
Calafato, Raes. 2019. The non-native speaker teacher as a proficient multilingual: A critical review of research from 2009–2018. *Lingua* 227. Elsevier B.V. https://doi.org/10.1016/j.lingua.2019.06.001
Canagarajah, Suresh. 2018. Translingual practice as spatial repertoires: Expanding the paradigm beyond structuralist orientations. *Applied Linguistics* 39 (1). 31–54.
Canagarajah, Suresh & Adrian Wurr. 2011. Multilingual Communication and Language Acquisition: New Research Directions. *The Reading Matrix* 11 (1). 1–15.
Chomsky, Noam. (1965). *Aspects of the theory of syntax*. Cambridge, MA: MIT Press.
Chowdbury, Raqib & Phan Le Ha. 2014. *Desiring TESOL and international education. market abuse and exploitation*. Bristol: Multilingual Matters.
Cook, Vivian. 1991. The Poverty-of-the-stimulus argument and multi-competence. *Second Language Research* 7. 103–117.
Cook, Vivian. 1999. Going beyond native speaker in language teaching. *TESOL Quarterly* 33 (2). 185–200.
Cook, Vivian. 2002. Background to the L2 user. In V. Cook (Ed.), *Portraits of the L2 User*, 1–28. Clevedon: Multilingual Matters.
Cook, Vivian. 2003. The changing L1 in the L2 user's mind. In V. Cook (Ed.), *Effects of the L2 on the L1*. Clevedon: Multilingual Matters.

Cook, Vivian. 2012. *The native speaker and the second language user.* Sarajevo: Newcastle University Plenary talk at FLTAL.

Cook, Vivian. 2013. What are the goals of language teaching? *Iranian Journal of Language Teaching Research,* 1 (1). 44–56.

Cook, Vivian. 2016. Premises of multi-competence. In: Cook, Vivian & Li Wei (eds.) *The Cambridge Handbook of Linguistic Multi-Competence*, 1–25. Cambridge: Cambridge University Press.

Davies, Alan. 2003. *The Native Speaker: Myth and Reality.* Clevedon: Multilingual Matters.

Davies, Alan. 2013. Is the native speaker dead? *Histoire Épistémologie Langage* 35 (2). 17–28.

De Angelis, Gessica. 2011. Teachers' beliefs about the role of prior language knowledge in learning and how these influence teaching practices. *International Journal of Multilingualism.* 8 (3). 216–234. DOI: 10.1080/14790718.2011.560669

De Angelis, Gessica. & Ulrike Jessner. 2012. Writing across langauges in a bilingual context: A dynamic systems theory perspective. In R. Machon (Ed.) *L2 writing development: Multiple perspectives*, 47–68. Berlin, New Yori, NY: Mouton de Gruyter.

Dewaele, Jean-Marc. 2017. Why the dichotomy 'L1 versus LX user' is better than 'nativeversus non-native speaker'. *Applied Linguistics* 39. 10.1093/applin/amw055.

Edwards, John. 1994. *Multilingualism.* London: Routledge

De Angelis, Gessica. & Ulrike Jessner. 2012. Writing across langauges in a bilingual context: A dynamic systems theory perspective. In R. Machon (Ed.) *L2 writing development: Multiple perspectives*, 47–68. Berlin, New Yori, NY: Mouton de Gruyter.

Ferguson, Charles. (1983). Language Planning and Language Change. In Cobarrubias, Juan and Fishman, Joshua A. (eds.), *Progress in Language Planning*, 29–40. Berlin, Boston: De Gruyter Mouton.

Garcia, Ofelia. 2009. *Bilingual education in the 21st Century. A Global Perspective.* Chichester: Wiley-Blackwell.

Garcia, Ofelia & Li Wei. 2014. *Translanguaging: Language, bilingualism, and education.* 5–18 New York, NY: Palgrave MacMillan

Garcia, Ricardo L. 1984. Countering Classroom Discrimination. *Theory Into Practice*, 23 (2), 104–109. Retrieved October 21, 2020, from http://www.jstor.org/stable/1476438

Gogolin, Ingrid. 1998. Sprachen rein halten-Eine Obsession. In: Gogolin, Ingrid, Graap, Sabine & Liste, Günther (eds.), *Über Mehrsprachigkeit.* 72–96. Stuttgart: Stauffenburg Verlag.

Gogolin, Ingrid. 1997. The "monolingual habitus" as the common feature in teaching in the language of the majority in different countries. *Per Linguam* 13 (2). 38–49.

Grosjean, Francois. 1985. The bilingual as a competent but specific speaker-hearer. 467–477. *Journal of Multilingual and Multicultural Development*, 6 (6). 467–477.

Grosjean, Francois. 2008. *Studying bilinguals.* Oxford: Oxford University Press.

Grosjean, Francois. 2010. *Bilingual: Life and reality.* Cambridge: Harvard University Press.

Hall, Stephen. 2012. Deconstructing aspects of native speakerism: Reflections from in-service teacher education. *Journal of Asia TEFL* 9. 107–130.

Herdina, Philip & Ulrike Jessner. 2002. *A Dynamic Model of Multilingualism – Perspectives of change in psycholinguistics.* Clevedon: Multilingual Matters.

Holliday, Adrian. 2005. *The struggle to teach English as an international language.* Oxford: Oxford University Press.

Holliday, Adrian. (2006). Native-speakerism, *ELT Journal*, 60 (4), 385–387.

Holliday, Adrian. 2015. Native-speakerism: Taking the concept forward and achieving cultural belief. In Anne S., Aboshiha, Pamela & Holliday, Adrian (eds.) *Encountering Native-speakerism: Global Perspectives*. 11–25. Basingstoke: Palgrave Macmillan.
Hua, Zu. 2019. *Exploring intercultural communication: Language in action*. London and New York: Routledge
Kachru, Braj B. 2004. Asian Englishes: Beyond the canon. Hong Kong: Hong Kong University Press.
Jessner, Ulrike. 2006. *Linguistic awareness in multilinguals: English as a third language*. Edinburgh: Edinburgh University Press.
Jessner, Ulrike. 2008a. A DST Model of Multilingualism and the Role of Metalinguistic Awareness. *The Modern Language Journal* 92 (2). 270–283.
Jessner, Ulrike. 2008b. Teaching Third Languages: Findings, Trends and Challenges. *Language Teaching*, 41 (1). 15–56.
Jessner, Ulrike. 2014. On Multilingual Awareness or Why the Multilingual Learner is a Specific Language Learner. In Pawlak, Miroslaw; Aronin, Larissa (eds.). *Essential Topics in Applied Linguistics and Multilingualism. Studies in Honor of David Singleton*. 175–184. Wien [u.a.]: Springer.
Jessner, Ulrike. 2016. Multicompetence approaches to language proficiency development in multilingual education. In García, Ofelia, Lin, Angel, May, Stephen (eds) *Bilingual and multilingual education. Encyclopedia of Language and Education*. Springer.
Jessner, Ulrike, Elisabeth Allgäuer-Hackl & Barbara Hofer. 2016. *Emerging multilingual awareness in educational contexts: From theory to practice*. Canadian Modern Language Review 72 (2). 1–26.
Jodai, Hojat, Javad Pirhadi & Mehdi Taghavi. 2014. Attitudes towards native speaker norms: Evidence from an Iranian context. *Procedia Social and Behavioural Sciences* 98. 789–798.
Kramsch, Claire. 1998. The privileges of the intercultural speaker. In Byram, Michael & Flemming, Michael (eds.). *Language Learning in the Intercultural Perspective: Approaches through Drama and Ethnography*. 16–31. Cambridge: Cambridge University Press.
Kusters, Annelies, Massimiliano Spotti, Ruth Swanwick & Elina Tapio. 2017. Beyond languages, beyond modalities: transforming the study of semiotic repertoires. *International Journal of Multilingualism* 14 (3). 219–232, DOI: 10.1080/14790718.2017.1321651
Leonard, Josie. 2019. Beyond '(non) native-speakerism': Being or becoming a native-speaker teacher of English. Applied Linguistics Review, 10 (4), 677–703.
Leung, Constant. 2005. Convivial communication: Recontextualising communicative competence. *International Journal of Applied Linguistics* 15 (2). 119–143.
Mack, Molly. 1997. The monolingual native speaker: not a norm, but still a necessity. *Studies in the Linguistic Sciences* 27 (2). 113–146.
Makoni, Sinfree & Alastair Pennycook. 2005. Disinventing and (Re)constituting languages. *Critical Inquiry in Language Studies* 2. 137–156. 10.1207/s15427595cils0203_1.
Matsuda, Paul Kei. 1999. Teacher development through native-speaker-nonnative speaker collaboration. *TESOL Matters* 9 (6). 1–10.
Medgyes, Péter. 2017. Foreword. In Martinez Agudo, Juan de Dios (ed.). *Native and Non Native Teachers in English Language Classrooms. Professional Challenges and Teacher Education*, x–xi. Trends in Applied Linguistics 26. De Gruyter Mouton.
Modiano, Marko. 2017. English in a post. *Brexit European Union*. 36, no. 3, p. 313–327, doi:10.1111/weng.12264.

Moussu, Lucie & Enric Llurda. 2008. Non-native English-speaking English language teachers: History and research. *Language Teaching* 41 (3). 315–348.
Nemser, William. 1971. *Approximative Systems of Foreign Language Learners*. IRAL 9. 115–123. http://dx.doi.org/10.1515/iral.1971.9.2.115
Otwinowska, Agnieszka. 2014. Does multilingualism influence plurilingual awareness of Polish teachers of English? *International Journal of Multilingualism* 11 (1). 97–119
Paikeday, Thomas. 1985. *The native speaker is dead!* Toronto-New York, Paikeday Pub. Co.
Pasfield-Neofitou, Sarah. 2013. "Digital natives" and "native speakers": Competence in computer-mediated communication. In Sharifian, Farzad & Jamarani, Maryam (eds.) *Language and Intercultural Communication in the New Era*, 138–159. Routledge Studies in Language and Intercultural Communication 1. Abingdon Oxon UK: Routledge.
Pennycook, Alastair. 1998. *English and the discourses of colonialism*. London: Routledge, 133–144.
Pennycook, Alastair. 2012. *Language and mobility: Unexpected places*. Bristol: Multilingual Matters.
Pennycook, Alastair & Emi Otsuji. 2015. *Metrolingualism: Language in the city*. Abingdon, U.K/New York: Routledge, 255. https://doi.org/10.1111/josl.12220
Pennycook, Alastair. 2017. *The cultural politics of English as an international language*. Taylor & Francis: Routledge Linguistic Classics.
Philipson, Robert. 1992. *Linguistic imperialism*. Oxford: Oxford University Press
Piller, Ingrid. 2001. Who, if anyone, is a native speaker? *Anglistik* 12 (2). 109–121.
Prensky, Marc. 2001. *Digital natives, digital immigrants. On the horizon*. MCB University Press, Vol. 9, no. 5.
Rampton, Ben. 1990. Displacing the "native speaker": Expertise, affiliation and inheritance. *ELT Journal* 44 (2). 97–101.
Riodan, Emma. 2018. *The non-native speaker language teacher*. In: Language for Teaching Purposes. Palgrave Macmillan, Champ. 113–145.
Selvi, Ali Fuad. 2011. The non-native speaker teacher. *ELT Journal* 65 (2). 187–189. https://doi.org/10.1093/elt/ccq092
Shohamy, Elana. 2006. *Language Policy: Hidden Agendas and New Approaches*. London: Routledge.
Sharifian, Farzad & Maryam Jamarani. 2013. *Language and intercultural communication in the new era*. New York, London: Routledge.
Stavans, Anat, Maya Eden & Lior Azar. 2021. Multilingual Literacy: The Use of Emojis in Written Communication. In Esther Breuer, Eva Lindgren, Anat Stavans and Elke Van Steendam (eds.). *Multilingualism and Literacy*. Bristol: Multilingual Matters.
Statistik Austria. Kinder in Kindertagesheimen nach der Staatsangehörigkeit 2018/19. https://www.statistik.gv.at/web_de/statistiken/menschen_und_gesellschaft/bildung/kindertagesheime_kinderbetreuung/index.html. (accessed 23rd March 2020)
Vetter, Eva. & Ulrike Jessner (eds). 2019. *International Research on Multilingualism: Breaking with the Monolingual Perspective*. Berlin: Springer.
Wenz, Sebastian & Kerstin Hoenig. 2020. Ethnic and social class discrimination in education: Experimental evidence from Germany. Research in Social Stratification and Mobility 65. https://doi.org/10.1016/j.rssm.2019.100461
Wieser, Jasmin. 2019. *The relevance of the native speaker in language teaching in South Tyrol*. Diploma thesis unpublished, University of Innsbruck.

Joan Pujolar
Chapter 3
New speakers: New linguistic subjects

Abstract: In this chapter, I take up the exercise of analyzing the experience of "new speakers" from the perspective of studies on subjectivity. "New speakers" constitutes a new social category that emerged in the last decades in contexts where regional minority languages were spoken in Europe. The category designates those speakers of the minority language that have acquired it through formal learning and, therefore, are seen as different from the traditional community of native speakers. I argue that studies on subjectivity are relevant to understand the new speakers' phenomenon because these perspectives provide a critique of the ideologies of modernity that constituted the category of "native speaker" besides the conventional hierarchies of race, gender and sexuality. As such, the study of speaker identities arguably makes a distinct contribution to intersectionality studies. To develop this argument, I discuss the implications of Thomas Bonfiglio's (2010) history of the native speaker concept and I point at the connections with the debates on "non-native" speakers and varieties in Applied Linguistics. After this, I bring in some biographies from new speakers of Catalan that experience the process of adopting their new language as being in tension with their other language-based identities. These tensions emerge much more acutely with new speakers who can be constructed as racially different. This shows, I argue, that the processes of subjectification associated with modernity still favor durable and consistent forms of identity in which becoming and hybridity find no space. However, today's increasing mobility and diversity fill the social landscape with these in-between subjects that must constantly travel across boundaries and categories.

Keywords: new speakers, subjectivity, Catalan, native speaker

---

Acknowledgements: Research leading to this chapter was funded by the the Spanish Ministerio de Ciencia e Innovación for the project "Las mudas lingüísticas: una aproximación etnográfica a los nuevos hablantes en Europa." 'Linguistic "mudes": an ethnographic approach to new speakers in Europe'. Ref. FFI2015-67232-C3-1-P. The chapter has benefitted from ongoing discussion on the "new speaker" theme as part of the EU COST Action IS1306 network entitled "New Speakers in a Multilingual Europe: Opportunities and Challenges".

Joan Pujolar, Universitat Oberta de Catalunya, e-mail: jpujolar@uoc.edu

https://doi.org/10.1515/9781501512353-004

1 Introduction

Sociolinguistics has been a latecomer to the debates on subjectivity that have dominated the social sciences at the turn of the millennium. Debates on subjectivity have been central to the literature on gender, sexuality, colonialism or race within the social sciences. These debates concern themselves with how forms of social categorization inform people's lives and how people respond to them. Although sociolinguists often address the same issues, they draw upon different vocabularies, predominantly focusing on issues of "identity" or on the critique of language ideologies.

Debates on subjectivity have mainly focused on the construction of gender and race (Brah 1993; Butler 1990), but here I will focus specifically on language-based ethnicity. What I see in the literature on subjectivity is a range of analytical tools and procedures of object formation that enable nuanced understandings of how people experience, conform to, or disrupt social categorizations. In this chapter, I take up the thread of sociolinguists such as Alison Phipps (2006), Claire Kramsch (2009), Brigitta Busch (2012), Luisa Martín-Rojo (2016) and, more recently, Tim McNamara (2019) to strengthen the case for the incorporation of a subjectivity perspective in work on multilingualism. To do so, I will draw on my current research on new speakers of Catalan.

Work on "new speakers" has recently developed in Europe amongst researchers of regional minority languages (O'Rourke, Pujolar, and Ramallo 2015). "New speakers", in its most restrictive sense, refers to non-native speakers, i.e. people who have learned a given language not by family or early socialization, but through other means such as schooling, adult education or other forms of later socialization. In communities such as the Basques, Galicians, Occitans, Irish, Welsh and Bretons, new speakers have become a distinct group in the sense that they are generally identified, characterized, criticized or defended in political debates. In some communities, there are widely known terms to name them: *Euskaldunberri* in the Basque Country, *Neofalantes* in Galicia, *Neo-brétonnants* in Britany. Sociolinguistic interest in new speakers can be traced to earlier articles by Robert (2009) on Welsh learners, by Moal (2009) on the *nouveaux locuteurs* of Breton, and to the work of O'Rourke and Ramallo (2011, 2013) on the new communities of speakers in Galicia and Ireland. These works basically pointed out that new speakers were perceived as a problematic category, a form of belonging to the speech community that was at odds with received notions of national identity and linguistic authenticity.

New speakers do not constitute a new phenomenon in the sense that there have always been multilingual people. However, it seems relevant to ask why they are salient now as a social category, and what the implications are. I would argue that new speakers emerge as a kind of anomaly within modernist paradigms of linguistic rationality, and this is why interesting connections can be explored with current debates and social movements on gender, sexuality or race. Moreover, attention to language-based identities arguably complements the conversation on intersectionality (Yuval-Davis 2011) by expanding the range of experiences in which axes of power interact in complex ways.

In this chapter, I explore the specific experience of linguistic embodiment of first-language speakers of Spanish who undertake to speak Catalan in their social lives in Catalonia, an officially bilingual region in North-Eastern Spain. I purposely address the experience of people who cannot be differentiated by any feature other than language to explore the specific affordances that language-based categorizations may arguably offer to subjectivity debates. By doing so, I hope to make evident the conditions and processes that make social categorizations both resilient and negotiable in specific contexts. In Catalonia, most Spanish speakers are conversant in Catalan; but their possibilities of *acting* as speakers of Catalan are not proportional to their competence. To become speakers of Catalan *in practice* demands delicate work to circumvent or confront subtle symbolic boundaries.

In the first part of this chapter I put forward a hypothesis on why the category "new speakers" has become salient now. O'Rourke, Pujolar and Ramallo (2015) and Martín-Rojo and Márquez-Reiter (2019) contend that debates on new speakers respond to inherited notions about "native speakers" that have been reproduced by modern nationalism. So, I begin by exploring the genealogy of the concept of the "native speaker" and discuss the connections between the "new speaker" phenomenon and the ongoing debates on "non-native speakers" in applied linguistics. My argument is that these debates emerge as a dissonance in the face of nationalist and colonialist understandings that co-naturalize (Rosa 2019) language and culture. As such, they query received understandings about language that are characteristic of modernity, a condition that they share with the alternative forms of experiencing and politicizing gender, race and sexuality in the current world.

After this, I add a conceptual summary of the ideas that I take from the literature on subjectivity that addresses how subjects confront culturally constructed categories, which I apply in this case to speaker categories. This is where I move on to briefly describe the Catalan context, with a specific focus on how the linguistic categorizations of people have been historically enacted and transformed. I provide examples of narratives of new speakers of Catalan that I analyze by drawing on the language of the subjectivity literature. On this basis, I describe the subtle ways through which speakers confront and circumvent the traditional ethnic boundaries associated with speaking either Catalan or Spanish. I additionally note that visible minorities experience more difficulties to enact these same strategies, and I finally reflect on the fact that the main forms of social classification inherited from modernity get increasingly contested in contemporary society.

2 Speakers: a history

Historian Thomas Bonfiglio (2010) has reconstructed the historical contingencies that led to the emergence of the concept of "native speaker" during the eighteenth and nineteenth centuries along with nationalist and evolutionist ideologies that supported the articulation of national states and colonial rule. The term (together with the older "mother tongue") was transferred from the vocabularies of the scientific disciplines into the political discourses and administrative procedures that characterized the new forms of governance. However, it was never critically examined, even when it played a key role in drawing the political map of Europe after the First World War. For many decades, it was also assumed that "normal" native speakers were generally monolingual, as hybridity was considered a moral anomaly. Moreover, both "mother tongue" and "native speaker" presuppose that ancestry or biological reproduction are important, and it is not by chance if they were used in the construction of racial and colonial hierarchies. These notions only began to be queried by linguists during the 1980s with the work of Kachru (1982) on the emergence of "new" English-speaking communities in former colonies, and with Paikeday's (1985) original survey about the ideas that leading linguists had (or rather, didn't have) about what constituted the ideal native speaker of generative grammarians. Phillipson (1992) and Pennycook (1994) later contended that the idea of the native speaker was being mobilized in the world of English language teaching in a way that benefitted (largely) white British or American teachers as well as the economic interests of Universities and Publishers from the Anglo-Saxon "core" countries.

This is a short appraisal of a long and intense debate that has, at some points, transcended the boundaries of the English language teaching world and inspired the work of sociolinguists working on migration, race relations or globalized cultural expressions (Doerr 2009; Androutsopoulos 2004; Rampton 1990; Creese, Blackledge, and Takhi 2014). As Widdowson (1994) pointed out, this is not so much a linguistic problem but one of "ownership." In Bordieuan terms, it affects the processes of recognition as to what categories of social actor are invested with the right to establish what constitutes appropriate linguistic capital or appropriate linguistic performance. In the world of foreign language teaching, this is not just a conceptual or abstract problem; but one with palpable implications as to who can teach, what curricular targets must be set, what evaluation criteria should be applied, who can publish educational resources or distribute accreditations, and what persons and institutions can act as leaders in the field. This is why one productive line of inquiry has focused on the pedagogical affordances of "non-native" language teachers (Medgyes 1994; Braine 1999). This line of enquiry has produced comparisons of teaching styles, analyses of perceptions or ideologies of participants and stakeholders in education, of institutional hiring practices, and so on (see Moussu and Llurda 2008 for a detailed review). Much less attention has been paid to professions associated with translation (but see Pokorn 2004; Cronin 2003), or other forms of linguistic boundary crossing, such as translinguistic or multilingual literary writing (Grönstrand, Huss, and Ralf Kauranen 2019).

3 The speaking subject

The concept of "subjectivity" overlaps in multiple ways with that of "identity" and it does not seem prudent to contrast them in their definitions, but rather in the questions and themes addressed (McNamara 2019). It is a conversation that began with Foucault's (1983) works on power, which raise the question of how people can resist or change power relationships. The basic concept of the subject seems to refer to the works of Georg W. F. Hegel, in the idea that no social status can be assumed without the recognition of an other. Master and slave, for example, need each other to assume and enact their status. Foucault focused on the ideas of "normality", which defines what state of affairs is in consonance with the dominant discourse, and that of "abnormality", i.e. its deviations. For Foucault, institutions played an important role in shaping the subject through discourse and disciplinary procedures, and this emphasis on processes of organized inculcation has brought many readers to dub him as determinist.

In the late 20th century, the concept of subjectivity became the axis of three main themes: colonial relations, racial relations and gender relations, which has evolved into "queer theory" and other themes. Edward Said's (1978) "Orientalism" is seen as post-colonial studies' seminal work. Said was interested in how specific forms of academic knowledge had participated in the articulation of colonial projects. He attributed an important role to 19th-century philologies in the production of modern forms of anti-Semitism and racism. Said, like his predecessor Frantz Fanon (1952), supported his arguments with great doses of introspection, so that the analysis of the phenomenon was unfolding in a very personal key. The same can be said of Butler (1990), who contributed to the appropriation of the concept of subjectivity by social movements linked to gender and sexuality. Butler explored the processes that force a person to assume a gender/sexual identity or, alternatively, provoke their proscription from it. Each society possesses a repertoire of behaviors and ideas associated with being a man or a woman, and with "normal" sexual practice, and persons are either forced to assume these normalities or live with the consequences of abnormality. One important aspect of this social categorization is that they are inculcated and evaluated through practices and dispositions that get necessarily repeated in daily life, and for this reason they must be continually reaffirmed (or transgressed): how people dress, move, eat, interact with others. They are *performative* identities in so far as they are embodied in the ways in which people enact their social persona in everyday life (Butler 1990).

From Fanon, through Said and Butler, to Jacques Derrida (1996) with his book *Le monolinguisme de l'autre*, theorists of subjectivity have debated about language and its projection towards both the intimate and the political. Fanon (1952), for example, brought up the question of how the subjects of the colonies, being black, could be recognized as normal people just by adopting the normative ways of speaking and behaving, as well as obtaining the relevant educational qualifications, which defined the modern model of the civilized man (and, therefore, of the archetypal French citizen in his case). Being himself of this profile, Fanon noted that a full recognition was beyond his reach. Among the means he gathered and deployed to achieve and display his desire for recognition, the most prominent was language. Having grown up in Martinique, his social status had largely depended on avoiding speaking Creole and avoiding all traces of Creole in his French. More than any other attribute of the physical, the gestural and associated artifacts, language was the element that more repetitively and insistently inscribed him in what he wanted to be.

Thus, being a specific speaker profile, or performing as such, constitutes a condition that symbolically and morally places people in one or another social category and way of life. Fanon's experience, from this point of view, does not present essential differences with those of new speakers as presented above. Bhabha's (1994) notion of "mimicry" in the colonial relation seems also relevant here. Mimicry refers to the fact that the metropoles typically lend its colonial subjects their own practices, symbology and values, thus setting a model towards which these subjects must refer to and strive to resemble; but which they can never fully achieve. Otherwise, the relation of domination would get dissolved.

This idea seems applicable, as I will try to develop below, not just to Fanon's ambivalent position; but to new speakers as they strive to appropriate models that are by definition unattainable. Despite the fact that linguistics in the early 20th century eventually dispensed with the racial concerns of its 19th-century forefathers, or emphasized descriptivism over prescriptivism, language has never ceased to be mobilized in the reproduction of social categories that informed inequalities in terms of class (Bourdieu 1982) or race (Lippi-Green 1997). In these axes of difference, divergence from linguistic norms has remained in a space of ambivalence between the cultural and the biological; and this has allowed the subaltern to be treated both as "natural" speakers and as culturally disabled in different contexts, so that assimilated profiles such as Fanon's could be constructed as unnatural or fake.

Some new speakers, however, are not vulnerable to racialization or class categorizations, and therefore they point to the ways in which language is specifically inscribed in the production of otherness.[1]

In the following paragraphs, I will review the literature on how people can or cannot become speakers of some European minority languages. Later, I focus on the Catalan context, one which provides added layers of complexity. Generally, these considerations bring the issue of subjectivity into the terrain of language and ethnicity. Ethnicity issues have important continuities with issues of race. In this exploration, however, I have willfully excluded race from the data to appreciate how ethnicity gets mobilized even when bodies cannot provide perceptible articulations for boundary making.

4 New speakers: the vampire in the mirror

Josep-Anton Fernàndez (2008) argues that Catalan identity is constitutively queer because it leads an existence outside the institutional logic of the nation state and its forms of legitimization. In the procedures that are institutionally and publicly devised to reflect back their image and contours (the mirror), Catalans do not see any reflection of themselves. This psychoanalytic language is applicable to any speaker of a minority language, and probably to many other forms of subalternity.

---

[1] For reasons of space, I chose not to discuss the specific position of gender categorization with regard to linguistic normativity. See Cameron (1992) for a discussion of the debates in the 1980s between the "difference" and the "power" approaches. Through this discussion, we can appreciate how, since women speech was not vulnerable from the viewpoint of linguistic normativity, alternative criteria of evaluation were developed to "naturalize" male dominance.

New speakers can arguably be presented in similar ways, as they have no legitimate space or position within the traditional and predominant conceptions of what language communities are. Between 2013 and 2017 a large network of European sociolinguists addressed these "new speakers", citizens who, by engaging with languages other than their "native" or "national" language(s), need to cross existing social boundaries and adapt to new sociolinguistic spaces (COST 2013). This definition potentially encompasses any type of multilingual, but it was the specific profiles of new speakers amongst regional minority communities that provided the most productive line of work. To my knowledge, the oldest popular denomination of "new speakers" stems from the Basque Country (in northern Spain). Since the 1980s, those who participated in the mass movements to "relearn" Basque in adult schools were called *euskaldun berri* 'new Bascophone'. The phenomenon, however, was not critically examined as such until more recently (Gatti 2007). O'Rourke and Ramallo (2011) observed that, in Galicia, the term *neofalante* 'neo-speaker' was used in opposition to "native speaker" to express the experience of speakers who did not fit with traditional assumptions about these speech communities: i.e. people who had acquired Galician through formal learning rather than conventional family transmission. These people were generally local people who identified with the movement for linguistic revitalization for political and/or sentimental reasons. Most would have some family memory of the language being spoken by grandparents or relatives, and they typically "relearnt" the language in adult classes and sought minority language schools for their children.

O'Rourke and Ramallo also studied new speakers of Gaelic in the Irish context. They observed that language planning authorities rarely considered new speakers in their policy design, and they also perceived that there were sometimes tensions between "new" and "native" speakers. Further research in different contexts showed that this was a general trend amongst similar regional minorities in Europe. Native speakers showed implicit or explicit ambivalence towards what they saw as a new specimen of recruit to their communities. More so when these new speakers were becoming the actual majority, as happens in the Basque Country or in Ireland (Ortega et al. 2015; Walsh 2012). In Brittany (McDonald 1994; Hornsby 2009; Timm, Ball, and Müller 2010) and Occitania (Costa 2010a, 2010b), "old" and new speakers are arguably in open conflict. In Scotland, Gaelic-medium educated adults often do not identify with the original Gaelic speaking community and still regard native speakers as backward (Dunmore 2016). Both in Scotland and Ireland, new speakers often complain of being excluded by native speakers, who often refuse to speak in Gaelic to them (McEwan-Fujita 2010; O'Rourke and Walsh 2015).

Most of these minority settings exemplify what Gal and Woolard (2001) characterize as struggles over "authenticity", whereby different voices compete "as the embodiment of a particular community" (Ibid., 7). This competition has two main focal value sources: "authenticity", as those practices that claim a bond to place, rurality and tradition; and "anonymity", as when the language is presented as a widely accessible means of communication. New speakers usually learn the standard form of the minority language, which by definition avoids local or particularistic forms of expression, and hence may come across as placeless or anonymous. On the other hand, standards of minority languages typically require speakers to drop the vocabulary and grammar that speakers have adopted from the majority language. A tension emerges here with new speakers, as they formally adhere to this "purified" variety but present many other indicators of linguistic interference. Thus, traditional speakers of Galician reportedly express high regard for new speakers because they are literate in the language and come across as more educated (Ramallo and O'Rourke 2014). However, Galician "*neofalantes*" consider that the speech of native speakers is more authentic than their own (O'Rourke and Ramallo 2013). The same may happen amongst new speakers of Basque or Irish, who may even actively pursue to learn local dialects (Ortega et al. 2014; Lantto 2016; Urla 2012; O'Rourke and Walsh 2015). Traditional native speakers can present a genuineness associated with the display of fluency and spontaneity, as well as the use of idiomatic expressions (Lantto 2016; Urla et al. 2017), while new speakers may obtain legitimacy from their mastery of the "standard language", which have their own claims to genuineness substantiated by expert linguists. In some contexts, relations may become more strained: in Britany and Occitania, either group even orient to separate linguistic standards (McDonald 1994; Costa 2010a).

One key factor of (mostly) implicit differentiation between old and new speakers is socioeconomic background. New speaker communities mostly stem from middle class urban families who engage in movements to "relearn" or "reclaim" the minority language. Most of them may be descendants of native speakers who performed language shift in the past, typically rural migrants to cities; but these descendants now possess significant symbolic and economic capital. They are multilingual and socially mobile. As such, they embody the modernization of the community, but also the disengagement of the minority with the values of authenticity, and with the specific bonds with the land and its sublimated heritage that traditional speakers represented. From this angle, the significance of class in these controversies seems clear, and hence the need to interpret the phenomenon from an intersectional perspective.

There is however a paradox in the way that new speakers emerge as a result of a process of modernization while they embody at the same time a break with the conception of nationality inscribed in modernity. Most of these minorities suffered from industrialization and nation state formation. The former brought about migration to urban centers and a gradual incorporation of minority speakers into the industrial workforce; the latter imposed the dominant languages through universal schooling, conscription, bureaucracy and even political repression. Thus, native speakers of these languages were until recently associated with people in the peripheries in every sense of the word: political, geographic, economic (employed in primary sectors) and cultural, as possessors of devalued forms of cultural capital (Grillo 1989; Pietikäinen and Kelly-Holmes 2013). The later part of the 20th century saw the development of policies of linguistic revitalization after the so-called "ethnic revival" of the 1960s, with many European states following the proposals of the Council of Europe's Charter of Regional and Minority Languages. The spread of minority language schooling, bilingual or immersion schools was the most visible result of these policies, which are largely responsible for the formation of new speaker communities. This is why the division between native speakers and new speakers disorients the managers of linguistic policies that were based on the assumption that minority language communities needed access to the resources of modernity: schools, institutions, media, cultural industries and . . . a standard language with no ostensible connection to locality.

This is what gives rise to contradictions such as the one observed by Jaffe (2015) in the Corsican context. The learners of Corsican that she observed came from very diverse backgrounds (newcomers from France or abroad, spouses of locals, or both) and, although most identified with the value of Corsican as heritage or even as a national symbol, this need not necessarily mean that they saw it as part of their own cultural heritage. This had an important implication in terms of the model for language learning enacted in schools or in adult classes. Corsica has a long tradition of a "polynomic" standard that allows for regional variation to resolve tensions between different dialect areas. However, many learners of Corsican were not interested in these local forms of the language and reportedly preferred to learn a unified variety (Jaffe 1999).

If new speakers stick out within some minority communities, this is because community leaders have traditionally drawn on classical nationalism to make sense of their situation. Most of these communities project historical narratives of national oppression and draw from the same ideologies about language, nation, identity and territory that established nation states drew from the works of Herder and Humboldt (Heller 1999). Consequently, they fully concur with the above-mentioned, biologically-inspired conceptions of the national body. Within this frame, new speakers have no meaningful place, as national belonging is and has always been implicitly inherited, not learned.

Even when they may subscribe to conventional nationalist ideas about language and nation, new speakers bring in a different form of consciousness and engagement with language and tradition from that of native speakers. As Costa (2015) observes in relation to communities of young Occitanists who create rock bands, folk fusion bands, or organize running events and the like, these are "post-traditional speakers" associated with new lifestyles and forms of consumption who re-invent traditions in ways not unlike those identified by Hobsbawm and Ranger (1983). Hobsbawm and Ranger's collection reviews a number of cases in which specific forms of ritual, celebration or performance were developed in the 19th Century as representations of national traditions in public life. Although these practices were often presented as immemorial, they were also to a large extent (re)created as new rituals of collective representation and recognition. New speakers, according to Costa, are actually producing reenactments of local identity by associating this identity with contemporary forms of leisure.

The contradictions that new speakers bring to the surface suggest that minority speakers have no positions from which to claim full legitimacy, be it because native speakers must inevitably stay locked in a traditional niche inscribed in peripherality, or because those who emerge from outside this niche are constructed as impostors. Thus, provided that current discourses on cultural diversity enable some form of visibility to minorities, it still seems that minority speakers cannot hope to obtain from their mirrors figures other than either puppets or monsters. It is these seemingly intractable tensions that I try to address by drawing on the literature on subjectivity. The situation of new speakers recalls Bhabha's (1994) notion of "mimicry", of the colonial subject that pursues a legitimacy that she or he cannot hope to attain.

5 New speakers of Catalan

My characterization of new speakers of minority languages so far has been purposely restrictive, as it does not fully reflect the experience of a few minority contexts such as Catalonia, Flanders or Quebec. These contexts cannot be characterized as so categorically peripheral. They are mid-way between regional minorities and nation state language communities. In addition to their larger demographics, their speakers historically retained important footholds in the economy and in political institutions, and hence a substantial presence amongst the urban lower and middle classes. They did not experience massive language shift to the dominant language. They were not successfully dubbed as backward and rural for centuries (although some nation states tried to present them as such), and they do not display today the same internal ambivalences towards modernity.

Catalan speakers, however, have a subaltern status within the Spanish state after 300 hundred years of political exclusion. In an ethnography conducted at the end of the 1970s, Woolard (1985) considered it exceptional that the community still "recruited" speakers given the demographic superiority of Spanish and after 40 years of Francoist persecution. She claimed that this was because Catalan was locally associated with social mobility and that the language had played an important role in anti-Francoist political mobilization. However, both being and becoming a speaker of Catalan at the turn of the 1980s was not an easy task. For decades, Catalan speakers had withdrawn from using the language publicly but had kept speaking it amongst themselves. Speakers of Spanish were generally military personnel, bureaucrats or migrant workers (by far the most numerous), all from other parts of Spain. Thus, speaking Catalan and *being* Catalan, a member of the local group, became intimately associated, bearing in mind that other differences in terms of race or religion were not present. Even when most Spanish speakers could understand the language, "Catalans" would speak Spanish to any of these "outsiders"; but they would strictly adhere to Catalan amongst themselves, sometimes through subtle skills that foreigners often found bemusing, such as people switching languages as they moved their gaze from one participant to another at a dinner table (see Woolard 1989: 64).

Woolard characterized this pattern of language use as a marker of ethnicity, that is, as behavior that signaled belonging to the Catalan group and that defined its boundaries strictly: Catalans were those who spoke Catalan amongst themselves.

At the time, however, important political changes were to push for change: Catalan became a co-official language and the main language of instruction in schools. This was accompanied by a local autonomous administration that associated Catalan with a national identity, one that was not necessarily incompatible with Spanish identity, but often in tension with it. As Catalan nationalists took the wheel of the official administration, they treated the *whole* population as "Catalan", not just a part of it. The fact that so many were unable to speak Catalan was seen as an anomaly. So, the new administration mobilized education in the production of Catalan nationals through language, like any other nation state (although it did not address the ambivalence derived from people's accompanying adscription to Spanish national identity).

Sociolinguistic studies in the early 1990s attested to the momentous changes in the country's sociolinguistic structure. Basically, the whole school population was growing up bilingual, not just first-language Catalan speakers anymore (Woolard and Gahng 1990; Boix 1993; Vila 1996; Pujolar 1997). Moreover, all these studies were ascertaining that first-language speakers of the two languages were socializing together, that their language choices were less categorical than earlier, and that their predisposition to speak each other's language had improved. Woolard and Gahng (1990) demonstrated through a matched-guise experiment that, in contrast with the results of an earlier study (Woolard 1989), young adolescents did not evaluate negatively anymore the speakers of either language that were using their *other* language.

However, all was not so rosy, particularly for those who expected Catalan to become once again the main national language. Demographic trends expanded the numbers of first-language speakers of Spanish. Today, these make 55% of the whole population against 31% of self-declared Catalan speakers, 2.4% of "both" and 11.3% of "others".[2] Moreover, young Spanish speakers were learning Catalan at school and they were using it successfully for academic purposes; but they generally did not adopt it for everyday ordinary talk. Most of them were geographically concentrated in urban areas where the numbers of Catalan speakers were low. Therefore, by codeswitching between Spanish and Catalan according to context, they were effectively drawing symbolic lines and keeping linguistic spaces separate, like Catalan speakers had done during the years of oppression.

Gonzàlez et al. (2009), in a study based on life history interviews, claimed that it was difficult for many speakers of Spanish to access the conditions where they could practice Catalan even if they actively sought to do so. The first issue was the availability of other practitioners of the language in their own networks of family, friends and colleagues. The second issue, also very important, was that Catalan speakers were not especially collaborative and would often respond to them in Spanish. Despite years of Catalan-dominant schooling, native speakers of Catalan were more fluent in Spanish than the reverse, and most still tended to keep Catalan instinctively to themselves.

There were potential grounds for frustration here, given that Catalan was important for the participation in cultural, economic and political life, and to enter and generate trust in valuable local networks. The experience of wanting to speak Catalan, but failing to do so, affected many people (although we do

---

[2] Data from the 2013 language survey: *Enquesta d'Usos Lingüístics de la Població*, available on-line at http://www.idescat.cat/pub/?id=eulp.

not know how many). The competence was in principle there; but there was no social space to enact it, either because so few Catalan speakers were available, because self-confidence diminished with lack of practice, or because one was already categorized by others as someone to whom Spanish had to be spoken to (Gonzàlez et al. 2009).

6 Linguistic mudes: linguistic appropriations

The González et al. (2009) study was the beginning of the line of work that lead to these considerations (Martínez et al. 2012; Pujolar and Gonzàlez 2013; Pujolar and Puigdevall 2015). The material reproduced below has been selected out of a total of 87 life history interviews and 18 group discussions centered on people's experiences of learning and using new languages. I have focused on how Spanish speakers born and raised in Catalonia have developed their relationship with Catalan, which means that linguistic competence can be presupposed, and issues of race or religion are not relevant. Spanish-speakers born in Catalonia may be able to speak and write Catalan in theory, but many of them grow up functionally monolingual in social life because they have little or no opportunities to use the language informally and conversationally.

The excerpts reproduced below corresponded to cases where the respondents had a story to tell on how they managed to include Catalan in their lives. "Linguistic muda" is how some colleagues and myself named this process of staking a claim for recognition of a speaker identity. We drew from the family of meanings of the Catalan verb *"mudar"*, i.e. to change places, or fur or skin for animals, or dress for special occasions (Gonzàlez et al. 2009; Pujolar and Gonzàlez 2013). The main challenge for these potential bilinguals was to escape from a corner demarcated by either a self-categorization or an *other*-categorization (or by both). The self-categorization was active in terms of considering oneself not adept to produce a Catalan-speaking persona, that is, feeling insecure, that one's competence or fluency is inadequate. Other-categorization would correspond to other people rejecting one's own claim to act as a Catalan speaker. Typically, this involved Catalan speakers simply responding in Spanish to statements in Catalan. Given the monolingual hegemonic assumption that conversations must stick to a single language, any address in a given language is functionally a request to respond in that language. The experience of seeing such requests ignored or rejected is common amongst people whose claim to being Catalan speakers is not regarded as solid enough. In everyday conversation, code-switching (dropping Catalan words or even engaging in short impersonations) was common for everybody; but this did not really qualify one as a Catalan speaker. Such code-switches required no reciprocity or continuity. Obtaining recognition as a Catalan-speaking interlocutor required to speak it consistently and durably.

This process of adopting a new language, the muda, connects with the vast anthropological literature on identity and role transformations in terms of "rites of passage" (Van Gennep 1909), although there is the important qualification that no established rite seems to be available here. Otherwise, the literature on subjectivity and processes of subjectification avail us of a wider toolkit to understand the tribulations of subjects throughout the process of muda.

For instance, one of the key issues for new speakers of Catalan is that it is a position that requires reiterated confirmation. Being a Catalan-speaker presupposes a competence and a disposition that is durable and stable, so that any sign that emerges as evidence to the contrary may frustrate the claim to being one. From this perspective, knowledge of biographical details or partial competence may emerge as a threat in need of prevention measures. Alfonso's family was from Chile and he had spoken in Spanish up to his late teens, even though most of his schoolmates spoke Catalan in the Northern town where he lived. At one point, he moved to Barcelona to attend university:

Extract 1
Alfonso: amb el que me'n vaig a viure a Barcelona és amb un dels que vaig conèixer als aiguamolls quan tenia dotze anys i per tant ja parlàvem català i per tant · és molt més fàcil · estic en un entorn que ningú me coneix · que ningú pot decidir quina és la meva llengua o vehicular i quina no · començo a parlar en català i ja està · quan torno a girona ja hi estic acostumat i . . .

Alfonso: *I Shared a flat in Barcelona with one guy I had already met at the moors [an environmental movement] when I was twelve and therefore we were already speaking Catalan and for this reason · it is way easier · I am in a milieu where nobody knows me · no one can decide what my Language, my vehicle, and which it isn't · I start speaking Catalan and that's it. When I go back to Vilagran I have gotten accustomed to it and . . .*

Alfonso's account implies that he had spoken Catalan earlier in the past, in the restricted milieu of an environmentalist summer camp, a place separated from his usual social milieu. Separation is a common feature of rites of passage, though here no ritual or visible symbolisms were performed. Now, to follow his plan of becoming a more stable speaker of Catalan, he used the new separation caused by this moving temporally to Barcelona to study. In my data, language *mudes* tended to be hidden from view: students would use the opportunity of changing to a new school (high school, college) and speak Catalan to new acquaintances, or act in job interviews (and in the new job environment) as if they had spoken Catalan all their lives.

Alfonso's final point that he had to get "accustomed" to speaking Catalan is also important. He had used the chance to acquire fluency. Fluency was not important just to get his message across comfortably, but crucially to make his Catalan performance convincing: stumbling, stuttering into Spanish, excessive borrowings would potentially lead the audience to switch to Spanish and mar the project. The Barcelona flat, therefore, served the purposes of a refuge, a safe space (Puigdevall, Colombo, and Pujolar 2020), from which Alfonso could train a new identity and also construct for himself a new history.

There are other sides to this assumed continuity of linguistic identity. In Catalonia, it is generally accepted that one can speak different languages to different people; but one must respect each specific personal linguistic history, as Uri discusses in extract 2. Uri and Franc below, who were Catalan speakers, reflected on how difficult it felt for them to speak Catalan to Spanish speakers in certain situations.

Extract 2

Uri: bueno · no sé · · després també em passa o em passava més abans això típic de què coneixes una persona i- · i has començat parlant-hi en castellà i continua aix . . .

Franc: costa molt canviar.

Uri: després canviar el xip costa molt · sí que és veritat · amb gent ho he aconseguit i amb altres és que sembla que fem teatre

Uri: Well, I don't know . . . it also happens or used to happen more before the typical thing that you meet someone and, and you started speaking Castilian (Spanish) and you go on that way . . .

Franc: It is hard to change.

Uri: It is hard to change gear afterwards. This is certainly true. I have managed to do it with some people and with others it looks as if we are acting [literally: "doing theatre"].

Uri's account attests to the experience that the language chosen with a given person gets inscribed in the performance style that defines the personal relation with this person. He seems to lack the words to describe and justify this obstacle; probably because we are all too saturated by the classical linguistic notion that language simply conveys information. Thus, changing the language in this particular case is felt as incongruent. It seems that all social relations based on actual interaction must gradually enregister their own expressive style inscribed in a specific language choice, so that the relationship is not always readily translatable into other languages. The experience of changing language in this case seems akin to the impression that people get when they see familiar characters in cinema dubbed into other languages.

In short, deciding what language to speak to someone, when such a choice exists, is consequential for an indefinite future. This seems to be true for any speaker, but new speakers experience it in a distinct way, as I will show below. In the following extract, we got the account of Lídia, born to a Spanish-speaking family in a Catalan-speaking small town. Lídia spoke Catalan to practically everyone she knew, except for her parents and other close family. I asked her how she reacted on occasions when she found herself speaking in Catalan with someone who she later discovered to be a first language speaker of Spanish like her:

> Extract 3
> **Lídia**: no · segueixo català · segueixo català perquè m'estimo més- · · · i penso · sort que tots dos hem començat- · · · que he començat parlant català · · millor · encara que els dos sabem castellà · no vull · va · ara parlem castellà · · no · parlem català que anem més bé
>
> *Lídia: No, I go on in Catalan. I go on in Catalan because I prefer- ·· And I think "it is lucky that we both started- · · that I started speaking Catalan." · · Much better. Even if we both know Spanish, I don't want "come, let us now speak Castilian." · · No, we speak Catalan and so much the better.*

New speakers of Catalan must not only perform the language convincingly and acquire a track record as such but must also decide what to do with other parts of their linguistic life that can potentially be interpreted as incongruent. Lídia's family language still ascribed her to a category of people that could potentially trigger demands to speak Spanish on the basis of this shared feature. Although her close acquaintances knew about her family and this did not unsettle their language choices, she had to prevent the detail from being known to new acquaintances because she generally preferred to speak Catalan.

Confronting the danger of an undesired categorization can of course get complicated in contexts where the information cannot be isolated or controlled. Judith was born and raised in a big town in which Spanish was the predominant language and did not speak Catalan until she started to study journalism at the university. Extract 4 exemplifies her experience at the office of a Catalan newspaper with old and new colleagues:

> Extract 4
> **Judith**: llavors al diari al principi tenia una sèrie de gent molt puntual amb els que tenia amistat que parlàvem castellà · llavors jo notava que quan alguna persona al diari es volia acostar a mi o volia sentir-se més propera · parlaven en castellà ·saps? i jo insistia en que- perquè clar · per mi era molt dolent · perquè em sentia com si no sapigués parlar català · no? i jo no- però pel tema com qualsevol- potser ells ho feien més- de dir una via d'aproximació

de- eh, podem ser col·legues' o 'no m'importa parlar-te castellà' i jo em sentia molt violenta · no? això sempre m'ha violentat molt. (· · ·) es una cosa que la gent que- la catalanoparlant es pensa que et fa un favor i realment és una putada

> **Judith**: and then at the newspaper at the beginning there were a few people specific cases that we had been earlier friends and spoke Castilian. Then, I noticed that when somebody at the office wanted to approach me or wanted to feel closer, they would speak in Castilian, you know? And I insisted in the- because of course. For me this was bad, because it felt as if I could not speak Catalan, right? And I didn't- but this is the issue for anyone- maybe they do it rather for- say a way of doing closeness about- "Hey, we can be pals" or "I don't mind speaking in Castilian to you" and I felt very violent, right? This has always felt real violent (. . .) It's something that Catalan-speaking people think that they are doing you a favor and it is a load of shit.

Judith attests to the fact that adscriptions are often ambivalent and hence negotiable, but that this does not make them less problematic. Her account suggests that she instinctively reacted in emotionally strong terms to a perceived threat of exclusion, because accepting an address in Spanish in that context had implications for subsequent interactions and for her whole image about her availability and capability to speak Catalan in the workplace.

The four extracts show that language competence was a subsidiary condition when it came to explaining language choice amongst Catalan people. What seems important is that the language chosen still involved a claim to act from a given position. The old positionalities of language choice had changed and now there were new ones that seemed more complex and subtle. Catalan-Spanish bilinguals could in principle choose to speak one language or the other; but there were plenty of constraints that determined what were generally regarded as reasonable, consistent, or acceptable choices.

7 Discussion: subjects on the move

The literature on subjectivity has primarily focused on particularly recalcitrant forms of subjectification affecting gender or race. Subjectification (or subjection) is the term commonly used to describe the process whereby institutions or society in general lead people to adopt specific social positions so that they themselves actively engage in producing and reproducing them. It stems from Butler's (1995) idea that subjection is double sided: it is to yield to the dominant order but also to adopt the position imposed as the basis for one's active engagement in society. As such, it is an approach that leans heavily on how the social order imposes a repertoire of subjects and thereby reproduces itself.

This angle is vulnerable to criticisms similar to those that have been directed to Foucault's alleged determinism.

The idea of subjectification is typically applied to processes in which the materiality of the body, namely anatomy, plays a key role. Discourses of gender are anchored in bodily organs and anatomical features constructed as sexual, and those of race rely on phenotypic characteristics. In these constructs, through a metonymic operation, the body is recruited in a way that it is made to constantly signal the positionality of the subject. Social actors are therefore sentenced for life into acting out a sex and a race within their hegemonic configurations, or else they must be constantly responding to this hegemony and hence can never really be fully free from it.

In contrast, the examples provided in this chapter did not rely on any kind of anatomical signing. Language choice was clearly inscribed in some kind of ambivalent or negotiable positionality that bore a historical relation with ethnicity and with projects of nation-state construction. There is in modern public life a process of production of linguistic subjects, and hence of linguistic subjectification, that is just as ubiquitous and insistent as any imposition of categories of gender, sexuality or race (see Billig 1995).

All these processes of subjectification share a specific trajectory in the ways in which they have been constructed in the modern period as defining mutually exclusive categories, with institutions constantly applying normativity regimes to maintain the boundaries between genders, sexualities, races, ethnicities and even languages themselves (Martín-Rojo 2016). The critiques of these normativity regimes since the 1960s have had a clear sociolinguistic correlate: the increasing advocacy for, and the social prestige of bilingualism and multilingualism (although some multilingualisms are admittedly more valued than others).

In principle, speaking a language is objectively independent from anatomy. Granted, it is an *embodied* disposition inscribed into the multimodal forms of bodily and machine-mediated communication, one that recruits subtle cognitive, articulatory and aural procedures that operate in refined ways within interpersonal engagements and synchronizations. This is probably why accents acquire a disproportionate significance as specific traces of these processes of embodiment from which specific trajectories can be hypothesized and thereby loaded with symbolism in social encounters.

Be that as it may, what the Catalan material suggests is that linguistically-based identities, in the absence of anatomical or phenotypic components, provide a substantial leeway for self-transformations not found in the referred literature on subjectivity. Many current speakers of Catalan do have a past as Spanish-speakers and there is no realistic prospect that their present position is ever set in doubt. To put it bluntly, they are successfully assimilated. Linguistic boundary crossings or transformations are possible, and they happen. The local version of sociolinguistic common sense requires a convincing performance, maybe a minimal Catalan-speaking network too, but not an ascendancy certificate. The old categorical ethnic distinctions based on language that Woolard (1989) had identified have barely appeared in the stories that have been collected during the last 15 years (Pujolar and Gonzàlez 2013; Puigdevall et al. 2018; Woolard 2016). The categories "Catalan" and "Castilian" are now very rarely used, as they are considered politically incorrect and descriptively flawed when used in that old sense. Thus, being a native speaker of Catalan does not qualify anymore as defining Catalan-ness, and whatever language(s) a person learnt from their tutors will not be expected –in principle– to determine her language choices or even her accent.

Indeed, the Catalan context is often hailed as one in which national or cultural identity has been substantially pushed away from the traditional essentialisms associated with these constructs (Castells 1997; Cabré 1999; Fuchsel and Martín-Rojo 2003; Guibernau 2004; Woolard 2016). Castells characterizes Catalan nationalism as "based on flexibility and adaptability" and on the recognition of the "variation and interpenetration of cultures"; while Woolard presents Catalan nationalism as a new form of "rooted cosmopolitanism" that seeks to transcend the enlightenment's dichotomy between modernity and tradition by allowing more negotiable forms of investment around place and language.

And yet, the data shown above also qualifies such categorical remarks and provides a more ambivalent picture. The evidence of assimilation is indeed proof that Catalan identity is accessible (and Alfonso, Lídia and Judith spoke mostly Catalan in their lives); but not that such in-between positions have ceased to be problematic. All the examples remind us that language choice was anchored in people's trajectories and that this fact forced individuals to treat their own past as problematic. Uri felt out of place if trying to speak Catalan with people with whom he had been speaking Spanish and Lídia thought it best not to disclose her family background in certain situations. The knowledge of her background by workmates was creating difficulties for Judith to manage her language choices at the office. I must acknowledge that these circumstances were experienced more as annoyances than significant threats; that is, the participants were not worried about their livelihoods being endangered by linguistic mishaps which, at the end of the day, most people would treat as something about which each person's wishes could easily be granted. Close acquaintances and workmates, close friends and relatives, would generally accept someone's option to speak Catalan no matter how much detail of a Spanish-speaking past they were privy to. The experience reported also implies that uncertainties about language choice were common in encounters with strangers or more distant acquaintances.

Alfonso's case provides room for some more detail: he had used the separation from his usual environment in Girona as an opportunity to develop the habit, to train himself. He was not worried about going back and find that people refused to speak Catalan to him. Rather, the implication was that he wanted to get rid of the common indicators of lack of fluency that brought acquaintances to speak Spanish to him.

What this evidence suggests, on the whole, is that Catalan was indeed accessible for new speakers; but that the accession was fraught with obstacles and the final stage always open to vulnerabilities. That some new speakers had to hide their past in certain contexts reveals that the classical native speaker construct was still holding some ground. That some had to subtract themselves from their everyday environment to rehearse their vocabulary and grammar (and hence their Catalans-speaking personae) reveals that the "learner" did not have a stable legitimate ground from which to act. Speaking as a learner was difficult because there was always this alternative language that people could resort to.

Because the status of the Catalan speaker was expected to be firm and solid, it could not be imagined as a provisional state, in terms of "becoming" (Khan 2018), as something in which the subject can work on, and spend a while in transit. This affected both learners and expert new speakers, and this is why they must systematically delete their footprints to prevent their status as speakers to be set in doubt.

This also explains why sociolinguistic research routinely finds, similarly to racial stereotypes, new popular denominations and turns of expression that appear to act as substitutes of the expression that has become politically incorrect. In Catalonia, the term "català-català" 'Catalan-Catalan' appears often in interviews to name someone for whom the language is supposed to be deeply imprinted in the family or close social milieu. In youth culture, a context in which categorizations are continually invented, a number of language-based or language-informed categories have been identified: *catalufo* (for "a Catalan"), *indepe* (as for a Catalan independence supporter) or, for Spanish-speakers, "*quillo*" (with negative class connotations) or "*fachas*" (a popular term for a "fascist" or a "Spanish nationalist"). (Sabaté i Dalmau 2009; Woolard 2008; Boix 1993; Gonzàlez et al. 2014).

The connection between these processes and racial political correctness is relevant if we move the focus to what happens to new speakers who are anatomically exposed to racialization. As I was writing these lines in August 2019, the Twitter hashtag *#NOEMCANVIISLALLENGUA* 'do not change the language for/to me' had been rolling for many weeks after a TV documentary (Bassa and Díaz 2019) voiced the concerns of many new speakers who were frustrated because most Catalan-speakers spoke to them in Spanish. The Twitter posts featured people with either dark skin, oriental or Latin American features or some other mark of otherness in bearing or dress, such as wearing a hijab, who requested to be spoken to in Catalan. This was the result of the most recent wave of international migration that started in the late 1990s. Thus, even while local language policies and grassroots initiatives were successfully accomplishing the de-ethnicization of the Catalan language, a new trend towards racialization was gathering pace (Pujolar 2009; Rovira et al. 2004). Actually, there were already cases of young people for whom Catalan was in practice a "first language" but who were systematically addressed to in Spanish by Catalan speakers.

What this new development teaches us is that linguistic ethnicity in Catalonia was not gone but dormant. The accounts of Alfonso, Lídia and Judith, I would argue, pointed at the ways in which institutional action, grassroots mobilization and individual initiatives had subdued and circumvented the contradictions of traditional linguistic nationalism and created space for new speakers. As such, their trajectories show that it was possible to contest the subjectification to essentialized ethnicity; but that the ideology had not been fully dismantled. Alfonso, Lídia and Judith had been able to assert their status as Catalan speakers partly by erasing their trajectory as Spanish speakers or having their acquaintances suspend the relevance of their past. Alfonso had managed this even while he maintained the use of the Spanish form of his name ("Alfonso" rather than "Alfons"), which is unusual. However, most newly arrived new speakers had their trajectories, their otherness, imprinted in their bodies. This means that their encounters in public spaces could not rely on the ambivalences that former new speakers could exploit.

8 Concluding remarks

In this chapter, I undertook to explore how people managed linguistically-defined ethnicities in Catalonia in daily life and what this told us on how linguistic categorizations get mobilized in the construction of social difference in contemporary societies. I suggested that the experience of Catalan speakers could productively draw from the literature on subjectivity, given the rich debates that this literature contains on how social subjects are produced through the operation of institutions but also through the multifarious forms of inclusion and exclusion that operate in other social settings. I took the experience of "new speakers" of Catalan as the embodiment of the model of a speaker that was potentially dissonant with inherited notions about how language embodied national identity through its native speakers.

To argue the potential relevance of subjectivity debates and their primary foci on gender and race, I posited the hegemony of a modernist genealogy of the native speaker concept within linguistics and in nationalist politics. I also reviewed how the native/new speaker dichotomy had played out in the political contentions around non-native speakers of English and new speakers of minority languages. Thus, as with debates on gender and race, I argued that linguistically-defined identities had arrived to us in the forms in which they had been articulated with ideologies of colonialism and nationalism, as part and parcel of the conceptualization of modern subjects under the operation of normalizing institutions and specific forms of knowledge. This was a trajectory that these non-canonical speaker identities arguably shared with gendered and racialized identities. These ideologies were instrumental in the production and reproduction of symbolic hierarchies that legitimized the cultural and economic hierarchies of modern capitalism and colonial/national governance.

As we know, these ideologies have all come under criticism in the last decades and important changes have taken place in how institutions and expert knowledge participate in their reproduction. However, they also appear to be very resilient in different contexts of society as they continue to be mobilized to reproduce inequalities. The Catalan experience of the last forty years provides an interesting case to appreciate the resilience of old ideologies about what constitutes a legitimate speaker. First language speakers of Spanish grew up with the competence to speak Catalan but often without the opportunities and the legitimacy to act out this competence in social life, where first language speakers of Catalan still associated the language with very specific social trajectories. Thus, new speakers of Catalan must constantly be aware that their language choice could be contested when the dissonant aspects of their trajectories was made available, such as accent or family history. Despite these obstacles, however, many first language Spanish speakers were in practice able to speak Catalan in their everyday life with the support of their closer acquaintances.

The arrival of new immigrants in the last two decades has revived the logic of linguistic boundary making as Catalan speakers treat visible minorities as linguistic others, and hence speak Spanish to them. Again, these new "new speakers" can also fight their way into recognition, and they are likely to find many allies to do so; but this shows us that language seems to always be available as a resource to create difference.

I pointed out earlier that, particularly for small regional minorities, new speakers brought up important contradictions within nationalist frameworks of understanding of linguistic revitalization. They embodied the ideal of a modernized community even as they undermined the standing of the native speakers that modernity had idealized as emblems of identity and tradition. A similar paradox can be identified in relation to the so-called "non-native" speakers of English, both the sign of success of colonial cultural agendas and the source of contention about what constitutes the English-speaking community. New speakers of Catalan present a similar challenge in that they are the product of the policies of linguistic nationalization, but this is a project that is hardly viable if the Catalan-speaking community is not effectively redefined as a multiracial and multilingual space.

The parallels in the genealogy and crises of modern conceptions of gender, sexuality, race, class or disability have been amply documented in the literature on intersectionality. In this chapter, I have presented arguments that support the notion that linguistic identities should be added to the list, particularly as language is commonly mobilized to signal these contested positionalities. All these modes of identification are contested as social movements advocate for more flexible boundaries or for the possibility of multiple belongings and hybridities; but the old frameworks appear to be fairly resilient for reasons that are still to be convincingly explained. The Catalan material shows that it is possible to cross boundaries but not so much to live in these boundaries, that new speakers repeatedly face expectations that linguistic identities must be durable and cohesive. The management of linguistic classifications remains within parameters in which hybridity and ambivalence are still treated as problems that need solving, not as positions from where to speak. These latest new speakers of Catalan have to confront racialization head on, and assume a situation in which they are seen as "mimickers" in Bhabha's sense, which is arguably what happens to most racialized migrants in Europe and North America as is attested in the recent debate on raciolinguistics (Rosa 2019). Undoing linguistic ethnicity, according to the evidence examined, seems to be as complex and paradoxical as undoing gender or race (Butler 2004).

And yet, against the current experience of increasing mobility and diversity in our societies, how long can such expectations last? As Appadurai (1996) observes, modernity is "at large" and it is through these multiple forms of appropriation that a different order seems to emerge in which the old North-Atlantic hegemony is gradually displaced. Thus, as new speakers and "non-native" speakers become the overwhelming majority in their respective linguistic markets, it may well be that identities *"in becoming"* constitute the rule rather than the exception.

Author's Positionality

Joan Pujolar is professor of Sociolinguistics at the Universitat Oberta de Catalunya. He has always done research on the politics of language in Catalonia as experienced by social actors in daily life. Being a speaker of Catalan himself, he was a language activist already as an adolescent at the time in which the autonomous government of the country was being reestablished in the early 1980s. After taking his undergraduate studies in Catalan and English at the *Universitat Autònoma de Barcelona*, he obtained his PhD at Lancaster University in 1995. This trajectory complexified his intellectual outlook, which had been initially marked by the emancipatory sociolinguistics proposed by Lluís V. Aracil and Rafael L. Ninyoles amongst European linguistic minorities. At Lancaster he incorporated the linguistic anthropological perspective of Marilyn Martin-Jones and the emerging Critical Discourse Analysis proposed by Norman Fairclough. For his PhD he conducted an ethnography that explored how young Spanish speakers in Barcelona were experiencing the fact that Catalan had become an official language. He analyzed how different forms of gender identity were mobilized in the production of specific forms of youth culture, and how these processes had linguistic implications that were also connected to class differences. This study made him aware of the need to adopt an intersectional perspective in the study of multilingualism, in which Bourdieu's ideas on inequalities and reproduction would gradually become central. Later on, he also studied language courses for immigrants in a Catalan town, where he pointed out how the organization and practice of such activities was invested by a colonial ethos. He also worked with Monica Heller, Sari Pietikäinen and Kathryn Jones on the commodification of language and identity, thus building connections between the Catalan experience and phenomena emerging amongst Francophone minorities in Canada, the Sami in Finland and the Welsh.

He became interested in the concept of the native speaker in the early 2000s when he noticed that public debates on language and identity in Catalonia left other profiles of speakers out of the conversation. He eventually focused on people's linguistic biographies and proposed the concept of "muda" to designate moments of transformation of a person's repertoire. A number of international collaborations eventually developed along these lines until, with Bernadette O'Rourke and other colleagues, funding was obtained from the EU COST agency to set up a research network on "New Speakers in a Multilingual Europe" (2013–2017), in which more than 300 scholars participated from 28 European countries. It was in the context of this network, participated by people working on multilingualism from many different perspectives, that an intense debate took place on issues associated with different profiles of speakers and the social implications of linguistic categorization. From here on, he is now working to conceptualize "speakerness" and "linguistic subjectivity" as theoretical constructs in a bid to focus research primarily on speakers rather than on linguistic practices.

References

Androutsopoulos, Jannis 2004. Non-Native English and Sub-Cultural Identities in Media Discourse. In Helge Sandøy (ed.), *Den fleirspråklege utfordringa/The multilingual challenge*, 83–98. Oslo: Novus.

Appadurai, Arjun. 1996. *Modernity at Large: Cultural Dimensions of Globalization*. Minneapolis: University of Minnesota Press.

Bassa, Mariona & Víctor Díaz. 2019. 30 Minuts: Llenguaferits». Catalonia: Corporació Catalana de Mitjans Audiovisuals, SA. https://www.ccma.cat/tv3/alacarta/30-minuts/llenguaferits/video/5879592/.

Bhabha, Homi K. 1994. *The Location of Culture*. London/New York: Routledge.

Billig, Michael. 1995. *Banal nationalism*. London: SAGE.

Boix, E. 1993. *Triar no és trair. Identitat i llengua en els joves de Barcelona*. Barcelona: Edicions 62.

Bonfiglio, Thomas Paul. 2010. *Mother Tongues and Nations: The Invention of the Native Speaker*. The Hague: Mouton De Gruyter.

Bourdieu, Pierre. 1982. *Ce que parler veut dire*. Paris: Fayard.

Brah, Avtar. 1993. Difference, Diversity, Differentiation. In, John Wrench and John Solomos (eds.), *Racism and Migration in Western Europe*, 195–214. Oxford: Berg Publishers.

Braine, George. 1999. *Non-Native Educators in English Language Teaching*. Mahwah, N.J.: Lawrence Erlbaum Associates.

Busch, Brigitta. 2012. The Linguistic Repertoire Revisited. *Applied Linguistics* 33 (5): 503–23.

Butler, Judith P. 1990. *Gender Trouble: Feminism and the Subversion of Identity*. New York: Routledge.

Butler, Judith P. 1995. Contingent Foundations. In Seyla Benhabib, Judith Butler, Drucilla Cornell and Nancy Fraser (eds.), *Feminist Contentions: A Philosophical Exchange*, 35–58. London/New York: Routledge.

Butler, Judith P. 2004. *Undoing Gender*. London/New York: Routledge.

Cabré, Anna M. 1999. *El sistema català de reproducció: Cent anys de singularitat demogràfica*. Barcelona: Proa.

Cameron, Deborah. 1992. *Feminism and Linguistic Theory*. London: The Macmillan Press Ltd.

Castells, Manuel. 1997. *The Information Age: Economy, Society and Culture. Volume II: The Power of Identity*. Malden, Massachusets: Blackwell.

COST, European Cooperation in Science and Technology. 2013. *Memorandum of Understanding for the Implementation of a European Concerted Research Action Designated as COST Action IS1306: New Speakers in a Multilingual Europe: Opportunities and Challenges*. Belgium. https://e-services.cost.eu/files/domain_files/ISCH/Action_IS1306/mou/IS1306-e.pdf.

Costa, James. 2010a. Des Derniers Locuteurs Aux Néo-Locuteurs: Revitalisation Linguistique En Europe. *Faits de Langues*, no. 35–36: 205–23.

Costa, James. 2010b. Revitalisation Linguistique: Discours, Mythes et Idéologies. Approche Critique de Mouvements de Revitalisation En Provence et En Ecosse. PhD. Thesis. Université Stendhal – Grenoble III. https://tel.archives-ouvertes.fr/tel-00625691

Costa, James. 2015. New Speakers, New Language: On Being a Legitimate Speaker of a Minority Language in Provence. *International Journal of the Sociology of Language* 2015 (231): 127–45.

Creese, Angela, Adrian Blackledge & Jaspreet Kaur Takhi. 2014. The Ideal "Native Speaker" Teacher: Negotiating Authenticity and Legitimacy in the Language Classroom. *The Modern Language Journal* 98 (4): 937–51.

Cronin, Michael. 2003. *Translation and Globalization. Contemporary Sociology*. Oxon/New York: Routledge.

Derrida, Jacques. 1996. *Le Monolinguisme de l'autre*. Paris: Galilée.

Doerr, Neriko Musha. 2009. *The Native Speaker Concept: Ethnographic Investigations of Native Speaker Effects*. Berlin: Walter de Gruyter.
Dunmore, Stuart S. 2016. Immersion Education Outcomes and the Gaelic Community: Identities and Language Ideologies among Gaelic Medium-Educated Adults in Scotland. *Journal of Multilingual and Multicultural Development*. 38 (8): 726–741.
Fanon, Frantz. 1952. *Peau Noire, Masques Blancs. 1952*. Paris: Editions du Seuil.
Fernàndez, Josep-Anton. 2008. *El malestar en la cultura catalana: La cultura de la normalització*. Barcelona: Empúries.
Foucault, Michel. 1983. The Subject and Power. In Hubert Dreyfus and Paul Rabinow (eds.), *Beyond Structuralism and Hermeneutics*, 208–26. Chicago: University of Chicago Press.
Fuchsel, Hector Grad & Luisa Martín-Rojo. 2003. "Civic" and "Ethnic" Nationalist Discourses in Spanish Parliamentary Debates. *Journal of Language and Politics* 2 (1): 31–70.
Gal, Susan & Kathryn Ann Woolard. 2001. *Languages and Publics: The Making of Authority. The Making of Authority*. London/New York: Routledge.
Gatti, Gabriel. 2007. *Identidades Débiles: Una Propuesta Teórica Aplicada Al Estudio de La Identidad En El País Vasco*. Madrid: Centro de Investigaciones Sociológicas.
Gonzàlez, Isaac, Joan Pujolar, Anna Font & Roger Martínez. 2009. Entre la identitat i el pragmatisme lingüístic. Usos i percepcions lingüístiques dels joves catalans a principis de segle. Research Report. Generalitat de Catalunya. Barcelona.
Gonzàlez, Isaac, Joan Pujolar, Anna Font & Roger Martínez. 2014. *Llengua i joves. Usos i percepcions lingüístics de la joventut catalana*. Estudis. Barcelona: Generalitat de Catalunya.
Grillo, Ralph D. 1989. *Dominant Languages: Language and Hierarchy in Britain and France*. Cambridge: Cambridge University Press.
Grönstrand, Heidi, Markus Huss & Ralf Kauranen. 2019. *The Aesthetics and Politics of Linguistic Borders. Multilingualism in Northern European Literature*. London/New York: Routledge.
Guibernau, Montserrat. 2004. *Catalan Nationalism: Francoism, Transition and Democracy*. London: Routledge.
Heller, Monica. 1999. *Linguistic Minorities and Modernity: A Sociolinguistic Ethnography*. London: Longman.
Hobsbawm, Eric J. & Terence Ranger. 1983. *The Invention of Tradition*. Cambridge: Cambridge University Press.
Hornsby, Michael. 2009. The Appearance of Neo-Speakers: Breton and Gaelic Perspectives. *Studies in Celtic Linguistics: Perspectives on Celtic Languages* 6: 199–294.
Jaffe, Alexandra Mystra. 1999. *Ideologies in Action: Language Politics on Corsica*. Berlin: Walter de Gruyter.
Jaffe, Alexandra Mystra. 2015. Defining the new speaker: theoretical perspectives and learner trajectories. *International Journal of the Sociology of Language* 231: 21–44.
Kachru, Braj B. 1982. *The Other Tongue: English across Cultures*. Indiana: University of Illinois Press.
Khan, Kamran. 2018. *Becoming a citizen : linguistic trials and negotiations in the UK*. London: Bloomsbury.
Kramsch, Claire. 2009. *The Multilingual Subject*. Oxford: Oxford University Press.
Lantto, Hanna. 2016. Conversations about Code-Switching: The Contrasting Ideologies of Purity and Authenticity in Basque Bilinguals' Reactions to Bilingual Speech. (Draft). *Multilingua* 35 (2): 137–161.

Lippi-Green, Rosina. 1997. *English with an accent: Language, ideology, and discrimination in the United States.* London/New York: Psychology Press / Routledge.

Martín-Rojo, Luisa. 2016. Language and Power. In eds. Ofelia García, Nelson Flores and Massimiliano Spotti (eds.), *The Oxford Handbook of Language and Society,* 72–102. Oxford: Oxford University Press.

Martín-Rojo, Luisa & Rosina Márquez-Reiter. 2019. Language and Speakerhood in Migratory Contexts. *International Journal of the Sociology of Language* 257 (4): 1–16.

Martínez, Roger, Joan Pujolar, Isaac Gonzàlez & Anna Font. 2012. El Poder de La Normalitat: Sobre Els Joves i La Llengua a Catalunya. *Journal of Catalan Studies. Revista Internacional de Catalanística* 15: 1–28.

McDonald, Maryon. 1994. Women and Linguistic Innovation in Brittany. In, Shirley Ardener, Pauline Burton and Ketaki Kushari Dyson (eds.), *Bilingual Women. Anthropological Approaches to Second Language Use,* 85–110. Oxford/Providence: Berg Publishers.

McEwan-Fujita, Emily. 2010. Ideology, Affect, and Socialization in Language Shift and Revitalization: The Experience of Adults Learning Gaelic in the Western Isles of Scotland. *Language in Society.* 39 (1): 27–64

McNamara, Tim. 2019. *Language and Subjectivity.* Cambridge: Cambridge University Press.

Medgyes, Péter. 1994. *The Non-Native Teacher.* Houndsmills: Macmillan.

Moal, Stefan. 2009. Locuteurs Traditionnels et Nouveaux Locuteurs de Langue Bretonne : Un Auto-Odi Peut En Cacher Un Autre. In Carmen Alén Garabato and Romain Colonna (eds.), *Auto-Odi. La « haine de Soi » En Sociolinguistique,* 119–44. Paris: L'Harmattan.

Moussu, Lucie & Enric Llurda. 2008. *Non-Native English-Speaking English Language Teachers: History and Research. Language Teaching.* Vol. 41 (3): 315–348.

O'Rourke, Bernadette. 2011. Whose Language Is It? Struggles for Language Ownership in an Irish Language Classroom. *Journal of Language, Identity and Education.* 10 (5): 327–345.

O'Rourke, Bernadette, Joan Pujolar & Fernando Ramallo. 2015. New Speakers of Minority Languages: The Challenging Opportunity. *International Journal of the Sociology of Language,* Special issue on New speakers of minority languages,, no. 231: 1–20.

O'Rourke, Bernadette & Fernando Ramallo. 2011. The Native-Non-Native Dichotomy in Minority Language Contexts: Comparisons between Irish and Galician. *Language Problems and Language Planning.* 35 (2): 139–59.

O'Rourke, Bernadette & Fernando Ramallo. 2013. Competing Ideologies of Linguistic Authority amongst "New Speakers" in Contemporary Galicia. *Language in Society.* 42 (3): 287–305.

O'Rourke, Bernadette & John Walsh. 2015. New Speakers of Irish: Shifting Boundaries across Time and Space. *International Journal of the Sociology of Language* 231: 63–83.

Ortega, Ane, Estibaliz Amorrortu, Jone Goirigolzarri, Jacqueline Urla & Belen Uranga. 2014. Nuevos Hablantes de Euskera: Identidad y Legitimidad. *DigitHum* 16: 86–97.

Ortega, Ane, Jacqueline Urla, Estibaliz Amorrortu, Jone Goirigolzarri & Belen Uranga. 2015. Linguistic Identity among New Speakers of Basque. *International Journal of the Sociology of Language* 2015 (231): 85–105.

Paikeday, Thomas M. 1985. *The Native Speaker Is Dead!: An Informal Discussion of a Linguistic Myth with Noam Chomsky and Other Linguists, Philosophers, Psychologists, and Lexicographers.* 2003 ed. Vol. 70. Toronto/New York: Lexicography, Inc.

Pennycook, Alastair. 1994. *The Cultural Politics of English as an International Language.* London: Longman.

Phillipson, Robert. 1992. *Linguistic Imperialism.* Oxford: Oxford University Press.

Phipps, Alison. 2006. *Learning the Arts of Linguistic Survival.* Vol. 1. Multilingual Matters.

Pietikäinen, Sari & Helen Kelly-Holmes. 2013. *Multilingualism and the Periphery*. Oxford, UK: Oxford University Press.

Pokorn, Nike K. 2004. Challenging the Myth of Native Speaker Competence in Translation Theory. In Daniel Gile Gyde Hansen, Kirsten Malmkjaer (eds.), *Claims, Changes and Challenges in Translation Studies. Selected Contributions from the EST Congress, Copenhagen 2001*, 113–24. Amsterdam/Philadelphia: John Benjamins.

Puigdevall, Maite, John Walsh, Estibaliz Amorrortu & Ane Ortega. 2018. "I'll be one of them": Linguistic mudes and new speakers in three minority language contexts. Journal of Multilingual & Multicultural Development 39 (5): 445–57.

Puigdevall, Maite, Alba Colombo & Joan Pujolar. 2020. Espacios de Adopción Del Catalán. Una Aproximación Etnográfica a Las Mudas Lingüísticas En Cataluña. In Fernando Ramallo, Estibaliz Amorrortu, and Maite Puigdevall (eds.), *Neohablantes de Lenguas Minoritarias En España*: 111–130. Madrid: Iberoamericana / Vervuert.

Pujolar, Joan. 1997. *De què vas, tio?* Barcelona: Editorial Empúries.

Pujolar, Joan. 2009. Immigration in Catalonia: Marking Territory through Language. In edited by Jim Collins, Stef Slembrouk, and Mike Baynham (eds.), *Globalization and Languages in Contact: Scale, Migration and Communicative Practices*, 85–106. New York: Continuum International.

Pujolar, Joan & Isaac Gonzàlez. 2013. Linguistic "Mudes" and the de-Ethnicization of Language Choice in Catalonia. *International Journal of Bilingual Education and Bilingualism* 0 (0): 1–15.

Pujolar, Joan & Maite Puigdevall. 2015. Linguistic Mudes: How to Become a New Speaker in Catalonia. *International Journal of the Sociology of Language* 2015 (231): 167–87.

Ramallo, Fernando & Bernadette O'Rourke. 2014. Perfiles de Neohablantes de Gallego // Profiles of New Speakers of Galician. *Digithum* 16.

Rampton, Ben. 1990. Displacing the "Native Speaker": Expertise, Affiliation, and Inheritance. *ELT Journal* 44 (2): 97–101.

Robert, Elen. 2009. Accommodating "New" Speakers? An Attitudinal Investigation of L2 Speakers of Welsh in South-East Wales. *International Journal of the Sociology of Language* 2009 (195): 93–115.

Rosa, Jonathan. 2019. *Looking like a Language, Sounding like a Race. Raciolinguistic Ideologies and the Learning of Latinidad*. Oxford: Oxford University Press.

Rovira, Marta, Eva Castellanos, Marta Fernàndez & Enric Saurí. 2004. *El català i la immigració. Anàlisi de l'oferta decursos de català als immigrats adults extracomunitaris*. Barcelona: Editorial Mediterrània.

Sabaté i Dalmau, Maria. 2009. Ideologies on multilingual practices at a rural Catalan school. *Sociolinguistic Studies* 3 (1): 37–60.

Said, Edward W. 1978. *Orientalism*. Vol. 1. Harmondsworth: Penguin.

Timm, Lenora A., Marin J. Ball & Nicole Müller. 2010. Language, Culture and Identity in Brittany: The Sociolinguistic of Breton. In Lenora Timm (ed.), *Ethnic Identity and Minority Language Survival in Brittany*, 2nd ed., 712–52. Abingdon: Routledge.

Urla, Jacqueline. 2012. *Reclaiming Basque: Language, Nation, and Cultural Activism*. Reno.: University of Nevada Press.

Urla, Jacqueline, Estibaliz Amorrortu, Ane Ortega & Jone Goirigolzarri. 2017. Basque Standardization and the New Speaker: Political Praxis and the Shifting Dynamics of Authority and Value. In edited by Pia Lane and James Costa (eds.) *Standardizing Minority*

Languages: Competing Ideologies of Authority and Authenticity in the Global Periphery, 24–46. New York: Routledge.

Van Gennep, Arnold. 1909. *Les Rites de Passage: Étude Systématique Des Rites*. Paris: Éditions A. & J. Picard.

Vila, Francesc Xavier. 1996. When Classes Are Over. Language Choice and Language Contact in Bilingual Education in Catalonia. PhD Thesis. Faculteit der Letteren en Wijsbegeerte. Vrije Universiteit Brussel.

Walsh, John. 2012. *Contests and Contexts: The Irish Language and Ireland's Socio-Economic Development*. 2nd edition. Bern: Peter Lang.

Widdowson, Henry G. 1994. The Ownership of English. *TESOL Quarterly* 28 (2): 377–89.

Woolard, Kathryn A. 1985. Language Variation and Cultural Hegemony: Towards an Integration of Sociolinguistics and Social Theory. *American Ethnologist* 12 (4): 738–48.

Woolard, Kathryn A. 1989. *Doubletalk: Bilingualism and the Politics of Ethnicity in Catalonia*. Stanford: Standford University Press.

Woolard, Kathryn A. 2008. Language and Identity Choice in Catalonia: the Interplay of Contrasting Ideologies of Linguistic Authority. In Kirsten Süselbeck, Ulrike Mühlschlegel and Peter Masson (eds.), *Lengua, nación e identidad: la regulación del plurilingüismo en España y América Latina*, 303–24. Madrid-Frankfurt am Main: Iberoamericana-Vervuert Verlag.

Woolard, Kathryn A. 2016. *Singular and Plural: Ideologies of Linguistic Authority in 21st Century Catalonia*. Oxford: Oxford University Press.

Woolard, Kathryn A. & Tae-Joong Gahng. 1990. Changing Language Policies and Attitudes in Autonomous Catalonia. *Language in Society* 19 (3): 311–30.

Yuval-Davis, Nira. 2011. Power, Intersectionality and the Politics of Belonging. *FREIA-Feminist Research Center in Aalborg. Aalborg University, Denmark. FREIA Working Paper Series, Working Paper*, no. 75.

Part two: **Practices and representations**

Jean-François de Pietro
Chapter 4
Is there a native speaker in the class?
A didactic view of a problematic notion

Abstract: The aim of this didactic contribution is to show why it is important and how to move beyond certain concepts of the notion of the native speaker in the school context in order to ensure greater fairness in teaching the language that, in the French-speaking part of Switzerland, we now call the *language of schooling*. After illustrating the problem with two concrete examples, I mention some sociolinguistic studies based on the observation of interactions that question the notion of a "native speaker" by showing its deficiencies but also by observing its presence in the speakers' representations, be they conscious or not. I then focus on the situation that prevails today in the school context and present what I feel is desirable to develop in concrete terms to take into account what actually lies behind the notions of native speaker and especially mother tongue. I briefly explain the theoretical framework that underpins my approach and illustrate my remarks with examples of activities designed in the context of French-speaking Switzerland and that on the whole enhance pluralistic approaches to languages. In the conclusion, I return – from a socio-didactic perspective aiming to reconcile efficiency, relevance and fairness of teaching – to the notion of the native speaker and the fate that should ultimately be reserved for it in the school context.

Keywords: mother tongue, language representations, pluralistic approaches to languages

---

Acknowledgements: Many thanks to Vanessa Boutefeu for the excellent translation of this text from French into English and to Verónica Sánchez Abchi (IRDP) for her commentaries after reading an earlier first version of the chapter.

Jean-François de Pietro, Institut de recherche et de documentation pédagogique (IRDP, Neuchâtel, Suisse), e-mail: Jean-Francois.dePietro@irdp.ch

https://doi.org/10.1515/9781501512353-005

> For the foreign language to be perceived at the same time as *a language* and as *another*, it is necessary for the first language to also be *another* language in a certain way.[1]
>
> (Py, 1992: 116)

1 Introduction

In this contribution I will look at the notion of the "native speaker" (henceforth NS) from a perspective that is primarily didactic, or rather socio-didactic, by analysing what it specifically covers in the school context, examining the role – usually implicit – it plays there and then mentioning some current guidelines that allow it to be put in its "proper" place. As we will see, it has in fact to do with reconciling the need to take into account the "objective" relation of students to the languages involved in various ways during their learning curriculum and certain social representations of languages and speakers that prevail in our societies. The desired aim is to propose a fairer approach in teaching which recognises and legitimises all students affected by this problematic issue of the native speaker. On the way, we will make a detour into interactional sociolinguistics in order to gain a better understanding of what is in play with this notion when the actual practices of interlocutors in interactions involving more than one language are focused on.

However, to start right at the heart of the matter, I will begin by presenting two examples that in my opinion clearly illustrate the issues the notion of "native speaker" raises in teaching/learning contexts – or rather the difficulties caused not by the notion itself but very often by the internalization of language behaviours and representations linked to it.

2 A certain ethnocentrism of native speakers

The first example is borrowed from a text by Michel Launey who describes a moment in the teaching of French, the language of school learning, in a school in French Guiana.[2] For her first work placement, the teacher, a recent graduate

---

[1] In the original : Pour que la langue étrangère soit perçue à la fois comme une *langue* et comme *autre*, il est nécessaire que la première langue soit aussi d'une certaine manière une *autre* langue. (Py, 1992: 116).

[2] The example is taken from a didactic insert in the magazine *Babylonia* (see bibliography). I have copied the author's text as closely as possible.

of IUFM [Institut universitaire de formation des maîtres] in Cayenne, is working in a CP class ("preparatory class", students aged 6–7). Trained in the importance of spatial structuring for the psychological development of the child, in the following exchanges she asks her students to comment on some pictures:
- Tu vois, Marilène,[3] le chien est dans la maison. Répète: le chien est dans la maison.
- Le chien est dans la maison, dit Marilène.
- Bien, dit Valérie. Dis-moi encore: Où est le chien?
- Il est dans la maison, dit Marilène.
- Maintenant, dis-moi, Marilène, où est le livre?
- Il est dans le sac, dit Marilène.

Satisfied, the teacher moves on to a third picture in which a fish, apparently cooked and ready to be eaten, can be seen on a plate. [NB: in French, the preposition here is 'in' *dans* not 'on'].
- Et le poisson, là, où est-il ?
- Je sais pas, dit Marilène, visiblement embarrassée.
- Comment ça s'appelle, ça, tu sais bien, pourtant?
- Oui, une assiette.
- Donc tu sais: où est le poisson ?
- Non, maitresse, je sais pas.

The teacher is surprised, baffled: how could the student have forgotten a word she had seemed to have good control of? And such a common word as *dans* [in/on]. Does she have attention difficulties? Spatialisation problems? In order to understand the issue better, the teacher continues:
- Mais enfin, voyons, le poisson, il est dans l'assiette!

Marilène looks stupefied then, stuttering, she asks:
- Il est dans l'assiette?
- Mais oui, bien sûr, dit l'enseignante, il est dans l'assiette. Maintenant (passant à une nouvelle image montrant un crayon posé sur une table), dis-moi, où est le crayon?
- Il est dans la table? risque Marilène après une longue hésitation.
- Non, non, on ne peut pas dire ça, dit l'enseignante. Tu vois, regarde, il est *sur* la table. (. . .)

---

[3] Marilène is a young girl who speaks Palikúr (an Amerindian language).

This first example clearly shows the teacher's confusion when confronted with a student who certainly possesses the rudiments of French as a second language but who is not a "native speaker" and whose first language is an Amerindian language which structures space in a very different way to French. The following table will enable the reader to have a better idea:

Le livre est *dans le sac*	**agiku sak**	L'assiette est tombée *sur le sol*	**amadgat wayk**
Le poisson est *dans l'assiette*	**amadga miruk**	J'ai posé le seau *sur le sol*	**amadgat wayk**
Le marteau est *sur la planche*	**amadga parak**	Il est tombé *à l'eau* (ou *dans l'eau*)	**ahakwat un**
La mouche est *dans l'eau*	**ahakwa un**	Il est sorti *de l'eau*	**ahakwatak un**
La fourmi est *dans le sucre*	**abet suku**	J'ai mis du sucre *dans le café*	**ahakwat kafe**
J'ai mis le livre *dans le sac*	**agikut sak**	J'ai mis le sirop *dans le couac*	**abetit kuwak**
Il est entré *dans le trou*	**agikut miyokwiye**	Je suis tombée *dans la boue*	**abetit ibug**
J'ai pris le livre *dans le sac*	**agikutak sak**	J'ai repris mon livre *dans la boue*	**abetitak ibug**
Le rat est sorti *de son trou*	**agikutak miyokwiye**	Je suis sortie *de la boue*	**abetitak ibug**
Il s'est mis *dans le hamac*	**amadgat pudig**		

What can we learn from such an example? Teachers generally do not have much training in how to deal with this type of situation. This calls into question the status of the language they are teaching as the language of learning but which very often they tend to treat as if it were the mother tongue, a language already known by the students. However such situations, in which the teacher does not have "native speakers" in front of them and has trouble envisaging the difficulties the students might encounter, are increasingly frequent and are even tending in certain places to become the norm. What we see here then is the manifestation of a certain, largely unconscious, linguistic ethnocentrism in which one comes to consider one's native language as the *true* representation of the world, enclosing us in this perception and preventing us from imagining other ways of structuring it. However, teaching the language of schooling, which is still envisaged all too often as being the students' mother tongue, tends at times to function in this way, a sort of unjust blindness of the person who possesses the power of the "native speaker".

3 A monolingual norm at the service of the native speaker?

The second example illustrates a comparable situation but at a very different level. Who, at least among those readers who teach in the context of an *Haute École* [a higher education institution, for example, a university or a professional school], has never been disappointed when they are correcting exam papers and wondered if the "problems" detected have arisen from the content being assessed or because of the difficulties faced when formulating their answers by students whose *linguistic biography* is not necessarily known? Is it a student who has encountered real problems in understanding and/or structuring the content? Or a "non-native" student who encounters some difficulties in formulating their thoughts? And here the range of nuances is infinite: is it a so-called "allophone" student but one who has taken all their classes in the region of the Haute École? Or a visiting student, for instance on an Erasmus programme, for whom French might only be their third, fourth or even fifth language? How then should one assess such exam papers?

The situation does have certain points in common with that of our Palikúr student: some students' mastery of the language may certainly pose a problem but sometimes it may also be the modalities of text structure or argumentation. These can differ from one language to another thus leading the student to structure their text in an 'exotic' way, incomprehensible to the "native" teacher.

But this example also raises other questions: how to ensure all the students are treated equally and fairly? And how to ensure the equity of the assessment? How to define what is expected in terms of linguistic correctness and text structure? As the introduction of this book reminds us, monolingual norms and assumptions (of the notion of the native speaker) are flawed or inequitable in a global super-diverse world. However, such norms are still ubiquitous in educational, institutional, and social settings, in political structures and in research paradigms. In other words, the (monolingual) norm of the native speaker very often acts as a unique norm without taking into account the overall linguistic competences of the speakers and without questioning our relationship to the norm in an increasingly plurilingual world.

4 Should we do away with the native speaker?

These two examples show us clearly that there are certainly "native speakers" but that this notion – as Louise Dabène already noted in 1994 – is in any case not (or no longer?) sufficient to deal with the teaching and learning situations we find in today's societies.[4]

---

[4] Let us add to this that all the "native speakers" of the "same" language are not in fact equal, as if there were some "super native speakers", holders of "the" native norm of the language: I myself am certainly a native speaker of French but from a very small region (less than 1% of the world's French speakers!) where a "peripheral" French is spoken – a French language about which a

It is important today to propose new ways of envisaging the teaching of the *language of learning* – which, in order not to prejudge its status for the students, we now term in Switzerland the "language of schooling" (*cf. infra*) – and revisit this notion of "native speaker" to eventually give it a place in a new, didactically relevant, conceptual apparatus. The challenge is considerable, but the aim is to render teaching more equitable and also more efficient. It is even more important as well in the current social context where, increasingly, in numerous European countries mastery of the "national" language has become a determining criterion when it comes to deciding on the reception of migrants and the "naturalisation" of foreigners: the native speaker thus tends to become the standard for an identity norm and acquires a significance that is more political than linguistic.[5]

As we can see, the reflection to be undertaken on the subject of this notion would appear to be inseparable from a more global, ecological (de Pietro 2018) reflection on teaching objectives, cultural norms and plurilingualism.

However, before considering new avenues, we will first briefly examine this notion from a sociolinguistic point of view and present some observations – the result of various research studies – relating to how it can be manifested in the actual behaviour of speakers (§5). Then we will consider how it has been – and often still is – used in the classroom context of French-speaking Swiss schools as well as the notions and tools that for several years now have been developed to take us beyond the initial unfair concept (§6). Finally, we will then give some reflections and present some views for the current and future school (§7).

5 Some preliminary sociolinguistic considerations

The notion of the NS has, as we well know, been called into question within the framework of "emergentist" sociolinguistic studies (Lüdi 2011; Pekarek Doehler 2005). The very notion of language, and mother tongue, is discussed in the

---

journalist could write that we were but tenants! It is moreover likely that the situation in which the Swiss live, like numerous other French speakers, gives them a particular sensitivity in regard to linguistic variation, the relationship to norms and the power relations that ensue from this. Ultimately, who are the "true" native speakers of French? And of which French? See, on this subject, de Pietro 1995 and 2008, Meisoz 1999, Singy 1997, Thibault 1998, etc.

5 See, for example, what is said in Wikipedia about "français langue d'intégration" (FLI) [French as an integration language]: https://fr.wikipedia.org/wiki/Fran%C3%A7ais_langue_d%27int%C3%A9gration consulted on 11 March 2020.

theories of (trans)languaging as Blommaert and Rampton mention: "So although notions like 'native speaker', 'mother tongue' and 'ethnolinguistic group' have considerable ideological force (and as such should certainly feature as *objects* of analysis), they should have no place in the sociolinguistic toolkit itself." (Blommaert and Rampton, 2011: 5) Is this justified?

5.1 Some forms of communication that call into question the notion of the NS

To examine this question, I will return to some slightly older studies in which I was an active participant and which I will attempt to re-examine from the perspective of this contribution. These concern the work of the research team led by Professors Lüdi and Py ("Neuchâtel-Basel team") that dealt with the linguistic aspects of "external" migration (nationals coming from other countries) and "internal" migration between the different language areas of Switzerland.[6] These studies are both numerous and varied and have contributed particularly to a better understanding of the way in which communication in such contexts functions. Long before the term *translanguaging* was coined, we tried to describe, by means of an original notional apparatus (*endolingual, exolingual, 'marque transcodique', code switching*, etc.), what happens when speakers who do not necessarily share the same language construct meaning together or, at times, somehow push the person who is the weak partner in the exchange into a "non-native" status. We therefore proposed a model of communication that, in a certain way, called into question two implicit presuppositions of Jakobson's model of communication: predetermination of the code and the sharing of the same code by the interlocutors. In such situations, among other structuring factors, communication is constructed according to two axes, each of which forms a continuum:
- a monolingual/bilingual, or even multilingual, axis depending on whether the interlocutors keep, more or less rigidly, to only one language or resort, to a variable extent, to more than one language to ensure the communication develops well;
- an endolingual/exolingual axis depending on whether the interlocutors share a similar linguistic repertoire overall or, on the contrary, whether the differences between their respective linguistic repertoires are sufficiently significant that adjustment and adaptation strategies are deemed necessary.

---

6 See for example: Alber and Py 1986; del Coso *et al.* 1985; de Pietro 1988 a and b; Grosjean and Py 1991; Lüdi 1986 and 1992; Lüdi and Py, 1986; Lüdi *et al.* 1995; Py 1986; etc.

The link between these different axes and our problematic can be seen straight-away. In any communication that is at the same time monolingual and exolingual, one of the partners (who we therefore designate as a NS) occupies a "strong" position that allows them to lead the exchange adopting variable stances whose sociolinguistic significance is very different: taking advantage in a certain way of their position, they can correct their "non-native" interlocutor (a *purist* position), finish their utterances for them, address them in a childish style that is demeaning and so on; but they can also adjust their behaviour to the difficulties of their partner, even if it means putting aside their usual normative expectations, by helping them to formulate their thought better or by accepting their resorting to other languages, gestures, etc. (an *attentive, open* position).

The two following examples illustrate these different possibilities:

Example 1: The "strong" partner asserts his NS status by correcting his interlocutor.

A[7]	euh : . . . pendant le . les dernières vacances euh . je : . . . euh . j'ai été
LN	été
A	été
LN	je suis allé
A	à . Kenya
LN	au Kenya
A	au Kenya oui . oui en : . . au pr[ʒ]temps ?
LN	au printemps
A	au printemps oui (Neuchâtel-Basel corpus)

Example 2: The "strong" partner puts aside his status and favours the shared construction of meaning.

A	(. . .) qu'est-ce qu'on a diné ?
LN	(. . .) qu'est-ce qu'on a fait encore ? . qu'est-ce qu'on a diné ? ouais
A	oui
LN	alors eh : qu'est-ce qu'on a diné ? . du poisson ? (. . .) (Neuchâtel-Basel corpus)

In a bilingual, or even multilingual, communication on the other hand even the status of the NS is called into question since each speaker in turn becomes the strong partner, the NS, or even both of them become a type of NS of a pluralistic

---

[7] A = non-native speaker, *alloglot*; LN = native speaker; other letters = different speakers. We have limited transcription conventions here to facilitate the reading. Note, however, the two following conventions: (.) = pause; (:) = lengthening (marking a hesitation, searching for a formulation or a word. . .). All our examples are taken from the huge corpus developed between about 1980 and 1995 within the framework of the work done by the research team; this corpus consists of a variety of exchanges collected in diverse contexts and according to diverse modalities (research interviews, school exchanges, etc.), mainly in the Basel and Neuchâtel regions.

repertoire that allows them to communicate in an equal manner (a sort of *translanguaging* position):

Example 3: In this extract from a conversation in a Neapolitan family settled in Neuchâtel (French-speaking Switzerland), the different interlocutors share the same overall pluralistic repertoire and exploit it in their exchanges.
X   sì pure per me è così
Y   (rire) ah mais lui poi è quello che la sorella fanno lo stesso cammino (rire)
Z   ah sì sono legati
W   attaccatissimi
Y   lo stesso cammino . quella lì si butta nel lago l'autre fa la même chose (rire)
W   c'est normal (. . .)   (Neuchâtel-Basel corpus)

In the context of these studies, especially to describe the exolingual interactions between speakers who did not share a common code to the same degree, we frequently used the notion of the native speaker – as well as that of the non-native speaker – to designate the partners of the exchanges we analysed. We should perhaps have spoken rather of strong and weak partners. In fact our analyses already clearly suggested the limits of these categorisations as Lüdi has pointed out in a recent article: "The boundary between so-called native and non-native speakers had already been called into question by what certain people have called metonymically 'the Neuchâtel-Basel team'" (2011: 51). Above all, in the situations we termed *endolingual-bilingual*, however, the exchanges observed made us think that the speakers allowed language changes precisely because they considered they shared *on the whole* the same codes, whether to the same degree or not, and no longer would one of the parties be defined *a priori* as the strong partner: the notion of the native speaker is evidently not pertinent – unless you consider the speakers as being double native speakers, or even native speakers of a *mixed* code, which since Sankoff and Poplack (1979) is known to at least be based on some sort of grammar![8]

In fact, even in a number of exolingual situations in which the partners in the exchange do not obviously share the same codes to the same degree, a classification that is too rigid can turn out to be problematic; for example, when the speaker who is dominant in the language of the interaction resorts in some way or another to using the language of his partner to ensure the exchange develops

---

[8] Thus, given an utterance like "Espère-moi su' l'corner, j'traverse le chmin et j'viens right back" [Attends-moi au coin, je traverse la rue, je reviens bientôt / Wait for me at the corner. I'm crossing the road and I'll be right back], one could ask if there are "native speakers" of *Chiac*, the mixture of English and French spoken in New Brunswick and even found in literature and comics. (See https://fr.wikipedia.org/wiki/Chiac, consulted on 8 June 2020)

well, thereby "accepting" to (re)define the situation as exolingual-bilingual and through an inversion of roles to become the weak partner.

5.2 The perspective of the actors

However, the studies of our team also showed – sometimes positively, sometimes negatively – that the NS/NNS distinction is at times really relevant from the point of view of the actors themselves. Certain communicative behaviours observed actually suggest – without explicitly referring to them – that they in fact make these notions real:

- At one extreme, certain speakers behave rather like the guardians of the temple, thereby consolidating their status as the legitimate speaker – a status they very often attribute to themselves for the sole reason that they are "native". Among these behaviours, which can become violent, are the refusal to understand an interlocutor who does not express him/herself in exactly the same code[9] or constant correcting that might go as far as to become a "putsch énonciatif" [a sort of *utterance takeover or even a putsch*] consisting of usurping the place of the weak partner by completing their interventions for them (de Pietro et al. 1989/2004). This is a summary of the negative aspects of the status that this notion underpins which, although generally remaining implicit, has come to constitute one of the foundations of linguistic inequalities.
- In a more positive vein, certain speakers make an effort – sometimes rather clumsily, for example when they excessively simplify their way of speaking – to help the "weak" partner in the exchange, who thus appears, at the very least, as *less native* than them, for instance by using syntactic structures perceived to be accessible, reformulations,[10] slowing down the delivery, stressing

---

[9] See for example the recent case of the French politician Jean-Luc Mélanchon in 2018 who publicly mocked the accent of a French-speaking journalist from the South-West who asked him a perhaps slightly embarrassing question. He refused to understand the question she asked him then continued: "Quelqu'un a-t-il une question formulée en français (. . .)" [Does anyone have a question in French?]. This brief exchange caused a buzz on the Internet (see for example: https://www.huffingtonpost.fr/2018/10/18/melenchon-se-moque-de-laccent-du-sud-mais-cest-loin-detre-le-plus-discrimine_a_23564822/ consulted on 16.07.2020) and provoked numerous reactions mentioning, among other things, the notion of *glottophobia* (Blanchet 2017).

[10] We also observed on several occasions in our data a very interesting phenomenon that makes us think that these speakers, with the best will in the world, also see themselves as native guardians of the language: faced with an interlocutor who does not understand a question marked solely by intonation, such a speaker reformulates using an inversion this time; another, in a comparable situation, reformulates an utterance adding the negative "ne" [not] (de Pietro, 1988b).

intonation, etc. The *didactic contract* sometimes established (more or less explicitly) between interlocutors who have unequal mastery of the language of communication is characteristic of this specific case and to a certain extent establishes one of the interlocutors as a NS and the other as a NNS (de Pietro *et al.* 1989/2004).

Analysis of the interactions thus shows that the interlocutors themselves frequently define the interlocution situation as being unequal, involving a speaker of the language and a weaker partner – who could in a way be considered as a native speaker and a non-native speaker.

5.3 What to do with the notion of the NS?

What comes out of this brief digression to these sociolinguistic studies is that the notion of the NS is certainly debatable and even loses all relevance in certain situations – bilingual/plurilingual-endolingual communication – but retains a significant presence in the representations of the speakers; in most of the situations involving interlocutors who do not share the same linguistic repertoire, whatever behaviours – for the purpose of dominating or for equalitarian reasons – they might adopt, they are aware of the *constitutive* inequality of the situation. Thus, despite the radical positions taken by certain sociolinguistic currents, examination of linguistic data (conversational, representation . . .) cannot simply be used to conceal the notion of the native speaker: it is known, at least since Labov (1976), that representations are a constitutive component of sociolinguistic reality.

Our examination highlights some very diverse behaviours, some of which certainly transgress the boundaries between languages, but this does not necessarily mean that languages no longer exist and, especially according to the speakers themselves, that there will no longer be any native speakers. Moreover, I am convinced of the answers a large majority of people would give to the two following questions: Do languages exist? Do "native speakers" of French exist? Sociolinguistics should take account of these realities even if they are called into question by such practices as endolingual-bilingual communication or 'translanguaging'.

However, even if it is not a question of totally renouncing this notion, sociolinguistics rightly invites us to relativise it. The issue then is, as the title of this work suggests, more a question of ascertaining this "changing face of the native speaker". Perhaps it is therefore a matter of considering speakers – including teachers and students – before all else as neither "de simples 'actualisateurs' ou 'mobilisateurs' d'une variété pré-existante" [simple 'actualisers' or 'mobilisers' of a pre-existing variety] (Lüdi 2011: 51), of which they would in fact be NS or NNS, but as actors moving in a (pluri)linguistic space defined by practices (which sometimes transgress borders) and representations (which endow these borders with a certain reality), as if they were "des acteurs se mouvant dans un monde ouvert et prenant le risque de sortir des voies traditionnelles de parler et de faire preuve de créativité, dans le cadre de modèles linguistiques plus participatifs" [actors moving in an open world and taking the risk of moving away from the traditional paths of speaking and demonstrating creativity in the framework of more participatory language models] (Lüdi 2011: 51). The emphasis would no longer then be placed only on a predefined code and a unilateral, definitive allocation of interlocutory roles, with the result being to give the NS all the powers and advantages, but rather moved to practices, resources, styles and repertoires to activate, implement, develop, value and so on.

Are schools ready to move in this direction? This is what we are now going to address by asking what this notion of *native speaker* may become within this framework.

6 At school, different challenges

As we have already suggested, the challenges in the school context are of a very different kind. In effect, it is less a question of discussing the reality of this notion, of knowing for example if "true" NSs of French exist, than of asking what such a notion could bring to teaching along with the consequences that arise from its implicit presence in certain practices that are still in use.

This will lead us to ask ourselves about the terms to use, about the way to consider the marks of *alterity* that some of the students' formulations may contain and the steps to implement so that each student feels they are recognised in their own identity even while participating in the construction of a common language community combining representations that are open to diversity with diversified practices. We will see in so doing that there are approaches today that fall within such a movement and that specifically try to make bridges between languages without concealing the representations relating to them and without denying certain power relations and certain inequalities.

6.1 Behind the NS lies a mother tongue . . .

In fact, the notion of the NS seems to be barely used, nor discussed, in the school context, at least not explicitly. For example, there is not a single mention in the current curriculum of the school of the French part of Switzerland (PER; CIIP 2010). However, as we have already underlined, it cannot be dissociated from the notion of the mother tongue which has played – and very often still plays – an important role in the conception of learning contents and teaching practices. Before returning to the native speaker, our reflections and analyses will therefore now turn to the subject of the notion of mother tongue and its uses in the school context – without forgetting, however, that behind each mother tongue "native speakers" are sort of hidden.

In relation to the school context of the French-speaking part of Switzerland,[11] the "mother tongue" can in fact refer to very different realities, (very) unequally taken into account:
1) French (as used in Switzerland) as the first – if not only – language acquired by a certain number of students;
2) French as the main, official language of the region and school;
3) Certain of the languages linked to migratory movements when these possess a sufficient level of standardisation – whether they correspond to the languages effectively practised as the first language by migrant students or not;
4) The linguistic *practices*, whatever they may be, that will effectively be those of the children's first socialisation.

So, as we shall see below, one of the causes of the "problem" of the native speaker comes from the fact that it is often the first acceptation above, partially mixed with the second, that underpins teaching practices – the immediate consequence of which is to overlook all the mother tongues of students who do not have French as their first language of socialisation. This is why from here on we will avoid talking of *mother tongue*, a notion at the very least ambiguous that constitutes a harmful pedagogic fiction (de Pietro 2001).[12] The frequently encountered term *first language* also holds quite a few ambiguities: Is it the first language acquired by the child? Is it their main language? Is it the first language taken into account at school? . . . The notion of *language of schooling* (which can be used in the plural in bilingual teaching contexts) better describes French within the school framework: the main language in which the students express themselves and in which they study the majority of subjects.

---

11 The part called Romandy Switzerland or *Suisse romande*; for a presentation of the language situation in Switzerland, see, for example, Schläpfer [Ed.] 1985.
12 Furthermore, one can also add the sexist connotations this notion transmits (Dolz 2000; Simard 2000)!

6.2 The Romandy school context

In a rather arbitrary way, we will begin by compiling a brief description of the situation as it was in the years 1970–1980 at the time when numerous school systems in Europe were undergoing major changes.

In the *Romandy school context*[13], as elsewhere, the "traditional" teaching of languages underwent important changes at that time. German, the dominant national language, was now taught in primary school and English was more widely introduced at the secondary level. Teaching was centred on communication but each language remained viewed *in isolation*, in a cloistered way without any links to the other languages taught or merely presented in class – rather as if communication ought of necessity to remain enclosed within the borders of a single language. This was particularly the case of French which, still explicitly considered at the time as the "mother tongue", remained completely apart even though there were already many students of other linguistic origins in the classes at this time and even though it was firmly stated in the work that founded the regeneration of the teaching of French that "[à] l'école, il s'agit de poursuivre un apprentissage commencé dans la famille" [at school, it is a question of pursuing a learning begun in the family] (Besson *et al.* 1979: 1). In general, the textbooks written within the framework of this regeneration did not take into account at all the linguistic and cultural plurality of the classes. More serious still – and this is an indirect consequence of this categorisation – French was taught as if all the students were "native speakers", in effect as if they already knew the language. As we have seen at the beginning of this chapter with the preposition example borrowed from Michel Launey,[14] this leads to certain language phenomena (noun gender, tense value . . .) being ignored for the simple reason that they would be considered evident, acquired "naturally" during the students' first language development, even though they could pose problems for many students.

Such an approach, making French – the mother tongue of those who are in effect native speakers – the assumed starting point for teaching is obviously a

---

13 Switzerland is made up of 26 cantons which form the basic entities of the political system and enjoy genuine power, notably in the school domain. The 7 cantons in which French acts as the language of schooling – for the whole or part of their territory –as well as the Italian-speaking canton of Ticino are therefore grouped together under the aegis of the "Conférence intercantonale de l'Instruction publique" [Intercantonal Conference of Public Education] (CIIP) in order to define common objectives and share to a large extent their approaches and resources.
14 On the subject of the polysemy of the preposition *de* and its correspondences in German, see also Roulet 1980.

source of inequality and serious iniquity. The sociolinguistic evolution of society, illustrated by statistical data on the composition of classes,[15] has therefore led the school authorities to take this new challenge into account. It should be emphasised that the context is relatively favourable in Switzerland for a reflection on plurilingualism, language boundaries and, *a fortiori*, the notion of the native speaker. First of all – and this might seem trivial but . . . – there are no native speakers of the *Swiss language*. The country does not define itself, unlike France for example, by any linguistic nativeness whatsoever, but rather thinks of itself from the outset as being plural, plurilingual.[16]

Let us remember that Switzerland is fundamentally and constitutively a multilingual or, to be precise, a quadrilingual country.[17] There is therefore no "Swiss" language, contrary to what people sometimes ask, but four national languages of which three are official – German, declared as their "main" language by around 63% of the population according to the latest 2016 data from the *Office fédéral de la statistique* (OFS), French (23%), Italian (8%) and one "semi-official" language, Romansh, mentioned by 0.5% of the population.[18]

Moreover, added to this internal, endogenous complexity is, as we have seen, the increasingly strong presence of numerous languages linked to migratory movements and the influx of refugees. Understandably, the notions of mother tongue and native speaker are proving very difficult to grasp in such a context. This is what has made various authors (Weinreich 1953; Lüdi and Py 1990) comment that Switzerland is a veritable *laboratory* in which to deal with questions linked to plurilingualism!

---

15 In the primary level classes of the canton of Geneva for example, for the 2014–2015 school year, about 40% of the 31,000 students state they have a first language other than French; among these are primarily Portuguese (3783), Spanish(2030), Albanian (1543), English (952), Arabic (889) and Italian (778), but also Russian (331), Somali (203), German (203) – and Swiss German (90) –, Tamil (156), Chinese (114), Mongolian (57), etc.
16 This does not mean that all its citizens are themselves plurilingual and naturally does not exclude certain tensions between the different linguistic regions.
17 *Cf.* Article 4 of the Federal Constitution: "Les langues nationales sont l'allemand, le français, l'italien et le romanche." [The national languages are German, French, Italian and Romansh.]
18 See https://www.bfs.admin.ch/bfs/fr/home/statistiques/population/langues-religions/langues.html. Note that the people questioned could mention several "main languages"; however, no data exists based on the notion of "mother tongue" or "first language". In fact, the linguistic configuration is even more complex, in particular for the German-speaking region where the first language acquired by children is generally a regional dialect substantially different to German, which is essentially acquired at the time of entering the school system. Let us also highlight that 22% of the population mention a *non-national* language among their main languages.

6.3 Some paths developed in Swiss schools

The notion of the native speaker clearly appears to be very difficult to define in this context. Progressively, Swiss schools, notably in the French-speaking part, have introduced different notions and tools that enable them, to a certain extent, to avoid the obstacles and negative effects of the use of the notions of NS and mother tongue.

Let us retrace some stages in this slow evolution:
- In 1991 some other mother tongues are clearly recognised and envisaged no longer from the perspective of a return to the country but as a right: "[La *Conférence suisse des directeurs cantonaux de l'Instruction publique* (CDIP)] souligne que l'intégration doit intervenir dans le respect du droit de l'enfant au maintien de la langue et de la culture du pays d'origine." (1995: 207 [1991]). [The *Conférence suisse des directeurs cantonaux de l'Instruction publique* (CDIP) emphasises that integration should operate to respect the right of the child to maintain the language and culture of their country of origin.]

This first movement clearly expresses recognition of other mother tongues, but the languages are still noticeably separated, inherited and, in some way, assigned.
- The situation evolves more noticeably at the turn of the century. In 2003, the *Conférence intercantonale de l'instruction publique de la Suisse romande et du Tessin* (CIIP) states in an official "Declaration" that teaching "participe au développement chez l'élève de compétences de communication opérationnelles dans plusieurs langues (plurilinguisme)" [contributes to the development in the student of operational competences of communication in several languages (plurilingualism)]. French naturally remains the priority concern of teaching but it is no longer defined from the start as the mother tongue: "L'enseignement du français, langue véhiculaire et de culture du lieu ainsi que langue d'intégration, est objet d'une attention particulière tout au long de la scolarité, de l'école enfantine à la fin du cursus de formation de chaque élève." [The teaching of French, the vehicular language and language of culture of the place as well as the language of integration, is given special attention throughout school education, from infant school to the end of each student's educational program.][19]

---

19 *Déclaration de la CIIP relative à la politique de l'enseignement des langues en Suisse romande du 30 janvier 2003* (https://www.ciip.ch/La-CIIP/Documents-officiels/Declarations-politiques, consulted 26 July 2021).

- This document also makes use of new and significant notions: plurilingualism, "local" and "vehicular" language, language "of culture of the place" and "of integration" to designate French, integrated didactic methods, awakening to languages, etc. with regard to the teaching approaches to be implemented.

Through this document, a new conception of teaching can be seen to emerge ever more distinctly. It no longer consists only of gaining mastery of a larger number of languages, each separated from each other, but also of taking into account all these languages, including the first languages of the children of migrants in a common, integrative approach that includes establishing bridges between languages. This evolution is clearly confirmed in the new curriculum introduced in Romandy in 2010: in fact, several elements in the curriculum clearly express a willingness to propose integrated learning objectives beyond the learning of several languages, a plurilingual aim and an awareness of students' first languages. However, as the examples below show, the existence of different languages – and, implicitly, the fact there are then native speakers of these languages – is not called into question at any point:

> La présence d'une multiplicité de langues dans l'école et, plus largement, dans l'environnement quotidien des élèves **implique une approche plurilingue des langues** (. . .). Les diverses langues enseignées s'insèrent dans un **curriculum intégré des langues** (L1, L2, L3, langues d'origine des élèves allophones, langues anciennes. . .) incluant également une **réflexion sur les relations entre les langues**.
>
> [The presence of multiple languages in the school and, more broadly, in the students' daily environment **entails a plurilingual approach to languages** (. . .). The various languages taught are part of an **integrated language curriculum** (L1, L2, L3, languages of origin of allophone students, ancient languages. . .) including a **reflection on the relationship between languages**.]   (*PER, Langues, Commentaires généraux*, 2010)
>
> Le domaine contribue ainsi à la constitution d'un **répertoire langagier plurilingue**, dans lequel **toutes les compétences linguistiques – L1, L2, L3, mais aussi celles d'autres langues, les langues d'origine des élèves bi- ou trilingues en particulier** – trouvent leur place.
>
> [The domain[20] therefore contributes to the constitution of a **plurilingual language repertoire** in which **all language competences – L1, L2 and L3 as well as those of other languages, the languages of origin of bi-or trilingual students in particular** – have a place.]   (*PER, Langues, Commentaires généraux*, 2010)

---

[20] This is the "Languages" domain which brings together all the languages found within the school system, including French (another novelty).

In relation to the issue of the native speaker, which is what interests us here, the most significant evolution seems to be the introduction of a new axis, termed *Interlinguistic approaches,* among the axes structuring the teaching of languages. In effect, this axis added to the more usual ones (*Reading – Writing . . .*) involves *all* the students and is explicitly centred on *establishing connections* between various languages and the development of plurilingual learning components (comparison, listening in the various languages, etc.).

Its concrete content is mainly supported by teaching tools developed some years before under the term EOLE (Éveil et Ouverture aux Langues à l'Ecole; Perregaux *et al.*, 2003). These manuals fall within the didactic approach of "language awareness" started in Great Britain by Eric Hawkins (1984). The activities they propose do not directly call into question the existence of languages and speakers who would be natives, but several of them invite the students to engage in a genuine reflection on their language repertoire, on "language mixing", etc. Below are four examples:

Le papagei [The parrot]
This activity is aimed at very young students, aged between 4 and 6. First of all, they are familiarised with the texts – in this case short poems – which include words from other languages, as in the two examples below:

Le Papagei	Un moustique
– Connaissez-vous	A piqué
Le Papagei	Le bout de mon nez.
Qui dit ja, ja	Pauvre nose !
Et so wie so ?	Il a l'air tout enrhumé !
Connaissez-vous	
Ce drôle d'oiseau ?	
– Ja, ja, ja, ja	
Et so wie so.	

The pupils must "simply" listen to the poems, notice and repeat the words uttered in languages other than the base language of the poem and have fun mixing several languages. (*cf.* http://eole.irdp.ch/activites_eole/le_papagei.pdf)

Le rap des langues de ma classe [The languages of my class rap]
At the heart of youth culture today, rap is a form of musical creation that often uses linguistic diversity as a creative resource. In this activity, the students, aged 9–10, begin by listening to a rap that mixes several languages that they try

to recognise. Then they themselves create new verses based on the languages present in their class.

Figure 1: Le rap des langues de ma classe [The languages of my class rap].

In so doing, they are invited to reflect on the relations they have with these languages and to make the class an open "plurilingual space" (Perregaux 1995) in which the students want to enter and express themselves. (*cf.* http://eole.irdp.ch/activites_eole/rap_langues.pdf; see Appendix)

Parlez-vous europanto? [Do you speak Europanto?]
This activity[21], also aimed at students aged 9–10, goes further in a sort of reconsideration of the notion of the native speaker since it deals with the students understanding a joke written in *Europanto*, the "language" made up of all European languages that was created by Diego Marani, a translator in European institutions, who had fun mixing these languages in texts written for various media.

For the students it is of course a game, but a game that invites them to implement various comprehension strategies and develop their ability to understand such mixtures as in the example below:

---

21 Originally, this activity was developed within the context of a European project *Socrates Lingua* (called Evlang) that aimed to produce didactic support for awakening to languages. *Parlez-vous europanto?* was conceived by Marinette Matthey from the Swiss team of the Evlang project, then adapted to fit the framework of the published EOLE manuals. See also Candelier 2003.

Prénom : _____   *Document élève 1a*

Toto et sa little sorella

Die Mutter van Toto lui demande to go shopping y le donne una liste de cosas zu kaufen. Seine Mamma le dice auch :
– Bring la tua sorella mit !

Toto geht zum magasin, kauft todas las cosas, aber cuando er kommt zurück, seine little sorella tombe dans un loch und disappear.

Cuando Toto arrive at home, seine Mutti le dice :
– Wo ist ta little sorella ?

Toto answers :
– Elle est dans un loch gefallen.

– Aber porque du hast elle nicht help um zu sortir ? dice la mother.

– Porque no estaba escrito sur la liste ! answers Toto.

Figure 2: Parlez-vous europanto? [Do you speak Europanto?].

Next, when they in turn make up new plurilingual jokes, it is the linguistic knowledge of the whole class that is exploited this time, thereby showing their creative abilities. (*cf.* http://eole.irdp.ch/activites_eole/europanto.pdf)

Hanumsha, Nora, Jean-Yves: histoires de langues [Hanumsha, Nora, Jean-Yves: stories of languages]

The activity chosen for this last example falls within what has become almost a classic of plurilingual didactics: language biographies (Perregaux 2002; Jeanneret 2010; Molinié 2015; etc.). The students, aged 11 to 13, first of all work on the biographies of Hanumsha, Nora and Jean-Yves. With the help of a diagram they observe which language(s) these three young people express themselves in according to who they are communicating with, the places and domains referred to, etc. They therefore become aware of different types of rapport to languages.

The activity allows the students, no matter their own language situation, to reflect on the relationship they have with the languages in their environment. Moreover, it enables them to be sensitised to the existence of plurilingual practices whose forms are often unknown to, or even undervalued by, not only monolingual speakers but also the plurilingual speakers themselves. The situations that are presented allow the often limited concept of bilingualism or plurilingualism, which in fact excludes most plurilingual people, to become broader. It is interesting to

Figure 3: Hanumsha, Nora, Jean-Yves: histoires de langues [Hanumsha, Nora, Jean-Yves: stories of languages].

highlight that one of the biographies, that of Jean-Yves, is produced by a "monolingual" speaker – who nevertheless possesses some rudiments in other languages.

At the end, with the help of the diagram, the students are invited to write their own language biography and to compare it to those of their fellow students.

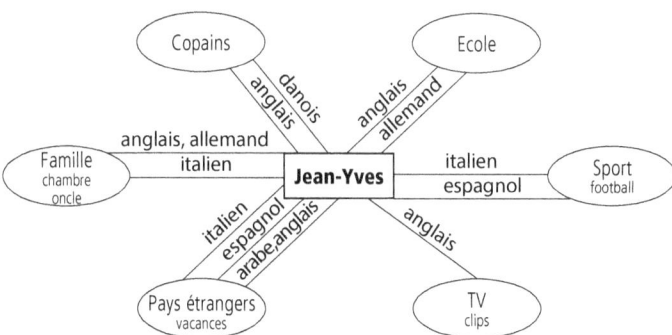

Figure 4: Diagram for stories of languages (cf. http://eole.irdp.ch/activites_eole/hanumsha.pdf).

7 Reflections and perspectives

And so finally is there a native speaker in the class? Does this notion still make sense? My reply is a very Swiss-like compromise: yes and no!

YES. The notion of the NS, envisaged with the necessary precautions, remains pertinent despite certain practices that have been observed that clearly show its limits and consequently would invite it to be called into question or even abandoned. As we have seen, this notion lies in fact behind various behaviours – be they conscious or not, voluntary or not – found simultaneously in the school context when each language that is taught is isolated in rigid monolingual compartments or when the students are treated as if they were all NSs of the language of schooling. This also applies in certain "exolinguistic" exchanges – when the "strong" partner behaves de facto like a native speaker, at times going so far as to adopt a purist position as the guardian of the temple of nativeness – and in the representations that most speakers make of the world's languages.

The essential contribution of sociolinguistics is to describe objectively what is effectively happening and taking place in the interactions – in terms of identity and the power relationships expressed in the various positions – and to further our understanding of language behaviours and their consequences for the status of the speakers. In particular, this leads us, as Georges Lüdi (*op. cit.*) and proponents of translanguaging have invited us to do, to conceive of language as *partly* emerging and *partly* recreated during each communicative exchange. But sociolinguistics also reminds us of the weight of normative constraints that affect the behaviour of the social actors. To completely abandon the notion would result in masking the importance of the representations of the speakers. But it is precisely the notion of the "native speaker", including everything it harbours that is fantasy, which allows us to understand and make visible certain language functions and representations that underpin inequalities between the speakers and the injustices that affect "*non*-native speakers" above all.

NO. This from a didactic perspective, however, in which it seems important to avoid this notion and even more the use of the notion of *mother tongue* to designate the language of teaching. Here, on the contrary, it is important to develop pluralistic approaches that lead students to become aware of the diversity of language repertoires and to exploit all the resources available to them, including multilingual and multimodal ones.

The initiatives described above for the Swiss context are a clear step towards opening up to diversity, recognition of allophone children's first language and creativity, thereby helping to make the system fairer. Contrary to the recurrent findings that highlight the difficulties of students coming from migration backgrounds or who have a first language different to the language of schooling, several studies undertaken in the last few years suggest in fact that, at the very least, plurilingualism could be an advantage rather than an obstacle in everyday life and at school. This is the case, for example, of the young Italian-speaking woman in her twenties who, when interviewed within the scope of a research project and talking about the problems of the French digraphs *en, em, an, am,* etc., said: "And so, it was practical for me to write in French because Italian helped me with French spelling." In this actual example, it is precisely the fact of not being a native speaker of French that helps her spell better.[22]

Many people thus spontaneously develop strategies and tricks to better manage and deal *with, between* and *beyond* the languages in their repertoire. Refusing to isolate languages from each other and not favouring those students categorised as natives should be the school's role in order to ensure that it is so for the greatest number. These approaches are not necessarily more "effective" and do not of course eliminate all the inequalities but at least they do not exclude anyone.

Such approaches have been developed for some thirty years now in various places and they fall perfectly within the guidelines defined by the Council of Europe, in particular in view of the construction of a "plurilingual, complex and composite repertoire" (Council of Europe 2001: 129). And today there are specific operational tools that make these guidelines possible. "A Framework of Reference for Pluralistic Approaches to Languages and Cultures" (CARAP; Candelier *et al.* 2012), developed under the aegis of the European Centre for Modern Languages (ECML), describes for example what must be developed through teaching so as to endow learners with competences that have proved to be key in the numerous communication situations characterised by the presence of speakers who have unequal knowledge of the language(s) being used: "managing communication", "negotiating", "adapting one's behaviour", "decentring", "making sense of unfamiliar linguistic and/or cultural elements", etc. It then also describes specifically the *resources* (Knowledge, Skills and Attitudes) that can be developed within the framework of specific school activities such as those we have presented above or those included in the database of didactic materials on the CARAP website (https://carap.ecml.at/Accueil/tabid/3577/language/fr-FR/Default.aspx). Below are some examples of resources that can be relevant and that in a certain way call into question the notions of mother tongue, native speaker and of course plurilingualism:

Knows that each individual belongs to at least one linguistic community and that many persons belong to more than one linguistic community (K 2.2)
Knows that one must adapt one's own communicative repertoire to the social and cultural context within which communication is taking place (K 3.3)
Knows that there exists language means to facilitate communication {simplification / reformulation etc.} (K 3.4)
Can communicate "between languages" (S 6.4)

---

22 See, on this subject, de Pietro (2011).

Can activate bilingual or plurilingual communication in relevant situations (S 6.5)
> Can 'vary / alternate' 'languages / linguistic codes / modes of communication' (S 6.5.1)
> Can produce a text in which registers / varieties / languages alternate functionally (when the situation allows it) (S 6.5.2)

The will to verbalise / discuss representations one may have of certain linguistic phenomena (loans / "mixing" of languages etc.) (A 8.4.2)
The will to adapt / to be flexible in one's own behaviour when interacting with persons who are linguistically / culturally different from oneself (A 13.1)
Accepting a bi-/plurilingual / bi-/pluricultural identity (A 16.2.2)

Whether in terms of knowledge, skills or attitudes, such resources involve the whole encounter with more than one language and the ways to handle it. They relativise the boundaries between languages and transcend them by comparison, adaptation and decentring. In so doing, they enable the notion of the native speaker to be bypassed – or at least relativised. In fact, there are only actors, communicators and/or learners, who manage pluralistic repertoires in communication situations that are often characterised by divergent representations, misunderstandings or inequalities of access to the language of communication by exploiting the resources they have available or that the school helps them develop.

However, on account of their unquestionable sociolinguistic reality, it can again be noticed that these resources do not directly call into question the notion of native speaker and even less that of mother tongue. But they support plurilingual practices that transcend the boundaries between languages and allow them to be relativised while becoming aware of their existence. Looking at it from this perspective, incidentally, is why I have chosen to use an extract from a text by Bernard Py as the epigraph to my contribution: to recognise and accept non-native speakers in their own identity supposes in some way that one's own language also becomes *another* language ... and consequently to *review* one's own status of supposedly being a native speaker.[23]

Therefore, as the framework text suggests, the face of the native speaker certainly does not disappear but it is well on the way to changing in favour of becoming a speaker who is now sensitive to:

---

[23] What can be recognised here is the closeness of this idea to Goethe's famous quote ("Wer fremde Sprachen nicht kennt weiss nichts von seiner eigenen", *Maximen und Reflexionen*, II, 23) and to how Vygotsky (1934, 374–376) considers the learning of a foreign language and its impact on the relationship to the first language.

- the pluralistic nature of the language repertoire of every individual and the composite nature of plurilingual competence;
- the phenomena of domination and exclusion that are potentially present in all situations linking a plurality of codes in more or less exolingual and plurilingual interactions as well as the means to prevent them;
- the creativity that such situations can give rise to if the speaker accepts moving away from the "traditional paths" (Lüdi 2011) and creates original ways to ensure the common construction of meaning in communication situations that have thus become more egalitarian.

The challenge, which does not sound much, is important and – from a sociodidactic perspective – goes a long way beyond the simple use of scientific notions. Édouard Glissant (1993, quoted by Perregaux 2004: 147) sums the issue up particularly well:

> it is not a matter of speaking languages, that is not the problem. One can speak no languages other than one's own. It is rather the very way of speaking one's own language, of speaking it in a closed or open way; of speaking it while ignoring the presence of other languages or in the prescience that other languages exist and that they influence us even when we don't know it.[24]

Author's Positionality

Most of the authors of this book certainly have a strong personal experience of plurilingualism, which probably influences their background and their perception of the question of the native speaker. This is not my case . . . Although I read English and German without much difficulty, understand Italian relatively well and a little bit of Spanish, Catalan and Portuguese texts, I remain, fundamentally and to my great regret, a 'not really plurilingual' French speaker. I could therefore appear to be a perfect prototype of the native speaker, with a fairly good mastery of his 'mother tongue', who could judge what is or is not said in French and who deserves to be considered a native speaker of French . . .

However, on various occasions, I have experienced, to a lesser degree, what speakers whose first language is not the legitimate form of the 'native speaker's' language may live through: I come from a peripheral region of the French-speaking world, a region where a

---

[24] Original quotation: "ce n'est pas une question de parler des langues, ce n'est pas le problème. On peut ne pas parler d'autres langues que la sienne. C'est plutôt la manière même de parler sa propre langue, de la parler de manière fermée ou ouverte; de la parler dans l'ignorance de la présence des autres langues ou dans la prescience que les autres langues existent et qu'elles nous influencent même sans qu'on le sache."

journalist once said that we are not owners but only tenants of the French language. Indeed, we are sometimes taken to task by 'real' French speakers about certain words and mocked for our accent. Despite my strong roots in the French-speaking world, and my strong attachment to the French language, part of my sensitivity to the issues of the book certainly comes from there, from these experiences of "marginality", of a certain "illegitimacy" . . .

But this is not the main reason for my sensitivities to the issues that this book addresses. The reason is primarily related to my professional and intellectual background and is reflected in the dual orientation of my contribution. One of these two orientations comes from my participation in the work of the Neuchâtel-Basel team, directed by Professors B. Py and G. Lüdi, on the linguistic (and social) situation of migrants, first of all Spanish migrants in Neuchâtel, and then 'internal' migrants within the various linguistic regions of Switzerland. There I could observe migrants' ways of managing their multilingual repertoire, their ease in alternating their codes and, also, sometimes, their difficulties in the French or German language, the difficulties for their integration and identity. This has had a profound effect on my way of conceiving of language, communication and norms, and has helped me develop a fundamentally open variationist notion of language competence.

The second orientation in my contribution is linked to my involvement, for several years, in the didactics of French within an institute linked to the educational authorities of the French-speaking part of Switzerland. There, I came across the issues of this book above all through the difficulties encountered by pupils from migrant backgrounds at school: stigmatisation as 'non-French speakers', failure to take into account their knowledge of other languages and their plurilingual competence, etc. I have since tried, with others of course (Chr. Perregaux, M. Candelier, J. Billiez, etc.), to change this situation by fighting against certain preconceived ideas and for the recognition of the multiple skills of these pupils. And that with some success: it's (almost) no more question in our schools of "non-French-speaking pupils", nor of the teaching of French as a "mother tongue"; French – as the language of schooling – is now integrated into a 'Languages' field which encompasses all the languages taken into account, including the languages of migration, and so favours the development of a more integrated approach to language teaching. The main contribution, however, seems to me to lie in the creation of the collection Éducation et Ouverture aux Langues à l'École "Education and opening up to languages at school" (EOLE; see bibliography), which includes 36 language awareness activities, now explicitly included in the official curriculum. These activities encourage openness to the diversity of languages, particularly those present in the classroom, and thus make possible, at the very least, to put the status of native speaker into perspective.

Thus, it is above all a social, socio-didactic commitment that leads me to be interested in the problematic of this book. The school context requires us to remain close to the reality experienced by the actors. In this context, the notion of language, for example, cannot be discussed: 'French' is taught, 'German' is taught, etc. My struggle is therefore with the idea of teaching these languages, but not as separate entities, isolated from each other, but as constituent parts of a plural, multimodal competence, always under construction and in movement.

What I find interesting in my case is that the issues addressed in this book are also addressed by researchers who are not necessarily themselves multilingual and multicompetent: the fight against 'native speakerism' must also come from persons who might enjoy a status of native speaker and the symbolic and social capital that this has given them for far too long!

Appendix: Text of the 'Languages of my class' rap activity

Le rap des langues de ma classe

Buongiorno ¿ Como estas ? Ouria
Mir, come with me
On va faire un tour au-delà des frontières
De nos jours, le langage ne doit plus être une barrière
Au contraire il est comme une échelle sur laquelle
Tout le monde monte, parle, chante et s'appelle
On peut même s'exprimer par le langage des signes
Sayōnara, Viedemo se, Auf wiedersehen

C'est le rap des langues de ma classe
La différence est une grande richesse
C'est le rap des langues de ma classe
De tous pays, d'origines et de cultures diverses

Pour s'exprimer il y a tellement de langues
De dialectes, de patois sans compter les slangs
On peut dire Nangadef, As salaam allaikoum
Sawadee kup, Namasté ou encore Vannakkam
Y a-t-il une meilleure façon parmi 360 degrés ?
Chacune est différente, chacun s'exprime à son gré
Pourtant elles ont en commun qu'elles permettent aux êtres humains
De communiquer et de marcher main dans la main

C'est le rap des langues de ma classe
La différence est une grande richesse
C'est le rap des langues de ma classe
De tous pays, d'origines et de cultures diverses

Amigo, sahbi, my friend, mon ami
Aujourd'hui on peut le dire qu'importe le temps qu'on a mis
Toda, Obrigado, Teşekkür ederim
Pas de frontière de langages, juste de l'amour et des rimes.

Cf. http://eole.irdp.ch/activites_eole/rap_langues.pdf [The audio version of this rap may also be accessed here.]

References

Alber, Jean-Luc & Bernard Py. 1986. Vers un modèle exolingue de la communication interculturelle: interparole, coopération et conversation. *Études de linguistique appliquée* 61. 78–90.

Besson, Marie-Josèphe, Marie-Rose Genoud, Bertrand Lipp & Roger Nussbaum. 1979. *Maîtrise du français*. Neuchâtel: Office romand des éditions et du matériel scolaire.

Blanchet, Philippe. 2017. *Discriminations: combattre la glottophobie*. Paris: Éditions Textuel.

Blommaert, Jan & Ben Rampton. 2011. Language and Superdiversity. *Diversities* 13(2). 1–21. https://newdiversities.mmg.mpg.de/?page_id=2056 (consulted 23 July 2020)

Candelier, Michel (Coordinateur), Antoinette Camilleri-Grima, Véronique Castellotti, Jean-François de Pietro, Ildikó Lőrincz, Franz-Joseph Meißner, Artur Noguerol & Anna Schröder-Sura (avec le concours de Muriel Molinié). 2012. *Le CARAP. Un Cadre de Référence pour les Approches Plurielles des Langues et des Cultures – Compétences et ressources*. Graz, Conseil de l'Europe, 104 p. (English edition: *CARAP – FREPA. A Framework of Reference for Pluralistic Approaches to Languages and Cultures – Competences and resources*) https://carap.ecml.at/Accueil/tabid/3577/language/fr-FR/Default.aspx (consulted 23 July 2020)

Candelier, Michel (Dir.). 2003. *L'éveil aux langues à l'école primaire. Evlang: bilan d'une innovation européenne*. Bruxelles: de Boeck.

Conférence intercantonale de l'instruction publique de la Suisse romande et du Tessin (CIIP). 2010. *Plan d'études romand: Langues*. Neuchâtel: CIIP. http://www.plandetudes.ch/ (consulted 13 February 2020)

Conférence suisse des directeurs cantonaux de l'Instruction publique (CDIP). 1995. *Recommandations et décisions*. Berne: CDIP. https://edudoc.ch/record/24417?ln=fr (consulted 20 April 2021)

Conseil de l'Europe. 2001. *Cadre européen commun de référence pour les langues (CECR)*. Strasbourg: Conseil de l'Europe. https://rm.coe.int/16802fc3a8 (consulted 23 July 2020)

Dabène, Louise. 1994. *Repères sociolinguistiques pour l'enseignement des langues: situations plurilingues*. Paris: Hachette FLE (Collection F/références), 191 pp.

Del Coso-Calame, Francine, Jean-François de Pietro & Cecilia Oesch-Serra. 1985. La compétence de communication bilingue. Étude fonctionnelle des code-switchings dans le discours de migrants espagnols et italiens à Neuchâtel /Suisse). In Elisabeth Gülich & Thomas Kotschi, *Grammatik, Konversation, Interaktion – Beiträge zum Romanistentag 1983*, 377–398. Tübingen: Max Niemeyer Verlag.

De Pietro, Jean-François. 1988a. Vers une typologie des situations de contacts linguistiques. *Langage et Société* 43. 65–89.

De Pietro, Jean-François. 1988b. Conversations exolingues: une approche linguistique des interactions interculturelles. In Jacques Cosnier, Nadine Gelas & Catherine Kerbrat-Orecchioni (Éds), *Échanges sur la conversation*, 251–267. Paris: Éditions du CNRS.

De Pietro, Jean-François. 1995. Francophone ou Romand? Qualité de la langue et identité linguistique en situation minoritaire. In Jean-Michel Eloy (Éd.), *La qualité de la langue? le cas du français*, 223–250. Paris: Champion.

De Pietro, Jean-François. 2001. Le français: LANGUE maternelle ou langue première? *L'Éducateur* 4. 6–8.

De Pietro, Jean-François. 2008. L'école face aux variétés du français: réflexions à partir de la situation en Suisse francophone. In Gisèle Delage [Éd.], *La langue française dans sa diversité*, 181–208. Québec, Secrétariat à la politique linguistique.

De Pietro, Jean-François. 2011. Quand parler une autre langue aide à écrire en français. *L'Éducateur 1.* 28–31.
De Pietro, Jean-François. 2018. L'école peut-elle contribuer à une écologie des langues? *Dialogues et cultures – Écologie du français et diversité des langues. Florilège du IVe congrès régional de la CAP, Kyoto 2017.* 25–44.
De Pietro, Jean-François, Marinette Matthey & Bernard Py. 1989. Acquisition et contrat didactique: les séquences potentiellement acquisitionnelles dans la conversation exolingue. In *Actes du troisième Colloque Régional de Linguistique*, 99–124. Strasbourg: Université des Sciences Humaines. (Reprinted in 2004 in Laurent Gajo, Marinette Matthey, Danièle Moore & Cecilia Serra (Éds), *Un parcours au contact des langues: textes de Bernard Py commentés*, 79–93. Paris: Didier)
Dolz, Joaquim. 2000. De la difficulté de «couper avec la mère» chez les didacticiens du français. Plaidoyer pour un changement de dénomination de la discipline. *Lettre de la DFLM 27.* 29–31.
Glissant, Édouard. 1993. Entretien avec Lise Gauvin. *Littératures 12.* Strasbourg: Édition spéciale du Carrefour des littératures européennes.
Grosjean, François & Bernard Py. 1991. La restructuration d'une première langue: l'intégration de variantes de contact dans la compétence de migrants espagnols à Neuchâtel (Suisse). *La Linguistique* 27 (2). 35–60.
Hawkins, Eric. 1984. *Awareness of language: an introduction.* New York: Cambridge University Press.
Jeanneret, Thérèse. 2010. Trajectoires d'appropriation langagière et travail identitaire: données et analyses. *Bulletin suisse de linguistique appliquée.* n° spécial tome 1. 27–45. http://doc.rero.ch/record/11876/files/bulletin_vals_asla_2010_special_1.pdf (consulted 20 July 2020)
Labov, William. 1976. *Sociolinguistique* (A. Kihm, trad.). Paris: Minuit. (Original published in English in 1972).
Launey, Michel. 2010. Je ne sais où . . . Deviner, comprendre, analyser – À la découverte des langues du monde. Encart didactique 64, *Babylonia* 4. http://babylonia.ch/fileadmin/user_upload/documents/2010-4/Baby4-2010encdid64.pdf (consulted 16 July 2020)
Lüdi, Georges. 1986. Forms and functions of bilingual speech in pluricultural migrant communities in Switzerland. In Joshua A. Fishman, Andrée Tabouret-Keller, Michael Clyne, Bhadriraju Krishnamurti & Mohamad Abdulaziz (Eds), *The Fergusonian Impact: In Honor Of Charles A. Ferguson On The Occasion Of His 65th Birthday*, 217–236 (vol. 2: Sociolinguistics and the Sociology of Language). New York: Mouton de Gruyter.
Lüdi, Georges. 1992. Internal migrants in a multilingual country. *Multilingua* 11 (1). 45–73.
Lüdi, Georges. 2011. Vers de nouvelles approches théoriques du langage et du plurilinguisme. *Travaux neuchâtelois de linguistique* (TRANEL) 53. 47–64. http://www.unine.ch/files/live/sites/tranel/files/Tranel/53/47-64_Ludi_VersionFinale2.pdf (consulted 23 July 2020)
Lüdi, Georges & Bernard Py. 1986. *Être bilingue.* Berne, Lang.
Lüdi, Georges & Bernard Py. 1990. La Suisse: un laboratoire pour l'étude de la dynamique des langues en contact. *Langage et Société* 50/51. 87–92.
Lüdi, Georges, Bernard Py, Jean-François de Pietro, Rita Franceschini, Marinette Matthey, Cecilia Oesch-Serra & Christine Quiroga. 1995. *Changement de langage et langage du changement.* Lausanne, L'Age d'Homme.
Meizoz, Jérôme. 1999. Le droit de mal écrire. *Babylonia 3.* 57–62.

Molinié, Muriel. 2015. La méthode biographique: de l'écoute de l'apprenant de langues à l'herméneutique du sujet plurilingue. In Philippe Blanchet et Patrick Chardenet (Dirs.), *Guide pour la recherche en didactique des langues. Approches contextualisées*, 144–154. Paris: Éditions des archives contemporaines / Agence universitaire de la francophonie (AUF, Montréal).

Pekarek Doehler, Simona. 2005. De la nature située des compétences en langue. In Jean-Paul Bronckart, Ecaterina Bulea & Michèle Pouliot (Éds), *Repenser l'enseignement des langues: comment identifier et exploiter les compétences?*, 41–68. Villeneuve d'Ascq: Presses universitaires du Septentrion.

Perregaux, Christiane. 1995. L'école, espace plurilingue. *Lidil* 11. 125–139.

Perregaux, Christiane. 2002. (Auto)biographies langagières en formation et à l'école: pour une autre compréhension du rapport aux langues. *Bulletin VALS-ASLA 76*. 81–94.

Perregaux, Christiane. 2004. Prendre appui sur la diversité linguistique et culturelle pour développer aussi la langue commune. *Repères 29*. 146–166.

Perregaux, Christiane, Jean-François de Pietro, Claire de Goumoëns & Dominique Jeannot [Dirs.] (2003). *EOLE: Éducation et Ouvertures aux langues à l'école*. Neuchâtel: CIIP (2 volumes avec CD audios + Fichiers de documents et 1 brochure d'accompagnement). http://eole.irdp.ch/eole/ (consulted 23 July 2020)

Py, Bernard. 1986. Making sense: interlanguage's intertalk in exolingual conversation. *Studies in Second Language Acquisition* 8. 343–353.

Py, Bernard. 1992. Acquisition d'une langue étrangère et altérité. *Cahiers de l'Institut de linguistique et des sciences du langage* 2. 113–126.

Roulet, Eddy. 1980. *Langues maternelles, langues secondes, vers une pédagogie intégrée*. Paris: Hatier (Collection LAL).

Sankoff, David & Shana Poplack. 1979. A formal grammar for code-switching. *Papers in Linguistics* 14 (1). 3–46.

Schläpfer, Robert (Ed.). 1985. *La Suisse aux quatre langues*. Genève: Éditions Zoé.

Simard, Claude. 2000. Pour une appellation moins connotée et plus appropriée au contexte actuel. *Lettre de la DFLM* 27. 31–32.

Singy, Pascal. 1997. *L'image du français en Suisse romande. Une enquête sociolinguistique en Pays de Vaud*. Paris: L'Harmattan.

Thibault, André. 1998. Légitimité linguistique des français nationaux hors de France: le français de Suisse romande. *Revue québécoise de linguistique* 26 (2). http://andre.thibault.pagesperso-orange.fr/LegitimiteFrSR.pdf (consulted 23 July 2020)

Vygotsky, Lev Semionovitch. 1934–1997. *Pensée et langage*. Paris: La Dispute.

Weinreich, Uriel. 1953. *Languages in Contact*. New York: Linguistic Circle of New York.

Maria Zerva
Chapter 5
On the paradox of being native speakers of two "competing" languages: Turkish as the mother or the father tongue of Greek nationals

Abstract: This chapter focuses on the notions of mother tongue and national identity. It draws on a sociolinguistic survey and semi-structured interviews in two Greek villages inhabited by Greek orthodox descendants of Asia Minor refugees, originated from today's Turkey, who resettled in Greece in the mid-1920s. Turkish as the "mother" or the "father tongue", is integrated in a complex network of relationships between affection and rejection. Building on theories of identity construction in discourse and of language evaluation and judgment, the chapter discusses the effects of myths naturalising the "mother tongue".

Keywords: national identity construction, discourse, agency, Greece, Asia Minor refugees, Greek language, Turkish language

1 Introduction

This chapter focuses on the association of designations such as "native speaker", "native language" and "mother tongue" with national identity (cf. Bonfiglio 2010). Our evidence comes from a sociolinguistic survey with semi-structured interviews in two Greek villages inhabited by Greek orthodox descendants of Asia Minor refugees originating from today's Turkey who were resettled in Greece in the mid-1920s. These populations, originally Turkish speaking, have shifted to Greek, the dominant national language, after four generations (Zerva 2011). Nevertheless, the Turkish language is present as part of the sociolinguistic situation and heritage, being spoken by elderly or middle-aged people or being sung at traditional feasts. The interviewees constantly refer to Turkish in their lives, trying to overcome the paradox, according to dominant national Discourses (De Fina, Schiffrin, and Bamberg 2006; Kiesling 2006), between a Greek identity and the Turkish language and

---
Maria Zerva, University of Strasbourg, e-mail: mzerva@unistra.fr

https://doi.org/10.1515/9781501512353-006

thus consolidate their position within the Greek nation. Turkish, as the "mother" or the "father tongue"[1] is thus integrated in a complex network of relationships, between affection and rejection. Building on theories of identity construction in discourse (Benwell and Stokoe 2006; De Fina, Schiffrin, and Bamberg 2006) and of language evaluation and judgement (*minoration – majoration*, see Blanchet 2000, 2005; see also the concept of Social Representations below), we discuss the pervasive effects of myths naturalising the "mother tongue", linked to the construction of national identities and the ideologies of homogeneity and exclusion of the Other in nation-states (Drettas 2008; Voutira 2007; Wodak et al. 1999).

2 The native speaker and the mother tongue metaphor

The term "native speaker" as well as its correlates, such as "native language" and "mother tongue", have been thoroughly discussed in the literature, mainly to denounce its ideological offshoots and politicisation (cf. Bonfiglio 2010, Blommaert and Rampton 2011, Muni Toke 2013b, Tabouret-Keller and Le Page 1986; see also Bono, this volume).[2] The very appearance of the "native speaker" in modern linguistics seems to be related to Bloomfield (Love and Ansaldo 2010: 589), probably due to a sensibility towards migrant communities and their subsequent multilingualism (Drettas 2008: 465), though he interestingly enough avoids using the "mother tongue" expression. Thus, Bloomfield notes in the chapter on "speech-communities":

> An infant that gets into a group as a foundling or by adoption, learns the language of the group exactly as does a child of native parentage; as he learns to speak, his language shows no trace of whatever language his parents may have spoken. [. . .] The child learns to speak like the persons round him. The first language a human being learns to speak is his *native language*: he is a *native speaker* of this language. (Bloomfield [1935] 1973: 43)

The idealisation of the "native speaker" is definitively established by Chomsky in his *Aspects of the Theory of Syntax* (1965), with his famous *ideal* monolingual

---

1 We are translating the utterance used by our interviewees, who employed both the equivalent, in Greek, of "mother language" (*mitriki glossa*) and "father language" (*patriki glossa*).
2 An overview of the discussions and critiques of the "native speaker" is beyond the scope of this chapter. See, among others the recent volume of *Histoire Epistémologie Langage* (2013), especially the papers of Muni Toke (2013a and 2013b), Davies 2003, and Bonfiglio 2010, especially chapter 1, 8–20.

speaker-listener, possessing perfect competence in an idealised standard language (Muni Toke 2013a). Multilingualism and diversity have been dismissed for a long time from linguistic investigation following a long-standing tradition and mainstream use which considered them as "anomalies" (cf. Gadet and Varro 2006; Tabouret-Keller 2011). The native speaker has been legitimised not only as the informant of linguists, but also as the ultimate representative of the language in question, gaining real profits in the real world, as Bourdieu (2001) has put it, with subsequent inequalities (cf. Jessner, Hofer, and Malzer-Papp, as well as Dewaele, Bak, and Ortega, this volume). As we have already mentioned, beginning with Dell Hymes, critiques have abounded and have challenged the essentialist, politico-ideological and hierarchical view of the native speaker ever since, a view transposing on language cultural assumptions and also reminding us of the hazardous use in academic discourses of common-sense categories (Muni Toke 2013a: 6; Tabouret-Keller and Le Page 1986: 254; see also Dewaele, Bak, and Ortega, this volume).

One of the main problems linked to the "native speaker", speaking perfectly his "native language" or "mother tongue" that has been pointed out is the use of kinship and biological metaphors in relation to language, which is not a natural object but a cultural construct[3] (Tabouret-Keller and Le Page 1986; Drettas 2008; Bonfiglio 2010; Ortega 2014). These metaphors mislead research on language, transferring connotations of purity, exclusivity and innateness to the emotional aspects of language and reflecting the (idealised) biological relation of mother-child. Furthermore, the metaphors of feminine parentage have also been pervasive in the very foundation of linguistics itself and beyond, being also present today: in the comparative linguistics of the 19th century, languages were considered as mothers, daughters and sisters put in genealogical trees (cf. the French expression *langue-mère*, parent language), thus insisting on parthenogenesis, purity and primordiality; these assumptions extend and convey scientificity to previous quests for the adamic, paradisiac or original language (Drettas 2008; Tabouret-Keller and Le Page 1986; Bonfiglio 2010: 142–184 and passim, Tabouret-Keller 1988: 10–15).

The connotations mentioned above, conveyed to the "mother tongue" of individuals, are easily transferred to communities (Tabouret-Keller and Le Page 1986: 255; Drettas 2008: 465–467).[4] Thus, cultural attributes and practices are

---

[3] Of course, kinship, as well as the mother-child relationship, are also cultural constructs whose connotations are transferred to language.
[4] With remarkable ideological misuses, as in the case of National-Socialism (Drettas 2008: 465–467; Tabouret-Keller and Le Page 1986: 255).

naturalised in the modern context of nation-states, the dominant framework of community organisation since the 19th century. The "totemic relationship" between language and blood (Voutira 2007: 89), transferred to the community and incorporating romanticized views about nation, language, homeland, ethnicity, and racial descent (cf. Muni Toke 2013b; Bonfiglio 2010), has been at the very foundation of the nation itself. As Benedict Anderson puts it in his seminal work on nationalism: "The nation was conceived in language, not in blood, and [. . .] one could be 'invited into' the imagined community" (Anderson [1983] 2006: 145; cf. also Hobsbawm 1992: 54–58). Anderson points out that "much the most important thing about language is its capacity for generating imagined communities, building in effect particular solidarities" (2006: 133).

In this relationship, the language concerned is the national language, whose mastery is considered a birthright and tightly linked to the national territory (cf. Bonfiglio 2010). However, the national language is not only a birthright but also an obligation, as language is generally instrumentalised in the construction of nationalisms, even if it is not the only nor an obligatory emblem of nationality. Nevertheless, its mastery is on the whole firmly demanded by nation-states, which deploy important resources, in particular in relation to schooling, in order to eliminate linguistic diversity and promote the national standardised language among their citizens, as has been the case for France and Greece (on the importance of language in Greek national identity, see, among others, Mackridge 2009). Thus, the homogeneity to which nation-states strive is approached. The kinship metaphors and the meanings they convey, such as exclusivity and purity, work together and are compounded with national myths and precepts of national loyalty and ethnic purity, as opposed to hybridity, linked to multilingualism and the threat of the Other (cf., among others, Voutira 2007; Bonfiglio 2010; Bono, this volume). Of course, we do not intend to oversimplify the complex relation between language and identity (national or other) (for an overview, see Tabouret-Keller 1997). Identity is not homogeneous and may be based on multiple linguistic varieties (Blanchet 2000: 116). The emphasis on language as an identity marker varies according to individuals, communities and context (cf. Coulmas 2005: 175). Thus, some communities are more concerned with their language than others, while the importance of mastering a language to embrace the identity (including ethnic identity) of which that language is the symbol may also vary (Coulmas 2005: 180). In this chapter, we will examine the role played by two "native languages" or "mother tongues" in the particular context of construction of the Modern Greek identity in order to elicit identity construction processes and choices as well as the activation of agency.

But what does "mother tongue" actually mean in its various uses and who is the "native speaker" who holds it as his birthright? "Mother tongue" commonly means the first language learnt by an individual. However, as we have already seen, it can also mean the best-known language, as well as the most used or the language with which one identifies oneself (Jenniges 1995: 7–8; Jessner, Hofer, and Malzer-Papp, as well as Dewaele, Bak, and Ortega, this volume). Who is the "native speaker" who owns it? Ideally, he is all that together, embodying the absolute idealised model of a national in a nation-state, which promotes monolingualism through language policies and academic, educational and bureaucratic institutions. Nevertheless, this ideal is challenged by the linguistic diversity observed in the real world as well as by academic work. Moreover, the ambiguities linked to the terms in question are complemented by a further paradox: the "mother tongue" can also be "downgraded by being opposed to a classical literary language [. . .] or by being opposed to a standard language which is seen as the vehicle of nationhood or of ethnicity or both" (Tabouret-Keller and Le Page 1986: 255). In this context, "mother tongue" means a language different from the national language. In a similar vein, *native* can be opposed to *national*, operating as a synonym of *indigenous*: "the "natives" being denied the right to constitute a nation of their own, or to belong to the majority national group" (Muni Toke 2013b: 81[5]). Thus, effective negative connotations of the term "native" "leave one unable to explain how it could at the same time stand as the synonym for perfection in linguistic competence" (Muni Toke 2013b: 82[6]), reinforcing the paradox as well as the argument according to which such terms do not belong to the sociolinguist's toolkit (Blommaert and Rampton 2011: 5).

3 The empirical study

3.1 The sociolinguistic and historical context: Turkish-speaking Orthodox Christian Greeks

Our data concern two communities[7] (two villages) in Greece, Bafra, in the northwest of the country, near the city of Ioannina and Nea Bafra, in the northeast, near the cities of Serres and Drama. These villages were founded between 1924

---

[5] Muni Toke refers to Butcher, Carmen Acevedo. 2005. The case against the 'native speaker'. *English Today* 21 (2), 13–24.
[6] The author refers to Hackert, Stephanie. 2012. *The Emergence of the English Native Speaker: A Chapter in Nineteenth-Century Linguistic Thought*. Walter de Gruyter, p. 30.
[7] We are not entering the theoretical discussion about the concept of community (see, among others, Patrick 2004). We consider the two villages, Bafra and Nea Bafra, as *de facto* communities, because of their well-defined geographical and administrative borders, as well as because

and 1925 by refugees from Asia Minor who came to Greece following the Treaty of Lausanne (1923), providing for a compulsory population exchange between Greece and Turkey on the basis of religion:[8] all Orthodox Christians in Turkey had to reach Greece and all Muslims in Greece had to move to Turkey (automatically acquiring the nationality of the destination country), with some minor exceptions. The population exchange provided for on the margins of this Treaty was massive and profoundly marked the fate of Greece and the minds of its inhabitants; it involved about 1.2 million[9] people who arrived in a country that had barely 4.5 million people (for an introduction, see Hirschon 2003).

Among these 1.2 million refugees, there were 100,000 Turkish-speaking people who did not speak Greek nor a Greek dialect.[10] For them, the experience of being uprooted, which was in any case painful for all the populations concerned, had to be even more difficult because of the Turkish language (Marantzidis 2001: 87–91), not only for practical reasons, but also because the latter was incompatible with the Greek identity model, according to which a Greek must be Greek-speaking[11] and Orthodox Christian (Zerva 2010). The Turkish-speaking Greek Orthodox have therefore developed strategies to compensate for this "defect" in order to facilitate their integration into the Greek nation. At the centre of these strategies was linguistic assimilation, namely the abandonment of the Turkish language, but also the over-emphasis on religious belonging as well as a martyrological discourse, emphasising persecutions suffered during the Ottoman era (Zerva 2011). Within the latter is integrated the "history-myth" (Marantzidis 2001), a story, not historically proven, that circulates among these populations and explains Turkish-speaking as

---

of their relative linguistic homogeneity with regard to the population initially settled there in the 1920s (all were Turkish-speaking Orthodox refugees).

8 What was targeted behind religion was nationality.

9 According to the 1928 census, 5 years after the exchange (Hirschon 1998: 37). This number does not include Asia-Minor refugees who had resettled in the meantime in other countries or had passed away due to diseases and poor hygiene conditions.

10 It is not easy to define what was included in the label Greek at that time of the Greek language controversy (also known as "Greek diglossia"), i.e. in the 1920s. Greek is used here to cover the purist (learned through education) as well as the demotic varieties, and also non-standards considered to be Greek dialects or idioms.

11 The importance of the Greek language in the construction of Greek national identity is primordial, as it constitutes the link with Greek Antiquity (through Greek language and notably Greek "pure" language, that is katharevoussa). Greek nationalism of the 19th century was more tolerant towards ethnic and linguistic diversity and was focused on religion: all co-religionists (Greek orthodox) were welcome in the Greek nation independently from the language spoken, but *hellenisation*, that is, adopting the Greek language was *in fine* demanded (cf., among others, Veremis 2003).

a constrained choice, made by the ancestors at the time of the Ottoman empire, when the Turks forced them to choose between their language (naturally, Greek) and their religion: they chose religion, which was thus raised to the primordial national element. In that way, Turkish-speaking is justified, while the adoption of Greek is seen as a return to the "natural state".

Today, the relevance of the term "refugee" or even of that of "Turkish-speaking", while we are dealing with the third or fourth generation, is problematic. "Refugee" is only supposed to characterize people who are subjected to violent displacement from their native land to a foreign country. As with the term "generation", the extension of this denomination to descendants of immigrants can be criticised since the children and grandchildren of displaced persons often do not know the parents' country of origin and are given designations with which they do not always identify. However, the common use in the social sciences and also in the Greek reality leads us to speak of "generations" of refugees. Furthermore, in the Greek case of the 1922 Exchange of populations, the word "refugee" differs in some respects from its common international use: the "refugees", who fled Asia Minor in 1922 after the collapse of the Greek military front, and the "exchanged" people, who left Asia Minor after the Treaty of Lausanne in 1923, were assimilated under the term "refugee". Furthermore, all these people were considered as Greeks, the Greek State immediately granted them Greek nationality; they settled in Greece permanently and irrevocably. Despite objections to the adequacy of the term "refugee", it was finally established and conveyed a legal status, involving compensation for the goods left in Turkey and rights (Voutira 2006; Zerva 2011: 88–91). With regard to "Turkish-speaking", it can also be objected to as improper, because some of the people belonging to these communities have little or no knowledge of Turkish (especially those belonging to the 4th generation), while all of them speak Greek, which definitely prevails in their lives. However, we apply it by extension to the descendants of the first generation, who were the "real" Turkish-speaking people, for reasons of convenience: it facilitates the constituency of the group referred to in this work, and in all cases all members of the communities have been marked by this identification feature, independently from language mastery.

3.2 Theoretical, methodological issues and data analysis

Our sociolinguistic survey was conducted using semi-structured interviews with an interview guide as a framework for the conversation. We were in Bafra in February 2005 and in Nea Bafra April 2007, where we conducted in Greek 36 interviews of 922.5 minutes in total (Zerva 2011). Our interviewees were

2nd, 3rd and 4th generation refugees. The objective of this research was to highlight the sociolinguistic situation of Bafra and Nea Bafra, to trace the evolution of language shift over time and to detect the process of identity construction *in* and *through* discourse. Being aware that our corpus includes interviews, that is discourse *on* one's practices and attitudes, i.e. statements that may be out of step with actual practices, we have chosen to work with the notion of Social Representations (henceforth SR), with which French-speaking sociolinguists are used to working.

SR are defined as "a form of knowledge, socially elaborated and shared, with a practical aim and contributing to the construction of a reality common to a social whole" (Jodelet 1989: 36, our translation). The concept of SR has the advantage of insisting on the fact that the human does not grasp objective reality but constructs it, by representing it. This cognitive process is accessible through discourse, which allows us to follow the dynamics of SR construction (Moscovici 2001: 29; Matthey 2000: 23; Py 2004: 6–7). For the identification of SR, we combine thematic content analysis (Bardin [1977] 2003) and discourse analysis, inspired by the tools provided by enunciation linguistics (Kerbrat-Orecchioni [1980] 2002), discourse analysis (cf. Mainguenau 1991) and critical discourse analysis (cf. Fairclough 2003; Wodak et al. 1999).

The construction of SR is inseparable from interdiscursive memory and depends not only on present but also on previous discourses, on dialogue with others, whether real or imagined, and on the polyphony of all these voices (Bakhtine/Volochinov 1977). At the same time, "localized" discourses, produced *hic et nunc*, also enter into dialogue with Dominant Discourses, opposing or adhering to them. By Dominant Discourses, we mean sets of culturally shared discourses that circulate in a society, feed and, at the same time, constrain the local discursive production of subjects (the discourse with lowercase letters) (cf. Kiesling 2006: 261–265; De Fina et. al. 2006: 7). These discourses are closely linked to the dominant ideologies (Van Dijk 1998) as well as to the interdiscursive memory mentioned.

Like SR, identities are also constructed *in* and *through* discourse. Considered as a constant social and discursive construction, a dynamic process, and not an innate characteristic of individuals and groups, identities are constructed through constant negotiation between the individual and the social structures that encompass him/her, as well as other individuals and groups (Benwell & Stokoe 2006: 17–47; Wodak et al. 1999: 1–48; Mendoza-Denton 2002: 475). Depending on the context, the individual is positioning him/herself and is an actor, having a capacity for action (*agency*), despite the constraints of the context (Holland et al. 1998; Wodak et al. 1999). It is in this sense that we will examine the discursive (micro) and macro choices of the inhabitants of

Bafra and Nea Bafra. Their choices at the macro level, such as loyalty to a linguistic variety, but also at the micro level, as in the way they put thoughts in discourse, are part of their identity construction and positioning.

In that context, we also integrate into the analysis the theoretical model of *minoration* vs *majoration* of Philippe Blanchet (2000: 131–132 and 2005). According to that model, in cases of unequal multilingualism, a group can suffer from ethno-cultural depreciation, related to its language. This depreciation (*minoration*) is qualitative, relative to the status of the language and speakers, as well as quantitative, that is the reduction of speakers and utterances (cf. language shift) (Blanchet 2000: 131[12]). This situation can also lead to linguistic insecurity and cultural alienation, or even ignorance and rejection of the culture and language of origin (Blanchet 2000: 132). However, depreciation (*minoration*) is always accompanied by appreciation (*majoration*), either in the general social context (the depreciation of a group or of a practice means the appreciation of another group/practice) or within the group or practice itself (despite negative aspects associated with a language, positive aspects are also associated with it, for example emotional attributes or connotations of solidarity) (Blanchet 2005: 34).

In the next section, after presenting the "sociolinguistic profile" of the communities, we will focus on answers to our question "which language(s) did you acquire first?" or to quotes including the terms mother/father tongue, appearing during discussions about language acquisition, mastery and use. As a preliminary remark, it is interesting to note that we have only 7 quotes of the expression "mother tongue" and 5 quotes of "father tongue" in a total corpus of 20.653 transcribed lines / 485 pages (of 922,5 minutes of recorded interviews). A first comment about this remarkably limited appearance of the expression is undoubtedly related to the close link between mother tongue and national identity. However, the ambiguities mentioned above will be more clearly displayed below.

4 Constructing identities *with* and *despite* Turkish

At the time of our field survey (2005 and 2007), a total of 80% of our interviewees had a "solid command" of Turkish (declarations ranging from "very good"

---

[12] Blanchet (2005: 34) makes a distinction between different forms of depreciation: qualitative (*minoration*), quantitative (*minorisation*) and their combination (*minoritarisation*). Considering this terminology inconvenient, we will only use the term *minoration*/depreciation.

to "moderate") and only 5% had no mastery of Turkish at all (Zerva 2011: 207).[13] The inhabitants of Bafra and Nea Bafra learned Turkish at home and were schooled exclusively in Greek. They interacted in Greek with the inhabitants of neighbouring villages and towns but used Turkish with persons of Turkish-speaking origin (such as Greek refugees who spoke Turkish or Turkish people met in Greece or abroad). It is only with the 3rd generation that Greek was introduced at home and has definitely prevailed with the 4th generation, notably since the 1970s/1980s. Despite language shift within the youngest, Turkish was very present at the end of the 2000s: fluently spoken by a large part of the population, namely those above 35, it constituted a reality for everyone in the communities, whether Turkish-speaking or not.

As already mentioned, the main strategies put in place to integrate the "problematic" element of Turkish into the identity construction of the descendants of Turkish-speaking Orthodox speakers as genuine Greeks were namely language shift, over-emphasis on religion and martyrological discourse. We should add to these the depreciation (*minoration*) of Turkish and the constant efforts to distance oneself from this language. Turkish has been presented in discourse[14] as something linked to the past and as a constraint, its acquisition having been mandatory and not a matter of choice. In addition, the fact that people of Bafra and Nea Bafra have spoken or still speak Turkish has given rise to expressions of embarrassment, such as laughter, to comments, such as "it [Turkish] has remained engraved in my head, I can't forget it" or to justifications of that fact, such as the "history-myth". In addition, the vast majority of Turkish speakers underestimate their own skills and say either that they do not speak it well or that they have forgotten it now. Finally, the Turkish of the village, which is characterized as a daily language, far from the "pure" Turkish of Turkey, is depreciated. Are those marks of a sort of "linguistic insecurity"? As Blanchet (2000: 131–132) points out, in cases of "ethno-sociocultural depreciation" (*minoration*), two main symptoms can be observed: loss of linguistic self-confidence (linguistic insecurity), which can be accompanied by negative attitudes to the heritage language, and cultural alienation. Both of them can go as far as rejection and ignorance of the language and culture of

---

[13] However, language shift was active, as individuals born after 1970 did not have a good or any command of Turkish, except in rare cases.

[14] We should not forget that the interviewer is a young educated woman who is not Turkish-speaking nor of a refugee origin, thus "representing" the dominant group (Greek-speaking and of Greek origin, even if that is not checked during the interview; we shall not examine here more deeply the question of the diversity of ethnic origins in Greece and beliefs about purity in Dominant national Discourses).

origin together with an imagined total assimilation in the dominant group. In our question above, the answer cannot be simple. Our interviewees do not have self-confidence in the use of Turkish, when they master it at all, and have abandoned it collectively, but this is not seen as problematic and is rather considered as an asset. It seems to be part of a strategy of distancing oneself from a Turkish identity and of a positive, valued (Greek) identity construction in line with the Greek Dominant Discourses.

4.1 Turkish as a mother or father tongue, but not a national language

Turkish is characterised by some of our interviewees as their mother or father tongue, in the sense of their first or best-known language or as a language which they cherish, being the one spoken with their parents.

Thus, despite general depreciation (*minoration*), we met with some positive mentions of Turkish, denoting a strong emotional bond between the individual and the language: *of course (I love it)/ (how) not to love my mother tongue*[15] said a female interviewee from Nea Bafra, aged 67 (NBf67[16]), answering the question "do you like speaking or listening to Turkish?". Nevertheless, clearly positive mentions are rare.[17] Positive mentions of the emotive aspect of Turkish, as of any aspect of this language, are frequently accompanied by utterances which attenuate the emotive bond with it, a fact that belongs to strategies of depreciation (*minoration*). Loving Turkish is inevitable, for a large part of our interviewees, but stopping speaking it is due to "other reasons": *whatever we do it is our father's language / we can't not love it / but we don't speak it that's for another reason* ↑ (NBf79). These other reasons are not clearly specified, but the person

---

15 In addition to this expression (*mother tongue*), which indicates an emotional link with Turkish, there is another expression denoting this link found in the corpus: "our language", which is nevertheless also rarely used (five times in all).
16 The anonymisation of our interviewees required the codification of their identities. Locality (Bafra or Nea Bafra), sex and age were chosen. Thus, NBf67 means a woman (f) from Nea Bafra (NB), aged 67, while Bm80, means a man (m) from Bafra (B) aged 80 (80) at the time of the interview, and E means the interviewer. Quotes from our corpus are given in italics. For reasons of space, we only reproduce the translation of the excerpts that closely follows the Greek text and transcribes the hesitations and failures of the speakers. The transcription conventions are presented in the Appendix.
17 Only one other person mentioned this emotive aspect without any modifiers: Bf60 said *I like it, it is our father language*.

says immediately thereafter that it is "bizarre" to speak Turkish with young people: language shift appears to be not only inflicted, which undoubtedly was the case due to linguistic ideologies (cf. Tsitsipis 1998), but also chosen as part of identity strategies, in order to conform oneself to the Greek identity model, even if this was a largely constrained choice.

Another interviewee, Bf48 also includes the expression "mother/father tongue" in her discourse: *talk to each other and say a few words OK*. However, according to her, they shouldn't speak Turkish *all the time* and in particular *in front of strangers*. The mentality of the Bafriotes must change; *it is now enough OK it is a mother/ fathe:r/ tongue::/ it came from there ↑ but it is over*. While acknowledging its emotional value, Bf48 therefore prefers that the use of Turkish be limited. Bf48's verdict leaves no doubt: Turkish is finished, not only for her, but for the communities in general. Despite the fact that many interviewees care about Turkish (taking into account those who have declared that they like to speak it, Bf48 included), and despite the fact that it is their mother or father tongue, Turkish is still destined to be abandoned. It is the interviewees themselves who are abandoning it. Moreover, many interviewees note that Turkish has no future and make predictions about the language shift that should take place in the near future. However, this does not seem to bother anyone. That is to say, the loyalty of Turkish-speaking refugees to Turkish is low, if not non-existent which is why language shift is unavoidable (on the relation between language shift or maintenance and language loyalty, see Fishman 1966). Loyalty to a language is a strong act of identity, which marks the identity affiliation of the individual or group. As the identity affiliation of our witnesses is undoubtedly the Greek national identity, Turkish no longer has a place in their language repertoire, other than as a foreign language. Indeed, one of the younger interviewees has learnt it in foreign language courses, while some of the older ones, who already have mastery of it, speak about its usefulness in contexts like a foreign trip abroad, where no other foreign language than Turkish is spoken and thus its knowledge proves helpful. Thus, the position of Turkish-speaking refugees towards the Turkish language does indeed show their identity affiliation. It is therefore this exteriority of Turkish in relation to the identity of Turkish-speaking Orthodox refugees that is underlined. The very weak mention of the expression "mother or father tongue", discussed above, also testifies to this exteriority.

Besides the emotional use of the terms presented, we can also find quotes meaning the best known or the first language. Thus, an aged interviewee (Bf76) said that, for example, they understand jokes better in Turkish, as it is their mother tongue. Yet, when it comes to the question concerning the first language acquired, we got an interesting answer:

E: [. . .] eu::h/ you when you were a child what language did you learn first;
Bm63: //// Greek ↑// but also the:/ mother tongue which was/ by misfortune / Turkish// because:: they did not allow the Greek language there/

From the point of view of thematic analysis, it can be noted that Bm63 acquired both languages at the same time, even if one may have some doubts about that, because according to his declarations, his parents spoke Greek poorly and it seems more likely that he learned Greek at school. Speaking of two first languages can be part of his identity construction, that is a strategy of depreciation (*minoration*), in order to mitigate the role of Turkish and emphasize the role of Greek in his repertoire. Moreover, attention to his discourse choices provides us with rich information. Word order is thus revealing: Greek is the first language to be uttered; it is mentioned alone, with an affirmative ascendant intonation, while Turkish is accompanied by axiological and justifying comments. Furthermore, Turkish is not named immediately; it is first suggested through a subjective and emotional qualification ("mother tongue") which could be both considered positive and negative (see section 2). His statement takes quickly a turn of definitely negative appreciation: this mother tongue was "by misfortune" Turkish. With this intrinsically axiological adverb (Kerbrat-Orecchioni 2002), Bm63 deplores the mastery of Turkish and depreciates it, while justifying this "disturbing reality" thereafter, alluding to the "history-myth". The argumentation serves to justify the regretted presence of the Turkish language by a force majeure, a fact that did not depend on the will of his ancestors, since Turkish was imposed – the third person in the plural must refer to the Ottomans/Turks. According to Wodak et al. (1999: 33), the justification strategy is generally mobilized for realities that are problematic and disturbing because of their incompatibility with the subjects' imaginary norms, a fact that is entirely confirmed here.

Another person of the 2nd generation used the expression "father tongue" with the sense of first language:

Bm80: when we are//// a little bit ↑/ the/ e[ld]erly people // we talk/ sometimes/ Turkish
E: mmm↑/mmm↓
Bm80: =and when/ we go out ↑ to an acquaintance again of my age / we talk again ↑ the:/ u::h/ Turkish
E: mmmmm
Bm80: that is to say/ it is not↑ that we love it/ like a father's language/

In order to describe when people from Bafra speak Turkish, this interviewee says that it is the elderly people who sometimes use it between them, thus limiting the use of Turkish to a certain group and some occasions. Thus Turkish is linked to the past. It is interesting to note that his statement – the presence of the Turkish language – is mitigated discursively twice (*a little bit*, *sometimes*): the surprising use of *a little bit* alongside the verb *to be*, which cannot be evaluated quantitatively (either we are or we are not), denotes in fact a subjective position (Kerbrat-Orecchioni 2002: 96–97) that reduces Turkish and its use. The depreciation (*minoration*) of the use of Turkish is evident, although rather discreet. The next statement continues in the same vein, affirming again the limited use of Turkish, though discursively further moderated with a hesitation marker (*uh::*). In the next turn, Bm80 explicitly depreciates Turkish. With a verb (*to love*) that is both emotional and axiological (Kerbrat-Orecchioni 2002: 115), he refuses both to aesthetically valorise Turkish (axiological aspect) and to recognize its proximity, an emotional link with the collective *us*: *it* "is not that we love it [but we speak it] like a father's language". The Turkish language, as well as the expression "father tongue", is deprived of its emotional assets[18] and its exteriority in relation to the community is underlined.

Thus, the examples discussed so far attest to the use of the expressions "mother/father tongue" for Turkish. As we have seen, the positive aspects of these expressions (emotional use, good mastery) are frequently undermined by processes of depreciation (*minoration*) or else denied as in the last example. Moreover, Turkish is referred to as the "mother or father tongue" by contrast to the national language, which is "naturally" Greek. Hence, the two languages of the "native repertoire" of the populations in question are clearly distinguished: there is the one inherited from the ancestors, the first language of the 2nd and for the majority of the 3rd generation, well mastered and emotionally associated with the parents and the cherished past,[19] although abandoned collectively, and the other, the national language, which has prevailed, with the assistance of national policies and ideology, the Dominant Discourses and the configuration of the linguistic market in the sense of Bourdieu, but also with the consent of the populations.

4.2 Turkish is not the mother tongue

The ambiguities of the expressions discussed above are evident also in the next examples, coming from a young person at Bafra, Bf30, who says that in the past,

---

18 The emotional functions of a minority language are one of the last functions existing before (and against) its abandonment.
19 The past plays a major role in the identity construction of refugees, as they constantly refer to it and to their lost homes and fatherland (Hirschon 1998, Zerva 2011).

people in the village spoke Turkish and adds "it was their mother tongue I believe". However, a few moments later, while the discussion is about the first generation,[20] Bf30 states that: *but even there where they were*[21]/ *they spoke Greek* ↑ *they didn' spea::k* ↓ / ↑ *they spoke TURKISH when they were forced // their mother tongue was Greek there too*. This evident contradiction,[22] not only with one's own statements but also with reality, testifies to the naturalisation and essentialisation of the Greek language for Greek identity. The essentialisation of the Greek language is related to the belief that the populations in question spoke this language before Turkish (or parallel to it), in a more or less undetermined past. The disturbing reality of Turkish is marginalised as something occasional and is also justified within the framework of a martyrological discourse: Turkish was a result of compulsion. Thus, Turkish is not a mother tongue. Greek as the national language is the only legitimate candidate to embody the exclusive link of a person with his/her mother tongue. Thus, the Greek national identity, anchored in the Greek language and the Christian orthodox religion, can be fully embraced.

That is exactly the point displayed in another quote, also taken from the interview with a young person. NBf25a says that Turkish, spoken in the village by the elderly,[23] may surprise or disturb people of non-refugee origin who are not familiar with it and asserts that even she was irritated by Turkish when she was younger, *but not anymore because these people it's not that they do it on purpose/ it's simply::: / it's now like / tch not like a mother tongue I can't say that / u:h it's simply because they're used to it*. Hence, Turkish cannot be a mother tongue of Greek nationals, it can at most be qualified as a "habit".

Moreover, purity is denied to the Turkish spoken by Greek-orthodox refugees (cf. Zerva 2014) in an interesting excerpt of an interview with a member of

---

20 During the interview, we had just addressed in the moments before the topic of written documents that the 1[rst] generation of refugees had eventually brought from Turkey, because at the beginning of the 20th century there was a literature in Turkish written with Greek characters ("Karamanlidika"). This question brought about comments on the illiteracy of the refugees. The above commented intervention of Bf30 comes suddenly without having been linked to a question or comment.
21 In Asia Minor.
22 This statement causes reactions from the friends of Bf30 also present during the interview who intervene to refute that the 1[rst] generation of refugees spoke any Greek.
23 It is interesting to note that she finds it "normal", given the vicissitudes of their lives and especially the refugee experience after 1922. However, in the rest of the discussion, she links this "habit" of older people to speak Turkish with their low educational level, which certainly results in the depreciation (*minoration*) of Turkish.

the local elite, NBm81,[24] who develops the "history-myth", although innovating on its content. He overbids the persecutions (even religion was prohibited as well as schools) and adds another argument in order to emphasize the group's Greekness. He actually claims that they (the ancestors) *created a language of their own ↑/ in TURKISH ↓/ it's not real Turkish / there's Greek in it ↑/ there's Pontiac in it ↑[let's say]/ Turkish// u::h other languages/ a_ mixed/ there are Muslims coming from ↑/ Bulgaria ↓/ here now it's full [a hundred] to work/ they speak Turkish/ we don't understand them ↑//// they can't understand us either// it's not the real Turkish language ↑ / it's a distortion ↓/ thanks to it they could communicate/ deceive/ the Turks / [say] that they really learned it // that happened in the Bafra region ↓/ and they lost the language (more slowly and more gently)/ but they kept the religion / they kept/ their/ nationality ↓/.*

Despite the multitude of elements that we could comment on about this extract, we will focus on the "trick" found by the ancestors to thwart the enemy who would have "forced" them to renounce Greek and speak Turkish: so they "pretended" to obey, but instead of really speaking Turkish, they created a mixed language, distinct from Turkish, with Greek, Pontiac Greek (Greek dialect) and Turkish elements (note that the Greek elements prevail here, as Pontiac is a Greek dialect). Thus, the so-called "history-myth" which serves to justify the presence of Turkish and to provide a solution to the paradox of Greek identity together with the use of Turkish, is here presented in an original version: the ancestors are not only martyrs, but heroes of the nation (instead of betrayers). Turkish-speaking is presented as an act of resistance that ultimately contributes to the group's appreciation (*majoration*), while Greek is constantly displayed as the natural mother tongue of Greeks. Furthermore, thanks to its essentialisation, Greek is retrospectively assigned a place in the repertoire of Turkish-speaking Orthodox Christians.

5 Conclusions

As we have seen, the inhabitants of Bafra and Nea Bafra are native speakers of two languages but refuse to be considered as native speakers of one of them,

---

[24] NBm81 is a local scholar who distinguished himself both by his remarkable studies and by the positions he held (teacher in the village, then, after studying law, senior civil servant in Thessaloniki). He is an indispensable reference in village affairs, especially in matters of history and culture: all the people we met told us to see him for "more complete information" (see also Zerva 2015).

Turkish, even those who acquired Turkish in their childhood and claim to speak it very well. Turkish is most frequently deprived of the nexus of the positive attributes of a "mother tongue": challenged by the elderly, these attributes are certainly not given to Turkish by younger people who no longer have an emotional link to it (as their parents spoke Greek to them). Along with appreciation processes (*majoration*), depreciation (*minoration*) is recurrent and denotes loose emotional links, distancing from Turkish, while its purity and exclusivity are denied, providing evidence of the ambiguities around the expressions "mother tongue" and "native speaker".

Turkish and Greek as named languages are naturalised mother tongues of two competing nation-states. As such, co-existence is rendered impossible and ambivalence is not permitted, according to an old mistrust of bilingualism, at least in Europe (Py & Gajo 2013: 74), linked to suspicions of national threat (Gadet & Varro 2006: 21). As soon as they settled in Greece in 1924–1925, Turkish-speaking refugees acquired the Greek citizenship, as the very reason for their expatriation from Asia Minor was their Greekness, even if this was refuted by a large part of the local Greeks of the time. Hence, they were not really a minority albeit they suffered discrimination due to language (even though language was not the only reason for this discrimination which operated along with other socio-economic factors). As with other minority language speakers, the Greek nation-state did not choose exclusion but assimilation through language shift in order to achieve homogeneity.

As a group, the Greek Turkish-speaking refugees chose to align with the mainstream national ideology of an exclusive relation between language and identity, particularly emphasised in the Greek case. Hence, they erased the "original" "mother tongue" and their bilingualism to fully integrate into the nation and demonstrate their national loyalty, as opposed to their low loyalty to Turkish. The essentialisation of the Greek language, raised to the innate, natural language of the community in a distant past, has led to the consideration of language shift as a return to the natural state of the community. Thus, the individuals and the groups adhere to the Dominant national Discourses, to the national ideology, but do not remain passive. They negotiate them and deploy their agency (cf. Holland et al. 1998) to build their identity under the best possible conditions (being genuine Greeks) and garner the maximum benefit. This arrangement allows them to find the balance between adhering to the Dominant Discourses and building an appreciated, positive identity (*majoration*), without completely denying the history of the group and self-depreciating themselves. Thus, they resolve the so-called paradox of being native speakers of two "competing" languages and show an interesting example of negotiation of the language shift in a strongly monolingual society.

Author's Positionality

Maria Zerva was born in Greece and raised monolingual, while attending classes in three foreign languages since childhood (not by accident "powerful" ones, that is English, French and German), though her parents were bilingual, speaking or having passive knowledge of a minority language besides Greek which they never transmitted to their children even if it did not seem to be a burden in their lives. She realised in adulthood the presence and loss of this language, but also the silence around it, sometimes weighty and "guilty", and also that this was not the only case in Greece, which led her to become interested in the minority languages of Greece and to conduct research on Greek descendants of Asia Minor refugees, speakers of Turkish or having this language in their families.

After studying Classics as well as Medieval and Modern Greek Literature and Linguistics (Greek Philology), she moved to Strasbourg, France, where she has been living since with a small interlude in Switzerland and has started a multilingual and multicultural family, where everyday life occurs mainly in three named languages: French, Greek and German. Quickly after her arrival in Strasbourg she became fascinated by the peaceful way of dealing with the difficult past between France and Germany, which challenged her and made her reflect on the relationship of the Greeks with their past. She also experienced in everyday life, but also in her courses in the University of Strasbourg, linguistic and cultural diversity as well as tolerance, but also discrimination due to otherness, including perception of linguistic otherness, especially foreign accent, linked to stark monolingual ideologies in France.

Her scholarly work is anchored in sociolinguistics and influenced by her aforementioned experiences, focusing on language as a social practice embedded in its socio-historical context. She is particularly interested in metalinguistic stances towards languages, variation and multilingualism, in language ideologies and nationalism, the construction of identities and Social Representations (SR) in discourse and the handling of individual and collective memory. The discursive construction of identities and SR has led her to enrich her analytical tools in Discourse Analysis with an eclectic combination of Critical Discourse Analysis as well as branches of Linguistics, such as Semantics and the French Theory of enunciation. This allows her to deepen her understanding of the often conflictual situations of social multilingualism linked to unequal relations of power and the ambivalent feelings of affiliation, loyalty or judgment on languages. She has also collaborated in the development of the multilingual series of the Textbook *Greek for you* for the Teaching of Modern Greek as a foreign/second language. In her work on the Greek language, she is trying to cope with the well-established monolingual scope of education and the "aversion" to variation but also translanguaging.

Appendix

Transcription conventions

/, //, /// more or less long break;
:,::,::: more or less long lengthening of the vowel or consonant preceding;
= resumption of interrupted speech;

↑ ascending intonation;
↓ descending intonation;
; ascending interrogative intonation;
() researcher's comment on voice quality or the environment;
[] uncertain utterance for which we make a listening proposal;
{ } overlapping utterances;
XXX unintelligible utterance;

CAPITAL LETTERS mark the beginning of proper nouns or, when applied to a word or letters of a word, denote an emphatic accent or a louder voice than for the rest of the statement.

References

Anderson, Benedict. 2006 [1983]. *Imagined Communities*. London & New York: Verso.
Bakhtine, Mikhail [Volochinov, Valentin N.] 1977. *Le marxisme et la philosophie du langage*. Paris: Les Editions de Minuit.
Bardin, Laurence. 2003 [1977]. *L'analyse de contenu*. Paris: Presses Universitaires de France.
Benwell, Bethan & Elizabeth Stokoe. 2006. *Discourse and Identity*. Edinburgh: Edinburgh University Press.
Blanchet, Philippe. 2000. *La linguistique de terrain. Méthode et théorie. Une approche ethno-sociolinguistique*. Rennes: Presses Universitaires de Rennes.
Blanchet, Philippe. 2005. Minorations, minorisations, minorités: Essai de théorisation d'un processus complexe. In Dominique Huck & Philippe Blanchet (eds), *Minorations, minorisations, minorités. Etudes exploratoires. Cahiers de sociolinguistique* n° 10, 17–47. Rennes: Presses Universitaires de Rennes.
Blommaert, Jan & Ben Rampton. 2011. Language and Superdiversity. *Diversities* 13(2). 1–21.
Bloomfield, Leonard. 1973 [1935]. *Language*. London: George Allen & Unwin.
Bonfiglio, Thomas Paul. 2010. *Mother Tongues and Nations: The Invention of the Native Speaker*. New York/Berlin: De Gruyter Mouton.
Bourdieu, Pierre. 2001. *Langage et pouvoir symbolique*. Paris: Fayard.
Chomsky, Noam. 1965. *Aspects of the Theory of Syntax*. Cambridge, Massachussets: MIT Press.
Coulmas, Florian. 2005. *Sociolinguistics. The study of speakers' choices*. Cambridge: Cambridge University Press.
Davies, Alan. 2003. *The Native Speaker: Myth and Reality*. Clevedon/Buffalo/Toronto/Sydney: Multilingual Matters.
De Fina, Anna, Deborah Schiffrin & Michael Bamberg (eds). 2006. *Discourse and identity*. Cambridge: Cambridge University Press.
Drettas, Georges. 2008. Langue maternelle ou paternelle? Réflexions sur les fonctions d'un contenu refoulé dans la sociolinguistique francophone. In Maria Theodoropoulou (ed.), *Thermi ke Fos/Licht und Wärme. In memory of A.-F. Christidis*, 455–472. Thessaloniki: Center of Greek Language.

Fairclough, Norman. 2003. *Analysing discourse. Textual analysis for social research*. London & New York: Routledge.
Fishman, Joshua A. (ed.). 1966. *Language Loyalty in the United States*. The Hague: Mouton.
Hirschon, Renée. 1998 [1989]. *Heirs of the Greek catastrophe. The social life of Asia Minor refugees in Piraeus*. New York/Oxford: Berghahn Books.
Hirschon, Renée (ed.). 2003. *Crossing the Aegean. An appraisal of the compulsory population exchange between Greece and Turkey*. New York/Oxford: Berghahn Books.
Gadet Françoise & Gabrielle Varro. 2006. Le "scandale" du bilinguisme. *Langage et Société* 116, 9–28.
Hobsbawm, Eric J. 1992 [1990]. *Nations and Nationalism since 1780*. Cambridge: Cambridge University Press.
Holland, Dorothy, William Jr. Lachicotte, Debra Skinner & Carole Cain. 1998. *Identity and Agency in Cultural Worlds*. Cambridge, Massachusetts/London, England: Harvard University Press.
Jenniges, Ricarda. 1995. *La langue, une histoire de famille. Transmission intergénérationnelle de la langue*. Bruxelles: Le Bureau pour les Langues Moins Répandues.
Jodelet, Denise. 1989. Représentations sociales: un domaine en expansion. In Denise Jodelet (ed.), *Les représentations sociales*, 31–61. Paris: Presses Universitaires de France.
Kerbrat-Orecchioni, Catherine. 2002 [1980]. *L'énonciation; de la subjectivité dans le langage*. Paris: Armand Colin.
Kiesling, Scott F. 2006. Hegemonic identity-making in narrative. In Anna de Fina, Deborah Schiffrin & Michael Bamberg (eds.), *Discourse and Identity*, 261–287. Cambridge: Cambridge University Press.
Love, Nigel & Umberto Ansaldo. 2010. The native speaker and the mother tongue. *Language Sciences* 32, 589–593.
Mackridge, Peter. 2009. *Language and National Identity in Greece, 1766–1976*. Oxford: Oxford University Press.
Maingueneau, Dominique. 1991. *L'analyse du discours. Introduction aux lectures d'archive*. Paris: Hachette.
Marantzidis, Nikos. 2001. *Yassassin Millet. Zito to ethnos. Prosfygia, katochi ke emfylios: ethnotiki taftotita ke politiki syberifora stous tourkofonous ellinorthodoxous tou Dytikou Pontou* [Yassassin Millet. Long live the nation. Refugees, Occupation and Civil War: Ethnic identity and political conduct of Turkish-speaking Greek Orthodox of the Western Pontus]. Iraklio: University Press of Crete.
Matthey, Marinette. 2000. Aspects théoriques et méthodologiques de la recherche sur le traitement discursif des représentations sociales. *TRANEL* 32, 21–37.
Mendoza-Denton, Norma. 2002. Language and identity. In J. K. Chambers, Peter Trudgill & Natalie Shilling-Estes (eds.), *The Handbook of Language Variation and Change*, 475–499. Oxford (UK)/ Malden (USA)/ Victoria (Australia): Blackwell Publishing.
Moscovici, Serge. 2001. Why a theory of Social Representations?. In Kay Deaux & Gina Philogène (eds.), *Representations of the social*, 8–35. Oxford/Massachussetts. Blackwell Publishers.
Muni Toke, Valelia. 2013a. Le locuteur natif et son idéalisation: un demi-siècle de critiques. *Histoire Épistémologie Langage* 35(2). 5–15.
Muni Toke, Valelia. 2013b. Native speaker: from idealization to politicization. *Histoire Épistémologie Langage* 35(2). 69–93.

Ortega, Lourdes. 2014. Ways forward for a bi/multilingual turn in SLA. In Stephen May (ed.), *The Multilingual Turn. Implications for SLA, TESOL and Bilingual Education*, 32–53. New York & London: Routledge.

Patrick, Peter L. 2004. The Speech Community. In J. K. Chambers, Peter Trudgill & Natalie Shilling-Estes (eds.), *The handbook of language variation and change*, 573–597. Oxford, Malden & Victoria: Blackwell Publishing.

Py, Bernard. 2004. Pour une approche linguistique des représentations sociales. In Jean-Claude Beacco (ed.) *Représentations métalinguistiques ordinaires et discours. Langages* 154, 6–19.

Py, Bernard & Gajo Laurent. 2013. Bilinguisme et plurilinguisme. In Jacky Simonin & Sylvie Wharton (eds.), *Sociolinguistique du contact. Dictionnaire des termes et concepts*, 71–93. Lyon: ENS Editions.

Tabouret-Keller, Andrée. 1988. Contacts de langues: deux modèles du XIXème siècle et leurs rejetons aujourd'hui. *Langage et Société* 43, 9–22.

Tabouret-Keller, Andrée. 1997. Language and identity. In Florian Coulmas (ed.), *The Handbook of Sociolinguistics*, 315–326. Oxford/Massachusetts. Blackwell Publishers.

Tabouret-Keller, Andrée. 2011. *Le bilinguisme en procès, cent ans d'errance (1840–1940)*. Limoges: Lambert-Lucas.

Tabouret-Keller, Andrée & Le Page, Robert. 1986. The mother-tongue metaphor. *Grazer Linguistische Studien* 27. 249–260.

Tsitsipis, Lukas D. 1998. *A linguistic anthropology of praxis and language shift: Arvanitika (Albanian) and Greek in contact*. Clarendon Press: Oxford.

Van Dijk, Teun A. 1998. *Ideology. A multidisciplinary approach*. London/Thousand Oaks/New Delhi: SAGE Publications.

Veremis, Thanos. 2003. 1922: Political Continuations and Realignments in the Greek State. In Renée Hirschon (ed.), *Crossing the Aegean. An appraisal of the compulsory population exchange between Greece and Turkey*, 53–62. New York & Oxford: Berghahn Books.

Voutira, Eftihia. 2006. I 'epitychis' apokatastasi ton Mikrasiaton prosfygon [The 'successful' rehabilitation of Asia Minor refugees]. In Tsitselikis Konstantinos (ed.), *I ellinotourkiki antallagi plithysmon. Ptyches mias ethnikis syngrousis* [The exchange of Greek-Turkish populations. Aspects of a national conflict], 238–248. Athens: Kritiki.

Voutira, Eftihia. 2007. Ethnogenesis, exclusivity and the model of the mother tongue in the Balkans. In Anastassios-Fivos Christidis (ed.), *Glossa, Kinonia, Istoria: ta Valkania* [Language, Society, History: the Balkans], 87–98. Thessaloniki: Center of Greek Language.

Wodak, Ruth, Rudolph de Cillia, Martin Reisigl & Karin Liebhart. 1999. *The discursive construction of national identity*. Edinburgh: Edinburgh University Press. [Translated from German by A. Hirsch and R. Mitten. German edition 1998].

Zerva, Maria. 2010. Le citoyen grec *par excellence*. Conception normative du citoyen grec par l'Etat-nation grec et cas de marginalité. In Naoum Abi-Rached (ed.), *Normes et marginalités à l'épreuve*, 49–61. Strasbourg: Presses Universitaires de Strasbourg.

Zerva, Maria. 2011. *Les Grecs turcophones orthodoxes: une étude sociolinguistique*. Strasbourg: University of Strasbourg. Vol. I & Vol. II. PhD Thesis.

Zerva, Maria. 2014. Représentations du multilinguisme en Grèce au début du 21ème siècle à partir de discours épilinguistiques. In Romain Colonna (ed.), *Les locuteurs et les langues: pouvoirs, non-pouvoirs et contre-pouvoirs*, 275–286. Limoges: Editions Lambert Lucas.

Zerva, Maria. 2015. Le rôle des élites locales dans la consolidation du sentiment national. *Cahiers balkaniques* (Hors-série/Special edition), 287–299.

Olga Kagan, Miriam Minkov, Ekaterina Protassova, Mila Schwartz

Chapter 6
What kind of speakers are these? Placing heritage speakers of Russian on a continuum

Abstract: It is commonly presupposed that one's first/home language is acquired easily, but there are numerous prerequisites for this "ease of acquisition": multifaceted purposes and a high frequency of use, a broad spectrum of speakers and situations, developing the habit of receiving information about the world in the language (the primary socialisation and verbally-mediated cognitive development), and shaping one's behaviour through this means of communication. Today, Russian develops as a pluricentric language with multiple centres of contact with languages of environment, e.g., in the USA, Israel, Germany, and Finland, as is demonstrated in this study with teenager bilinguals with the goal to show what is native-like and what belongs to their special proficiency. The debate upon pluricentricity strongly interrelates with the notions of norms/standards and native/heritage speakers in diaspora. Heritage speakers often report that they struggle to recognize their language imperfections. The position of the heritage speakers between the L1 and the L2 speakers/learners of a language is both emotionally and practically vulnerable. The concept of a native speaker of Russian should be rethought, and the multilingual speakers who claim to have Russian as their first language should be offered placement on the scale between native and non-native performance, as part of a continuum and not positioned on one end of this continuum.

Acknowledgments: The writing was enabled with a grant from the University of Helsinki, Finland, and supported by the Research and Evaluation Authority, Oranim Academic College of Education, Israel. We would like to express our gratitude to the colleagues of Olga Kagan at the UCLA, Susan Bauckus, Susan Kresin, Anna Kudyma, Kathryn Paul, and Sasha Razor. We would like to thank Elena Skudskaya, Elena Heiskanen, Katharina Meng and Artjom Chistjakov for their help in the collection and transliteration of these materials.

Olga Kagan, University of California Los Angeles
Miriam Minkov, Oranim Academic College of Education, e-mail: miryamminkov@gmail.com
Ekaterina Protassova, University of Helsinki, e-mail: ekaterina.protassova@helsinki.fi
Mila Schwartz, Oranim Academic College of Education, e-mail: milasch@post.bgu.ac.il

https://doi.org/10.1515/9781501512353-007

Keywords: Russian language, pluricentricity, transmission, heritage speaker, heritage language, Israel, Finland, Germany, USA

1. Introduction

The political, social, and economic reforms of the late 1980s followed by the collapse of the Soviet Union in 1991 produced a considerable surge of Soviet migrants and refugees, commonly called "the fourth wave" (Ben-Rafael et al. 2006). This chapter looks at the growing population of Russian *heritage speakers* (HSs) from a linguistic and sociolinguistic perspective and attempts to clarify the concept of HSs, as opposed to the concept of native language (NL) speaker, by thoroughly analysing the characteristics of the Russian speech of four groups of teenagers that speak Russian as a *heritage language* (HL) and English, Hebrew, German, or Finnish as dominant languages.

The notion of HSs has become problematic in recent years due to the globalization of migration (e.g., Kagan et al. 2017; Kasstan, Auer, and Salmons 2018). Migrants arrive with hundreds of languages and continue to speak them to their children at home in their new countries. Nevertheless, after two or three generations, many of these languages are lost. In general, large immigrant communities can either support bilingualism or impede integration into the majority of society. The number of speakers, political structures, and access to technology influence the linguistic vitality of a language (cf. Laleko 2013).

Several hundred million people speak Russian (about 150 million speak it as a first language, and an equal number speak it as a second or a foreign language). According to Aref'ev (2019), the number of Russian language (RL) speakers is in decline. While Aref'ev refers to learners of Russian and to those who already speak Russian, he does consider those who are bilingual from childhood to be a special group. Learners of Russian as a second or foreign language who studied it at some point, but may not use it anymore, still qualify as speaking some Russian. Individuals who speak Russian fluently, having learned it as their mother or second tongue at school during the Soviet era, might nowadays, for political, identity or language shift reasons, say that their dominant language and their NL are not Russian. These are complex processes related to identity, socio-political, and economic factors, among others, and are not always directly related to one's language proficiency.

The idea of linguistic pluricentricity (existence of a language with multiple centres of development, often in codified varieties, e.g. Kamwangamalu, this volume) was developed theoretically by Clyne (1992) and Muhr (2012); they mentioned Russian as a potentially pluricentric language. Today, Russian displays multiple centres of contact with the local language all over the world (Kamusella 2018; Mustajoki, Protassova, and Yelenevskaya 2020; Zybatov 2017). According to Coulmas (1981), linguistics cannot exist without the authority of the native speaker (NS), who decides about the quality of a construction, relevance of a word entry, or adequacy of emerging meaning. For Ortega (2019), this is valid only because we constructed the NS that way, in a monolingual paradigm of linguistics that changed a lot. Davies (2003) explains that the language individuals learn first can be or become neither their dominant language nor the most important language for them, making a case for a more dynamic view of language biographies and concepts usually used to refer to languages.

Due to the unique history of Russian-speaking expansion and emigration, many countries with communities of Russian speakers have developed policies for Russian Language (RL) and culture (Ryazanova-Clarke 2014; Yelenevskaya and Protassova 2015). Such communities are generally heterogeneous and embrace an ethnically diverse population of all waves of migration. Russia uses the umbrella term *compatriots* (*sootechestvenniki*) to identify these people and tries to include them into the "Russian World", whose representation abroad is also formally promoted via sponsored structures and programs by the Russian government. There are media and educational institutions in Russian because their members value education in Russian and preserve Russian culture at the material (food, shops, books, et cetera) and spiritual levels. All these facilities promote RL intergenerational transmission (Nikunlassi and Protassova 2019).

This chapter is aimed at analysing the acquisition of a home language abroad taking as example Russian as a pluricentric language and elaborates on the notions of the HLs. We search to show whether we could name those persons NSs (of Russian). First, the chapter addresses the theoretical background of the notion of the HSs. After that, we discuss data from interviews with young Russian-speaking immigrants in four countries: the USA, Israel, Germany and Finland. In the last section, we compare results between the countries and draw conclusions concerning the differences in the acquisition of the HL in respective countries.

2 Theoretical concepts

2.1 Varieties of a home language

Transmitting a language through multiple generations in a diaspora is difficult. Developing and maintaining any language in a child or a close community of speakers within a broader other-language-speaking community requires the synergy of many individuals, institutions, and initiatives. This task needs to extend beyond the linguistic domain and includes outreach in the community, the global spectrum of cognitive potential, and the plenitude of cultural amalgamations. While research indicates that acquisition through reduced input outside the dominant language home country follows the same pattern as that of learning the language in a monolingual environment, it may stop earlier (Flores, Jesus, and Marques 2017; Montrul 2015: 208–248; Polinsky 2018: 1–16). Comparing the contexts surrounding HL acquisition can potentially reveal the veritable nature of language "fuelling": what helps to condition fully-fledged linguistic competence. On the other hand, the age of the children and the amount and quality of exposure to the language determines the volume of language they acquire.

The quality of language at home may vary, but HSs can attain levels of linguistic competence that are either never or rarely achieved by the learners with a non-native background, such as language learners (Brecht and Ingold 1998). Still, HSs often have gaps in their acquisition because it is nearly impossible to reproduce the full experience and structure of first language acquisition. The fact that a language was learned first but outside of Russia could imply that the individual speaks it at the same level as that of a NS (a monolingual speaker of Russian born in Russia). However, this criterion is not enough. The term HL was previously used to designate the language of a person's heritage; that is, the language of parents, grandparents or great-grandparents (cf. Dewaele, Bak, and Ortega, this volume). HL was juxtaposed to "home language", which is the language used by the family. Home languages differ from those of the environment in cases of immigration, expatriation, minority groups, or a foreign or other naturally- or artificially-introduced language. Today, the term HL usually refers to the language first spoken by the family and later fossilized, acquired, or forgotten by the child or individual despite its continued use at home. In the literature both concepts (home language and heritage language) are sometimes used interchangeably.

Research has usually not discerned between children growing up in multilingual or monolingual homes, which means that having one or more first languages was not an important component for many researchers of HLs. Children who receive dual linguistic input from the time of their birth are exposed to these languages as mother tongues, and these children's competence is expected to differ from those who come from a monolingual family that later switched to another language.

Parents influence the way their children gain proficiency in their language(s) by deciding how languages are introduced: in a separate institution outside school hours or in a bilingual pre-primary or primary school. In a HL context, some people are able to speak Russian, but they cannot read or write in Russian. Additionally, some may have visited Russia, while others speak only "kitchen Russian" (Pavlenko and Malt 2011). Regarding formal RL education, there are different types of textbooks available: L1 for monolingual, mother-tongue speakers in the countries where they live and for bilingual or multilingual speakers abroad; L2 for ethnic minorities and immigrants in Russia; and textbooks for foreign-language learners, typically, outside Russia (starting at different levels). These textbooks are published both in Russia and abroad.

Until now, researchers have found that factors affecting a person's knowledge of a language include the generational socio-economic status of the person's family (education, knowledge of other languages, occupations, and the number of the family members and generations living together), the length of the person's exposure to the language, the age at which the person was first exposed to the language, the quantity and quality of the exposure, identities (cultural, ethnic, and religious views), and attitudes about multilingualism and language use (Ansala 2019; Rhodes, Ochoa, and Ortiz 2005).

Individuals can, surprisingly, lose competence in their first languages if they cut ties to other speakers of the language, especially if these individuals are still children and have not acquired literacy (Gindis 2005; Lindquist, McComarck, and Shablack 2015). One negative aspect of language loss is that previous generations, including parents and grandparents, cannot pass down their knowledge and experiences. Success depends on the family language policy; usually, parents make their decisions based upon the conditions of their surroundings and their life conditions (see Haque and Le Lièvre 2019; Schwartz and Verschik 2013; Slavkov 2017 and references therein).

As a pluricentric language, Russian should have its own variety in every country, which could be taught as such at the local level. Russian speakers in diaspora are subject to at least two types of variation in their language: a variety that was imported from their former residence (dialect and regional varieties), and another variety that is the result of local influence (standard and non-standard varieties) (Andrews 1999; Makarova 2012). The curriculum for first / HL should acknowledge the co-existence of the different language varieties alongside with the school standard or norm.

The differences between HSs and NSs are vague yet clear. With HS, there is an intact zone in their language that corresponds to NL proficiency combined with some deficits and lacunae due to the way they have acquired the language. It is a useful construct if we want to underline that the first language developed abroad may be affected by the language(s) and the lifestyle of the surroundings. This can be thought of as a variety of bilingualism.

2.2 Oral versus written proficiency in the HL: The case of Russian HL

In this section, we touch upon some trends in the discussion about HL and very briefly present the scope of the research on HL relevant for our study. Kupisch and Rothman (2018) claim that dominance is not nativeness. In their view, "naturalistically acquired native grammars that are sufficiently developed for communication cannot be incomplete, only different – potentially drastically – from one another by comparison. HSs are native speakers of their HL" (Kupisch and Rothman 2018: 573). Polinsky and Scontras (2020a) critically approached and re-examined the notion of a HL from the point of view of the object and methods of analysis and its results. If HL replaces the term *unbalanced bilingualism*, it can be extended to any multilingual situation. According to Polinsky and Scontras, the quantity and quality of the input, and "the economy of online resources when operating in a less dominant language" trigger deviation from the relevant baseline (Polinsky and Scontras 2020a: 4). Meisel (2020: 34) argues that "exposure to a HL over a longer time may lead to more balanced bilingualism; but this concerns proficiency, not competence. Empirical research suggests that even when relative frequency of exposure amounts to no more than 30%, this need not lead to divergent attainment." In their response, Polinsky and Scontras (2020b: 50) state: "Some of the defining properties of HL systems include high regularity of grammatical paradigms, commitment to fully-compositional expressions, low tolerance of ambiguities at various levels of linguistic representation, preference for perceptually-salient forms over the ones that are perceptually weak, and related difficulty with silent (missing) material in linguistic forms".

It is widely known that the outcomes in one's first language for some monolingual speakers may be different from the outcomes for other monolingual speakers. For example, according to Hart and Risley (1995), there are considerable discrepancies in vocabulary growth among monolingual children with different socio-economic statuses. This indicates, by analogy, that some bilingual individuals may have larger linguistic inventories than other bilingual or even monolingual individuals. While there are parents who invest a lot of time and energy into the development of HL proficiency, others prefer that the shift to the dominant language happens as quickly as possible (e.g., Akifyeva 2016; Otwinowska et al. 2021). This is one of the factors that determines the variety of HL proficiency. Also fluency diverges among HS: some report that they feel at ease while speaking in their first language, while others regret that they cannot find the right words, have delayed reactions, or that they differ from NSs (De Jong 2018).

The research on HL shows that these bilingual speakers are competent to a certain degree in the language of the environment (the language of their daily life and formal education) and the home language (which can also be, at least partially, the language of formal education). Oral proficiency usually correlates positively with written language proficiency. Yet, not all parents are aware that their child's oral language should be supported with literacy or they are just happy that they are able to communicate orally. Because children have little contact with literacy practices, their language may diverge from the so-called norm.

Self-assessment by and internal/external assessment of HSs produces mixed results. Their learning trajectories obviously do not coincide in time with that of "monolinguals" who frequent schools and interact daily with the language in the countries where this language is a majority language. In an empirical study on this particular subject in Finland, we met with heritage learners who were considered fluent speakers of Russian but learned to "properly" read and write only at a later age (Protassova 2008). Their peers learning Russian as a foreign language made fewer errors in written Russian but were unable to attain the same level of oral expression as the heritage learners. When assessing such learners, the goals vary from the socio- and psycholinguistic to the practical. Kagan and Kudyma (2019) examined in detail the issue of teaching and assessing heritage RL learners and concluded that such students displayed unbalanced oral and written proficiencies, and that grammar markers varied widely, depending on the amount of schooling.

3 Young Russian adolescents with migration backgrounds and Russian as a HL in the United States, Israel, Germany, and Finland: a transnational state of the art

In order to expand our understanding of the concept of HS as opposed to that of the "native language speaker", we conducted descriptive analysis of the semantic and morpho-phonological characteristics of the Russian speech of four groups of teenagers who speak Russian as a HL and English, Hebrew, German, or Finnish as dominant languages. In the following section, we will briefly describe: i) the demographic situation in each country; ii) how immigration laws influence language maintenance policy; and iii) the state of the art of the studies conducted in each country about the Russian diaspora.

3.1 The United States

The number of Russian speakers in the United States is more than 0.9 million. There are no large, concentrated Russian-speaking communities in the U.S. outside of New York, New Jersey, and California. Less than one-third of Russian-speaking parents in the U.S. encourage their children to maintain Russian, and these children may have only a passive knowledge of it (Isurin 2011).

According to Romanov (2014), the motivation of heritage learners is undermined when their family members and educators emphasize their deficiencies in Russian (which is lexically poor and grammatically incorrect if compared with a native-speaker norm based on Russian from the Russian Federation). At home, they encounter the Russian world via access to Russian TV-channels, and some are active on Russian social media (e.g., Odnoklassniki, VKontakte, and Facebook). Place of birth also plays a key role. Romanov (2014) discovered that Russian students learning the RL want to learn their L1 because it is their NL, their parents and family members push them to learn RL at university, they want to maintain family ties, travel in Russia, use the language at work, or do business in Russia. With their relatives and acquaintances, they speak about education, family, friends, and free time; fewer responses were received concerning actualities, ways of life, and professions. Even fewer spoke about weather, health, history, films, books, or art, which indicates that students generally do not discuss these topics in Russian.

Carreira and Kagan (2011) showed that, on the all-national level, some respondents underscored the importance of communicating with relatives in the U.S. and abroad, as well as knowing their cultural and linguistic roots. This was a self-selected group of individuals who chose to take Russian in college and, therefore, not a fully-representative sample. Also, this survey is from some time ago, and there have since been some generational shifts. Among those students, the transition to English happened mostly after the age of 5, when parents put them into school (before age 5, many stay at home, have a Russian nanny, or attend Russian-language day care). Upon entry into school, these children switch to English, and their parents do not oppose it. Less than half of the school children still speak Russian, but they remain exposed to listening in Russian, and only 3% go to Russian-speaking countries at least once a year (Carreira and Kagan 2011). In the majority of the cases, the students did not learn literacy until college.

3.2 Israel

In Israel, about 1 million inhabitants speak Russian. Spolsky and Shohamy (1999) describe Russian as one of the most frequently spoken languages in Israel, with significant infrastructure. Niznik (2011: 103) writes that "the younger their age at migration to Israel, the greater their Hebrew proficiency, yet all respondents have retained some basic communication skills in Russian," with more than 90% retaining literacy skills in Russian. The RL in Israel possesses defining features (Naiditsch 2004), is weaker (Meir 2018) and evolves in both the public and private spheres (Yelenevskaya 2015). Socio-linguistic trends in bilingual development have been studied by Schwartz (2012, 2017) while Meir and Polinsky (2019) discovered a robust dependence on the age of onset on bilingualism in the grammar of the HS of Russian in Israel.

3.3 Germany

Estimates of Russian speakers in Germany range up from 2 million. Russian-speaking immigrants to Germany include numerous diverse nationalities from former Soviet republics, currently independent countries. Isurin and Riehl (2017) summarized the multifaceted conceptions of Russian-speaking immigrants in Germany, including language maintenance, emerging identities, measurements of social inclusion, linguistic integration, and bilingual practices. Russian-German bilinguals experience language attrition and are described as having certain gaps in Russian-language acquisition (Anstatt 2011; Brehmer and Mehlhorn 2015; Brüggemann 2016, 2018). The grammatical features of their Russian are affected by varying exposure to Russian, matriculation into school and literacy acquisition in the local language (Gagarina and Klassert 2018). Scholars generally show a large spectrum of variation in the HSs' performance in Russian.

3.4 Finland

In Finland, about 80 thousand people are speakers of L1 Russian. For children, it is possible to frequent a bilingual daycare centre, a Russian-speaking circle, a group in kindergarten, or attend a bilingual school (there are six such schools in Finland) and receive instruction in Russian as a foreign language from ages 7–8, 12–13 or 17. All schoolchildren in Finland have the right to receive two lessons per week in their mother tongue (called *home language*) from age 6–19. These measures invigorate performance in HL.

As Moin et al. (2013) reflected, parents expect that children acquire multilingual abilities and maintain Russian on a high level. Some peculiarities of Russian spoken by different generations of bilinguals in Finland are uniform and stable due to the influence of the Finnish language and way of life, some vary, and some are caused by the complexities of the Russian grammar or emerge because of lexical lacunae (paronyms) (Protassova 2009). Rynkänen and Pöyhönen (2010) reinforced the argument that psychological and social factors partly shape linguistic and behavioral characteristics of young Russian speakers in Finland.

4 Empirical study: research aims and methodological approach

In the present study, which represents a multi-site research, we analysed the different backgrounds of adolescent HSs of Russian in the four countries presented before (the United States, Israel, Germany, and Finland), which, as we saw, have considerable Russian-speaking minorities. We then compared the outcomes of language acquisition and tried to embark on a conceptual discussion as to whether or not participants can be considered NSs of Russian.

We conducted interviews (see Appendix), provided self-evaluations for the participants, and collected narratives from 56 immigrant adolescents who either were born to Russian-speaking families or immigrated as small children to the U.S. (12), Israel (13), Germany (15), and Finland (16). Each session with a participant lasted about one hour, during which we conducted a structured interview for approximately 30 minutes. Participants were selected by the snowball method, starting from the researchers' acquaintances. The interviews were conducted individually at home, at school, or in public spaces. Professor Olga Kagan composed the written and oral questionnaires. Questions on narrative abilities of the participants are analysed elsewhere (Minkov et al. 2019). Here, we concentrate on the participants' answers about themselves. All of the data was transcribed, and each author analysed the materials. The qualitative analysis focused on describing the semantic and grammatical features of the adolescents' speech.

5 Results

5.1 General description of the commonalities across countries

Below is a snapshot of some themes that came up in the interviews conducted with the participants in the four countries. This summary will serve as a background to the more specific results presented by country below.

All of the interviewers' parents and children had multilingual backgrounds. On their own initiative, participants sometimes briefly judged the quality of the RL of their families that immigrated from the former Soviet Union. A young man from Israel mentioned, for example, that his parents' Russian was "broken" because when they visit Russia, everyone immediately recognizes them as "not from Russia." While answering questions, participants generally evaluated their Russian as being slightly accented; some said that they pronounced the sound *r* differently and they were aware that other Russian speakers recognize something strange in their speech. One remarked that her tone of voice changes when she switches to another language and, in consequence, she becomes a kind-of different person. They stressed that their Russian proficiency develops in the course of communication with NSs (e.g., "the language learned from my mother is my native language") and it should be perfect, and they regret to make mistakes. Adolescents noted that they have difficulties understanding fluent speech, such as what is said on television or by guests from Russia. They felt that they spoke better Russian when they were younger. Several individuals mentioned that they learned other languages besides Russian successfully. Writing, as they acknowledged, is often absent or problematic (while, for those who learn Russian as a foreign language, writing tends to be easier than speaking). One girl from Germany commented that she had not attained a high level of Russian; she mentioned that she reads insufficiently, misses some words, cannot formulate complex sentences, and cannot converse on many topics. She is able to do these things at school in German, but not in Russian, as she explains. Other participants mentioned that some borrowings from their other languages into Russian occur spontaneously, and their parents often criticize them. Some expressed interest in visiting their countries of birth/parents' origin in Russia.

The methods for acquiring literacy in Russian that their parents once used range from hiring a babysitter or coach to frequenting a bilingual school, either on Sundays or more regularly during the week; it was easier to learn the language if they watched Russian television at home and everybody used Russian exclusively in the household. Some respondents dropped their literacy studies early while others did so once they started high school. Their arguments in favour of learning Russian vary: knowledge of any language, especially one not widespread, is useful; knowing (Russian) is better than ignoring (it); the family language should be maintained, not just learned; better communication with family and other people; benefits for the younger children in the family; and being able to pass it on to their future generations.

5.2 Snapshots of results per country

5.2.1 The United States

Sample

We interviewed 12 teenagers aged 13 to 18 (seven girls and five boys) selected from a summer course in Russian at the University of California, Los Angeles (UCLA). Half of these students were born in the U.S. (of these, one was born in Canada), and the other half had arrived before school age. At home, Georgian, Ukrainian, Armenian, and Uzbek were spoken along with Russian. In the cases where the parents came from Belarus or Moldova, the students were less likely to use the former local languages at home. The parents usually spoke English, but not all of the grandparents did.

Findings

The students noted that they reply to their parents in Russian and English and speak with their grandparents primarily in Russian. Generally, grandparents watched TV in Russian but parents did so less frequently. Some of the students attended Russian preschools, took afternoon classes, or had Russian-speaking friendships that continued after preschool, although these students reported that they had lost contact with many of those friends unless they were children of their parents' friends. Some had Russian-speaking sports coaches.

We observed a number of examples of code-switching: in their Russian discourse, some participants used English words like *carpool, downtown, biology, summer, permit, assignment, application, report, credit, contact, appointment, population, director, babysitter, elementary school, high school, college, university, community, apartment, art, musical, my part for humanity, patient, open heart surgery, hospital, outside, wheelchair, seriously wounded, moody, separate, popular,* and *different*. They used the English discursive markers *like, you know* as well as the names of movies, festivities, books, and (geographic) locations. Thus, code-switching takes place in semantic fields served principally in the English language (namely, realities of their urban, school, and professional lives).

In addition, the choice of words, verbal agreement and tense, gender, number, case, the pronunciation of cognates or rare items, incorrect overgeneralizations, word formation (prefixes, suffixes), intonation, aspect, and stress were often deviant from a monolingual native-speaking norm. Combinations of English and

Russian words emerged, for example, when participants spoke about school subjects (*alfabit, kemija, bajologia* instead of *alfavit, himija, biologija*) or other countries (*Russija, Bulgerija* instead of *Rossija, Bolgarija*). Verbs with general meanings, like *delat'* (make) and *xodit'* (go), replaced verbs with more specific meanings. Some participants used calques like *ja 15 let* (I am 15 years old, not *mne 15 let*).

5.2.2 Israel

Sample

We interviewed 13 adolescents, seven boys and six girls. Not all of them could read and write in Russian, although a few had acquired academic skills in it. Most of them were born in Israel. All the participants were involved in after-school Russian-learning settings.

Findings

The adolescents seemed fluent in Russian and could communicate freely. Hebrew words entering the Russian discourse usually involved the names of shops, newspapers, universities, musical groups, hospitals, foundations, programs, terms for alternative and volunteer service, ambulance, as well as quotes from other people's speeches. The participants had studied Russian at *mofit, basmat, shiton* (names of the educational chains of institutions operating in Russian). Some expressions were translated from Hebrew: e.g., *vysokij ivrit* (high Hebrew) instead of *vysokij uroven' ivrita* (high level of Hebrew), *ja beru neskol'ko let opyta* (I have several years of experience) instead of *ja nabiraju neskolko let stazha*; an extra preposition *dlja* (for) appeared in the clause, *tam pomogal dlja uroki delat'* (there, I helped with the homework).

In addition, in trying to explain local realities, sometimes the participants employed too many words and thus the meaning of their statements was not easy to recover occasionally. Child-like errors emerged while using difficult cases of Russian declension, like *soldatov* instead of *soldat* (Gen. Pl. 'soldiers'), *musul'manov* instead of *musul'man* (Gen. Pl. 'Muslims'), and conjugation, like *iskaju* instead of *ishchu* (1. Sg. 'search') and *hochem* instead of *hotim* (1. Pl. 'want'). There were cases of non-standard agreement, prepositions, aspect, and so on.

5.2.3 Germany

Sample

We interviewed 15 teenagers aged 13 to 19 (five boys and ten girls), most of whom were born in Germany and whose parents came predominantly from Ukraine, and some Russian-German families repatriated from Kazakhstan. Many of them spoke Russian and had Russian-speaking friends and relatives; they frequented bilingual primary schools or took courses at the Russian House or elsewhere. One preferred not to take Russian as a foreign language at school because, she stated, the teachers "know the language worse than the students".

Findings

All participants were able to converse freely with the researcher. The German participants produced some grammatical forms using incorrect models, similar to those small children use. For example, the participants used *zahlebnyvajus'* instead of *zahljobyvajus'*, and *analizirovaesh'* instead of *analiziruesh'*. They invented hybrid pronunciation cognates like *inzhenjor* for *inzhener* (Germ. *Ingeneur*), *intenzivno* for *intensivno*, or they pronounced German words with a Russian accent (*gimnazium* instead of *gimnazija*). We found creative expressions, like *ne vedi nizhe plintusa, eto znachit ne vedi duraka*, produced from *ne vedi sebja ploho* (don't behave badly) + *nizhe plintusa* (below the plinth = at an all-time low) + (this means) *ne valjaj duraka* (don't mess around). Some participants confused the sounds *i* and *y*, used a middle *l* (between Russian hard and soft consonants, like in German), employed calques from the German language, copied German verbal agreements, and employed words with general, unspecific, meanings or overgeneralized animacy of nouns in Russian. Many used German words like *Termin* (appointment [missing in Russian]), *Nikolaus* (Nikolaj – the name of the saint who comes on December 6, a tradition that does not exist in Russian Orthodoxy), *Silvester* (December 31), and the terms *Jura, Rechtswissenschaft* (jurisprudence, law), *Duales Studium* (when a person works and studies at the same time), *Musikwissenschaft* (musicology), *TU, Technische Universität* (Institute of Technology), *Realschule* (a type of school in the German system), *Physik* (physics – a school subject), and *Pfleger* (nurse). The use of these terms means that they were learned and employed in a German context. The word *privat* (in private) was used as such and in the Russified form, *privatno*. The term *Abitur* (a certificate of the final examinations at school) was used to denote the German word (with German pronunciation) as well as the Russified masc. *abitur* or fem. *abitura*.

5.2.4 Finland

Sample

We interviewed 16 participants, ages 15 to 17 (nine girls and seven boys). 13 were born in various places in Finland, and three were born in Russia (Karelia and St. Petersburg). Most of them spoke Russian with their family members and friends, some had relatives with whom they spoke Finnish, and one had a Finnish-speaking father (and self-assessed his Russian skills as very low). Most expressed a desire to improve the proficiency in Russian, which was said to prevail over Finnish. Their knowledge of Russian was based on home communication and lessons at school (from two to five lessons per week; half of the participants abandoned this instruction). One learned Russian as a foreign language, some of the respondents' families employed a teacher, and one started learning Russian formally only at the age of 14. Most of the parents had repatriated to Finland as Finns from Russia. All of the participants wanted to have a future career that would, in some manner, employ Russian.

Findings

Most of the participants' conversational contributions were correct. The lexical lacunae were filled in with Finnish words: the festivity, *pääsiäinen* (Easter); the occupation, *marjastus* (berry collecting); historical events like *itsenäisyys* (independence), *ruokapula* (famine), and *työvoimapula* (workforce deficit); terms of school life, such as *ylä-aste* (classes 7–9), *lukio* (high school), *ammattikoulu* (college). One boy said that it was difficult for him to translate Finnish terms. In some cases, there was no grammatical agreement. In Finnish, there is no grammatical gender, and the participants sometimes get confused by this. They invented new words: a common case in Finnish is the production of nouns derived from verbs and signifying actions. We encountered *puteshestovanie* (traveling), *igranie* (playing), and *byvanie* (being), which are absent in standard Russian. When trying to produce a longer stretch of speech, some participants had difficulties formulating their thoughts.

6 Discussion: comparing and interpreting the results

As in previous studies (e.g., Nikunlassi and Protassova 2014), our participants in this multi-site research had difficulties expressing time, finding the proper adjectives, and constructing complex sentences. In addition, they confused reflexive and non-reflexive verbs, the grammatical gender of nouns, places of stress, and some nuances of negation; they used verbs with general semantics for a variety of other words: *vzjat'* (take) for rent, travel, hire, buy, receive, and choose; *delat'* (make) for put, set, and place; *pojti* (go) for ride, travel, and fly; some confounded *znat'* (know) and *umet'* (can).

From the point of view of 'normative' Russian, all four groups displayed borrowings, calques, pauses, and wavering while choosing the right word. They all made grammatical errors, especially with numerals (also with age), gender, and they frequently confounded the terms for older/younger siblings (they say *bol'šaja sestra* [big sister] or *malen'kij brat* [little brother] instead of *starshaja* [elder] and *mladshij* [younger]). They employed terms denoting nationality after the model *russkij* 'Russian', which is both a noun and adjective in Russian: for example, they said *nemeckij* (German) for a citizen of Germany, which should be *nemec* or *grazhdanin Germanii*, and *finskij chelovek* (Finnish man) for a Finn, which should be *finn*. The participants in all of the groups used *esli* (if) when introducing indirect speech or a clause without a conjunction (in Russian, this should have the particle *li*). We found numerous examples of placement of the preposition *ot* (from, of) instead of synthetic Genitive (*ot soseda balkon* [of the neighbor's balcony] instead of *balkon soseda* [the neighbor's balcony]); for *iz* (from) (*priehala ot Baku* [came from Baku] instead of *iz Baku*); or for possessive constructions (*dedushka ot papy* [grandpa from dad] instead of *papin dedushka*).

Many of our participants utilized special forms to express how one speaks a language: *ona bol'she russkij, chem ja, govorit* (she speaks Russian more than me), which should be *ona govorit po-russki bol'she, chem ja*); *po-ivritski* (in Hebrew), which should be *na ivrite*; *po-anglijskij* or *po-anglijskomu* (in English), which should be *po-anglijski*. Many would say *familija* (family name) to denote 'family', which is *sem'ja* in Russian; *pianino* was shortened to *piano*. Instead of *odnazhdy*, we repeatedly encounter *odin den'* (one day).

Overall, these inaccuracies, which are quite often reported by other researchers of non-standard Russian (in Russia and abroad), seldom impeded communication. Since the participants were born to Russian-speaking families, the local populations abroad consider them to be NSs. For Russian speakers in Russia, their language can seem incomplete, possibly primitive, with a touch of "foreignness". As Carreira and Kagan (2011) put it, they study Russian because they want to communicate, search for information, study their ancestral culture, read Russian literature, talk with family and friends in other countries, watch Russian TV, talk with the Russian speakers in the community, and follow Russian-language church services.

7 Conclusion

This chapter was aimed to analyse the acquisition of Russian as a heritage language abroad by comparing first and heritage languages. Our analysis showed a complex relationship between the two notions, native speakers and heritage speakers. Thus, on the scale of NSs to foreign language learners, most of the interviewees fell on the side of native speakers. Considering the overall amount of knowledge acquired by the participants, as well as their academic level and readiness to learn, they should not be considered incompetent speakers of Russian. Still, a couple of our teenagers struggled to express themselves adequately in Russian and felt that the RL was their mother tongue although they cannot perform in it at a level that they wanted to attain. If we accept the idea of pluricentricity, this could still be *their* language, if they choose to call it so.

For Bloomfield (1933: 43), a native speaker is one who speaks a language as a first language. In the case of HSs, we see that their first language is a language that they acquired sequentially or in parallel to a different majority language. Thus, while not matching the ideal, it is not a foreign language. Cook (1999) argues that teaching should consider the needs and abilities of the L2 learner rather than think about him or her as the failed native speaker, proposing the designation of "multicompetent speaker".

To distinguish between NSs and HSs may be still useful practically (Houghton et al. 2018). Theoretically, it should deal with a continuum of HSs and pluricentricity as well (Singh 1998). The ideal RL speaker, the so-called "bearer of the norm", is as much a myth as any other NS. The body of research on the reality of the RL use in each country is growing as these countries increasingly encounter such students in their school and university curriculums.

To conclude, it is currently difficult to estimate to what extent multilingual speakers whose Russian is their first language are "true" (in their own words) NSs of Russian throughout the world. Our study showed that the linguistic features of their speech are specific, partly common for all HSs, and they have the right to speak and name any language as their own. The current study searched to answer the question of whether the HSs could be characterised as NSs as well within a context of only one (although huge) linguistic diaspora. Future studies are necessary to continue exploring the nature of the relationship between NSs and HSs.

Authors' Positionalities

Olga Kagan (written by Anna Kudyma): Originally from Moscow, Olga Kagan received an MA from the Moscow Pedagogical Institute and began her career teaching English as a foreign language. After emigrating to the U.S. in 1976, she taught Russian as a lecturer, first at UC Riverside and then at UCLA starting in 1981. In time she earned a PhD, became a full professor, undergraduate advisor and director of language programs in her department, and director of the UCLA Center for World Languages, the Russian Flagship Center, and the National Heritage Language Resource Center (NHLRC), funded by the Department of Education's Title VI. NHLRC was founded to offer effective, research-based approaches to teaching heritage language speakers and providing teacher education. Olga coauthored over 10 Russian-language textbooks, published many articles and book chapters in heritage language studies, and founded the Heritage Language Journal.

She developed an interest in heritage language education after noticing an increasing number of Russian heritage speakers in UCLA Russian classes. While many instructors saw heritage speakers as disruptive and cynical, Olga looked more deeply and saw a fascinating human and pedagogical need and intriguing research questions. She often said, "If they come for an easy grade and that's what we give them, it's our fault, not theirs." She designed a class for heritage speakers at UCLA, which advances heritage speakers to high-level Russian coursework in one year by building on what students know rather than harping on their deficiencies.

Olga's work with these students and her publications made her a widely respected leader in the field. She won several awards for her work, two from the American Association of Teachers of Slavic and East European Languages (AATSEEL) for the Best Contribution to Pedagogy (in 2001 and 2004 for her books), another from AATSEEL for Excellence in Teaching in 2003, and one for Distinguished Service to the Profession from the Modern Language Association in 2014. She was a gifted teacher of foreign and heritage language students on all levels. Olga's work in heritage language studies was informed by her vision for language study for all students: that language can be a medium for discovering the world and oneself. That vision is also the guiding principle of UCLA Russian Flagship Center, one of eight in the U.S. that teach undergraduates to high levels of proficiency in Russian. Her gifts for interaction were evident in her genius for collaborating with many people simultaneously on multiple projects. She loved sharing ideas, designing projects and seeing them come to life, and mentoring students, officially and unofficially. She served on and chaired numerous dissertation committees and wrote thousands of letters of recommendation. Olga's sterling integrity of character could be seen in the integrity of her work. She was also intensely curious, immensely well-read and informed, and saw a staggering workload as a good time. She loved solving problems and was a true scholar in that she was fascinated and pleased to find unanticipated results. She practiced active goodness and was great fun to work with.

To our great grief, Olga Kagan passed away in April 2018. As we were working on this paper, we were not only comforted by her colleagues at UCLA but encouraged to continue.

Miriam Minkov is PhD student at the Tel Aviv University, Israel. Her research focuses on heritage language and the acquisition of early literacy in the context of bilingualism. Currently she is working on the research of the teaching of heritage languages in the early age.

Ekaterina Protassova holds Ph.D. in Philology and Hab. in Pedagogy. She is Adjunct Professor in Russian language at the University of Helsinki. She has authored and co-authored over 300 monographs, articles and book chapters, headed and participated in various international and national projects investigating language pedagogies, child and adult bilingualism, and the role of language and culture in immigrant integration. Her service to the profession includes editorial work for various journals and publishers and organization of seminars and conference panels. Her diverse interests brought her to collaborate with researchers and serve as Ph.D. advisor in Estonia, Germany, Israel, Italy, Kazakhstan, Latvia, Russia, the USA, and other countries. Her work has received multiple awards, including awards for disseminating bilingualism and biculturality among minority bilingual education and language revitalization in Russia.

Mila Schwartz is a Professor in Language and in Oranim Academic College of Education (Israel). Her research interests include language policy and models of early bilingual/multilingual education; linguistic, cognitive, and socio-cultural development of early sequential bilinguals; family language policy; and language teachers' pedagogical development. Recently, she has proposed and elaborated on the following theoretical concepts: language-conducive context, language-conducive strategies and child language-based agency. In addition, Prof. Schwartz has taken an active part in several international projects. For example, international projects entitled *Language Conceptions and Practices in Bilingual Early Childhood: Swedish-Finnish Bilingual Children in Swedish-medium Preschools in Finland* (2013–2017) and *Listening to the Voices of Teachers: Multilingualism and Inclusive Education across Borders* (2018-present). Furthermore, she has recently been invited to act as an international advisor in a new research project called *Language Policies and Practices of Diverse Immigrant Families in Iceland* and their implications for education, led by Prof. Hanna Ragnarsdóttir. She held the position of Secretary of the Steering Committee of the International Symposium of Bilingualism from 2015 to 2019, and currently she acts as Convenor of the MultilingualChildhoods network. In addition to her academic work, Prof. Schwartz is an Academic Adviser of "Hand in Hand: Center for Jewish-Arab Education" and the Russian-Hebrew speaking bilingual preschools in Israel.

Appendix

The questionnaire for participants (original is in Russian)
(1) Where does your family come from?
(2) What languages do you speak at home and with friends?
(3) How do your parents and grandparents react if they hear errors in Russian?
(4) How have you learned Russian and other languages?
(5) Which languages are beneficial?
(6) What do you want to do in the future?
(7) Which subjects do you enjoy studying?
(8) What do you celebrate at home?
(9) Do you listen to the Russian music?

(10) Do they know any Russian singers?
(11) Have you travelled to Russia or the country of your parents' origin? If yes, what are your impressions?
(12) What do your parents say about the life in the former Soviet Union?
(13) How do you identify yourself?
(14) Do you have a best friend? Can you talk about him/her? How did you meet?
(15) What did you do yesterday? What are you going to do tomorrow?
(16) If you are to have children, would you want them to speak Russian?

References

Akifyeva, Raisa. 2016. Child-rearing practices of Russian-speaking women from a migration perspective. St. Petersburg. Basic Research Programme. National Research University Higher School of Economics. *Basic Research Programme. Series HUM "Humanities"*, 140. 1–22.

Andrews, David R. 1999. *Sociocultural perspectives on language change in diaspora. Soviet immigrants in the United States*. Amsterdam: Benjamins.

Ansala, Laura. 2019. Maahanmuuttajien lasten ja suomalaistaustaisten lasten välisiä kouluttautumiseroja selittävät saapumisikä, perhetausta ja asuinalueet [The age of arrival, the family background and the place of dwelling explain differences in the education of the immigrant and Finnish-background children]. *Kvartti*, August 29. www.kvartti.fi/fi/artikkelit/maahanmuuttajien-lasten-ja-suomalaistaustaisten-lasten-valisia-kouluttautumiseroja (accessed 29 August 2019)

Anstatt, Tanja. 2011. Sprachattrition. Abbau der Erstsprache bei russisch-deutschen Jugendlichen. *Wiener Slawistischer Almanach* 67, 7–31.

Aref'ev, Aleksandr L. 2019. *Sociologija jazyka. Russkij jazyk. Sovremennoe sostojanie i tendencii rasprostranenija v mire*. [Sociology of language. Russian language. The state of art and the tendencies of development.] Moscow: Jurajt.

Ben-Rafael, Eliezer, Mikhail Lyubansky, Olaf Glöckner, Paul Harris, Yael Israel, Willi Jasper & Julius Schoeps. 2006. *Building a diaspora: Russian Jews in Israel, Germany and the USA*. Leiden: Brill.

Bloomfield, Leonard. 1933. *Language*. New York: Holt Rinehart Winston.

Brecht, Richard D. & Catherine W. Ingold. 1998. Tapping a national resource: Heritage languages in the United States. *ERIC Digest*. Washington, DC: ERIC Clearinghouse on Languages and Linguistics. https://files.eric.ed.gov/fulltext/ED424791.pdf (accessed 21 May 2021)

Brehmer, Bernhard & Grit Mehlhorn. 2015. Russisch als Herkunftssprache in Deutschland. Ein holistischer Ansatz zur Erforschung des Potenzials von Herkunftssprachen. *Zeitschrift für Fremdsprachenforschung* 26 (1), 85–123.

Brüggemann, Natalia. 2016. Herkunftssprache Russisch. Unvollständige Grammatik als Folge mündlichen Spracherwerbs. In Alena Bazhutkina & Barabara Sonnenhauser (eds.), *Linguistische Beiträge zur Slavistik. XXII. JungslavistInnen-Treffen in München*, 37–58. München: BiblionMedia.

Brüggemann, Natalia. 2018. SchreibanfängerInnen im herkunftssprachlichen Russischunterricht. In Anka Bergmann, Olga Caspers & Wolfgang Stadler (eds.), *Didaktik der slawischen Sprachen*, 177–192. Innsbruck: Innsbruck University Press.

Carreira, Maria M. & Olga Kagan. 2011. The results of the National Heritage Language Survey: Implications for teaching, curriculum design, and professional development. *Foreign Language Annals* 44, 40–64.

Clyne, Michael. 1992. *Pluricentric languages. Different norms in different countries*. Berlin: Mouton de Gruyter.

Cook, Vivian. 1999. Going beyond the native speaker in language teaching. *TESOL Quarterly* 33 (2), 185–209.

Coulmas, Florian. 1981. The concept of native speaker. In Florian Coulmas (ed.), *A Festschrift for native speaker*, 1–28. The Hague: Mouton.

Davies, Alan. 2003. *The native speaker: Myth and reality*. Clevedon: Multilingual Matters.

De Jong, Nivja H. 2018. Fluency in second language testing: Insights from different disciplines. *Language Assessment Quarterly* 15 (3), 237–254.

Flores, Cristina, Ana Lúcia Santos, Alice Jesus & Rui Marques. 2017. Age and input effects in the acquisition of mood in Heritage Portuguese. *Journal of Child Language* 44 (4), 795–828.

Gagarina, Natalia & Annegret Klassert. 2018. Input dominance and development of home language in Russian-German bilinguals. *Language Sciences, Frontiers in Communication* 3 (40), 1–14. doi: 10.3389/fcomm.2018.00040

Gindis, Boris. 2005. Cognitive, language, and educational issues of children adopted from overseas orphanages. *Journal of Cognitive Education and Psychology* 4 (3), 291–315.

Haque, Shahzaman & Françoise Le Lièvre (eds.). 2019. *Politique linguistique familiale. Enjeux dynamiques de la transmission linguistique dans un contexte migratoire*. München: Lincom.

Hart, Betty & Todd. R. Risley. 1995. *Meaningful differences in the everyday experience of young American children*. Baltimore, MD: Paul H. Brookes.

Houghton, Stephanie A., Damian J. Rivers & Kayoko Hashimoto. 2018. *Beyond native-speakerism: Current explorations and future visions*. New York: Routledge.

Isurin, Ludmila. 2011. *Russian diaspora: Culture, identity, and language change*. Berlin: de Gruyter.

Isurin, Ludmila & Claudia M. Riehl (eds.). 2017. *Integration, identity and language maintenance in young immigrants. Russian Germans or German Russians*. Amsterdam: Benjamins.

Kagan, Olga, Maria M. Carreira & Claire C. Hitchens (eds.). 2017. *The Routledge handbook of heritage language education: From innovation to programme building*. Abingdon, UK: Routledge.

Kagan, Olga & Anna Kudyma. 2019. Assessment and curriculum for heritage language learners: Exploring Russian data. In Paula Winke & Susan M. Gass (eds.), *Foreign language proficiency in higher education,* 71–92. Cham: Springer.

Kamusella, Tomasz. 2018. Russian: A Monocentric or Pluricentric Language? *Colloquia Humanistica* 7, 153–196.

Kasstan, Jonathan R., Anita Auer & Joseph Salmons. 2018. Heritage-language speakers: Theoretical and empirical challenges on sociolinguistic attitudes and prestige. *International Journal of Bilingualism* 22 (4), 387–394.

Kleyn, Tatiana & Beth Vayshenker (eds.). 2013. Russian bilingual education across public, private and community spheres. In Ofelia García, Zeena Zakharia & Bahar Otcu (eds.), *Bilingual community education and multilingualism: Beyond heritage languages in a global city*, 259–271. Bristol: Multilingual Matters.

Kupisch, Tanja & Jason Rothman. 2018. Terminology matters! Why difference is not incompleteness and how early child bilinguals are heritage speakers. *International Journal of Bilingualism* 22 (5), 564–582.

Laleko, Oksana. 2013. Assessing heritage language vitality: Russian in the United States. *Heritage Language Journal* 10 (3), 89–102.

Lindquist, Kristen A., Jennifer K. MacCormack & Holly Shablack. 2015. The role of language in emotion: Predictions from psychological constructionism. *Frontiers in Psychology* 6, doi: 10.3389/fpsyg.2015.00444.

Makarova, Veronika (ed.) 2012. *Russian language studies in North America: New perspectives from theoretical and applied linguistics*. London: Anthem Press.

Meir, Natalia. 2018. Morpho-syntactic abilities of unbalanced bilingual children: A closer look at the weaker language. *Frontiers in Psychology* 9 (PMC6099692). doi 10.3389/fpsyg.2018.01318

Meir, Natalia, & Maria Polinsky. 2019. Restructuring in heritage grammars. Adjective-noun and numeral-noun expressions in Israeli Russian. *Linguistic Approaches to Bilingualism*, doi.org/10.1075/lab.18069.mei. 1–37.

Meisel, Jürgen M. 2020. Shrinking structures in heritage languages: Triggered by reduced quantity of input? *Bilingualism: Language and Cognition* 23 (1), 33–34.

Minkov, Miriam, Olga Kagan, Ekaterina Protassova, & Mila Schwartz. 2019. Towards a better understanding of a continuum of heritage language proficiency: The case of adolescent Russian heritage speakers. *Heritage Language Journal* 16 (2), 211–237.

Moin, Victor, Ekaterina Protassova, Valeria Lukkari, & Mila Schwartz. 2013. The role of family background in early bilingual education: The Finnish-Russian experience. In Mila Schwartz & Anna Verschik (eds.), *Successful family language policy: Parents, children and educators in interaction*, 53–82. Dordrecht: Springer.

Montrul, Silvina. 2015. *The acquisition of heritage languages*. Cambridge: Cambridge University Press.

Muhr, Rudolf. 2012. Linguistic dominance and non-dominance in pluricentric languages: A typology. In Rudolf Muhr (ed.), *Non-dominant varieties of pluricentric languages. Getting the picture. In memory of Michael Clyne*, 23–48. Frankfurt am Main: Lang.

Mustajoki, Arto, Ekaterina Protassova & Maria Yelenevskaya. 2020. *The soft power of the Russian language: Pluricentricity, politics and policies*. London: Routledge.

Naiditch, Larisa. 2004. Vybor jazyka, perekljuchenie koda, leksicheskie zaimstvovanija: russkij jazyk emigrantov poslednej volny v Izraile [Language choice, code switching, lexical borrowings: the Russian language of the last wave émigrés in Israel]. In Arto Mustajoki & Ekaterina Protassova (eds.), *Russkojazychnyj chelovek v inojazychnom okruzhenii* [Russian-speaking person in an other-language environment], 108–122. Helsinki: University of Helsinki.

Nikunlassi, Ahti & Ekaterina Protassova (eds.). 2014. *Instrumentarij rusistiki: oshibki i mnogojazychie* [Instrumentarium of Russistics: errors and multilingualism]. Helsinki: University of Helsinki.

Nikunlassi, Ahti & Ekaterina Protassova (eds.). 2019. *Russian language in the multilingual world*. Helsinki: University of Helsinki.

Niznik, Marina. 2011. Cultural practices and preferences of 'Russian' youth in Israel. *Israel Affairs* 17 (1), 89–107.
Ortega, Lourdes. 2019. SLA and the study of equitable multilingualism. *The Modern Language Journal* 103 (Supplement 2019), 23–38.
Otwinowska, Agnieszka, Natalia Meir, Natalia Ringblom, Sviatlana Karpava & Francesca La Morgia. 2021. Language and literacy transmission in heritage language: Evidence from Russian-speaking families in Cyprus, Ireland, Israel, and Sweden. *Journal of Multilingual and Multicultural Development* 42 (4), 357–382. https://doi.org/10.1080/01434632.2019.1695807.
Pavlenko, Aneta, & Barbara C. Malt. 2011. Kitchen Russian: Crosslinguistic difference and first language object naming by Russian-English bilinguals. *Bilingualism: Language and Cognition* 14 (1), 19–45.
Polinsky, Maria. 2018. *Heritage languages and their speakers*. Cambridge: Cambridge University Press.
Polinsky, Maria, & Gregory Scontras. 2020a. Understanding heritage languages. *Bilingualism: Language and Cognition* 23 (1), 4–20.
Polinsky, Maria, & Gregory Scontras. 2020b. A roadmap for heritage language research. *Bilingualism: Language and Cognition* 23 (1), 50–55.
Protassova, Ekaterina. 2008. Teaching Russian as a heritage language in Finland. *Heritage Language Journal* 2 (5), 127–152.
Protassova, Ekaterina. 2009. Russian as a lesser used language in Finland. In Bert Cornillie, José Lambert & Pierre Swiggers (eds), *Linguistic Identities, Language Shift and Language Policy in Europe*, 167–184. Leuven: Peeters.
Romanov, Artemi Y. 2014. Motivacija studentov-bilingvov iz russkogovorjashchih semej k izucheniju russkogo jazyka v SSha [Motivation of bilingual students from the Russian-speaking families towards learning of the Russian language in the USA]. *Sociokul'turnye i filologicheskie aspekty v obrazovatel'nom i nauchnom kontekste* [Sociocultural and philological aspects in the educational and scientific context], 528–535. Kyoto: University Kyoto Sangyo.
Rhodes, Robert L., Salvador Hector Ochoa & Samuel O. Ortiz. 2005. *Assessing culturally and linguistically diverse students: A practical guide*. New York: The Guilford Press.
Ryazanova-Clarke, Lara. (ed.) 2014. *The Russian Language outside the nation: Speakers and identities*. Edinburgh: Edinburgh University Press.
Rynkänen, Tatjana & Sari Pöyhönen. 2010. Russian-speaking young immigrants in Finland: Educational and linguistic challenges for integration. In Mika Lähteenmäki & Marjatta Vanhala-Aniszewski (eds.), *Language ideologies in transition: Multilingualism in Finland and Russia*, 175–194. Frankfurt am Main: Lang.
Schwartz, Mila. 2012. Second generation immigrants: A socio-linguistic approach of linguistic development within the framework of family language policy. In: Mark Leikin, Mila Schwartz & Yishai Tobin (eds.), *Current issues in bilingualism. Cognitive and sociolinguistic perspectives*, 119–135. Dordrecht: Springer.
Schwartz, Mila. 2017. Rationalization of the first language first model of bilingual development and education: The case of Russian as a heritage language in Israel. In Olga Kagan, Maria M. Carreira & Claire C. Hitchens (eds.), *The Routledge handbook of heritage language education: From innovation to programme building*, 191–203. Abingdon, UK: Routledge.

Schwartz, Mila & Anna A. Verschik (eds.) 2013. *Successful family language policy: Parents, children and educators in interaction*. Dordrecht: Springer.

Singh, Rajendra (ed.). 1998. *The native speaker: Multilingual perspectives*. New Delhi & Thousand Oaks, CA: Sage.

Slavkov, Nikolay. 2017. Family language policy and school language choice: Pathways to bilingualism and multilingualism in a Canadian context. *International Journal of Multilingualism* 14 (4), 378–400.

Spolsky, Bernard & Elana G. Shohamy. 1999. *The languages of Israel: Policy, ideology, and practice*. Clevedon: Multilingual Matters.

Yelenevskaya, Maria & Ekaterina Protassova. 2015. Global Russian: Between decline and revitalization. *Russian Journal of Communication* 7 (2), 139–149.

Zybatow, Gerhild. 2017. Auslandsvarietäten des Russischen. In Kai Witzlack-Makarevich & Nadja Wulff (eds.), *Handbuch des Russischen in Deutschland*: Migration – Mehrsprachigkeit – Spracherwerb, 261–281. Berlin: Frank & Timme.

Sofia Stratilaki-Klein
Chapter 7
The out-of-sight of "native speaker": A critical journey through models of social representations of plurilingual identities

Abstract: Contemporary educational systems, particularly in European societies, are faced nowadays with the challenge of coping with different forms of plurality. These various forms of plurality are important in many respects for young children entering school as they already have a complex experience of language forms und uses, even if this experience naturally differs from one child to another. Yet, these children, even without any prior knowledge of the language of schooling, know about the plurality of languages, they possess a somewhat rich and diversified linguistic repertoire that school and other instances of socialization have difficulties to support and, therefore, often choose to ignore or stigmatize, especially when it comes to the languages of "migrants". Establishing bridges between their first repertoire and the school language can only assist the process of inclusion of these young learners. In this chapter, we analyze the representations of plurilingualism of young children. The analysis confirms that their needs are specific and require an acknowledgement of singularities and pluralities in the school inclusion: singularities in the sense that each young newcomer has his own trajectory and history of migration, and pluralities because he/she has an experience of plurilingualism that the school cannot continue to ignore under the pretense of the native speaker model.

Keywords: plurilingual repertoire, social representations, identity, language biography, enunciative space

---

Acknowledgements: The present study was carried out by the author as part of the European PLINSCO research project (Plurilingualism and School Inclusion, project leader: Sofia Stratilaki-Klein, France/Luxembourg) and was co-funded by the European Social Fund (2017–2020). I am grateful to the children and parents that have graciously and generously shared with me their language experiences. I also thank the editors of this volume for their precious comments and constructive feedback.

Sofia Stratilaki-Klein, Université Sorbonne Nouvelle, DILTEC / Université du Luxembourg, e-mail: sofia.stratilaki@sorbonne-nouvelle.fr

https://doi.org/10.1515/9781501512353-008

1 Introduction

The linguistic opposition between "native" and "non-native" speaker can no longer be seen as clear-cut, but rather as a continuum expressing various linguistic trajectories and situations. But what does this mean in a globalised world? What are the social issues still at stake? How were they constructed? In other words, how do they belong both to the categories of common sense and to the "indigenous" categories of teaching/learning language(s)?[1] The ideological background of these constructs is a very distant one, historically speaking, and underlies that dichotomous divisions are convenient but simplifying labels. A brief review of the most relevant articles (Doerr 2009) shows that it is founded on the "native speaker myth" and received wisdom that monolingualism represents a general state, intended by God (ever since the construction of the tower of Babel, Genesis 11: 6–7) and/or politically legitimised by human beings.[2] By extension, this conception was also applied to the linguistic behaviour of bilingual people as a pluralisation of monolingualism (Pennycook 2010). Grosjean (1985: 467) defines language mode as "the state of activation of the bilingual's languages and language processing mechanisms at a certain point in time". In other words, the bilingual can be in a complete monolingual mode at one end of the continuum (when he/she is interacting with monolinguals) and in a bilingual language mode at the other end of the continuum (when communicating with bilinguals who share the two languages). Within this framework, individual plurilingualism is perceived as a challenge and "successful" plurilingualism would become rare or difficult to achieve.

Over the last decades, even though there is a considerable body of evidence (Dervin and Liddicoat 2013; Hall, Hellermann, and Pekarek-Doehler 2011; Hélot

---

[1] Franceschini (2001: 114) argues: "Languages are to be understood here as individual languages, which denote historically developed systems and are to be regarded as the production of the underlying linguistic ability of humans." She underlines (*op. cit.*) that: "the brain has no difficulty in absorbing more languages; if it does, the difficulties lie in the social circumstances in which languages are used and, in the ideologies, believed around languages".

[2] The term *native speaker* emerged in the Western world in the middle of the nineteenth century (Hackert 2013). It was understood as owning the language based on the territory from which one has been socialised and speaking it in a natural, authentic matter (see also Bonfiglio 2010; Muni Toke 2013). According to Bourdieu (1991, 2001), the term is deeply embedded in social representations and monolingual schemes or social habits about certain speech acts. Train (2009: 47) specifies: "as the Latin etymon *nativus* (from the verb 'to be born') suggests, the nativeness of language as something one is born with is closely tied to notions of naturalness and authenticity (related to *natura* and *naturalis*), as well as notions of belonging to a tribe, species, nation, etc. (*natio*)."

and Erfurt 2016; Mondada and Pekarek-Doehler 2004, among others) demonstrating that prior language knowledge is beneficial to the language learning process and that language contact between languages plays a very important and recognised role in language history as a source of creativity and enrichment (Weinreich 1953), "the ideologies and practices embodied in the Native Standard Speaker have continued to furnish educators and linguists with an implicit or explicit model for native competence in L1 as well as for ultimate attainment among non-native speakers or L2 learners" (Train 2009: 47; see also Franceschini and Miecznikowski 2004). Blommaert and Rampton (2011: 6) underline that "[a]lthough notions like 'native speaker', 'mother tongue' and 'ethnolinguistic group' have considerable ideological force (and as such should certainly feature as objects of analysis), they should have no place in the sociolinguistic toolkit itself". Despite differing views, the notions of identity, biography and belief[3] are particularly explored in the literature on plurilingualism, which concerns the school but also social situations. As Horwitz (1999: 562) suggests in her work on learners' beliefs about languages, "perhaps there is a world culture of language learning and teaching which encourages learners of many cultural backgrounds to perceive language learning very similarly". These beliefs concern not only languages but also the speakers of those languages. We also know that narratives play an important role in the negotiation of identities and "offer a way to impose an imaginary coherence on the experience of dispersal and fragmentation, which is the history of all enforced diasporas" (Hall 1990: 224). As Hall (1990: 225) points out, they are also inherently longitudinal: "the names we give to the different ways we are positioned by, and position ourselves within, the narratives of the past".

In this chapter, we try to understand why, even though we recognize the intrinsic link between languages and identities, the school continues reproducing social inequality by refusing to acknowledge the benefits of plurilingualism other than communicative skills in each language. From an epistemic point of view, the concept of communicative competence (Hymes 1962) is related to cultural anthropology. Hymes considered social function to be the source of linguistic form and so conceptualized language as context-embedded social action. He

---

3 According to Hymes (1991: 154–155) "Identity implies identification, a belief or a desire to be like that with which one identifies. One of the contributions of a sociolinguistics grounded in the problems and needs of individuals could well be to determine the extent to which the identifications they seek or assume are realized. Light shed only on individual competence would not suffice. It would also be necessary to know what value individuals attribute to the competences of other individuals. Locating what constitutes these group norms would be – is, in fact – essential for the orientation of learners and teachers of language."

coined the concept communicative competence to refer to the capacity to acquire and use language appropriately. Nonetheless, the dominant tendency in language teaching and learning has been to interpret it in (firmly) linguistic rather than cultural terms. As Young (2003) and others (He and Young 1998; Lüdi 2006; McNamara and Roever 2006) have noted, the various components of communicative competence have, by and large, been treated as static, cognitive properties of individuals, thereby rendering invisible their social foundations. Coste (1997: 90) explains this point of view in terms of the native speaker model, which prevails in educational systems in Europe: "communicative competence is then characterised as adding to the strictly linguistic competence sociolinguistics and pragmatic abilities, knowledge and dispositions of speakers who are implicitly assumed to be monolingual natives or who are at least regarded as operating in circumstances of endolingual communication (i.e. communication involving persons deemed to have a perfect, homogenous command of the resources of the medium used, namely their first language)".[4] Castellotti (2017: 132) writes: "The 'native', by virtue of his or her status as *indigenous* is in a way a linguistic expert of divine right, just as the aristocrats were noble by birth under the Ancien Régime: it is also his or her birth, and in particular the place of birth, that confers hereditary virtues on him or her (Detienne 2003)". Yet, in multilingual contexts, we argue that we cannot adopt a monolingual nor a purely bilingual conception of the relationship between first language and foreign language or language of schooling with regard to learners, since it often states a relationship of power between languages, interpreted generally by a greater proficiency in the first language. In contrast, communicative practices in multilingual settings rely on individual multilingualism. As research in conversation analysis has shown, there can also be shifts in time. The plural experience with languages can be then considered as a "capital" (see Bourdieu and Passeron 1970) that is unique for each speaker and that serves to represent his or her identity in a particular space-time line.

In our analysis, we propose to differentiate between three types of language identities: imposed identities (according to the monolingual perspective of the native speaker, that is not negotiable in terms of means of communication), assumed identities (according to the plurilingual perspective, that is the speaker is exposed to different linguistic variants and cultural variation in the course of his or her life) and negotiable identities (according to the capacity to perceive,

---

4 Coste (2004: 78) argues: "Describing a communication skill may have consisted in making an inventory of the communicational skills of a kind of idealized super-native, capable of managing with as much finesse as adequacy, both written and oral, diversified situations where speaking acts, covert and written scripts presuppose a particularly developed skill in language, textual genres, of uses in a social context."

observe and objectivise this multiplicity in his/her discourse, when circumstances permit it). Identity is therefore constructed in the speaker's ability to interpret the context, to adapt to it as required by playing locally with the linguistic-cultural resources at his or her disposal. Coste (1997: 91) argues that "while the knowledge of one foreign language and culture does not always lead to going beyond what may be ethnocentric in relation to the 'native' language and culture, and may even have the opposite effect, a knowledge of several languages is more likely to achieve this, while at the same time enriching the potential for learning". For instance, Bono (2011) showed in her research on third language acquisition how individuals acquire pragmatic competence by identifying different illocutionary values during the acquisition of a *non-native* language (for an overview see also Cenoz 2003). Furthermore, Bono supports (this volume) that we should not "underestimate the emotional toll, the feeling of tragic loss that can be felt by the impossible property of (a) language". These observations lead to the more general question that our paper addresses: Is the notion of native speaker a linguistic category or, more precisely, a social construction specific to the linguistic field of education?

Most studies on multilingualism argue that plurilingual identity is in perpetual dynamic of construction. We also know how much immigrant children are in search of academic and social success, without abandoning their language(s). The focus of this study is the school context in France. In fact, the children rely on school to maintain or amplify their bi-/plurilingualism by learning French, the sole language of schooling in France. The analysis attempts to demonstrate that all the discourses about "the native speaker expectations" that surround the socialisation of immigrants are constitutive of their representations as plurilingual speakers. In order to do so, we seek to establish whether the central position of French as school language is likely to change children's representations towards a monolingual or a plurilingual conception of their linguistic resources, i.e., a more or less dynamic conception of their plurilingual competence as a structured set of partial and unbalanced competences, diversely acquired and solicited in the learning process. To summarise the findings, we argue that it is essential to understand that the language biography of immigrant children is highly individualized, since it is related to their personal history, while being influenced by social/cultural practices in various historical contexts. As such, biography will be considered in terms of three complementary levels of analysis: biography as lived reality (the Socratic *bios*, i.e., the art of self-knowledge), biography as discourse and staging, and biography as learning process.

In Section 2, we briefly review the relevant literature and delineate a conceptual framework for the study of social representations of language identities by immigrant children. Most publications that will be mentioned in this chapter do not consider plurilingual identity in a static way. Depending on subjectivities, the shape of identity evolves, becomes enriched with new biographical components and leaves others to wither way. It is in this perspective also that the concept of individual experience in a language is meaningful, while considering these experiences to be permeable to social representations and language attitudes produced by the individuals who frequent them. Section 3 provides a description of the empirical study, including the educational context and methodology, the participants and the data as well as the analytical categories and tools that have been used. Section 4 is divided into three parts: social and personal identity, continuity and self-constancy, the need to be part of a group; they indicate that there are different ways of constructing one's identity, according to the pupils' backgrounds and the different educational and cultural traditions. Sections 5 and 6 provide further elements of discussion and sum up the results of the present study. The findings support that the plurilingual identity of an immigrant child is dynamic in that its' components are constructed in discourse and shared with social group members in specific communicative contexts, far beyond the static native speaker's competence.

2 Social representations and biographical stories: interpreting language identities

In Europe, in the late 1990s, interest in plurilingualism was emerging, in line with the work on interlanguage of learners (Corder 1981) and on the notion of social identity (Gumperz 1982). Cook's (1992) notion of multicompetence sought to describe a unique form of language competence that is not necessarily comparable to that of the native speaker. Cook defended the idea that bilingual speakers' knowledge of their L1 and L2 differs from that of monolingual speakers, and that bilinguals develop a different metalinguistic awareness compared to monolinguals. In the 2000s, notably with the publication of the *European Framework of Reference for Languages* (2001), the research on the concepts of translanguaging (Lewis, Jones, and Baker 2012) and plurilingual and pluricultural competence (Coste, Moore, and Zarate 1997; 2009) (both appearing almost at the same time – a curious coincidence?[5] – suggesting the valorisation of plurilingualism as an

---

5 Cf. *CEFR Companion volume with new descriptors* (Council of Europe 2017: 28).

individual proficiency of several languages to varying degrees), was popularized within the institutional and educational spheres.[6] It is an important paradigmatic shift as both concepts focus on the acquisition of languages through awareness and valorisation of multilingual practices. At the same time, the authors underline the decisive role of history, both individual and collective, in the development of language practices and skills. According to this perspective, the question is no longer to understand plurilingual competence as it is given once and for all, but as it is negotiable and as it can evolve in the very course of individual trajectory and learning process at school. This point of view endorses clearly the perspective of social actors and seeks to describe the way in which they make interpretable through their language practices the relevant features of their identity (see Moore and Gajo 2009, for an overview).

Social representations and practices of languages are well documented in the literature. Traditionally, the key themes, and perhaps the most common, include code-alternation, language choice and language crossing (Scotton 1983; Pavlenko 2001; Rampton 1995, among others). This current of work concentrates on the individual rather than the community as it seeks alternative paths for language education. Several models of interpretation have been published over the last thirty years depending on the perspectives adopted. Among the various approaches, the theoretical and experimental francophone work of Abric and Morin (1990), that of Flament (1981), Doise (1990), Guimelli (1994), and De Rosa (1988), based on the structuring of representations, are most often used as references. In sum, these authors propose to enrich the initial theoretical framework proposed by Moscovici (1984) by taking up the idea of the figurative nucleus (or model), a schematization of psychoanalytic theory which can be defined as "an assemblage of pictorial notions relating to the object and which can be conceived as the centre of gravity of any social representation" (Moliner 2001: 10). Moscovici (1984) shows how representations change when confronted with communication systems. Focusing on communication processes and forms of sociability within the community, he analyses the social character of representation and its determining role in the formation of the social image to be created or modified. In particular, the author shows that the formation of an image depends both on the *social* object that gives rise to it (for example, a social event or fact), on

---

6 Coste (2004: 78) underlines: "Whereas the notion of plurilingual competence implies different, dynamic and evolving profiles and where the native speaker, if it exists at all in canonical form, is only one case among others [. . .]. This shift in representation, if taken fully seriously, is perhaps the most important determinant of the plausible consequences, in the field of language teaching/learning, of the notion of plurilingual competence". (my translation).

the *individual* or group that expresses it (including elements of an affective, behavioural and emotional nature) as well as on the *interactions* that will lead to the construction of common knowledge. Social representations thus have a communication function and are themselves, at their origin, communications. They are born and develop in everyday conversations related to cultural and historical circumstances. According to his theory, the constituent elements of a reality are selected, categorized, and hierarchized in the representational system in such a way that determines both their meaning and their role at the process of interpretation. Afterwards, these various elements of information can be rearranged differently. This framework enables individuals to understand reality through their own system of references (Abric 1976). This framework of interpreting reality was adopted by other researchers. Several decades later, Ricoeur makes the dynamic aspect of representations as one of the defining elements of the human being by writing: "To be human is to be capable of transfer to another centre of perspective" (Ricoeur 1990: 251). Delory-Momberger (2005: 107) associates representations with the notion of "biographical capital", which she defines as: "a pool of available knowledge acquired through previous experiences and a system that constructs representations and the resulting knowledge".

At the same time, the idea of variation of the constituents of a representation appears: for certain themes, in certain contexts, there is a "mute zone" of the representation made up of peripheral elements that are not spontaneously verbalized by the subjects. It can be defined as a "specific subset of beliefs which, while available, are not expressed by the subjects under the normal conditions of discursive production [. . .] and which, if expressed, could call into question moral values or norms valued by the group" (Guimelli and Deschamps 2000: 48). This dynamic perspective on perception is consistent with the idea that some elements of the core may be "inactivated", "masked" or even mobilized only in certain situations (e.g., affective aspects such as emotions or feelings). From this perspective, social representations can be defined as "fundamental frameworks of reasoning" or "opinions" (Rouquette 1994) with a stable structure that can be presented in different ways depending on the circumstances, namely three elements: information, the field of knowledge and the attitudes of individuals towards the object of representation. The first of these elements is defined by the information available to individuals about the object of representation. This information becomes source for evaluating and judging the quality of social objects. Then, there is the hierarchization and organization of the information in a "field of knowledge", i.e., a structure that organizes, articulates, and ranks the elementary units of information among themselves. This organization varies according to each individual and the social, geographic or historical context. Finally, the attitudes of individuals towards the object of representation, whether favourable or unfavourable, play a decisive role in its creation (Stratilaki 2014; Stratilaki-Klein 2019). In this sense, representation becomes a mirror for interpreting social reality, while contributing to the development of its features through personal experiences.

Researchers in social sciences are interested in the process in which the individual as social actor understands an object, an opinion, an ideology, or a behaviour. Drawing on their findings, it is possible to study the discourse on languages in its communicative functions (Py 2000), construction of identity (Stratilaki 2011) or its impact upon attitudes (Blanchet 2018) and social relationships (Bourdieu 1982). Other studies, from a different perspective, have provided substantial theoretical support for the research on interaction as a means of elaborating skills and discourse strategies (Nussbaum 1999; Mondada 1998). By doing so, they opened promising paths as to how representations are intimately linked to learners' experiences, language practices and the "processes" of giving meaning into words (Byrd-Clark and Stratilaki 2013; Molinié 2015). Hence, one of the pedagogical goals in using forms of biographical narrative (through interviews, for example) and in encouraging learners to reflect on their plurilingual life, is to help them become conscious actors in their own learning process.

In order to describe the role of self-reflection in the learning process, Delory-Momberger (2013) uses the metaphor of the *walker in the landscape*. According to her theory, for the walker, the landscape exists only in the *temporal* unfolding of his walk; in other words, in the successive and cumulative perception of the points of view that he/she crosses as he/she goes along. In the same way, for the individual, the social world only becomes a reality in the temporal succession of his personal experiences. Thus, biographical research would have the task of understanding how the walker constructs the landscape; in other words, how the individual in the course of his/her experiences over time constructs himself/herself as a social actor. In our study, we argue that it is in the discourse that the individual is experiencing (again) the most important moments of his/her plurilingual identity. It is therefore essential to take into consideration the symbolic power that is endowed on languages so as to understand the language biography of a speaker. This symbolic power emanates from people's representations, but it is also clearly linked to their linguistic habitus. Indeed, language and words act as a kind of semantic Trojan Horse that conveys all sorts of attitudes, representations and values that are powerful. The native speaker paradigm is still used either as a linguistic category or as a social category and can influence the language identity of a speaker.

3 Context, data and methodology

The plurilingualism inherent in French society has long been rejected and fought against by the educational institution (Puren 2004). French, for mainly historical and political reasons, is a factor of social promotion, whereas the first language, spoken in the family, does not enjoy real social status (Spaëth 2008; Lahire 2012). French at school is at once the language of fundamental learning (literacy skills), the language of school communication (depending on the context and speakers) and the language of instruction. The newly arrived pupils are compelled to encounter a new language, on which the construction of their knowledge (as language of schooling) will be based. However, the question of school success in the French system is sometimes strictly a matter of linguistic competence, i.e., native speaker competence. Additionally, the languages of migration are linked to the social value attributed to them (Garcia and Kleyn 2016). And, as is well known, this value is not the same for all languages. These elements provide the grounds for understanding that it is not the same process as being multilingual in valued or stigmatized languages. But what about the characteristics of the situations concerned? Before going further, a note of caution needs to be made here: Our study does not attempt to change stereotypes on plurilingualism of immigrant children or expectations on native competence in the educational system. We acknowledge that they are part of our human way of translating our experience of the world into signs or words. We rather seek to make them overt, to confront them in order to better interpret or explain them.

In Paris, around 3,000 newcomer pupils are enrolled each year in more than 150 primary and secondary schools. In this multilingual context, we carried out a study entitled Plurilingualism and School Inclusion (2017–2020). The main objective of this study was to explore representations of the plurilingualism of allophone children and their families and to relate them to the representations and declared pedagogical practices of their teachers. We qualitatively analysed oral data collected during semi-directive audio-recorded interviews with pupils from 15 schools (a sample of 37 pupils), which were conducted in French and/or in the first languages of the participants. The interviews were transcribed and coded before analysis and were translated into French. In 2017, first, we interviewed the children, either in groups or individually. In the second stage, we conducted interviews with the children and their parents. In 2019, we interviewed only the children of the sample. The interview protocol (15 questions) dealt with biography, practices and language representations which can be divided into two main parts. The first part (questions 1–7) aimed to elicit information on children's beliefs about the advantages or disadvantages of multilingualism, teachers' perception of parents' and pupils' attitudes towards home language

maintenance, as well as teachers' classroom practices in relation to home language maintenance. The second part (questions 8–15) elicit different types of information such as children's biographical data (age, gender, years of schooling, ability to speak French and other languages) and teachers' and parents' interests towards languages. In particular, the main following questions were raised:
- What are the representations of children and their parents on issues related to bi-/plurilingual education?
- What are teachers' beliefs about the role of mother tongues, native competence, and prior language knowledge in language learning?
- How similar are teachers' beliefs across actors in educational system?
- How useful do children and parents perceive plurilingual competence and language knowledge to be?
- Do teachers' beliefs seem to inform and influence teaching practices?

The study is based on a sample of children (10–12 years old), who have been in France for a maximum of 18 months, which allows us to gather recent socialising experience as well as close language contact experiences. The interviews were conducted in 2017–2019, so as to see the changes of beliefs with regard to plurilingualism, for two years. In particular, we conducted semi-directive interviews crossing two dimensions, a synchronic study (i.e., the horizontal axis of temporality, which focuses on their plurilingualism at a given moment, this moment being situated to the beginning of their schooling in French) and a diachronic study (i.e., the vertical axis, which is constructed by their representations of plurilingualism and of the self in relations with others). The data has been transcribed entirely according to the transcription conventions commonly used in conversation analysis (see Pekarek-Doehler and Pochon-Berger 2011). Since the study is too complex for all aspects to be examined in this paper, we will leave some issues for future consideration. The qualitative analysis presented here focuses only on selected excerpts of a child/parent corpus. In our study, we found out that among some children and their parents, the rather positive representations of plurilingualism differ from the negative discourse of certain actors in the education system such as directors, principals or inspectors.

As in most European countries, schools in France have implemented specific classes for French as a Second or Foreign Language, called Teaching Units for Newly Arriving Allophone Pupils (henceforth, Upe2a).[7] This immersive type

---

[7] These structures have existed since the mid-1960s, officially 1970 for the first degree and 1973 for the second. Primary school facilities cater for children from 7 to 13 years of age, while secondary schools cater for children from 11 to 16 years of age.

of schooling in the French language (lasting one year, according to the Education Law 2012) is intended to prepare them for the common school curriculum and aims at rapid mastery of the language for everyday communication on the one hand, and for learning other school subjects on the other.[8] Allophone pupils thus build up their knowledge of French and continue to learn the other subjects, in Upe2a and in the ordinary classes, according to their school level, without exceeding an age gap of more than two years with the reference age corresponding to these classes. The choice of using the pupils' languages in the learning activities is left to the teacher's discretion. In practice, therefore, this can vary widely from one class to another, from one year to another, depending on the age, numbers and/or language level (in the first language) of the pupils, but also on the teachers and their conception of bi/plurilingual education. All the learners of our study (in total 37, as pointed out) attended the Teaching Units in 2017. We also interviewed 38 parents, 31 teachers in schools (elementary and secondary schools) in which pupils are enrolled (Upe2a and other subjects, including mathematics, biology, sport, Spanish), 10 directors (elementary school) and 5 principals (secondary school) of the same schools, as well as 10 primary school inspectors. The teachers are well aware that classrooms are rarely homogeneous, especially in terms of language and social background. However, this heterogeneity leaves them perplexed as to how to handle it: they are very often caught between curricula designed for native speakers of French and a much more complex pedagogical reality. In what follows, we consider French from the perspective of plurilingual education rather from the point of view of building knowledge as a native speaker which involves analysing representations of identities as a central component of language learning.

In order to better understand our data, we propose to the reader two complementary levels of analysis, individual and social. These two levels show, in our view, that speakers do not abstractly represent objects to themselves; on the contrary, they create enunciative spaces in which various enunciative positions are distinguished. Before going further to our analysis, let us define briefly what we mean by *enunciative space*. To address the individual aspect, we argue

---

[8] Education Law 2012: "The aim is that he [the allophone pupil] should be able to follow all the lessons in a class of the school curriculum as quickly as possible, with, if necessary, a more flexible support system. A pupil admitted to a UPE2A can therefore enter a class of the ordinary curriculum at any time of the year as soon as he or she has acquired a sufficient command of French, both orally and in writing, and as soon as he or she has become sufficiently familiar with the operating conditions and rules of life of the school or establishment".

in particular that each pupil has a story, his or her own story of migration, made up of personal experiences, socializations and identifications (imagined, attested or described) with values, languages, norms, models in which the subject recognizes himself or herself, and groups with which the subject interacts. In immigrant families, it is mainly different stories that meet, long before languages, and these histories are constitutive of the competence of the individual who knows how to adapt to a new situation. Beyond the individual level, we question the dynamics of the social level in our research, because the discourses on plurilingualism and learning languages are very socially charged. They create or even support social representations, stereotypes and attitudes that condition the relationship of individuals to their language(s), to the language(s) of their environment and to those of others. This discursive approach enables us to work both on the meaning that learners themselves give to plurilingualism in their private and public "zones" of socialisation (school and family) and on the meaning that actors in the education system give them according to their own opinions and values. Do the participants in our study share the same understanding of plurilingualism or are there essential differences? What kinds of identities are identifiable in the statements made by the participants?

The stories the pupils tell us about their multilingualism show a "gap" between family and school, between the languages that were already there from the first experiences of life and French. These narratives are based upon ordinary representations of French as the language of schooling and incorporate the idea of competition, risk, and shame. But the stories also show alternative ways, individual realities, or personal choices, as the excerpts in the analysis illustrate. We remind that the interviews take place at school, i.e., in a context that generates specific expectations of language practices. We argue that considering all languages is essential, insofar as learning and plurilingual identity will be largely invested in and determined by these languages. Learning in the specific classes of Upe2a can therefore only be a temporary solution in an immersive context for plurilingual learners who, like all the others, but in more difficult social conditions, must learn French in school in all its linguistic dimensions. In our analysis, we will show that the construction of plurilingual skills should be based both on the diversified repertoires that children have (conceived in a holistic manner and not only on forms or varieties recognized by the school) and on a dynamic and constant inclusive approach, as part of a common project of the school.

4 Analysis

4.1 Plurilingual identity: an individual and a social point of view

To account for the complexity of plurilingualism in Upe2a, we propose to describe the way in which this social reality is thought out and (re)presented by the actors themselves in the education system. Multiple models of plurilingualism emerge in the discourse, where they are put into words by the children, who accept them, refuse them or adjust them to their personal experiences. These identities mean that the child (or his or her parents) has (have) a different affective relationship with each language in its (their) repertoire, which essentially – though not exclusively – translates into a hierarchical architecture between languages. In other words, one language may, at a given time, become a priority and others a little less so. This is the case for French as the language of schooling. But languages are also unequal because their status are unequal within French society, both autonomous and juxtaposed like "nesting dolls", without the question of their relationship being addressed systematically. These sociolinguistic inequalities are among the major factors of "internal conflicts" linked to plurilingualism (Dahlet 2008). The plurilingual speaker classifies his or her languages into separate compartments, building up a competence in managing this repertoire to which all knowledge and experience of languages contributes and in which languages are correlated, in terms of use and appropriation.

Without further ado, let us read the following excerpts (A and B) from an interview with a child and his father.[9] The child lives with her parents, sisters, and brothers in France since 2016. She has been attending the school in France for the first time. Though they still find it hard to express themselves in phonological and syntactic forms in French, they succeed in making themselves understood. Four languages are spoken in the home on a continual basis, French, Creole, Hindi and English, with a complex pattern of relationships. Above all, however, we note that, beyond the knowledge of languages, it is the openness to variation that is shown in the discourse.

Excerpt A

P: No, it's over there too, same thing. Because there was the school. Over there, it's a bit less, if she comes to France, you speak French. For education, for living, you need French.

---

9 P = Parent, R = Researcher, C = Child. The interviews were conducted in French, then translated in English for this paper.

It's not Mauritius [. . .]. Creole, a little bit French, but now it's French because I went back to Mauritius, I haven't adapted Creole now, I speak French here.

R: Do you understand Mom's language, Hindi?

C: Yes.

R: And you speak it? Do you also talk a little bit? Or not at all?

C: No.

R: Do you just understand it?

C: Yes [. . .]. My brothers and sisters too, they just understand, but they don't talk.

R: The first language you use, in a natural, spontaneous way, like this, when you want to talk to mum, what is it, that comes to you?

C: Creole.

R: Is there a language that you like the most? Do you like Creole, French?

P: Preferred, English.

C: English.

R: English? [. . .] You've always preferred English, right? Since Mauritius, in fact (laughs)

P: French too, but no longer English.

R: Because in fact, since you learned both at the same time, there's one that you prefer, that's why?

C: Yes.

R: You're not afraid she's going to lose her language?

P: No no, it's Creole, it stays Creole all the time, English, it's French, it's Creole, it stayed Creole. [. . .] Creole is in the family, it's always there, the language, it's not forgotten, it's native.

What is in evidence here is the father's attempts to be seen, in Bourdieu's (1972) terms, as a "legitimate speaker", even though there can be tensions between languages, at particular points in time. In other words, one way of looking constructively at these tensions is to understand plurilingual competence as an organizing principle of identity. As a heuristic framework, plurilingual competence makes it possible to account for both the stability of the self and its fluidity, to combine past experience with the present and the future, by highlighting the specific (or singular) place of the self in social and symbolic relations with others. In order to achieve this balance, it seems to us that there is one essential condition: that speakers should be aware that the construction of a plurilingual competence, in its continuity and complexity, owes more to a biographical trajectory, where mobility can be found, than to a fixed origin, associated with "native" competence. The father communicates his feeling in the following words: "it's always there, the language, it's not forgotten, it's native". In our data, the child and his father recognize, each in her/his own way, their skills in several languages, while expressing their preferences according to time, needs and socialization spaces (school/family, here/elsewhere): English being the preferred language, French the language of the school and Creole the family language, with transitions from one to the other.

However, whether P is considered a legitimate speaker in the French society is somewhat unclear: he has not succeeded to gain access to a social network at work, as he changes jobs frequently. We insist here on the question of identity and the relationship to time and space. In particular, the father can present himself in different profiles (in the sense of "face" of Goffman 1973, 1974), as a monolingual, bilingual or plurilingual speaker; that is, he uses simply discourse strategies in order to explain or negotiate his representations of languages while maintaining a sense of continuity and self-consistency, as the following excerpt shows. We understand also that the fear of devaluation often leads P to perceive situations as power relations where one risks being put in a situation of inferiority and weakness. How this will affect his child exposure to and practice in Creole, the family language, has yet to be determined.

Excerpt B

P: There you go. In Mauritius there's different English, there's French, Creole, Hindus, Tamils, and everything / X / but you come to France, you only speak French, not like over there. Only, 100%, it's not . . . but still, she knows everything, French, speaking it, everything, it's good. English too, Creole is the same, everything. [. . .]. You can speak French or be multilingual, when you want, it depends [. . .] precisely, in the future, she may say to herself, because she lives here, she needs the French language. She needs to speak it as native language, to speak as a native person, as a person born here. If she is interested in English, that is fine with me.

These data seem to suggest also that, in a way, plurilingual competence refers to an *emic* conception of the plurilingual repertoire: its features are at the same time composite, distinct, in contact with each other and capable of being mobilized *in situ* for communicational and identity purposes. A plurilingual is someone who can play with the plurality and heterogeneity of his or her experiences to deal with diversity. As such, P recognizes the value of plurilingualism in everyday life. It is significant, however, that as P becomes more comfortable and confident with the language, he sees French as becoming his "native language". Without such competence, his daughter will have difficulty finding better working conditions. Consequently, for him, the key to participation to the French community (and to all that membership entails) is to speak the language "as a native person": as a native speaker, one can relate to his language from a position of strength rather than a position of weakness. It is for this reason that his daughter should speak "100%" French. In other words, P conceives languages as separate entities and seems to believe that native speaker essentially signifies monolingualism, i.e., acquiring a language competence only in French, even though a social actor may speak multiple languages from birth.

4.2 Continuity and self-constancy

The following excerpt from an interview with a boy and his father, in the same Parisian school, shows how the two speakers negotiate, in and through discourse, the value of languages and how they seek to go beyond these identity conflicts to feel comfortable with their repertoire. In this excerpt, the 12-year-old child is from Afghanistan and lives alone with his father. At the time of the interview (March 2017), he has been attending school for 4 months in Upe2a. Let's read carefully the father's answers first:

> **Excerpt C**
>
> C: She says that in your heart, what is the language you love the most, your own language?
>
> P: In my heart there is French, because I live here.
>
> C: I told you your own language!
>
> P: My own language is my mother tongue. And I love French.
>
> C: You love it, but which one do you love the most?
>
> P: But I love it very much.
>
> C: Pashto.
>
> P: But Pashto is my own language, my mother tongue.

C: That's what she says. Don't you prefer Pashto?

P: Pashto is my mother tongue. Whether I like it or not is another question. But I like both, Pashto and French.

C: We're not in Afghanistan here.

P: I like both, French and Pashto.

C: Why do you like French? That's what they said, tell them, we don't talk about need.

P: I like French, because here . . .

C: It's easy

P: Yes, it's easy and there's another thing, I like the country, that's why I came. I like the country; I like the language and I like the people.

R: [. . .] do you afraid that he will speak only French?

P: yes, but it is a necessary evil so that he can stay here

The father came with his son to France, because he wanted a better life for his child. He had a quite different lifestyle in his home country. Before starting the interview, he stresses the fact that he was an educated person who had taught for many years. When asked to explain, he says that he strongly encourages his son to learn French, so that he can be integrated into the French society. Indeed, he sees Pashto as an essential link to the past, but not to the future. There are moments, however, when he expresses during the interview his concern that his son seems to be forgetting his "mother tongue", saying "a necessary evil so that he can stay here".

During the interview, the child speaks with his father in his mother tongue and then translates the exchanges into French. We notice his fluency and his motivation for the acquisition of this language. During the interaction, the child repeats and develops his ideas, adding significant information. In addition to Pashto, Farsi is part of his plurilingual repertoire (language spoken in his home country), but with different emotional ties and levels of proficiency. In school, he mainly uses French with his classmates and teachers, his school inclusion (conditioned by learning French) now becomes his main objective. English helps him to understand certain instructions, as part of his plurilingual repertoire. Moreover, the other two languages are never used in learning or school interactions. Despite this lack of awareness of plurilingualism on the part of the school, the pupil recognizes himself as a plurilingual speaker and is not afraid to forget his first tongue. He explained this in the interview with me:

Excerpt D

C: I am from Afghanistan.

R: That's right. So, at home everyone speaks Pashto?

C: There are only two of us at home.

R: Oh right. There you go. And have you ever learned another language before, have you ever been to school in Afghanistan?

C: Yes, I learned Farsi, that's a language of Afghanistan too.

R: Farsi, do you learn to read and write Farsi at school?

C: No, not all that, I can read a little, speak a little. [. . .]

P: Pashto and Farsi.

R: Have you started English?

C: But then I forgot. I'm talking with Mrs. X in English.

R: So now, it's ok, you're going to take English again.

C: Yes.

R: And French, when did you start learning it? When you arrived here, or did you start before?

C: When I arrived here.

R: Hat (laughs) [. . .] You speak like a French speaker.

C: Yes, before, I didn't speak French, it's been 3–4 months since I learned. [. . .]

C: With my classmates, at school, and talk, talk, talk, and whatever, well, that's how I learned.

R: And listening and writing French, is it difficult for you?

C: Dictation, writing, but that's a bit difficult for me. [. . .]

C: Yes, I much prefer French.

R: Because it's easier?

C: Yes. No. That's not it. It's harder than English, but [. . .] But still, I like it [. . .].

C: I like both languages. English and French. Yes, but English (sighs) . . .

R: A little less?

C: Yes.

R: What about Pashto in there?

C: Pashto is my favourite language. [. . .]

C: I speak a little English, a little French, Pashto and Farsi.

R: So, it's like dad, you'd be multilingual?

C: Yes, and I am very proud of it

4.3 The need to be part of a group: the balance of power and domination

In December 2018, we spoke again with the same pupil, to see if his representations had changed. The pupil is now enrolled in an ordinary class in the same school, with 2 hours/week of support in French given by the Upe2a teacher. He continues to speak Pashto with his father, as the rest of his family is still in Afghanistan. He remains attached to his mother tongue, as it is the language he has spoken "since he was a child", but he now ranks his languages according to their proficiency, recognizing especially his fluency in French. He's a motivated pupil, willing to succeed, who implicitly uses his or her plurilingual skills to understand difficult words in French. Not wishing to be categorised as a "bad pupil", he is ashamed to ask questions in front of his classmates. In physics, he has more difficulties in understanding instructions than in learning the discipline. He also values his knowledge of English, which he identifies as the language of work. During the interview, he compares the languages, their similarities and differences, apart from his "native tongue", which is for him a language apart (both emotionally and linguistically) by declaring:

Excerpt E

E: it doesn't help me, because it's different, then there are the other languages, it can help, but when I speak Pashto, it's not at all the same, there are no words, there's nothing, I don't know, I don't necessarily need to have my mother tongue [. . .]. I don't need to use it, it's my native tongue, because I am native speaker: I know it perfectly, but it doesn't help me. But French can help me learn Spanish, not necessarily German, but Spanish, in words, there are a lot of words, Spanish and French are a little bit the same. If the word is half French, half Spanish, I will understand directly what it means.

He wants to enrich his plurilingual repertoire by learning German. Even though he expresses his desire to return to his country to see his mother, he now realizes that he will stay in France. As for his plurilingual identity, he assumes it positively by declaring that he is "proud" of it. As he says in the following except:

Excerpt F

R: I show you three pictures. Which image best suits you?

C: The image where there are more than three languages.

R: Why did you choose this image?

C: If I can speak all these languages at the same level, that's great. As N said, if we go to a country we won't be blocked, or when we talk with someone who came to France, for example, and he doesn't know how to say something, I can help him. But even if I don't speak them very well, all languages perfectly, I can manage. I'm pretty much like a native speaker, except in two languages, French and English, I don't have the same level, the others, I know them, I speak them perfectly [. . .]. I do, in fact, see myself as plurilingual, because I speak several languages.

R: Are you proud to be one?

C: Yes, very proud.

The last sentence is highly significant. It depicts very clearly that a learner's identity is not only constructed by social interaction but is also constitutive of social interaction. Further, the corpus shows that the child had already begun to understand the world in his first language, when he arrived in France. As such, the language (or the languages) in which he has learned to speak/think is part of his linguistic identity, an identity that is not definitive and at the same time plural and in its initial state. It is then better to take these languages and their specificities (in terms of practices, affectivity, or functions) into account as constitutive of the child's identity and language biography instead of ignoring them, especially in primary school when it comes to young pupils.

In order to gain greater insight into the data, we questioned teachers in traditional classes about plural pedagogical practices. For, in our opinion, the school as the bearer of values, norms and rules structures the perception, feelings and behaviour of its pupils. Even if all teachers unanimously admit, in a politically correct manner, the social usefulness of plurilingualism, their pedagogy is more a matter of monolingual teaching, with (other) languages being ignored or never explicitly mobilized as resources in learning. These languages remain "outside the walls" of the school. In our corpus, discourses on plural practices consisting of activities comparing other languages with French are mainly held by Upe2a teachers. At least for these teachers, plurilingualism is a learning tool, a resource for managing heterogeneity, a starting point for reflection on French as a language of schooling. However, they sometimes find it difficult to make the inclusion of allophone pupils a real project for all those involved in the school, especially as certain negative representations of plurilingualism (involving minority languages) persist. In "regular" classes, allophone pupils are aware of the centrality of French because it is clearly seen as synonymous with academic and social success. In essence, teachers do not distinguish between the plurilingual allophone pupil and the monolingual francophone native speaker with learning difficulties. The language market leads them to believe that an allophone pupil is *de facto* disadvantaged by his or her L1 (especially with regard to the languages of immigration). In our corpus, the national education inspectors refer to the difficulties of these pupils as "social problems", as if the school were not part of society. And this representation, as perceived by the pupils, reinforces their insecurity (identity, language or status of L1). In class, they do not dare to ask for help; they are ashamed to assume their plurilingual and pluricultural background, especially if they are newcomers. In other words, they will seek to conceal anything that might make them look inferior (a different accent in French, for instance, which sometimes render immigrants voiceless and invisible). The result is a form of discouragement for some. Others, like our participant continue their efforts for success, although their plurilingual repertoire is often neglected or (temporarily) set aside in favour of the school language. Immigrant families believe that only time, hard work and courage will make a difference in their lives. Given this position, they are often bewildered when confronted with evidence that seemed to confirm the significance of the *native speaker competence* at French school. In sum, teachers nowadays seem more receptive to language variation. However, our study shows that, despite the Upe2a classes for newly arrived pupils, despite numerous studies on educational inequalities in France, despite the consensus on the benefits of L1 in the appropriation of knowledge, representations of plurilingualism and teaching practices are slowly evolving; in any case, too slowly to aim at real inclusion and recognition of linguistic and educational otherness in the classroom.

5 Discussion

Language is an essential element in an officially monolingual nation/state. The "native" speaker appears as an obvious argument of quality, a guarantee of success in learning at school since the beginning of the development of modern language teaching. Nevertheless, the French education system is faced nowadays with the challenge of coping with different forms of plurality (plurality of cultural and language references, in terms of values and principles, etc.). These various forms of plurality are important in many respects for young children entering school (especially when the main language of schooling is not their first language) as they already have a complex experience of language forms und uses, even if this experience naturally differs from one child to another. Yet, these children, even without any prior knowledge of the language of schooling, know about the plurality of languages, they possess a somewhat rich and diversified linguistic repertoire that school and other instances of socialization have difficulties to support and, therefore, often choose to ignore or stigmatize, especially when it comes to the languages of immigrants. Establishing bridges between their first repertoire and the school language and acknowledging the transversalities of spaces of socialization can only assist the process of school inclusion of these young learners. The qualitative analysis in Section 4 confirms that their needs are specific and require an acknowledgement of singularities and pluralities in the school inclusion: singularities in the sense that each young newcomer has his or her own trajectory and history of migration, and pluralities because he or she has an experience of plurilingual and pluricultural competence that the school cannot continue to ignore. In our study, two main characteristics emerge from the set of narratives:

Firstly, despite the evolution of the sociolinguistic situation and that of the school public that characterizes France today, teachers and pupils continue to be shaped by the monolingual ideology of the native speaker as it still manifests itself in the hexagonal educational system. As a result, teachers consider their pupils' languages only within the limited framework of informal interactions outside the classroom. Pupils try to conform to the dominant monolingual ideology, so as not to appear different or be ashamed in front of their classmates; they are often reluctant to use their (first) languages at school, in the presence of their teacher. Allophone pupils thus spontaneously place themselves in a situation in which French is the only language admitted at school and the dominant language of communication. Their narratives extend along a continuum from total indifference to the fierce desire to find their own plurilingual identity, without ever evoking a possible challenge to school's native speaker model.

The stakes of language learning, at their level, seem rather practical: to be integrated/accepted into the French school.

Secondly, we argue that language biographies and the spaces in which they unfold and relate should be taken into account in their variability. In our perspective, the question of time is to be thought of from the point of view of the pupils' histories, mobility, and social experiences. In fact, our data show that there is no one right way to learn, once and for all. The approaches vary according to learners' backgrounds and educational traditions. As Morin and Le Moigne (1999: 145) point out, "the importance of the choice of attitude shows that what is at stake is the way we look at otherness and the world". This includes also considering the emotional dimension of learning. For instance, one of the problems often mentioned in pupils' discourse is language insecurity. This derives from the teaching of French, which generally aims at learning the language as perfect as possible, according to France's monolingual political and ideological choices. At school, the learning of French as a second or foreign language is essentially aimed at reproducing the same exact process as it is supposed to be constructed for the acquisition of a first language in a monolingual school environment.

From our perspective, the explicit reflexive dimension, combined with pluralistic approach activities, encourages children to question their beliefs of language norms, as well as their ability to accept others, their language(s), values, and culture. As we know, language is an affective and symbolic mediator that participates in the construction of identity. If teachers devalue home languages, because they are minority languages, as is the case for most allophone children, they thus bring the children to integrate this perspective into their attitudes at school. In other words, tensions and conflicts between languages and identities result primarily from social representations. Embracing the plurilingualism of allophone pupils goes beyond teaching French as language of schooling: it also means diversifying the notion of native speaker when taking pedagogical decisions for plurilingual learners, without which it is, from our point of view, not possible to make identities and lived experiences of the language learner an integral part of classroom practice.

6 Conclusion

We show that Norton's (2013) notion of identity is essential in this study. It is understood mainly as "discursively constructed" and always socially and historically embedded. It is good to remember that plurilingual competence is not matter of "birth privilege and social class", as suggested by the notion of native speaker. If the fact of identifying where one comes from is indeed important in order to situate oneself in this encounter, but it is not so much from one's origin as from one's experience and history that one builds the relationship. In the narratives, a space of in-between in the construction of the plurilingual identity emerges: the school imposes by its standards a monolingual identity. The child can accept this position or negotiate his or her own identity, without total adherence to the monolingual model of the school or to his or her parents' background.

The data show also that it is not oral communication that represents the major obstacle to success for an allophone learner. All pupils were able to express themselves in our interviews. The acquisition of oral skills is greatly facilitated by the context in which the child is immersed and the difficulties at this level are, after a few months at school, of the same nature as those experienced by natives in a school system that most often neglects systematic work on oral communication. The main obstacle is gaining access to literacy, which represents the base for the acquisition of all subjects in the French school curriculum. And acquiring this skill takes time. Consequently, the schooling of allophone pupils is part of a longitudinal process, i.e., it consists of giving them the means to succeed by considering their language skills and previous experiences. Unfortunately, knowledge acquired outside school, and prior to schooling in France, is often ignored by teachers.

In a multilingual context, as is the school in France today, it seems essential to us to consider all the languages/cultures present for the following reasons:
- because they can be used to learn French and improve skills: language awareness activities, for example, facilitate the appropriation of a language in all its dimensions and variations. The learner pays attention on meaning, while at the same time gains access to form by specifying French in relation to other languages, developing a metalinguistic competence.
- because the general approach of comparing languages is based on the linguistic knowledge already existing in other languages: the extensive knowledge that pupils have of languages makes it possible to develop multilingual resources for the classroom and support intercultural teaching.
- because the knowledge acquired by allophone pupils contributes to the positive construction of their plurilingual identity: the interest shown in the languages of these pupils is more in keeping with their role as languages of communication and culture.
- because this approach guarantees success at school: in the process of learning other languages, oral and written comprehension activities are intricately

linked to the curricula (phonology, oral language, grammar), thus improving learning, in general.

By valuing the plurilingual and pluricultural competences of pupils and their families, these approaches place biography at the heart of learning; and thus become effective factors for the successful learning of French for *all* pupils in the classroom.

Author's Positionality

Sofia Stratilaki-Klein. I was born in Northern Greece, my grandparents were Greek immigrants of Smyrna, and, like any self-respecting Greek, languages came into my life relatively early, all of them learned formally. When I look back on the languages I studied today, I realise that their learning is still confined to the possibility of an encounter with an Other that I found difficult to imagine at the time. It was in Denmark, in Germany, in France, and more recently in Luxembourg that this fictitious, illusory – and sometimes even caricatured – image gave way to an Other with plural faces, experiences and paths. Since languages and cultures are inseparable from societies, it would seem legitimate to consider them as resources to a more (personal and social) human contact, knowing that cultural and linguistic diversity allows us to be as close as possible to people. In my research, I am interested in language biographies, discourses and life stories of plurilingual actors, because their power to turn back time leads to reflexivity, awareness of certain causalities and sometimes even to transformation. This awareness depends, in my opinion, on the educational cultures and values transmitted to our students and shared with our colleagues.

In Luxembourg, I work on a daily basis with transcultural, intercultural, out-of-school and life-long education concepts that germinated in me as a child and that have shaped my adult life. They allow me to mix erudition and intimacy, collective history and personal past, just like the two knitting needles, needing them both to expose what our relationship to the mother tongue says about us. After spending half of my life abroad, my mother tongue, Greek, has not become foreign. With humor, I encounter the prejudice that "one can only write an original work in one's native language". Which one, may I ask? I decided to learn a third language, French, to take stock of, and destabilize, the two poles of my linguistic balance, Greek and English. I didn't know, for instance, that the French language could make me laugh; French suddenly seemed very close to me because a language that makes you laugh stops being a foreign language. However, the social gaze of this prestigious language had made me forget a part of my plurilingual history. As Vassilis Alexakis wrote in *Paris-Athènes*: "We are delighted that French conquers foreigners, but we are not at all convinced that they can in turn conquer the language. They are considered more as representatives of another culture, ambassadors of a beyond, than as original creators, authors in their own right". I am wondering how is it possible to choose between the language of memory and that of the present, since the life of a researcher in human sciences requires a combination (at least minimal) of the two? My decision to live and teach in Luxembourg is to be seen as a desire to return "to the heart of myself", without denying to a certain linguistic realism. And I do hope that this enthousiasm would last forever.

References

Abric, Jean-Claude & Karren Morin. 1990. Recherches psychosociales sur la mobilité urbaine et voyages interurbaines. *Cahiers internationaux de psychologie sociale* 5, 11–35.
Abric, Jean-Claude. 1976. *Jeux, conflits et représentations sociales*. Thèse de Doctorat d'État. Aix-en-Provence: Université de Provence.
Blanchet, Philippe. 2018. Entre droits linguistiques et glottophobie. Analyse d'une discrimination instituée dans la société française. *Les Cahiers de la lutte contre les discriminations* (L'Harmattan) 7(2), 27–43. DOI: 10.3917/clcd.007.0027
Blommaert, Jan. & Rampton, Ben. 2011. Language and superdiversity: A position paper. *Diversities* 13(2). https://newdiversities.mmg.mpg.de/fileadmin/user_upload/2011_13-02_art1.pdf (accessed 22 December 2020).
Bonfiglio, Thomas. 2010. *Mother tongues and nations: The invention of the native speaker*, Berlin & New York: Mouton De Gruyter.
Bono, Mariana. 2011. Crosslinguistic interaction and metalinguistic awareness in third language acquisition. In Gessica De Angelis & Jean-Marc Dewaele (eds.), *New trends in crosslinguistic influence and multilingualism research*, 25–52. Bristol: Multilingual Matters.
Bourdieu, Pierre & Passeron, Jean-Claude. 1970. *Reproduction. Éléments pour une théorie du système d'enseignement*. Paris: Editions de Minuit.
Bourdieu, Pierre. 1972. *Esquisse d'une théorie de la pratique*. Genève: Droz.
Bourdieu, Pierre. 1982. *Ce que parler veut dire. L'économie des échanges linguistiques*. Paris: Fayard.
Bourdieu, Pierre. 2001 [1991]. *Langage et pouvoir symbolique*. Paris: Essais.
Byrd-Clark, Julie & Sofia Stratilaki. 2013. Complex and symbolic discursive encounters for intercultural education in plurilingual times. In Fred Dervin & Anthony Liddicoat (eds.), *Linguistics for intercultural education.*, 175–197. Philadelphia: John Benjamins Publishing.
Castellotti, Veronique. 2017. *Pour une didactique de l'appropriation. Diversité, compréhension, relation*. Paris: Didier.
Council of Europe, 2017. *CEFR. Companion volume with new descriptors*. Strasbourg: Council of Europe.
Cenoz, Jasone. 2003. The additive effect of bilingualism in third language acquisition: A review. *International Journal of Bilingualism* 7(1), 71–87.
Circulaire no 2012-141, 2 octobre 2012, Organisation de la scolarité des élèves allophones nouvellement arrivés. *Bulletin officiel* 37, 11-10-2012. http://www.education.gouv.fr/pid285/bulletin_officiel.html?cid_bo=61536 (accessed 10 December 2020).
Cook, Vivian. 1992. Evidence for multi-competence. *Language Learning* 42, 557–591.
Corder, Pit. 1981. *Error Analysis and nterlanguage*. Oxford: Oxford University Press.
Coste, Daniel. 2004. De quelques déplacements opérés en didactique des langues par la notion de compétence plurilingue. In Antoine Auchlin, Marcel Burger, Laurent Filliettaz, Anen Grobet, Jacques Moeschler, Laurent Perrin, Corinne Rossari & Louis de Saussure (eds.), *Structures et discours. Mélanges offerts à Eddy Roulet.* 67–85. Laval: Éditions Nota bene.
Coste, Daniel. 1997. Multilingual and multicultural competence and the role of school. *Language Teaching* 30(2), 90–93. doi:10.1017/S0261444800012817.

Coste, Daniel, Danielle Moore, & Geneviène Zarate. 1997. [1998] [Trad. 2009]. *Compétence plurilingue et pluriculturelle*. Strasbourg: Conseil de l'Europe.

Dahlet, Patrick. 2008. Les identités plurilingues: enjeux globaux et partages singuliers. In Pierre Martinez, Danièle Moore & Valérie Spaeth (eds.), *Plurilinguismes et enseignement. Identités en construction*. 23–45. Paris: Riveneuve.

De Rosa, Annamaria. 1988. Sur l'usage des associations libres dans l'étude des représentations sociales de la maladie mentale. *Connexions* 51, 28–50.

Delory-Momberger, Christine. 2013. Recherche biographique et récit de soi dans la modernité avancée. In Christophe Niewiadomski & Christine Delory-Momberger (eds.), *La mise en récit de soi*. 41–52. Paris: Septentrion.

Delory-Momberger, Christine. 2005. *Histoire de vie et Recherche biographique en éducation*. Paris: Anthropos.

Dervin, Fred & Anthony Liddicoat (eds.), 2013. *Linguistics for Intercultural Education*. Philadelphia: John Benjamins.

Detienne, Marcel. 2003. *Comment être autochtone. Du pur Athénien au Français raciné*. Paris: Le Seuil.

Doerr, Neriko Musha. (ed.). 2009. *The native speaker concept. Ethnographic investigations of native speaker effects*. Berlin: De Gruyter Mouton.

Doise, Willem. 1990. Les représentations sociales. In Rodolphe Ghiglione, Claude Bonnet, Jean-François Richard (eds.), *Traité de psychologie cognitive*, Tome 3, Cognition, représentation, communication. 111–174. Paris: Dunod.

Education Law 2012. *Circulaire n° 2012-142 du 2-10-2012: Scolarisation et scolarité des enfants issus de familles itinérantes et de voyageurs*. https://www.education.gouv.fr/bo/12/Hebdo37/MENE1234231C.htm (accessed 10 December 2020).

Flament, Claude. 1981. L'analyse de similitude: une technique pour les recherches sur les représentations sociales. *Cahiers de Psychologie Cognitive* 4, 357–396.

Franceschini, Rita. 2001. Sprachbiographien randständiger Sprecher. In Rita Franceschini (eds.), *Biographie und Interkulturalität. Diskurs und Lebenspraxis*. 11–125. Tübingen: Stauffenburg.

Franceschini, Rita & Miecznikowski, Johanna (eds.), 2004. *Leben mit mehreren Sprachen*. Berne: Peter Lang.

García, Ofelia & Tatyana Kleyn. 2016. *Translanguaging with multilingual students*. New York: Routledge.

Goffman, Erwing. 1973. *La mise en scène de la vie quotidienne*. Tomes I et II. Paris: Minuit.

Goffman, Erwing. 1974. *Les rites d'interaction*. Paris: Minuit.

Grosjean, Francois. 1985. The bilingual as a competent but specific speaker-hearer. *Journal of Multilingual and Multicultural Development* 6, 467–477.

Guimelli, Carmel & Jean-Claude Deschamps. 2000. Effets de contexte sur la production d'associations verbales: le cas des représentations sociales des Gitans. *Cahiers Internationaux de Psychologie Sociale* 47–48(3–4), 44–54.

Guimelli, Carmel (eds.), 1994. *Structures et transformations des représentations sociales*. Neuchâtel: Delachaux & Niestlé.

Gumperz, John. (eds.), 1982. *Language and social identity*. Cambridge: Cambridge University Press.

Hackert, Stephanie. 2013. *The Emergence of the English native speaker. Chapter in nineteenth-century linguistic thought*. Berlin: De Gruyter Mouton.

Hall, Joan Kelly, John Hellermann & Simone Pekarek-Doehler (eds.), 2011. *L2 Interactional Competence and Development*. Bristol: Multilingual Matters.
Hall, Stuart. 1990. Cultural identity and diaspora. In Jonathan Rutherford (ed.), *Identity, community, culture, difference*, 222–237. London: Lawrence and Wishart.
He, Agnes Weiyum & Richard Young. 1998. Language proficiency interviews: A discourse approach. In Richard Young & Agnes Weiyum He (eds.), *Talking and testing. Discourse approaches to the assessment of oral proficiency*, 1–24. Amsterdam: John Benjamins.
Hélot, Christine & Jürgen Erfurt (eds.), 2016. *L'éducation bilingue en France. Politiques linguistiques, modèles et pratiques*. Paris: Lambert-Lucas.
Horwitz, Elaine. 1999. Cultural and situational differences on foreign language learners' beliefs about language learning. A review of BALLI studies. *System* 27, 557–576.
Hymes, Dell. 1962. The ethnography of speaking. In Thomas Gladwin & William Sturtevant (eds.), *Anthropology and human behaviour*, 13–53. Washington: Anthropological Society of Washington.
Hymes, Dell. 1972. On communicative competence. In John Pride & Janet Holmes (eds.), *Sociolinguistics. Selected Readings*. [Reprint], 269–293. Harmondsworth: Penguin Modern Linguistics Readings.
Hymes, Dell. 1991. *Vers la compétence de communication*. Paris: Hatier.
Lahire, Bernard. 2012. *Monde pluriel. Penser l'unité des sciences sociales*. Paris: Seuil.
Lewis, Gwyn, Bryn Jones & Colin Baker. 2012. Translanguaging: Origins and Development from School to Street and Beyond. *Educational Research and Evaluation* 18 (7), 641–654.
Lüdi, Georges. 2006. De la compétence linguistique au répertoire plurilingue. Bulletin *VALS-ASLA* 84, 172–189.
McNamara, Tim & Carsten Roever. 2006. *Language Testing. The social dimension*. Malden, MA: Blackwell.
Moliner, Pierre. (ed.). 2001. *La dynamique des représentations sociales*. Grenoble: P.U.G.
Molinié, Muriel. 2015. *Recherche biographique en contexte plurilingue. Cartographie d'un parcours de didacticienne*. Paris: Riveneuve Editions.
Mondada, Lorenza. 1998. De l'analyse des représentations à l'analyse des activités descriptives en contexte. *Cahiers de praxématique* 31, 127–148.
Mondada, Lorenza & Simona Pekarek-Doehler. 2004. Second language acquisition as situated practice. *The Modern Language Journal* 88, 501–518.
Morin, Edgar & Jean-Louis Le Moigne. 1999. *L'intelligence de la complexité*. Paris: L'Harmattan.
Moore, Daniele & Laurent Gajo. 2009. Introduction – French voices on plurilingualism and pluriculturalism: theory, significance and perspectives. *International Journal of Multilingualism* 6(2), 137–153.
Moscovici, Serge. 1984. *Psychologie sociale*. Paris: P.U.F.
Muni Toke, Valelia. 2013. Le locuteur natif et son idéalisation: un demi-siècle de critiques. *Histoire Épistémologie Langage* 35(2), 5–15.
Norton, Bonny. 2013. *Identity and Language learning*. Bristol: Multilingual Matters.
Nussbaum, Lucie. 1999. Emergence de la conscience langagière en travail de groupe entre apprenants de langue étrangère. *Langages* 134, 35–50.
Pavlenko, Aneta. 2001. In the world of the tradition I was unimagined: Negotiation of identities in cross-cultural autobiographies. *International Journal of Bilingualism* 5(3), 317–344.
Pekarek-Doehler, Simona & Evelyne Pochon-Berger. 2011. Developing methods for interaction: A cross-sectional study of disagreement sequences in French L2. In Joan Kelly Hall, John

Hellermann & Simona Pekarek-Doehler (eds.), *L2 Interactional competence and development*. 206–243. Bristol: Multilingual Matters.

Pennycook, Alastair. 2010. *Language as a social practice*. New York: Routledge.

Puren, Laurent. 2004. *L'école française face à l'enfant alloglotte. Contribution à une étude des politiques linguistiques éducatives mises en œuvre à l'égard des minorités linguistiques scolarisées dans le système éducatif français du XIXe siècle à nos jours*. Thèse de doctorat sous la direction de Daniel Véronique. Université Sorbonne Nouvelle.

Py, Bernard. 2000. Représentations sociales et discours. Questions épistémologiques et méthodologiques. *TRANEL* 32, 5–20.

Rampton, Ben. 1995. *Crossing: Language and ethnicity among adolescents*. London: Longman.

Ricœur, Paul. 1990. *Soi-même comme un autre*. Paris: Seuil.

Rouquette, Michel-Louis. 1994. *Chaînes magiques. Les maillons de l'appartenance*. Neuchâtel: Delachaux & Niestlé.

Scotton, Carol. 1983. The negociation of identities in conversation: A theory of markedness and code choice. *Journal of the Sociology of Language* 44, 115–136.

Spaëth, Valérie. 2008. Le français "langue de scolarisation" et les disciplines scolaires. In Jean-Louis Chiss (eds.), *Immigration, école et didactique du français*, 62–100. Paris: Didier.

Stratilaki, Sofia. 2011. *Discours et représentations du plurilinguisme*. Francfort/Main: Peter Lang.

Stratilaki, Sofia. 2014. Discourse, representation and language practices: Negotiating plurilingual identities and spaces. In Patrick Grommes & Adelheid Hu (eds.), *Plurilingual education*. Philadelphia: John Benjamins Publishing, 139–160.

Stratilaki-Klein, Sofia. 2019. Distance vs proximité: le Luxembourg, un pays aux frontières des langues. In Mariella Causa & Sofia Stratilaki-Klein (eds.), *Distance(s) et didactique des langues. L'exemple de l'enseignement bilingue*, 75–105. Bruxelles: EME Editions.

Train, Robert. 2009. Toward a natural history of the native (standard speaker). In Neriko Musha Doerr (ed.), *The native speaker concept. Ethnographic investigations of native speaker effects*. 47–79. Berlin: De Gruyter Mouton.

Weinreich, Uriel. 1953. *Languages in contact, findings and problems*. New York.

Young, Richard. 2003. Learning to talk the talk and walk the walk. Interactional competence in academic spoken English. *North Eastern Illinois University Working Papers in Linguistics* 2, 26–44.

Sílvia Melo-Pfeifer

Chapter 8
Practice-proof concepts? Rethinking linguistic borders and families in multilingual communication: Exploiting the relationship between intercomprehension and translanguaging

Abstract: This contribution analyses intercomprehension practices in multilingual chat interactions. The aim is to challenge the concept of "native speakers" of a Romance Language (RL) in the literature on Intercomprehension (usually expressed through phrases such as "to speak their [own] language" or "French speakers that understand Italian speakers") in order to accommodate multilingual repertoires (reference to and use of complex linguistic constellations). This conceptual development involves likening "intercomprehension" to the concept of "translanguaging". Furthermore, the text presents chat sequences where multilingual participants discuss "linguistic borders" and "linguistic familiarity", showing that even when individuals *translanguage* between RLs, ideas of "native speaker", "native language" and languages as discrete realities are still pervasive.

Keywords: intercomprehension, translanguaging, Romance languages, multilingual communication, chat communication

1 Introduction

Many concepts have been used to refer to multilingual communication, some related to the simultaneous use of different languages (such as "parler bilingue", Lüdi 1987), others related to the ability of relying on receptive competences (such as "lingua receptiva", Ten Thije 2014) to collaboratively achieve meaning (see Melo-Pfeifer 2018 for a catalog of existing concepts). Intercomprehension, a concept used in language (teacher) education (Degache 2006; Doyé 2005; Melo-Pfeifer 2018; Ollivier and Strasser 2013), describes the processes of both understanding and using different languages in order to co-create meaning

---

Sílvia Melo-Pfeifer, University of Hamburg, e-mail: silvia.melo-pfeifer@uni-hamburg.de

within (preferably) multilingual interaction, i.e. when speakers share languages of the same linguistic family already existing in their repertoire.[1] This contribution analyses multilingual interaction in chat rooms within the Galanet Project, a scenario designed to foster intercomprehension between speakers from a linguistic *continuum*, that of Romance Languages (RL), including: French, Italian, Portuguese and Spanish, with sporadic occurrences of Catalan and Romanian. Intercomprehension is here understood as a multilingual communicative situation, where speakers interact using their "own" RL(s) – meaning the one they identify the most with – while aiming to understand the RL(s) of the other(s), based on the transparency that characterizes languages of the same family. Thus, intercomprehension challenges monolingual stances towards communication and highlights collaboration as a means of achieving co-constructed meaning in multilingual settings. Despite this fact, intercomprehension can still be understood as a scenario with fixed linguistic and communicative borders: first, privileging linguistic families over linguistic continua; second, distinguishing receptive and productive skills, associating the use of different languages to either type of skill; third, privileging native speakers of a RL in the production aspect of the scenario compared to foreign language speakers (Melo-Pfeifer 2016). In previous analyses of intercomprehension stances, the researchers argued that speakers don't always respect these restrictive borders (in other words, they don't always abide by the rules such borders imply, constituting the linguistic contract of the GALANET project), because they wish to make use of the full range of their linguistic repertoires. Additionally, they do not always acknowledge the validity of separating productive and receptive skills in one language or another (Bono and Melo-Pfeifer 2012; Melo-Pfeifer 2016 and 2018; Melo-Pfeifer and Araújo e Sá 2018). These observations led to approaching the concept of intercomprehension using a translanguaging lens, since it allows a description of the less constrained practices of speakers engaged in multilingual interaction. Despite this fact, we observed that discussions on linguistic borders, language families and languages as fixed objects were concomitantly taking place within the chatroom interactions, thereby constituting an interrogation of the definition of translanguaging (Melo-Pfeifer and Araújo e Sá 2018; see section 1 below for the working definition of translanguaging used in this contribution).

The observation of these tensions led to questioning the validity of such theoretical constructs as "intercomprehension" and "translanguaging", challenging them in light of the real practices of speakers engaged in multilingual interaction,

---

[1] Intercomprehension can also relate to receptive reading and listening skills (see Ollivier & Strasser 2013).

where the use of RL is mandatory. The main question in this contribution is whether translanguaging and intercomprehension are "practice-proof concepts" and how a close analysis of multilingual interaction challenges some of the main tenets of each. The research questions that will guide this contribution, exploring the connections between tranlanguaging and intercomprehension, are:
– Do speakers using different RLs in a multi-plurilinguistic context use languages following a pre-fixed distributed pattern?
– Do the observed translanguaging practices correspond to border- and family-free conceptions of languages and communication, namely in what concerns the distinction native/non-native?

The contribution starts by presenting the definition of translanguaging, noting some of the criticisms to its definition. The empirical section of the study focuses on an analysis of selected multilingual chat sequences illustrating how interaction resorting to RL cannot be described resorting to intercomprehension or translanguaging only, and how this particular scenario challenges the understanding of these concepts, taken as theoretical constructs.

2 Translanguaging: A new description of being plurilingual and doing plurilinguistically

Literature describing multilingual repertoires has been challenging old assumptions around the composition and organization of linguistic repertoires. Following García and Wei (2014) and Vogel and García (2017), three theories describing the plurilingual repertoire are presented below.

The first theoretical approach describing plurilingualism is called "traditional bilingualism", in which languages are seen as independent systems. Being independent and fixed systems, languages in this approach are said to possess distinctive characteristics, being juxtaposed in the plurilingual repertoire as "linguistic solitudes" (Cummins 2007; see MacLennan 1945) or "parallel monolingualisms". Such definition of language has been criticized by Blommaert as that of "language as a bounded, nameable and countable unit, often reduced to grammatical structures and vocabulary, and called by names such as "English", "French" and so on" (2010: 4). According to this model, a bilingual or plurilingual speaker will be a person having the same degree of proficiency in both languages, being (near) native in both. Despite decades of studies on linguistic transfer and code-switching, and on the achievements of the multicompetent speaker (Cook 1999;

see also Introduction to this volume), this conception of bilingualism and plurilingualism is still entrenched in social discourses and is, according to studies on bilingual children, the most accepted and reproduced (Melo-Pfeifer 2015 and 2017). As also acknowledged by Wei (2015), "despite the commonplace occurrence of multilingual practices in our everyday life, there is a pervasive belief in society, bilingual and monolingual alike, that languages are best kept separate, discrete and pure; mixing and switching between languages are seen as interference or trespassing which may have a detrimental effect on both individual users and the community they live in" (p. 195).

The second approach, also very influential, was developed by Cummins (2008) and was called "linguistic interdependence". According to this theory, languages of the plurilingual self are clearly interconnected and phenomena such as linguistic transfer and transcodic productions are the sign of a "Common Underlying Proficiency". Cummins' theory, however, is criticized by García and Wei (2014) for still conceiving languages as separate entities, with distinctive features that make them unique. According to the authors, a sign of this separateness and discreteness is the concept of *code-switching*: because this concept focuses on both the "code" and the "switching" from one to the other, the linguistic interdependence approach still conceives languages as single entities, possible to distinguish and to separate from each other. This criticism is highlighted in the fact that researchers within the linguistic interdependency approach analyze the code-switching grammar or try to identify the linguistic base (the dominant language of a speaker) being used to introduce other linguistic features (with concepts such as code-switching and borrowings, among others).

In their attempt to answer to criticism of these two models, García and Wei present a more dynamic and integrated vision of the plurilingual repertoire, more apt to respond to the dynamics of actual multilingual dispensation (Aronin and Singleton 2008). In their proposal, "there is one linguistic system (. . .) with features that are integrated throughout. (. . .) These linguistic features are then (. . .) often used in ways that conform to societal constructions of 'a language', and other times used differently" (García and Wei 2014: 15). In order to better illustrate the integration of the different linguistic resources, the authors propose replacing code-switching with translanguaging. Translanguaging would refer to the integrated and interdependent use of semiotic repertoires (not limited to so-called languages) in order to collaboratively achieve meaning in the social, plurilingual and intercultural interaction (García 2014; García and Wei 2014). This concept brings a major development to studies of multilingual interaction: acknowledgment that multilingual interaction is not just "lingual", integrating other *sense makers* and *sense containers* (Jewitt 2009). Despite these developments, it must be acknowledged that studies resorting to translanguaging as a heuristic tool still tend to focus on the linguistic accomplishments of speakers, the multimodal aspects of communication not being fully integrated in the analytical apparatus of the researcher:

> Discussions around the idea of translanguaging have largely focused on the ways in which the idea enables researchers to transcend predefined notions of language in favour of more fluid accounts of linguistic resources (. . .). The attention paid to the "languaging" part of the term, meanwhile, has largely focused on the ways in which it suggests a sense of language as action; this is not just about using language but about language as doing, as transformative (Li 2011). Less attention, however, has been paid to the scope of what is encompassed by the idea of language itself, or what translanguaging might look like if we took up an expanded version of language and attended not only to the borders between languages but also to the borders between semiotic modes".
>
> (Pennycook 2017: 269–270)

Despite the identification of such underdevelopment, translanguaging remains a powerful instrument to more accurately describe "the structure of people's repertoires and the patterns of multilingual language use, [which have] become less predictable and significantly more complex" (Blommaert 2010: 5).

According to a growing body of literature (Blackledge and Creese 2014; Canagarajah 2013; García 2014; García, Flores, and Woodley 2012; García and Li 2014; see Auer, forthcoming for a critique), translanguaging differs from codeswitching because:

- It focuses on individuals and their linguistic trajectories rather than on codes;
- It analyses the use of semiotic resources as an integrated practice (the semiotic resources are an ensemble whose parts cannot be fully understood when analysed separately);
- It sees those resources, namely the linguistic ones, as *hic et nunc* co-constructions (and not as pre-given);
- It describes how languages are used to communicate while at the same time offering a theoretical standpoint about how languages are processed;
- It adopts a socioconstructivist stance, based on collaboration between subjects (intersubjectivity) and the co-elaboration of meaning across modes that are contextually selected and used;

These advantages are rapidly gaining supporters among researchers of language learning and teaching. However, a consensus is still lacking (and will probably take time to achieve) regarding how languages are organized and processed in the brain and whether they actually form a single linguistic system, as posited by García and Wei (2014). In particular, a vision of the plurilingual system as unified and merged, challenging the understanding of languages, linguistic borders and designations is still considered problematic:

> In this debate, Aronin and Singleton (2012) assume that there is an important interaction and interplay among the multilingual's languages but they take issue with the idea of a strict unitary linguistic system. Some arguments they put forward are: formal differences among languages, language selection according to their interlocutor, code-switching not as a counter-example to the idea of language separation, and selective recovery of language due to aphasia which affects only one of the multiple languages or as a result of neglect in favor of another language.
>
> (Ruiz de Zarobe and Ruiz de Zarobe 2015: 399)

Some authors argue that taking the concept of translanguaging to its final consequences, in its strong version (see Vogel and García 2017 for a synthesis of the weak and strong versions of translanguaging), it entails the disappearance of concepts such as mother, second or foreign languages or even native and non-native speakers, as these become non-marked and non-distinctive features to describe plurilingual repertoires and the plurilingual self. Such predictions should nevertheless be received with caution, since subjects continue to employ such terminology to define themselves and the more radical views contained in a strong version of translanguaging may contribute to alienating individuals who feel strong identification with specific languages or, the other way around, will alienate researchers from the real world (Melo-Pfeifer 2019; also Auer, forthcoming).

The debate around the unitary conception of the linguistic repertoire has grown due to the contributions of certain researchers (see MacSwan 2017 and response by Otheguy, García, and Reid 2018; also Auer, forthcoming) concerning the question of whether "social duality [regarding the counting of languages] is not matched by a dual psycholinguistic one" (Otheguy, García, and Reid 2018: 3). As Vogel and García (2017) recognize, "there are also continued debates between scholars who have largely embraced translanguaging and those who resist the theory´s premises or have accepted them only partially" (2017: 1; see Auer, forthcoming and Wei 2018). Despite this, translanguaging is a powerful concept to describe how individuals make use of their repertoires as it shows the "integration rather than separation of the languages at the bi/multilingual's disposal" (Ruiz de Zarobe and Ruiz de Zarobe 2015, 399). It also posits that individuals have dynamic resources, linguistic or otherwise, at their disposal (Blommaert 2010: 102), instead of immobile and unchangeable languages. These elements shall be revisited during the analysis of our chat sequences.

3 Corpus and methodology

3.1 The GALANET project

GALANET[2] ("Plateforme pour le développement de l'intercompréhension en Langues Romanes") was a European project connecting students mastering at least one Romance Language (RL), either as a so-called mother tongue or as a "reference language" (that could act as "bridge" between RL speakers), through the means of an Internet platform created for this purpose. This platform included synchronous and asynchronous communicational tools allowing participants to exchange plurilingually: the linguistic communicative contract established that participants should productively use their "reference" RL (in fact, students were commonly identified as experts in a RL, even if they are not "native-speakers") and, at the same time, attempt to achieve comprehension of the RL of other participants. The idea behind this communicative contract was the definition of intercomprehension as the ability to speak *one's own* language and understand the languages of the others, within the context of communication resorting to languages of the same linguistic family.

The collaborative work in the platform which was integrated in the curriculum and the regular workload of different subjects at their home university (either language courses or foreign language teacher education) followed a project-oriented approach. Participants were meant to produce a multilingual "press dossier" on a previously negotiated intercultural theme (for example, humor in different RLs). In order to achieve this goal, participants had to communicate in the several languages of the project to produce a synthesis of the discussions on the platform, both in the forums and the chatrooms.

The platform followed two organizational themes: a temporal and a physical one. In terms of temporal representation, a GALANET session developed in four interdependent and sequential phases, lasting about four months (Araújo e Sá, De Carlo, and Melo-Pfeifer 2010; Melo-Pfeifer 2016): breaking the ice and choice of a theme; brainstorming; collecting documents and debate; and elaborating and publishing the press dossier.

---

[2] GALANET was a Socrates/Lingua Project, coordinated by Christian Degache of the Université Stendhal, Grenoble 3 (France). The same research group worked on two more recent projects: GALAPRO (www.galapro.eu) and Miriadi (https://www.miriadi.net/). More recently, an enlarged group of researchers engaged in a new project related to the assessment of intercomprehension competences through an European Erasmus Plus project, coordinated by Christian Ollivier (University of La Réunion), called EVAL-IC (Evaluation des compétences en intercomprehension, https://evalic.eu/).

Visually, the platform was organized around different spaces, each one being attributed a different functional task: a welcome desk (displaying information about the session), a private bureau (with the internal e-mail account and personal profile), a library and a resource center (both conceived as a self-paced individual learning center), a forum (to meet other participants following the discussion forum format), three meeting points (technologically conceived as three chat rooms) and a group meeting room (a space to complete collaborative tasks and produce the final "press dossier"). While the phases "breaking the ice and choice of a theme" and "brainstorming" would commonly take place in the discussion forums and three chat rooms, "collecting documents and debate" and "elaborating and publishing the press dossier" mostly took place in the group meeting room.

The three chat sequences analyzed in this contribution were produced during the second intercomprehension session on the GALANET platform, between February and May 2004 (called Canosession). In this session, 13 teams from six countries (Argentina, Belgium, France, Italy, Portugal, and Spain) participated in the interactions, with a total of 236 participants (students and tutors). As their thematic strand, participants chose to debate the following theme: *"Ridiamo per le stesse cose? . . . Y a-t-il un humour romanophone?"* (*"Do we laugh at the same things? . . . Is there a RL humour?"*).

Despite the fact that all languages should be considered equal, French was the most shared RL in all teams and also the most common "target language" (i.e., the language students were studying formally). Almost all participant teams share a bilingual experience as a minimum asset, as they have all learnt a RL as a foreign language. As in previous occasions, we describe the communicative setting as "multi-plurilingual" (Ehrhart 2010), because of its dual complexity: on the one hand, plurilingual individual repertoires meet each other; and, on the other hand, a multilingual social space is created according to specific communicative rules (Melo-Pfeifer 2016 and 2018; see the introduction to this volume about the distinction between multilingualism and plurilingualism).

3.2 Selection of chat sequences

At this stage, it should be recalled that the aim of this contribution is twofold: on the one hand, it aims at exploring whether speakers using different RLs in a multi-plurilingual context use languages following a previously fixed distributed pattern (RL only, production being attached to a dominant RL and reception being developed in all the other languages); on the other hand, analyzing the co-construction of intercomprehension from a translanguaging lens, this contribution intends to scrutinize whether the observed practices follow a border- and family-free conception of languages and communication. To sum up, the chosen sequences could help us to answer the question whether or not it is possible to define intercomprehension within multilingual but monoglossic RL-only norms, without taking into account subject agency and complete linguistic repertoires (Melo-Pfeifer 2018) and, at the same time, relate translanguaging practices to the linguistic ideologies and conceptions being displayed and openly discussed by the participants.

To achieve these goals, three chat sequences were selected that could provide signs of the hybridization of intercomprehension and translanguaging, based on an analysis of speakers' language use and metalinguistic and meta-communicative comments. As seen in previous analyses (Melo-Pfeifer 2018), the moment when speakers meet each other for the first time and present themselves and their linguistic biographies (all subjects participating in the project being plurilinguals) can be a particularly fruitful moment to observe the use of different languages and the reflection about languages and their connections. Such information are provided spontaneously or prompted by other participants. Therefore, three chat sequences that reproduce these typical moments of getting to know each other and their languages where chosen. Because of the variation of participants in each given chat conversation, these three sequences occurred in different phases of the collaborative work within the platform. The following criteria were crucial in the selection of the sequences for this contribution, as three "information-rich sequences":
– Sequences are multilingual;
– Individuals describe their linguistic biographies and their linguistic repertoires;
– Individuals shuttle between their semiotic resources, linguistic or other (such as smileys or capitalized letters);
– Individuals reflect about the communicative situation and the linguistic contract;
– Individuals question the relationship between different languages of the same linguistic family and/or between different linguistic families;

Nonetheless, it should be stated that our analysis focused both on what was said about languages and how languages were used. This analysis thus allows us to identify any mismatches between principles and practices, from the participants' perspectives, and to analyze the tensions between the practices and concepts being used to describe them (particularly intercomprehension and translanguaging), from a researcher's perspective. The analysis consists of chat sequence analysis of the three chat sequences, emphasizing the thematization of linguistic borders and families, as well as the similarities and differences between languages. In our analysis, the way these themes are introduced and how they are linguistically and discursively treated are of paramount importance in order to examine: i) plurilingual strategies and linguistic ideologies, and ii) how these ideologies and practices could be addressed through intercomprehension and/or translanguaging as theoretical constructs.

4 Analysis of chat sequences: translanguaging, linguistic borders and language families

The first sequence of the corpora presents an ongoing conversation between Ilaria and Laura (both from Italy) and Pau (from Spain). If the interaction contract were followed, Ilaria and Laura would speak in Italian and Pau in Spanish. However, as can be seen (excerpt 1), Ilaria and Laura express themselves both in Spanish and Italian (mostly in Spanish, in fact) and the interaction adopts a monolingual tone.

Excerpt 1. Chat sequence 1.

Sequence 1[3]	English translation
[ilaria] y que estudias ? (ES)	[ilaria] and what do you study?
[PauV] filologia francesa (ES)	[PauV] French philology
[PauV] pero de segunda lengua hago italiano (ES)	[PauV] but as a second language I am doing Italian
[ilaria] entonces sabes muy bien el frances? (ES)	[ilaria] you know French very well?
[laura] bravo (IT)	[laura] very good
[PauV] bueno . . . un pochino (ES & IT)	[PauV] well . . . a little
[PauV] jajaja	[PauV] hahaha
[PauV] hablo como lengua materna el catalan, luego hablo castellano, frances, ingles e italiano (ES)	[PauV] I speak Catalan as mother tongue, then I speak Spanish, French, English and Italian
[ilaria] per el italiano lo conoces bastante? (ES)	[ilaria] But you know Italian quite well?

---

3 Languages used are indicated in brackets: CAT= Catalan, DE= German, EN=English, ES=Spanish, FL=Flemish, FR=French, IT= Italian, PT= Portuguese. Nicknames as chosen by the participants are presented in square brackets. Excerpts presented in the orthography used by the participants.

[PauV] no se (ES)	[PauV] I don't know
[ilaria] ma si!!! (IT)	[ilaria] but of course!!!
[PauV] creo que puedo hablarlo mas o menos (ES)	[PauV] I think I can speak it more or less
[laura] catelan y castellano son muy diferentes? (ES)	[laura] are Catalan and Spanish very different?
[PauV] bueno, si . . . es bastante diferente, es como el frances y l'italiano o el portuges i el castellano, sabes? son lenguas latinas . . . tienen sus diferencias . . . (ES)	[PauV] well, yes . . . it is quite different, it is like French and Italian or Portuguese and Spanish, you know? They are Romance languages . . . They have their differences . . .
[ilaria] aquì conozco un chico que esPeruviano y ayer me decìa de hablar con el panol . . . mhhh . . . no me lo recuerdo muy bien!!! (ES)	[ilaria] Here I know a Peruvian guy and yesterday he told me to speak with him in Spanish . . . mhhh . . . I don't remember it that well!!!
[PauV] i el catalan tiene un acento muy fuerte (ES)	[PauV] and Catalan has a very strong accent
[laura] pero en espana la lengua oficial es el catalan o el castellano? (ES)	[laura] but in Spain, the official language is Catalan or Spanish?
[PauV] es el castellano (ES)	[PauV] it is Spanish
[ilaria] sobre todo no conozco muchas palabras en espanol!este ano tengo que hacer un examen de espanol (ES)	[ilaria] I especially do not know a lot of words in Spanish! this year I have to do a Spanish exam
[PauV] pero se hablan 3 lenguas mas: el gallego, el vasco y el catalan (ES)	[PauV] but 3 other languages are spoken: Galician, Basque and Catalan
[laura] ahora tengo que ir a la lecciòn de economia politica, a presto e fatti vivo!!!!!ciao (ES & IT)	[laura] now I have to go to the lesson on political economy, see you soon and keep in touch!!!!!bye
[ilaria] conmo es el vasco? (ES)	[ilaria] What is Basque like?
[PauV] pero el catalan se habla mucho, sobretodo en la zona donde yo vivo (ES)	[PauV] but Catalan is widely spoken, especially in the area where I live
[PauV] el vasco??? incomprensible (ES)	[PauV] Basque??? incomprehensible
[PauV] no se sabe de donde proviene (ES)	[PauV] it's not even known where it comes from
[laura] ciaoooo (IT)	[laura] byeeee
[ilaria] ah!bueno! (ES)	[ilaria] ah! well!
[PauV] es mas dificil que el aleman (ES)	[PauV] it is harder than German

In this sequence, despite the adoption of a predominantly monolingual tone, marks of linguistic hybridization through the combination of Spanish and Italian elements can still be seen (*PauV: bueno . . . un pochino*; *Ilaria: ahora tengo que ir a la lecciòn de economia politica, a presto e fatti vivo!!!!!ciao*). It should also be noted that the main theme of this sequence is the linguistic competence of the Spanish speaker, PauV, who describes his linguistic resources naming the languages of his repertoire as separate entities (*PauV: hablo como lengua materna el catalan, luego hablo castellano, frances, ingles e italiano*). Alongside listing these five languages, concepts such as "mother tongue" are also used, implying a better command of this language, which is named separately from the others ("*luego hablo*"/"then I speak"). So, if we believe this statement from PauV, those languages are not all at the same level of proficiency and he feels he has to distinguish them when referring to them. The status of mother tongue (in the case Catalan) seems also to explain why he is so renitent to define and recognize his linguistic level in Italian, because he seems to fear evaluation by the two "real speakers" of this language (*PauV: bueno . . . un pochino; no se; creo que puedo hablarlo mas o menos*). So, it seems that Pau not only acknowledges the special relationship he establishes with Catalan, but is also keen to believe in the special or privileged status of the native speaker, who can claim ownership of a given language. The students then go on to discuss the differences between RL, recognizing that they somehow belong together, but focusing more on the elements that make them unique and separable (*PauV: bueno, si . . . es bastante diferente, es como el frances y l'italiano o el portuges i el castellano, sabes? son lenguas latinas . . . tienen sus diferencias . . .*). One aspect mentioned is the accent, as a distinctive feature of a language, which serves as a distinctive characteristic (*PauV: i el catalan tiene un acento muy fuerte*). So, in this sequence social and political constructs such as "mother tongue", "accent" and "Romance languages" are used to recreate the social organization of the linguistic world and, at the same time, to refer to languages as identifiable objects. These aspects are heightened by the discussions about the languages spoken in Spain and their degree of mutual intelligibility (*PauV: el vasco??? Incomprensible*), learning difficulty (*PauV: es mas dificil que el aleman*) and origin (*PauV: no se sabe de donde proviene*). In addition, linguistic and geographical borders are frequently thematised and rebuilt as legitimate constructs to refer to languages and linguistic territories (*PauV: pero el catalan se habla mucho, sobretodo en la zona donde yo vivo*).

In different moments of this interaction, we observe the mediational role language education paths may have had in the creation and dissemination of linguistic ideologies and stereotypes. Ilaria, for instance, seems to believe the educational path is enough to ensure a good command of a language (*Ilaria: entonces sabes* **muy bien** *el frances?; pero el italiano lo conoces* **bastante**?; our emphasis added), which seems to be interpreted by Pau as a "native-like" command of the language, as explained above. Referring to her competences in Spanish, Ilaria automatically establishes a connection between knowledge of the foreign language and command of vocabulary, fearing her results in the Spanish test (*Ilaria: sobre todo no conozco muchas palabras en espanol!este ano tengo que hacer un examen de espanol*).

In the second sequence between a Portuguese tutor (Silvia M), two Italian students (Laura and Ilaria) and one Spanish student (PauV), the theme discussed is again the mutual intelligibility of RL, this time Portuguese. This sequence (excerpt 2) follows chronologically the previous one but is different in that another language is introduced. We also observe that all speakers shuttle between languages, because co-constructing intercomprehension is more difficult.

Excerpt 2. Chat sequence 2.

Sequence 2	English translation
[SilviaM] Alguém compreende Portugues? (PT)	[SilviaM] Does anyone understand Portuguese?
[SilviaM] Siques en Barcelona Pau? (ES)	[SilviaM] Are you still in Barcelona Pau?
[laura] dònde està Marensa? (ES)	[laura] where is Marensa?
[PauV] no, ahora estoy en manresa (ES)	[PauV] no, I am in manresa now
[SilviaM] Boa Pergunta!!!! Onde fica Marensa???? (PT)	[SilviaM] Good Question!!!! Where is Marensa????
[laura] No se (ES)	[laura] I don't know
[SilviaM] Não faço a mínima ideia:(é longe de Marcelona? (PT)	[SilviaM] I have no idea:(Is it far from Barcelona?
[ilaria] que dices tu en portuguese que no entiendo nada! (ES)	[ilaria] What are you saying in Portuguese, I don't understand anything!
[SilviaM] Que no tengo idea donde esta Marensa . . . . (ES)	[SilviaM] That I have no idea where Marensa is . . . .
[PauV] manresa i barcelona non sono longe, 45 minuti in macchina (IT)	[PauV] manresa and barcelona are not far, 45 minutes by car
[SilviaM] Não sabia que era tão difícil compreender-me:((((PT)	[SilviaM] I didn't know it was so difficult to understand me:((
[ilaria] es un poquito diferente del espanol . . . yo no imajinaba tan diferencias pero es un lenguage que me gustarìamucho comprender! (PT)	[ilaria] it is a little different from Spanish . . . I didn't imagine such differences but it is a language I would very much like to understand!
[laura] yo no lo comprendo (ES)	[laura] I don't understand it
[SilviaM] Que pena Laura!!!! (PT)	[SilviaM] That's a pity Laura!!!!
[SilviaM] Que línguas falas Laua? (PT)	[SilviaM] Which languages do you speak Laua?
[laura] gracias, pena significa mi dispiace? (ES, PT & IT)	[laura] thank you, pena means I don't like it?
[SilviaM] Pena = lastima!!!! Que pena! = Que lastima! (PT & ES)	[SilviaM] Pena = lastima!!!! Que pena! = Que lastima!
[laura] yo hablo; espanol; francés inglés y italiano poro no conozco tu idioma (ES)	[laura] I speak Spanish; French English and Italian but I don't know your language
[SilviaM] Me voy ahora! Arrivederci:) Buena charla!!!!! (ES & IT)	[SilviaM] I am leaving now! See you:) Have a nice chat!!!!!
[laura] ma che lingua parlava silvia? (IT)	[laura] Which language was silvia speaking?
[PauV] silvia parla portughese (IT)	[PauV] silvia speaks Portuguese
[laura] ah	[laura] ah

Here, to the question "*Alguém compreende Portugues?*" orienting the discussion to named languages, participants first respond with doubt (*laura: No se*) to subsequently deny any possibility of understanding (*Ilaria: que dices tu en portuguese que no entiendo nada!*; *laura: yo no lo comprendo*), despite the recognized proximity (*Ilaria: es un poquito diferente del espanol . . .*). And again, referring to linguistic repertoires resorts to listing named languages (*Laura: yo hablo; espanol; francés inglés y italiano poro no conozco tu idioma*) and it is interesting to note that belonging to the same linguistic family and even being considered close to Spanish, these are not sufficient conditions to ensure written comprehension. It can also be observed that the incomprehension experienced by Laura has to be given a name: *ma che lingua parlava silvia?*. Naming an unknown language serves perfectly as an alibi to justify the communication problems even if, in this author's opinion, in all of the utterances written by the Portuguese speaker, most of the words could be considered transparent words (compared to Spanish, the language shared by the three other chat participants): e.g. *Silvia: Não sabia que era tão difícil compreender-me:((* would be "No sabía que era tan difícil comprenderme" in Spanish. It may be concluded that being unable to identify the language and clearly acknowledge its familiarity seems to entail a denial of any competence whatsoever, even when the aim is to develop comprehension skills (*Ilaria: yo no imajinaba tan diferencias pero es un lenguage que me gustariamucho comprender!*). And even though SilviaM used Portuguese, Spanish and, to a lesser extent, Italian, Laura seems inclined to define her through one language only (*ma che lingua parlava silvia?*, in the singular form). This may, however, be an unintended effect of the project: first, the communicative contract establishes that participants should use one language productively; and, second, the project establishes that the students must identify their "reference and target languages", thus also understanding (or reproducing) languages as distinct realities. However, when PauV formulates his explanation in Italian (*PauV: manresa i barcelona non sono longe, 45 minuti in macchina*), he doesn't face this need – or even symbolic violence – of, as a plurilingual person, being identified to a single language. Picking up from the comments about his insecurity in the first sequence, it may also be simply that he has had time to process the „insecurity" and by now feels capable of „trying".

In this field of the discussion on linguistic borders and their perception by the participants, excerpt 3 presents a very interesting conversation on crossing family borders and linguistic boundaries. In this chat sequence, between two Portuguese tutors (SilviaM and Mokab) and one Belgian student (Annalisa), all participants express their openness towards languages, countries and speakers.

Excerpt 3. Chat sequence 3.

Sequence 3 (Original version)	English translation
[Annalisa] ciao a tutti! (IT)	[Annalisa] hello everybody!
[SilviaM] Olá Annalisa! (PT)	[SilviaM] Hi Annalisa!
[mokab] Olá Annalisa! De onde vens? (PT)	[mokab] Hi Annalisa! Where are you from?
[Annalisa] de belgica! (PT?)	[Annalisa] from Belgium!
[Annalisa] y tu? (ES)	[Annalisa] and you?
[SilviaM] Oh eu adora a Bélgica!!!!!! (PT)	[SilviaM] Oh I love Belgium!!!!!!
[SilviaM] Sou de Aveiro! (PT)	[SilviaM] I am from Aveiro!
[mokab] J'adore ce pays! On peut parler en français! (FR)	[mokab] I love that country! We can speak French!
[Annalisa] bien sur! (FR)	[Annalisa] certainly!
[SilviaM] De que parte da Bélgica es? (PT)	[SilviaM] Which part of Belgium are you from?
[Annalisa] de flandre, c'est le nord (FR)	[Annalisa] from Flanders, its the north
[SilviaM] Alors, tu parles le flamand???? (FR)	[SilviaM] so, you speak Flemish???
[mokab] Je viens d'Aveiro, une belle ville portugaise. Tu as déja visité mon pays? (FR)	[mokab] I am from Aveiro, a beautiful Portuguese city. Have you ever visited my country?
[Annalisa] oui (FR)	[Annalisa] yes
[SilviaM] Juste un peu, juste un peu . . . . (FR)	[SilviaM] Just a bit, just a bit . . . .
[SilviaM] Escreve algo em Flamand . . . . (PT & FR)	[SilviaM] Write something in Flemish . . . .
[Annalisa] non j ai de la famillen qui habite en algarve (FR)	[Annalisa] no, I have family living in algarve
[Annalisa] ok!	[Annalisa] ok!
[mokab] ecrit un petit peu en flamand! PLEASE!!! (FR & EN)	[mokab] Write a little bit in Flemish! PLEASE!!!
[SilviaM] Escreve flamanego:(Vá lá!!!!! (PT)	[SilviaM] Write Flemish:(Come on!!!!!
[Annalisa] hallo alles kits? (FL)	[Annalisa] hallo alles kits?
[Annalisa] ik ben 22 jaar. en jij? (FL)	[Annalisa] ik ben 22 jaar. en jij?
[SilviaM] Kits para ti também:))) (FL & PT)	[SilviaM] Kits for you too:)))
[mokab] Qu'est-ce que ça veut dire? (FR)	[mokab] What does it mean?
[SilviaM] Ich bin 26 jahre alt (DE)	[SilviaM] I am 26 years old [German]
[Annalisa] ohlala mais tu réponds en allemand! c'est pas la meme chose hè (FR)	[Annalisa] ohlala but you are answers in German! It is not the same thing hè
[mokab] Ik ben 24 jaar! Chouette, je sais parler déjà un petit peu de flamand! (FL & FR)	[mokab] I am 24 years old [Flemish]! Cool, I can speak a little bit of Flemish already!
[Annalisa] parfait! (FR)	[Annalisa] perfect!
[Annalisa] comment ça se fait? tu as des amis en belgique? (FR)	[Annalisa] and how is it so? Do you have friends in Belgium?
[mokab] A sílvia é poliglota: fala alemão, espanhol, frances . . . (PT)	[mokab] Silvia is a polyglot: she speaks German, Spanish, French . . .
[Annalisa] bien! (FR)	[Annalisa] well!
[Annalisa] et très pratique (FR)	[Annalisa] and very practical

[mokab] Non, je n'ai pas d'amis en Belgique, mais je suis passioné par la langue française et dons par les pays francophones! (FR)	[mokab] No, I don't have any friends in Belgium, but I am passionate about French and so about French speaking countries!
[SilviaM] Je sais, mais c'est quand-même pareil??? Non????? (FR)	[SilviaM] I know, but it is similar though ??? No?????
[Annalisa] non! pas du tout! (FR)	[Annalisa] no! not at all!
[SilviaM] Mais c'est proche!!!! Qu'en penses tu???? (FR)	[SilviaM] But it is close!!!! What do you think????
[mokab] J'ai la meme opinion de Sílvia! Je crois qu'il y a beaucoup de ressemblance entre ces deux langues! (FR)	[mokab] I have the same opinion as Silvia! I believe there are many similarities between these two languages!
[Annalisa] oui ça ressemble un peu, mais pas trop! (FR)	[Annalisa] yes, it has some similarities, but not too much!
[mokab] C'est un petit comme le français, le portugais, l'espagnol, l'italien: ce sont des langues différentes, mais quand meme très proches et pareilles. (FR)	[mokab] It's a bit like French, Portuguese, Spanish and Italian: these are different languages, but very close and similar though.
[Annalisa] exactement! (FR)	[Annalisa] exactly!

It is relevant to note that Belgium is quite automatically associated to the French language (*Mokab: J'adore ce pays! On peut parler en français!*), prompting Annalisa to explain that she comes from the (Flemish-speaking) North. So, a first strand in the conversation could involve the interdependence between linguistic and geographical borders, an exclusive language being attributed to each of the parts of the country and also a linguistic identity being immediately attributed depending on the geographic origin (*SilviaM: Alors, tu parle le flamand?????*, "alors" implying causality). Because Annalisa positively responds to the question asked by SilviaM, everyone engages momentarily in a side sequence of teaching and learning a language (*SilviaM: Escreve algo em Flamand . . . .*). As we note, this teaching and learning sequence follows characteristics of language learning in school environments: the communicative approach to the language and the separation of languages (in this case, German and Flemish). The first influence is apparent in the teaching of greetings in the language (*Annalisa: hallo alles kits? / ik ben 22 jaar. en jij?*) and the second in the ensuing discussion around the differences and similarities between the two Germanic languages. Clearly, Annalisa, here in the role of teacher, expert and perhaps even native speaker, doesn't seem to like Flemish being taken for German and to accept that communication may develop bilingually, following the principle of intercomprehension between Germanic languages, the same principle that is being practiced within RL (*Annalisa: ohlala mais tu réponds en allemand! c'est pas la meme chose hè*). This could be justified by the fact that the tutors explicitly asked her to violate the communicative contract and to speak a specific language, now disregarding her reluctance to violate the linguistic contract and her linguistic efforts (what may be understood as incoherent by Annalisa). At this point, some annoyance is visible: SilviaM tries to explain that both languages seem similar (*Je sais, mais c'est quand-même pareil??? Non?????*), to which Annalisa promptly answers through a clear denial (*non! pas du tout!*). Thus, it would appear that, unlike with RL, the Flemish language triggers Annalisa to a discussion on linguistic borders within the Germanic languages, these being almost emotionally defended, faced with someone who intends to blur them. Indeed, this linguistic border seems connoted with an idea of identity and identification with a certain linguistic community. But again, the project is about RL and not Germanic languages and she might think it is not appropriate to go so far in discussing another linguistic family.

We could carefully hypothesise that, while moving between RL seems to pose no problem to this student (she even agrees to the statement that "*C'est un petit comme le français, le portugais, l'espagnol, l'italien: ce sont des langues différentes, mais quand meme très proches et pareilles*), the same linguistic behaviour with "her" language is hard to be accepted (*Annalisa: oui ça ressemble un peu, mais pas trop!*). According to this interpretation, we could suppose that it is the native speaker of a language, whether monolingual or multilingual, that faces problems with the translinguistic practices of the Other. Another hypothesis to explain Annalisa's sensitive response to the use of German and comparison with Flemish could be the fact that Flemish has not been attributed an independent state (completing the trilogy language-country-people; see Bono, in this volume) and its speakers resent this since it may make them feel diminished. As before, the role of language learning at school, where each language is clearly separated from other languages (multilingual pedagogies still being rare), could once more be called upon to say that each language learning and teaching process (referring to the teaching role taken on by Annalisa within the chat sequence), is likely to be influenced by the system to which the agents were exposed throughout their linguistic biographies and experiences.

5 Synthesis and perspectives

The present analysis has pointed out that plurilingual subjects do not always use language consistently with the ways researchers theorize about it and teachers teach them. The analysis made clear that individuals neither abide by the perceived constraint and pre-given communicative rules underlying the intercomprehension contract, nor conceive their translanguaging practices as a family and border-free contact situation (they use social categories and dualities to explain and refer to the integrated use of their repertoires and to their learning processes), showing that "while named languages and traditional language ideologies are socially constructed, they still have material effects" (Vogel and García 2017: 6). As we claimed in another study related to the same corpus,

> Despite the openness of the (multilingual) communicative contract, our samples still show that multilingual communication is impregnated by monolingual and monoglossic viewpoints towards communication. Even in a situation that is substantially recognized as fostering multilingual literacies and despite the possibility of forging, claiming and performing a multilingual identity, the understanding of these multilingual literacies is still based on certain monoglossic norms, such as the recognition of languages as countable entities and the potential of singular language learning. (Melo-Pfeifer 2021: 178)

Indeed, the observed practices seem to suggest that "as participants engage in flexible bilingualism [or plurilingualism, we would add], the boundaries between languages become permeable" (Creese and Blackledge 2011: 17) but these borders are still constantly surveilled and are not easily trespassed, mainly because "native speakers", whether monolingual or plurilingual, are perceived or perceive themselves as the symbols of those borders. Thus, a theoretical crossing between the concepts intercomprehension and translanguaging seems useful to describe what is going on in these chat interactions. If we should guide our analysis by the way people use language, then we should avoid seeing our heuristic objects as too-fixed conceptual constructs. More precisely, both intercomprehension and translanguaging emerged from our analysis as conceptual hybridizations: in common, they have the principle of communication not being constrained to the use of a single language; but there are also differences between the two: regarding intercomprehension, users denote the preference given to languages of the same linguistic family and the belief that communication is possible resorting to the transparency which characterizes such languages (despite the obstacles described); regarding translanguaging, users do not limit their resources either to languages only, or, within these, to RL only, making use of a holistic semiotic repertoire. However, in terms of intercomprehension, communicative resources are not limited to RL, neither is the contract to "produce in one language and understand the other languages" seem to be consistently complied with, instead it is constantly challenged and negotiated. Furthermore, linguistic modus and metalinguistic and metacommunicative comments make it clear that aspects referred as artificial social constructs in the literature on translanguaging (notably named languages, linguistic families, linguistic borders, . . .) appear to have an explanatory adequacy as participants use them to define and construct the context, to distribute communicative roles, to achieve meaning and to define oneself as a (competent) speaker. So, a "clear speaker orientation at separate codes" (Auer, forthcoming: 2) is still visible. Using concepts such as "linguistic family" or referring to similarities and differences between named languages allows participants to refer to the multilingual world order they perceive to inhabit and are familiar with. This statement goes hand in hand with Auer's perspective, to whom

> languages' are social constructs in a certain understanding of the word, these constructs [being] (a) very real objects for the speakers and (b) constructed not only by language authorities and via state institutions (such as schools) but by the multilingual speakers themselves, through their multilingual practices. (forthcoming: 3)

By communicating in this somewhat regulated GALANET context, participants learn that languages as well as the very definition of intercomprehension are social and theoretical constructs. If our role, as researchers, is "to support people, enhance communication between them and create communicative contexts which would enhance people's abilities to carry out their activities" (García 2007: xiv), we should support them in their processes of co-construction of meaning and unite efforts in valuing these processes and practices, disregard the concepts being used as heuristic and ideological tools to describe them. In a previous contribution, we defended that

> it would be fruitful to engage in discussion where the different viewpoints on multilingual communicative practices come close. This dialogue would cross-fertilize research paths and views on different contexts, and legitimate multilingual interaction as a trustworthy research field, namely in language education and teacher training. Bringing all these perspectives together would highlight the 'normality' of interactions that resort to several languages and that activate the full plurilingual and strategic repertoires of social actors, as well as their consciousness about the interplay of linguistic and non-linguistic resources, ingredients of the context and situational constraints. (Melo-Pfeifer 2018: 165)

Ofelia García, recognizing the "multiplicities of multilingual interactions" (2018: 881), explains that "multilingual interaction takes place at different societal levels, in different social spaces, and with very different interlocutors" (García 2018: 882). Whereas tensions were visible in our analysis between named languages and named linguistic families, on the one hand, and translanguaging, on the other hand, the analysis of the three chat sequences illustrates the three main ingredients to achieve meaning in multilingual interaction: "an attitude of openness, flexibility and respect; an ability to shuttle among semiotic features (. . .); and, the use of strategies of negotiation" (García 2018: 886). If these features are to be developed in context, we should then conclude that there are no "practice-proof concepts", when it comes to definition and analysis of complex plurilingual and collaborative semiotic behaviors.

Author's Positionality

Please see the introduction.

References

Araújo e Sá, Maria Helena, Maddalena De Carlo & Sílvia Melo-Pfeifer. 2010. "O que diriam sobre os portugueses?????": Intercultural curiosity in multilingual chatrooms. *Journal of Language and Intercultural Communication* 10(4), 277–298.

Araújo e Sá, Maria Helena & Sílvia Melo-Pfeifer. 2018. Introduction: Multilingual interaction – dynamics and achievements. *International Journal of Bilingual Education and Bilingualism* 21(7), 781–787.

Aronin, Larissa & Singleton, David. 2012. *Multilingualism*. Amsterdam: John Benjamins Publishing.

Aronin, Larissa & David Singleton. 2008. Multilingualism as a new linguistic dispensation. *International Journal of Multilingualism* 5(1), 1–16.

Auer, Peter (forthcoming). 'Translanguaging' or 'doing languages'? Multilingual practices and the notion of 'codes'. In Jeff MacSwann (ed.), *Language(s): Multilingualism and its Consequences*. Bristol: Multilingual Matters. URL https://www.researchgate.net/publication/332593230_'Translanguaging'_or_'doing_languages'_Multilingual_practices_and_the_notion_of_'codes' (accessed 15 May 2021)

Blackledge, Adrian & Angela Creese (eds.). 2014. *Heteroglossia as practice and pedagogy*. London: Springer.

Blommaert, Jan. 2010. *The sociolinguistics of globalization*. Cambridge: Cambridge University Press.

Bono, Mariana & Sílvia Melo-Pfeifer. 2012. Language negotiation in multilingual learning environments. *International Journal of Bilingualism* 15(3), 291–309.

Canagarajah, Suresh. 2013. *Translingual practice: Global Englishes and cosmopolitan relations*. Oxon: Routledge.

Cook, Vivian. 1999. Going beyond the bative speaker in language teaching. *TESOL Quarterly* 33, 185–209.

Creese, Angela & Adrian Blackledge. 2011. Ideologies and interactions in multilingual education: What can an ecological approach tell us about bilingual pedagogy? In Christine Hélot & Muiris Ó Laoire (eds.), *Language policy for the multilingual classroom*, 3–21. Bristol: Multilingual Matters.

Cummins, Jim. 2008. Teaching for transfer: Challenging the two solitudes assumption in bilingual education. In Jim Cummins & Nancy Hornberger (eds.), *Bilingual education. Encyclopedia of language and education* Vol. 5, 66–75. New York: Springer.

Cummins, Jim. 2007. Rethinking monolingual instructional strategies in multilingual classrooms. *The Canadian Journal of Applied Linguistics* 10(2), 221–240.

Degache, Christian. 2006. *Didactique du plurilinguisme. Travaux sur l'intercompréhension et l'utilisation des technologies pour l'apprentissage des langues* [Didactics of plurilingualism. On Intercomprehension and the use of technologies in language learning]. Habilitation, Université Stendhal-Grenoble 3.

Doyé, Peter. 2005. *Intercomprehension – Guide for the development of language education policies in Europe: from linguistic diversity to plurilingual education. Reference Study.* Strasbourg: Council of Europe.

Ehrhart, Sabine. 2010. Pourquoi intégrer la diversité linguistique et culturelle dans la formation des enseignants au Luxemburg. In Sabine Ehrhart, Christine Hélot & Adam Nevez (eds.), *Plurilinguisme et formation des enseignants: une approche critique*, 221–238. Bern: Peter Lang.

García, Ofelia. 2018. The multiplicities of multilingual interaction. *International Journal of Bilingual Education and Bilingualism* 21(7), 881–891, DOI: 10.1080/13670050.2018.1474851

García, Ofelia. 2014. Countering the dual: transglossia, dynamic bilingualism and translanguaging in education. In Rani Rubdy & Lubna Alsagoff (eds.), *The global-local interface, language choice and hybridity*, 100–118. Bristol: Multilingual Matters.

García, Ofelia. 2007. Foreword. Intervening discourses, representations and conceptualizations of language. In Sinfree Makoni & Alastair Pennycook (eds.), *Desinventing and reconstituting Languages*, xi–xv. Clevedon: Multilingual Matters.

García, Ofelia & Li Wei. 2014. *Translanguaging. Language, bilingualism and education.* Hampshire: Palgrave MacMillan.

García, Ofelia & Nelson Flores & Heather Woodley. 2012. Transgressing monolingualism and bilingual dualities: translanguaging pedagogies. In Androula Yiakoumetti (ed.), *Harnessing linguistic variation to improve education*, 45–75. Bern: Peter Lang.

Jewitt, Carey. 2009. An introduction to multimodality. In Carey Jewitt (ed.), *The Routledge handbook of multimodal analysis*, 14–27. London: Routledge.

Lüdi, George (ed.) 1987. *Devenir bilingue, parler bilingue.* Tübingen: Niemayer.

MacLennan, Hugh. 1945. *Two solitudes.* Montreal & Kingston: Macmillan of Canada.

MacSwan, Jeff. 2017. A Multilingual perspective on translanguaging. *American Educational Research Journal* 54(1), 167–201.

Melo-Pfeifer, Sílvia. 2021. Developing multiliteracies in on-line multilingual interactions: the example of chatroom conversations in Romance Languages. In Esther Breuer, Eva Lindgren, Anet Stavans & Elke Van Steendam (eds.), *Multilingual literacy*, 165–186. Bristol: Multilingual Matters.

Melo-Pfeifer, Sílvia. 2019. *Business as usual?* (Re)conceptualizations and the multilingual turn in education. The case of mother tongue. In Eva Vetter & Ulrike Jessner (eds.), *International Research on Multilingualism: Breaking with the Monolingual Perspective*, 27–41. Dordrecht: Springer Nature Switzerland AG.

Melo-Pfeifer, Sílvia & Maria Helena Araújo e Sá. 2018. Multilingual interaction in chatrooms: translanguaging to learn and learning to translanguage. *International Journal of Bilingual Education and Bilingualism* 21(7), 867–880.

Melo-Pfeifer, Sílvia. 2018. When Non-Romance Languages break the linguistic contract in Romance languages chat rooms: Theoretical consequences for the studies on intercomprehension. In Judith Buendgens-Kosten & Daniela Elsner (eds.), *Multilingual computer assisted language learning*, 151–167. Oxon: Multilingual Matters.

Melo-Pfeifer, Sílvia. 2017. Drawing the multilingual self: how children portray their multilingual resources. *IRAL International Review of Applied Linguistics in Language Teaching* 55(1). 41–60.

Melo-Pfeifer, Sílvia. 2016. Translanguaging in multilingual chat interaction: opportunities for Intercomprehension between Romance Languages. In Congcong Wang & Lisa Winstead (eds.), *Handbook of foreign language research in the digital age*, 189–208. Hershey, Pennsylvania: IGI Global.

Melo-Pfeifer, Sílvia. 2015. Multilingual awareness and heritage language education: children's multimodal representations of their multilingualism. *Language Awareness* 24(3). 197–215.

Ollivier, Christian & Strasser, Margareta. 2013. *Interkomprehension in Theorie und Praxis*. Wien: Praesens.

Otheguy, Ricardo, Ofelia García & Wallis Reid. 2018. A translanguaging view of the linguistic system of bilinguals. *Applied Linguistics Review*, 10(4), 625–651. Doi.org/10.1515/applirev-2018-0020.

Pennycook, Alastair. 2017. Translanguaging and semiotic assemblages. *International Journal of Multilingualism* 14(3), 269–282.

Ruiz De Zarobe, Leyre & Yolanda Ruiz De Zarobe. 2015. New perspectives on multilingualism and L2 acquisition: an introduction. *International Journal of Multilingualism* 12(4), 393–403.

Ten Thije, Jan. 2014. The effectiveness of Lingua Receptiva (LaRa) in multilingual communication. *Applied Linguistics Review* 5(1), 125–129.

Vogel, Sara & Ofelia García. 2017. Translanguaging. *Oxford Research Encyclopedia of Education*. Doi 10.1093/acrefore/9780190264093.013.181.

Wei, Li. 2018. Translanguaging as a practical theory of language. *Applied Linguistics* 29(1), 9–30.

Wei, Li. 2011. Moment analysis and translanguaging space: Discursive construction of identities by multilingual Chinese youth in Britain. *Journal of Pragmatics* 43, 1222–1235.

Wei, Li. 2015. Complementary classrooms for multilingual minority ethnic children as a translanguaging space. In Jasone Cenoz & Durk Gorter (eds.), *Between language learning and translanguaging*, 177–198. Cambridge: Cambridge University Press.

Part three: **Policies and controversies**

Mariana Bono
Chapter 9
Provenance and possession: Rethinking the mother tongue

Abstract: The seemingly benign notion of *mother tongue* has always been a strong signifier of provenance and possession. In multicultural, pan-ethnic states, whenever the language of the mother does not coincide with the language of the nation, there is a presumption of foreignness, which installs a problematic geopolitical frame for those who have known several (linguistic) homes in their lives. One of the central tenets of multilingual studies has been the idea that monolingualism is not the norm, but rather an exceptional state of affairs. However, in large swaths of late capitalist societies, monolingualism remains the main vehicle for social promotion, and, as such, it retains all its advantages. Multilingual subjects continue to struggle with the rhetoric of privilege and subordination powered by nativist approaches to language. They must routinely content with the monolingualizing forces that undermine even the most progressive institutions, including our schools and universities, which purport to promote and protect linguistic diversity while remaining a key cog in an apparatus that constructs language as something which is a natural possession and towards which certain individuals can claim proprietary rights. This chapter focuses on the personal narratives of a group of multilingual first-year students at Princeton University. Because subjectivities are negotiated in and through language, I discuss the impact that their languaging experiences have had on their personhood. I pay close attention to the emergent dynamics between tongues and bodies in the semiotic practices of racialized minorities, both in their modes of identification and in their encounters with others.

Keywords: mother tongue, subjectivity, personal narratives, languaging domains

---

Acknowledgements: I am deeply grateful to the students in my "Mother Tongues" seminar for sharing their extraordinary experiences and invaluable perspectives with me. My gratitude also goes to the Freshman Seminars Program at Princeton University for their continued support.

Mariana Bono, Princeton University, e-mail: mbono@princeton.edu

https://doi.org/10.1515/9781501512353-010

> If thus, each language has its distinct national character, it seems that nature imposes upon us an obligation only to our mother tongue, for it is perhaps better attuned to our character and coextensive with our way of thinking. I may perhaps be able to ape haltingly the sounds of foreign nations, without, however, penetrating to the core of their uniqueness.
> J. G. von HERDER, *On Diligence in the Study of Several Learned Languages*, 1764

1 The need for "mother tongues"

A survey of the *Nassau Weekly*, the journal run by students at Princeton University that publishes essays on culture and politics, personal histories, travel journals, reviews of movies and music, humor, poetry and fiction – among other campus-related news and stories – reveals a number of recent autobiographical pieces with a shared concern with language as the defining element in their author's self-representation and social domains of interaction: Verbal Knockout, by Mina Kesen (*Language is a boxing match in my home*); A Mother's Love, Lost in Translation, by Jimin Kang (*When the mother tongue is tucked away to make room for other languages, what becomes of it?*); Mother Tongue, by Somi Jun (*A power imbalance mediated by language, a relationship done and undone in the webs of translation*); Speaker of Many, Master of None, by Jin Chow (*I slammed my 12-year-old fists onto the shiny Yamaha piano keys, the polyphonic dissonance echoing my frustration. "Would you please stop speaking Cantonese to me?" I yelled. "From now on, I only want you to teach me in Mandarin or English."*); J'ai Deux Amours, by Emily Lever (*My parents put in uncommon efforts to raise my brother and me completely bilingual*).

These student pieces offer an indication that issues of subjectivity and positionality in relation to language are a central preoccupation for an increasingly diverse student body. International students, students who arrived in the United States at an early age, second generation students born to immigrant families, students who participate in Princeton's Bridge Year Study-Abroad Program . . . all of them bring to our campus and to our classrooms languages known or lost, remembered or forgotten, desired or rejected. Sometimes, their life stories are carried in their voices. Often, there is little visible – or rather, audible – evidence to gauge the full impact that their languages have had on their personhood. By this, I do not mean simply that their voices bear no traces of an accent,[1] that symptom

---

[1] Reflecting upon the "failure" to sound completely like a native speaker, Rey Chow writes: "Having an accent is, in other words, a symptom precisely of discontinuity – an incomplete

of discontinuity that indexes foreignness and a fundamental disruption. I posit that some of our multilingual students are not only accent-less, but also language-less. Following Julia Kristeva's poignant observation that "between two languages, your realm is silence", I further argue that we need to listen to the silence of the polyglots[2] and to the monolingualism of the other,[3] to uncover what is left unsaid, what cannot be said, or will not be received.

Over the past six years, I have been witness to the myriad ways in which students' knowledge of and experience with language shape their academic and personal trajectories. In the fall of 2015, I began to offer a Freshman Seminar entitled "Mother Tongues", which focuses on languages as social institutions and instruments used by nation-states to homogenize populations, define citizenship, and create social hierarchies. Among other topics, the seminar explores language dynamics in national and colonial contexts, language allegiance and language shift, and the many ways in which language policy impacts schooling and citizenship in a transnational, interconnected world. My overarching goal in creating this course was to open up a dialogic space to rethink the figure of the native speaker, imagined to be in full possession of their language, and the idea of structural privilege that linguistic nativism entails. Student response has exceeded all my expectations. Many if not most of my students have first-hand experience of how subject positions are negotiated in and through language, and these issues resonate deeply with them. The so-called *heritage* speaker enrolled in an Arabic course to "learn" her mother tongue, the student from Manila who does not speak Tagalog, but whose repertoire includes English, Chinese, Bolivian Spanish, and some Quechua; the Korean student who hails from Hong Kong and speaks Brazilian Portuguese . . . they all share a deeply rooted desire to understand the influence of language in their (social, national, racial, generational) modes of identification. Their personal narratives, which constitute the basis of the present work, show them grappling with the notions of linguistic belonging

---

assimilation, a botched attempt at eliminating another tongue's competing copresence. In geopolitical terms, having an accent is tantamount to leaving on display – rather than successfully covering up – the embarrassing evidence of one's alien origins and migratory status" (2014: 58).

2 In *Strangers to ourselves*, Julia Kristeva describes the devastating effects of the linguistic *approximation* and the linguistic *insecurity* to which the bilingual subject is condemned in these terms: "Thus, between two languages, your realm is silence. By dint of saying things in various ways, one just as trite as the other, just as approximate, one ends up no longer saying them." (Kristeva 1991 [1988]: 15; see also Chow 2014: 136).

3 Jacques Derrida's *Monolingualism of the Other Or The Prosthesis of Origin* (1998 [1996]) informs my discussion of the loss of bilingualism that results from exclusive allegiance to the language of the nation.

and linguistic foreignness, building bridges and crossing lines between what is, should be, or could be, linguistically speaking, *theirs*.

In this chapter, I rely on theoretical developments from multilingual studies, linguistic anthropology, post-structural and postcolonial theory, combined with my own experience teaching "Mother Tongues" and those of the students who have taken this seminar, to build upon the idea that the notion of the native speaker originates within a monolingual paradigm which is, as this book's editors have noted, deeply flawed and inequitable. Despite its imperfections and inequities, and despite the fact that it is a relatively recent development in the history of humankind, the monolingual paradigm has proven to be immensely successful, for reasons that will be addressed below. Monolingual or monolingualizing practices are ubiquitous in our institutions, in our schools and universities, in the political structures of our societies, in our epistemological apparatuses. In all of these realms of human activity, the unexamined belief in the existence of native speakers of singular languages creates a dynamics of exclusion. The mother tongue as an othering device manifests itself in national debates on immigration and citizenship, whenever someone lends their support to the idea that monolingualism in English is the price that you have to pay to be American, or in conversations about language education, whenever American university administrators believe that their efforts to internationalize the curriculum need not involve languages other than English – to mention but a few examples that are close to my professional activity.

In the following sections, I review historical developments that explain the crucial role of language in the processes of nation-building, the social engineering of monolingual populations, the lot of linguistic minorities, language profiling in education, and the languages of our scholarly disciplines. Instead of separating the epistemological discussion from the empirical analysis, theoretical insights and students' personal narratives (within the context of the Freshman Seminar "Mother Tongues") are organically interwoven throughout the chapter. I approach students' written productions as a window into cultural and historical conceptions of language; they provide access to socially situated systems of representations that I aim to interrogate. I therefore choose to treat my students' life stories and itineraries as literature, on an equal footing with a number of scholarly sources, to lay down my claim that the most important implication underlying the idea of the mother tongue, namely, its ability to signal both *provenance* and *possession*, is inadequate to describe certain domains of languaging and the experiences of those who have had several homes and who have acquired several languages in the course of their lives.

2 Bilingual infidelity

> Any man who says he is an American, but something else also, isn't an American at all. We have room for but one flag, the American flag. **We have room for but one language here, and that is the English language . . .** and we have room for but one sole loyalty and that is a loyalty to the American people.
> – Letter from Theodore Roosevelt to the board of trustees of the American Defense Society, 1919. Theodore Roosevelt Papers, Library of Congress Manuscript Division; emphasis added

In this well-known and oft-cited passage, Roosevelt frames the possibility of having "deux amours" as utterly un-American. He seems to suggest that patriotic love can only be conveyed in English, the one and only language with territorial rights to this land. Besides the spatial metaphor – *languages take place*, Roosevelt's letter points to a linguistic ideology based upon the superiority of one language over all others to embody the values of the nation. Clearly, this ideology accounts for the all too familiar phenomenon of bilingualism as a transitional stage in immigrants' lives. It explains why the complete and unconditional surrender of the familial language that is enacted at some point between the first and second or third generation (as soon as possible, really) is perceived, with varying degrees of consciousness, as the sign of successful assimilation to the new homeland. For the national project to succeed, the mother tongue and the national language *must* coincide; the familial interests and the political will of the state *must* converge, or accusations of disloyalty will ensue. According to Anne-Emmanuelle Berger (2002: 63), the real question raised by modern nationalism is whether a national language can be successfully converted into a mother tongue, or, conversely, whether a mother tongue can assume the status of a national language.

A century has passed since Roosevelt wrote his missive. Linguistic nationalism is still strong, and the monolingualism of the state is still triumphant. In our current political climate, one may be tempted to throw the blame onto the resurgence of nativist and xenophobic politics. But an alternative explanation, namely, that far-right assimilationist politics alone cannot sustain the enduring grasp of monolingualism, should be entertained. As David Gramling (2019) has argued, a centrist, technocratic reinvestment in monolingual procedures is rife in the life of our institutions. This kind of monolingual bias is best illustrated by a 2011 speech on immigration reform by then president Barack Obama, in which he metaphorically states that undocumented Americans who wish to stay in the United States should "pay a fine" and "learn English." Gramling interprets this type of discourse as a confirmation that there is a progressive, common-sensical position that ensures the reproduction of the monolingual state, while claiming to promote or, at the very least, to protect, linguistic diversity:

> The President's formulation itself was such a faint and prosaic recitativ of Teddy Roosevelt's stances on assimilationism. Roosevelt's vivid rebuke of the specter of the US as a "polyglot boarding house" – and Obama's bland recasting of this – showed how subtle, understated, and yet unquestionable this thickened administrative monolingualism had become around citizenship, and how these modest-sounding procedural demands to *pay a fine and learn English* rest on these officials' self-assured presumption that they themselves are the ones attempting to combat monolingualism.
>
> (Gramling 2019: 3–4, author's emphasis)

The ideology of the nation that sustains these monolingual fortifications is one in which citizenship presupposes permanence and undivided loyalty. Movement across space – migration – and across languages – multilingualism – will be tolerated but, under certain conditions, can be punishable with a fine, and an injunction that is an imposition in disguise: that you acquire the monolanguage of the nation. If the mother tongue is, as I argue in the following section, a sign of provenance, the sooner someone can claim English as their mother tongue, the sooner they will be seen to belong to the national community. The national mother tongue, then, serves as a vital element in the imagination and the production of a homogeneous, cohesive nation-state.

3 The location of the mother tongue

In her critique of Anderson's discussion of the role of language in the emergence of nationalist movements and the nation-states, Berger reminds us that, assuming that the mother tongue is the language of the mother, the preposition "of" signifies both provenance and possession: the mother tongue is the language that comes *from* and belongs *to* the mother. Let us start by examining the idea of provenance introduced in the previous section. Taking her cues from Derrida, Berger asks a series of important questions:

> What becomes of the notion of mother tongue, and of the values of originality, authenticity, irreplaceability, permanence and identity that accompany and exalt it, when the mother's language is, strictly speaking, the language of the other? (2012: 14) What would happen if 'mothers', putting themselves into motion, abandoned the sphere of their confinement and began crossing frontiers, bound for the universe? (2012: 22) What is a 'mother tongue'? What becomes of its myth when mother-women speak and transmit more than one language, and not necessarily their language(s) of 'origin', thereby cutting the fantasmatic cord which ties the tongue of the mother, and the mother who transmits it, to a site that is defined, stable, homogenous, unsubstitutable – to the mother's resting place? (2012: 23)

Chapter 9 Provenance and possession: Rethinking the mother tongue — **239**

These questions invite us to consider the impact of population movements across the globe in the domain of languaging. People who have a hard time answering the question of their origins – *Where are you from?* – usually find it equally hard to come up with a straight-forward answer when asked about their first language – *What is your mother tongue?*, which raises the question of the kind of relations that can be posited between language and identity in the context of spatial, but also mental, dislocation.[4]

Some elements of response can be found in the following narrative, told by a 17 year-old student who was born in Richmond, BC, Canada, where she was raised by her recently-immigrated Chinese mother. At age six, she moved to Shiroi, Japan, where the family resided for three years. When the student was nine years old, they moved back to Richmond, and a few years later, they moved again, starting high school in conjunction with a new life in Vancouver. Along the way, she learnt Mandarin, English, and Japanese, and school gave her the opportunity to expand her repertoire by adding French to her known languages. About her lived experience, she wrote:

> Changing addresses and countries had quite a few benefits and drawbacks, including but not limited to becoming fluent in four languages and developing *suspicion* of any roots I put down. But one effect *snuck up* on me that I was never too sure what to make of: a *nebulous* national identity. Even now, whenever I try to have an introspective moment, I find my various experiences aggregating into *almost-discrete narratives*, pooling into the different imprints that each culture and its language have made in me. The *difficulty* I faced in connecting these narratives into one cohesive and confident being *plagued me* for most of my childhood. (FRS173 Student Essay; emphasis added)

Nativist approaches to language presuppose a stable and static origin for language itineraries. When people – or, following Berger's feminist reading, women – put themselves in motion, the Herderian continuity between language and territory is lost, and the subject is left unable to imagine a *cohesive and confident* self. If, as Anderson would claim, the nation is narrated to us, the possibility of telling the story in different languages complicates the narrative, creates suspicion, and clouds comprehension (Berger 2012; Anderson 2006). My student does identify fluency in more than one language as a positive outcome of migration. Is it possible, then, that language need not be territorialized, that the subject can locate herself *in* language? "It might be that the lesser the

---

4 See Kerschhofer-Pulaho and Slavkov (this volume) for an in-depth discussion of how educational institutions frame the "language question" for incoming children and their families, imposing labels and categories that leave little room for them to resist or challenge the monolingual orientation of the school.

attachment to one's 'place of origin' or to the 'native soil', the greater the attachment to language: to languages without lands, without limits, spoken and transmitted by families in mutation-migration" (Berger 2012: 24).

If, as Berger suggests, we can think of the subject as located in language, we should also envision language as located in the body. Many of my students, regardless of whether they were born in the United States or abroad, do claim English as their native language. Among them, a language-as-privilege narrative is common. These students are keenly aware of the advantages that English confers in terms of access to cultural, social, and economic capital, an awareness that is rendered even more acute by the fact that their own parents may have migrated to the United States as adults and lack fluency in English. But these young people are equally aware that theirs is a *finite* privilege. In the words of one of my students:

> In the United States, my fluency in English lends me a distinct – though finite – privilege. In Taiwan, this foreign lilt brands me as an outsider in my ancestral home. In the United States, I'm presumed a foreigner until I speak; in Taiwan, it's the other way round.
> (FRS173 Student Essay)

The privilege conferred by the world's most dominant language remains invisible because it is inaudible. In order to reap the benefits, the English-speaking subject must *speak*, and she must be heard. The privilege carried by her voice is not in her body, where it is overrun by another crucial marker of nationhood: race. Racialized minorities can claim membership to the national community *and* command of the national language, but, because they do not conform to normative racial ideals of Americanness, they are still *presumed foreigners, until they speak*.[5]

The co-naturalization of language and race is at play in these student narratives, whereby "languages are perceived as racially embodied and race is perceived as linguistically intelligible" (Rosa 2019: 2; see also Shuck 2006). For some, their non-conformity to normative representational tropes surfaces during their participation in that standard staple of an elite liberal arts education, the study-abroad program. In the following excerpt, another student reflects upon an interaction that she routinely had while studying abroad in Germany:

---

[5] Of course, when the listening subject engages in racial profiling, speech that falls perfectly in line with national standards is not going to suffice. In a May 2020 White House press conference, CBS News journalist Weijia Jiang asked Donald Trump a question about the Covid-19 pandemic, and he responded that she should "ask China." Ms. Jiang, an Asian American, followed up by asking the president why that response was *specifically* for her, which prompted Mr. Trump to abruptly end the press conference.

In Germany, where I spent the past eleven months of my life, I was somewhat of a linguistic unicorn. People who met me claimed to be verwirrt, confused. After revealing I was an exchange student, the question that often ensued was, "where in Asia are you from?" I'm American; I explained that, although Chinese was the first language I could coherently communicate in, I thought of English more as a "native language". I'd subsequently be introduced to others as "Chinese, but living in America", as if my Americanness was not entirely plausible. My classmates listened slightly bewildered as I posited that Chinese, technically my first language, did not diminish my identity as American. *I'm not special where I grew up. Many of my friends are also bilingual Americans. But relocate me to another culture, and it may be harder to explain myself to others.*

(FRS Student Essay, emphasis added)

Every year, American institutions of higher education send hundreds of thousands of students abroad, many of whom find themselves at odds with the global racial and linguistic stereotype of the American citizen. *I'm not special where I grew up* denotes confidence in and ease with one's bilingual ordinariness, but that certitude evaporates in a different locale: *relocate me to another culture, and it may be harder to explain myself to others*. On a similar note, a Hispanic student who was in Beijing to teach English to Chinese learners reported having his language credentials questioned more than once: *Are you sure you know this [language]?* He struggled to be taken seriously as an English instructor because his body negates his tongue. Since nationality and race compete as markers of linguistic ability and language loyalty, but linguistic ability and language loyalty are pre-conditions for being admitted into the national community, the question of the relation between language and territory raises all kinds of complexities, and complicates the ways in which subject positions are ascribed, claimed, and performed. "Place of birth," writes Jonathan Rosa, "is of little relevance when one's racially overdetermined body, primordially anchored in an imagined foreign elsewhere, demands to be accounted for" (2019: 14).

Transplanted, transnational languaging triggers suspicion and requires containment strategies (Yildiz 2012) in the form of administrative and procedural fortifications (Gramling 2019). Because monolingualizing forces are not exclusive to the United States, I will put my analysis of student narratives on hold to briefly discuss two European examples of attempts at managing and restricting multilingual practices. The first example is borrowed from Yasemin Yildiz's 2012 book *Beyond the Mother Tongue: The Postmonolingual Condition*. Yildiz tells of a state-endorsed media campaign launched in Germany in the spring of 2010 with the goal of encouraging immigrants to learn German. The campaign slogan was *Raus mit der Sprache. Rein ins Leben*, which translates as 'Spit it out. Throw yourself into life.'

> [. . .] the campaign slogan was superimposed on a series of photographs, each showing a more or less prominent minority figure in his or her twenties, thirties, or forties. Ranging from sports stars and politicians to hip-hop musicians and other entertainers, the depicted subjects appear as lively, excited, and happy, or hipster cool. The focal point of each of these largely grey-hued pictures, meanwhile, is the tongue: each subject sticks out a tongue that has been painted in bright stripes of the German national colors of black, red, and gold. In this manner, the campaign promises inclusion and enjoyment to those who allow their bodies to be painted in the national colors *exclusively*.
> (Yildiz 2012: 206; emphasis added)

'Spit it out' (literally 'out with the language') is an injunction to speak, usually addressed to someone who is reluctant to do so. In Yildiz's terms, "the campaign's message of 'speak already' thus construes an addressee who is willfully silent and who needs to be playfully challenged to give up that position" (2012: 206). The second part of the slogan, 'throw yourself into life,' promises a fun, blissful existence to those who agree to expel their foreign tongues. The inscription of the national tongue in the very bodies of the minorities pushes forward the narrative that their multiple tongues represent an obstacle to integration. Yildiz sees in this campaign a substitutional logic that promises inclusion and even happiness to those who accept to paint their tongues in the colors of the nation. But more interestingly, she reads it as an inadvertent admission of defeat, an acknowledgement that the nation is not, or is no longer, monolingual, hence the need for a monolingualizing intervention.

The second example comes from Spain, in the form of a rather laughable tentative by the Spanish Royal Academy to curb the use of English in the public domain. The 2016 institutional campaign, entitled *Lengua madre solo hay una* ('There is but one mother tongue'), features fake commercials that are supposed to trick the unwitting consumers who let themselves be lured by the sound of fancy English words into buying luxury goods which are either useless or ridiculously named (there is, for instance, a fake ad for sunglasses with a "blinding effect" – the latter two words in English). At one point, the screen is divided into several close-ups of white bodies, presumably Spanish, whose tongues form English sounds. The maligned anglicisms against which the Royal Academy is fighting its quixotic battle include words such as *target, briefing, packaging, input,* and *branding*.

It follows from these examples that two of the most defining aspects of late capitalism, mobility and globalization, threaten the *one language, one nation* premise upon which the European nation-states have been conceived. Both the German and the Spanish campaigns referenced above attempt to protect the national linguascape against what Rey Chow has labelled the *xenophone*, an emergent languaging domain that "bears in its accents the murmur, the passage, of diverse found speeches" and whose imprints, revealingly, "are already present everywhere" (2014: 59).

4 The impossible possession of language

Different modalities of communal, administrative, and institutional interventions are designed and implemented to strengthen the monolingual nature of the modern nation. Diasporic, multiethnic communities and families find themselves under pressure to give up their *alien tongues* so that they can cross the line between foreigner and citizen, non-speaker and speaker. But, because of the elusive, unattainable nature of linguistic nativeness, and because language is racialized, their gesture of surrender, however complete and unconditional, does not guarantee that they will be awarded the privileges of the native speaker. Those who succeed may find themselves speaking the *monolingualism of the other*, and those who fall short of reaching this target can be reduced to *a state of languagelessness*.

"I only have one language. Yet it is not mine." So begins Derrida's *The Monolingualism of the Other, or the Prosthesis of Origin* (1998). Derrida's only language was French, and in this borrowed, alien, distant tongue, that came from his mother but wasn't hers either, the philosopher sees "the threatening face and features of colonial hegemony" (1998: 69). An Algerian born to Jewish parents, Derrida would never feel at home in the French language, which he wrote with distinction, but spoke with an accent, a centrifugal force and a xenophonic mark that "gave him up" and immediately and automatically located him in the periphery of France's hyper centralized political imagination. Arabic, taught as a foreign language at his French *lycée* in Algiers, was also a language of alterity, as was Judeo-Spanish, the sacred but forgotten language of his Sephardic forbearers. Derrida describes his inability to anchor himself in any of these languages as a catastrophic dispossession with devastating effects, "a strangely bottomless alienation of the soul" (1998: 53). Throughout his life, Derrida would entertain a neurotic relationship with French. French was the language of the Other, but he never stopped trying to conquer it. By his own account, he would actually become a purist, intolerant of accents, improprieties and solecisms.

Clearly, the crucible so poignantly described by Derrida is not exclusive to a Jewish *pied noir* in Algeria. The expression "monolingual in someone else's tongue" brings to the foreground the experience of countless speakers with a linguistic and cultural "heritage" to their names. The word *heritage* points to an alterity, the memory of a distant place, and the possibility (the risk?) of being unfaithful towards the national community. At this point, I wish to return to my own work in the field of collegiate language education, and to the personal narratives that the students who have taken the Freshman Seminar "Mother Tongues" have graciously and generously shared with me. My experiences as a language scholar, a teacher and an adviser to undergraduate students at Princeton University have taught me that so-called "heritage" students grapple with a perceived dissonance between their names, their bodies, and their often times "perfect" monolingualism in English. Perhaps one of the most important lessons in Derrida's work is that we would be mistaken to underestimate the emotional toll and the feeling of tragic loss that results from the impossibility to *own* (a) language.

Ever since Chomsky issued his seminal programmatic statement that "linguistic theory is concerned with an ideal speaker-listener in a completely homogeneous speech community, who knows its language perfectly" (1965:3), theoretical linguistics and applied linguistics alike have been bound by an epistemological stance that equates nativism with authority and authenticity. To state the obvious, the "native" character of a language is not negotiable nor transferable. It is impossible to learn and thus cannot be taught. And, in terms of social value, "being native" beats all other available options, because the figure of the native speaker of a singular language comes closest to the ideal linguistic self. Within applied linguistics, and specifically in the field of language education, linguistic nativism has deeply affected the way in which multilingualism is perceived by teachers and students alike. For many teachers, a monolingual orientation appears to be an integral component of their professional *habitus* (Gogolin 1997). As for students, empirical studies analyzing visual representations of multilingualism among school-aged children have shown that, when asked to draw the multilingual brain, a majority of children will draw a map, with different languages occupying discrete spaces, not unlike national territories separated by political borders: "their drawings are made up of compartments, with each language occupying a specific area that is distinct from the others; plurilingualism appears to be constructed through juxtaposition rather than complementarity" (Castellotti and Moore 2002: 13; see also Castellotti & Moore 2009 and Melo-Pfeifer 2017).

Through formal education, we enter the world as viable social subjects. Faced with the explicit message of the supremacy of the national language over their home languages, "the subject in question is constituted in none other than a condition of being caught between languages – and further, between languages not simply as skills but as indexes of cultural superiority and inferiority" (Chow 2014: 39). Home semiotic practices are perennially construed as being in need of remediation (Valdes 2005; Garcia, Kleifgen & Falchi 2008), so much so that, early on, a linguistic heritage can become a burden, when society and its institutions signal that *some languages are better than others, and one language is better than many languages*. The following student reflection will allow me to discuss the impact of this pervasive monolingual, nativist model of subject formation:

> As a child, I could not speak English properly. [. . .] When I spent time with my mother, *we spoke with no regard for grammar*. Our language had become a mesh of Spanish and English: words from both tongues were *interchangeable* and the grammar of each respective language was similar enough to become equivalent in our minds. *Double* negatives, *misplaced* modifiers, and *misused* verb tenses flowed from one language into the other – and my mother never noticed. My earliest memories, however, provide me with the intimation that I had known for quite a while that *my English was far from standard*. Around my father, I had always tried to avoid making grammar errors that would prompt him to correct me. He simply always seemed to correct me. I just would not understand why until years later. In his twenties, my father had left behind a military dictatorship and communist insurrection in his native land of Peru. He had spent countless hours in his youth learning and practicing English and even German for the chance to study abroad. *He succeeded*. He was there when the Berlin Wall crumbled, and three years later, he was working in Los Angeles as an English teacher when the L.A. riots broke out.
>
> (FRS173 Student Essay; emphasis added)

In this narrative, there is – ab initio – an organic fluidity between English and Spanish, two languages with porous borders. This idiosyncratic blend has been well described in the literature of translanguaging (see, for instance, Otheguy, García and Reid 2015) and in memoirs of multilingual writers.[6] Soon enough, however, these practices are noticed and stigmatized (*"my English was far from standard"*), and the possibility of language without a grammar is entertained (*"we spoke with no regard for grammar"*). In a discursive movement linked to the normative pressure exerted by the school and embodied by the father – not coincidentally, a teacher himself, the othered language, Spanish, begins to fade, while the hegemonic language, English, is parsed and experienced as improper, inaccurate, and inappropriate.

Rey Chow's discussion of languaging in the postcolonial scene is particularly useful to analyze the treatment of linguistic minorities by the nation-state and its institutions (as the author points out, modern nation-states and colonial enterprises are similar in that they have made language a primary tool

---

[6] Hélène Cixous' *The names of Oran* (2002) offers a riveting example of multilingual effervescence by means of an ontological riddle: *I love my mother tongue – but which one*. If Derrida's linguascape is tragically monolingual, Cixous tells of an Algerian childhood in which French, German, Arabic, Berber, Hebrew, Spanish, and English merge to form "a language that makes use of everything it encounters, incomprehensible beyond the apartment", a language so radical in its creativity and hybridity that it must be renamed, and that Cixous rebaptizes "Westphaloberber Charabia" (2002: 190).

and coercive agent of national or colonial cohesion, whatever the grounds of their claim). Reflecting upon the ways in which schooling can instill a hierarchy of cultural values in which knowledge of standard English is deemed indispensable for social advancement, she writes that "to learn is to simultaneously alienate or strange from oneself what is closest to one" (2014: 45). In the cases where one or several home or community languages coexist with a dominant language, a dispossession, a loss of language, ensues. On his first year at Princeton, the student whose narrative I presented above enrolled in an intermediate Spanish course in order to satisfy the university's "foreign" language requirement. That the language of his early socialization has become a foreign language demands attention. Is he in better hands now? The answer may be yes, by some accounts. His is undoubtedly a story of success. He has succeeded at dominating the dominant language. He is pursuing a university degree at a prestigious institution. The Spanish he is being taught is what many consider to be the legitimate, cultivated, cosmopolitan variety, the language of symbolic power that will add cultural and linguistic capital to his academic credentials. The critical question is whether that original fluidity can be restored. His Spanish may be credible now, but can it be creative again?

The lived experience of my student is a good illustration of the damaging effects of the disconnection between early schooling and secondary and postsecondary education as far as language instruction is concerned. In the early stages of formal education, the languages spoken at home and in the community have to give way to the national language, the mastery of which is regarded as the *sine qua non* condition for overall academic achievement. When foreign language instruction is introduced in the curriculum, preexisting competences and their impact on further language learning are far from being a focal point, and when educators do pay attention to them, they overwhelmingly adopt a monolingual perspective whereby the less standardized and more informal language that is (or was) used at home is seldom recognized as a strategic asset. In the North American context, Cummins (2005) has described a "no win" situation by virtue of which the school system deprives children of the very same resources it aims to develop. There is a perverse logic in the way in which our educational institutions choose to ignore or to actively suppress bilingualism in schoolchildren, while simultaneously claiming to develop skills in foreign languages, "often the very same languages and often in the very same children" (Hornberger 2005: 606). A paradigmatic shift is needed for education to become a factor of change as opposed to being yet another fortification of monolingualism (Gramling 2019). We have to rethink the way in which we engage with pedagogical practices that may be purporting to develop multilingualism, but only *after* producing perfectly monolingual students, who are able to ascertain their normative monolingual privilege.

The final point I wish to make concerns not our language pedagogies, our roadmaps for the transmission of knowledge, but our languages of scholarship, that is, our approach to the production of knowledge. According to Mignolo (2012), the scholarly profession has collectively decided that the languaging practices of multilingual subjects constitute a worthy field of inquiry. But, he adds, the language of the disciplines must remain pure:

> What is permitted in literature is not allowed in cultures of scholarship. Cultures of scholarship [. . .] could make of hybridity an interesting topic of study, but the discourse reporting the finding cannot be hybrid itself! You cannot, for example, be a sociologist and publish an article in a prestigious and refereed sociological journal (or any other discipline for that matter) and write like Anzaldúa wrote *Borderlands/ La frontera* (1987).
>
> (Mignolo 2012: 222)

In other words, we can have a translingual imagination, but the text is only acceptable in a monolingual form. Mignolo's argument raises a crucial question: "Is it enough to describe the heterogeneity or hybridity of the enunciated, maintaining at the same time the homogeneity and purity of enunciation?" (2012: 256). Reflecting upon the discursive condition and linguistic materiality of our objects of study and of our intellectual tools, Germán Labrador asks similar questions:

> "What languages make theory? Which provide case studies? Is it necessary for Iberian Studies to be expressed in English or in a multitude of peninsular languages? Does it make sense that at a Galician Studies conference no one speaks publicly in Galician? In what language(s) are these pages written?" (Labrador 2016: 69)

About multilingual writing practices, Sylvia Molloy wrote that "one always writes from an absence, the choice of a language automatically signifying the postponement of another" (2003, np). In the domain of language, postponement can lead to erasure. If we continue to function within national or colonial geopolitics of language and knowledge production, if we keep trying to dominate the dominant language and enforcing native-speaking norms, we are condemning ourselves to mimic the monolingualism of the other and to reproduce dubious schemata that perpetrate inequity by acknowledging certain semiotic practices while denying others. For ourselves as well as for our students, bilingualism then stops being a way of life – as it was in the premodern era and still is in a large share of the postcolonial world – to become a skill in a resumé, worthy of institutional recognition, but sterile, without imagination.

5 Conclusion: the mother tongue and the reproduction of glotopolitical hierarchies

History teaches us that language was a vital element in the creation of the national community – a discursive community, according to Anderson (2006). A common language may have been the foundation of national cultures and political imaginations, but the rise of specific vernaculars as national languages was not the product of a natural evolution, and is better portrayed as a conscious exercise in social engineering (Hobsbawm 1990; Bonfiglio 2010). The German romantics believed that, when there is a language, there is a nation (the nation is a cultural formation and language incarnates the spirit of the people). The French positivists, on the other hand, thought that because the nation existed, it had to be given a language (the nation is a political formation and a common language guarantees its unity). However different in their conceptions of the relationship between language and the state, the two approaches led to a similar paradigm or model for nation-building: *one language, one nation*, a paradigm so powerful that it became one of the greatest narratives of the modern era (Judt & Lacorne 2004; Sériot 2014).

Since the early days of the nation-state, governmental structures have suppressed and concealed, without fully eliminating, the multilingual practices of the people. Throughout the modern era, the monolingualism of the state has produced more monolingual subjects, monolingual communities, and monolingual institutions. In Europe, to return to a geopolitical context that I have used to support my argument, not even the most coercive containment strategies – Robespierre's linguistic terror or Francoist-era castillianization come to mind – succeeded at erasing regional languages.[7] In present times, it is no longer acceptable to ask of immigrants that they relinquish their language rights to achieve a linguistically homogeneous citizenship. Instead, linguistic minorities are expected to display competence in the registers of the state, the academy, and the professions. At its most successful, "monolingualism *manages* other languages; it does not oppose them" (Gramling 2016: 11). To frame the common language as an instrument for national cohesion, the guarantor of civil rights, and a tool for social advancement may seem laudable. Nevertheless, this discursive trope does little to address a glotopolitical hierarchy that manifests itself in time and space. In the national discursive space, the only voices that are heard (that

---

[7] It is not a coincidence that, at the end of the twentieth century, Pierre Bourdieu relies on the portrayal of the mayor of the Southwest city of Pau giving a public speech in Gascon Bearnese to illustrate the condescending strategies of the French elites (Bourdieu 1982).

have the power to impose reception) speak the monolanguage of the state. Modes of representation and interaction are further complicated by the fact that, in the multi-ethnic modern state, many citizens don't look the way they sound, or don't sound the way they look. In terms of the temporal inscription of linguistic practices, every time we tell someone that a language, be it Spanish, Korean, or Guaraní, is their heritage, we are signifying to them that that language belongs to their past, to the familial archive. While some will want to tend to their heritage, others will feel disinherited, or refuse the legacy in favor of the more productive language, the language of promise.

Monolingualism is not a fashionable state of affairs. No one, except perhaps for members of the most reactionary social and political circles, would take pride in knowing only one language. However, as recent scholarly work suggests and the student narratives discussed in this chapter appear to confirm, "the *kind* of multilingualism that is often idealized in order to stave off [. . .] ostensibly monolingual parochialism is often deeply at odds with existing popular multilingualisms" (Gramling 2016: 194). There is a clear need to further interrogate the paradox of the monolanguage: if it is always defined as a negative, if no one wants it, if well-meaning policy-makers, educators, and families assign value to *not* being monolingual, why does, then, the monolingualism of the state always triumph? Has the idea of a *national mother tongue* become so naturalized as to make us forget its own history of production? Is it useful to cling to the notion that monolingualism is not the norm, when – as the main vehicle for social advancement – it retains all the advantages (Judt & Lacorne, 2004)? Robust interdisciplinary conversations, including the ones featured in this book, are currently offering important elements of response.

In closing, I would like to return to the notion of the native speaker. Rey Chow argues that, for the native speaker to become audible or discernible, nonnative speakers need to be present. For the mother tongue to come to the foreground "more than one language [has to be] already in play, explicitly or implicitly, as a murmur, and an interference" (Chow 2014: 58). How we respond to, regulate, and manage this polyphonic or *xenophonic* reality (Chow, 2014:59) has consequences for the maintenance or the loss of linguistic diversity at different levels of the public and private realms. Our educational institutions and pedagogical practices are a key element in an apparatus that constructs language as something which is a natural possession, and towards which certain individuals can claim proprietary rights. On the national stage, mother tongues other than the hegemonic language forever locate minoritized populations in an imagined foreignness, *someplace else*. To a large extent, the purpose of linguistic nativism is to anchor power in a particular category of speaker, born into the political matrix of the nation. To use the seemingly benign terms of "native speaker" and "mother tongue" unreflectively is to engage in a gesture of othering that operates on an axis of empowerment and disempowerment, to reproduce a debilitating rhetoric of exclusion for those who do not conform to the normative parameters upon which the national community was originally imagined.

Author's Positionality

Mariana Bono was born in Argentina and her first language was Spanish. She always thought her childhood to have been strictly monolingual (with the exception of the mandatory English lessons) but, later in life, she has come to recognize the constant, familiar presence of Italian, or rather, the Piedmontese dialect that had been her grand-parents' mother tongue, in the household. Italian is, to her, as intimate as it is unknown; neither her own, nor foreign. Whenever Italian is being spoken, provided that she doesn't attempt to parse the words, it *sounds* like the Spanish of her childhood. Her family's experience of language replacement resembles that of millions who cross oceans and national borders to start a new life elsewhere: monolingualism in the language of the host nation will always seem like a small price to pay for assimilation.

Learning English in Argentina was hard work. It took effort, and the rewards always seemed too meager. English was, for a long time, distant, out of reach. But English prepared her for French. Learning French at age 20 was a revelation. It happened at light-fastening speed. French came naturally to her, and she entered its realm with confidence and ease. These language learning experiences were so transformative that when the time came for Mariana, who by now was living in Paris, to settle on a topic for her doctoral dissertation, multilingualism and third language acquisition seemed an inescapable, self-evident subject. Her early work is a linguistic and pedagogical exploration of the factors that bear on instructed language learning by multilingual students.

Languages that were not originally her own opened up new pathways for emotional and intellectual growth. They offered opportunities for radical reinvention and gave her permission to imagine new versions of herself, to claim new subject positions. These lived experiences led her to mistrust the essentialist linkage of linguistic nativity (the "mother tongue") with authenticity, authority, and ownership. The paths by which speakers come to feel at home in a language are complex, subtle, and intimately connected to human trajectories. Mariana's has taken her from Argentina to France, the UK, and the United States. These experiences of relocation, integration, and discovery, together with her acquaintance with different cultures of scholarship (with different cultures *tout court*), and the linguistic insecurity that she has had to contend with along the way, have prepared her to recognize the plight of those, including her students, whose multilingualism is perennially construed as an othering device, devalued and pushed to the margins, and reinforced her commitment to work towards linguistic equity and language inclusion through her teaching and scholarly work.

References

Anderson, Benedict. 2006. *Imagined Communities*, 2nd edition. London: Verso.
Berger, Anne-Emmanuelle. 2002. The Impossible Wedding: Nationalism, Languages, and the Mother Tongue in Postcolonial Algeria. In Anne-Emmanuelle Berger (ed), *Algeria in others' languages*, 60–80. Ithaca, NY: Cornell University Press.
Berger, Anne-Emmanuelle. 2012. Politics of the Mother Tongue, *Parallax* 18(3), 9–26.
Bonfiglio, Thomas. 2010. *Mother tongues and nations: The invention of the native speaker*. New York, NY: Mouton de Gruyter.
Bourdieu, Pierre. 1982. *Ce que parler veut dire: L'économie des échanges linguistiques*. Paris: Fayard.
Castellotti, Véronique and Danièle Moore. 2002. *Représentations sociales des langues et enseignements. Guide pour l'élaboration des politiques linguistiques éducatives en Europe. De la diversité linguistique à l'éducation plurilingue. Étude de référence*. Strasbourg: Conseil de l'Europe.
Castellotti, Véronique and Danièle Moore. 2009. Dessins d'enfants et constructions plurilingues. Territoires imagés et parcours imaginés. In Muriel Molinié (ed), *Le dessin réflexif: éléments pour une herméneutique du sujet plurilingue*, 45–85. Cergy-Pontoise: CRTF: Université de Cergy-Pontoise.
Chomsky, Noam. 1965. *Aspects of the theory of syntax*. Cambridge, MA: MIT Press.
Chow, Rey. 2014. *Not like a native speaker. On languaging as a postcolonial experience*. New York, NY: Columbia University Press.
Cixous, Hélène. 2002. The Names of Oran. In Anne-Emmanuelle Berger (ed), *Algeria in others' languages*, 184–196. Ithaca, NY: Cornell University Press.
Cummins, Jim. 2005. A Proposal for Action: Strategies for Recognizing Heritage Language Competence as a Learning Resource within the Mainstream Classroom. *The Modern Language Journal* 89(4), 585–592.
Derrida, Jacques. 1998. *Monolingualism of the Other, or the Prosthesis of Origin*, trans. Patrick Mensah. Stanford, CA: Stanford University Press.
García, Ofelia, Jo Anne Kleifgen, and Lorraine Falchi. 2008. From English language learners to emergent bilinguals. *Equity matters: Research review* No. 1. New York: Teachers College, Columbia University.
Gogolin, Ingrid. 1997. The "monolingual habitus" as the common feature in teaching in the language of the majority in different countries. *Per Linguam* 13(2), 38–49.
Gramling, David. 2016. *The invention of monolingualism*. New York: Bloomsbury.
Gramling, David. 2019. "On Reelecting Monolingualism." Invited Lecture. Princeton University, Princeton, NJ, April 2019.
Hobsbawm, Eric. 1990. *Nations and nationalism since 1780. Programme, myth, reality*. Cambridge, UK: Cambridge University Press.
Hornberger, Nancy. 2005. Opening and filling up implementational and ideological spaces in heritage language education. *The Modern Language Journal* 89(4), 605–609.
Judt, Tony and Denis Lacorne. 2004. The politics of panguage. In Tony Judt and Denis Lacorne (eds), *Language, nation, and state: Identity politics in a multilingual age*, 1–16. New York, NY: Palgrave Macmillan.
Kristeva, Julia. 1988. *Etrangers à nous mêmes*. Paris: Gallimard.

Labrador Méndez, Germán. 2016. New directions in Iberian cultural studies? (Gloto)political peographies of Peninsular Hispanism after 2008. *Hispanic Issues On Line Debates* 6, 57–71.

Melo-Pfeifer, Sílvia. 2017. Drawing the plurilingual self: how children portray their plurilingual resources. *IRAL* 55(1), 41–60.

Mignolo, Walter. 2012. *Local histories/Global designs: Coloniality, subaltern knowledges, and border thinking*. Princeton, NJ: Princeton University Press.

Molloy, Sylvia. 2003. Bilingualism, writing, and the feeling of not quite being there. In Isabelle de Courtivron (ed), *Lives in translation. Bilingual writers on identity and creativity*, np. New York, NY: Palgrave Macmillan.

Otheguy, Ricardo, Ofelia García, and Wallis Reid. 2015. Clarifying translanguaging and deconstructing named languages: A perspective from linguistics. *Applied Linguistics Review* 6(3). 281–307.

Rosa, Jonathan. 2019. *Looking like a language, sounding like a race: Raciolinguistic ideologies and the learning of Latinidad*. New York, NY: Oxford Unversity Press.

Sériot, Patrick. 2014. Language and nation: two models. In Virve-Anneli Vibman and Kristiina Praakli (eds), *Negotiating linguistic identity: language and belonging in Europe*. Bern: Peter Lang.

Shuck, Gail. 2006. Racializing the nonnative English speaker. *Journal of Language, Identity, and Education* 5(4), 259–276.

Valdés, Guadalupe. 2005. Bilingualism, heritage language learners, and SLA research: Opportunities Lost or Seized? *The Modern Language Journal* 89(3), 410–426.

Yildiz, Yasemin. 2012. *Beyond the mother tongue: The postmonolingual condition*. New York, NY: Fordham University.

Nkonko M. Kamwangamalu
Chapter 10
The pluricentricity and ownership of English

Abstract: English is the most widely spread and spreading language around the world. As English has spread and new varieties of English have emerged in former British and American colonies as well as in countries with no colonial ties to Britain or the United States, questions have been raised about how to model this diversity of English and about who owns the language. In his 'new Englishes' paradigm, Braj Kachru has proposed three concentric circles of English – the inner circle, the outer circle, and the expanding circle – which some 'new Englishes' scholars equate with the ENL-ESL-EFL trichotomy. Kachru has argued that English belongs to all who use it, regardless of how the literature defines them, as natives or non-natives. This chapter critiques and calls into question the theoretical and functional usefulness of the distinction between native and non-native Englishes (NS/NNS). The chapter revisits the concept of English as a first language and argues that the term better captures the evolving nature and changing face of English in both post-colonial as well as non-colonial contexts, where English has also been acculturated and is used by some as first or only language in their daily language practices. Drawing on data from African Englishes, the chapter highlights some of the processes involved in the acculturation of English in support of the advanced argument, with a focus on lexical transfer from the indigenous languages into English, internal lexical creativity, idiomatic expressions, and selected syntactic features.

Keywords: pluricentricity, world Englishes, English as a first language, post-colonial and non-colonial contexts

1 Introduction

In his address to the 1999 TESOL Annual Convention in New York, David Crystal remarks as follows regarding the linguistic center of English: "the center of gravity for the language, which used to be in the US/UK, is now moving elsewhere, as speakers of English as a second/foreign language gradually become

Nkonko M. Kamwangamalu, Howard University, e-mail: nkamwangamalu@howard.edu

https://doi.org/10.1515/9781501512353-011

the majority (1999: 4)." As noted elsewhere (Kamwangamalu 2001: 46), at issue in Crystal's remarks is the *pluricentricity* of English, a topic that the literature on world Englishes has addressed over the years (McArthur 1987; Kachru 1992; 1996a; Mufwene 1994) and which continues to be the focus of investigations in the present (Buschfeld and Kautzsch 2017; Deshors 2018; Saraceni 2015). More specifically, the issue is whether with the emergence of new varieties of English in former British and American colonies, Britain and America can continue to claim to be the sole centers from which norms and innovations are created (Doeer 2009; Ferguson 1982; Hilgendorf 2019; Onysko 2019). The related issue concerns the ownership of English, whether any one center can claim sole ownership of English or whether, as Kachru (1986) puts it, the language belongs to all who use it, regardless of how the literature defines them, as natives or non-natives (Giri 2014; Holliday 2006). In this chapter, I call into question the distinction between native and non-native speakers of English (hereafter NS/NNS dichotomy or distinction). The very concept of 'native speaker' has been challenged and contested in the literature, and appears to be ideologically driven to maintain a monolithic vision of English (Bhatt 2019; Kachru 1996b; Kobayashi 2018). I propose that more encompassing concepts, such as *English as a first language*, be revisited to not only challenge the monolithic vision of English, but also to accommodate speakers of English in the Outer Circle, where some use English as first or only language to meet their daily communication needs. But, as a reviewer remarks, how beneficial is the distinction between 'first language' and 'native language'? Wouldn't 'first language' run into the same problem – clean-looking, monolithic view of English – just as 'native language' does? How about the term 'mother tongue'? How does it compare to 'native language' and 'first language'? I tackle these concerns first in Section 3, where I discuss the NS/NNS dichotomy, and I subsequently return to them in Section 4 and Section 5, where I present a case study of English as a first language in the context of the South African Indian community and Singapore, respectively.

The discussion of the NS/NNS dichotomy will be organized as follows. First, I offer an overview of the literature to provide the theoretical background against which the issues under consideration will be discussed, with the focus on new Englishes paradigm and world Englishes paradigm (Kachru 1996c, 1997). Next, I discuss the NS/NNS dichotomy against Kachru's concentric circles of English – Inner Circle, Outer Circle, and Expanding Circle – and contrast these with the ENL-ESL-EFL trichotomy. I argue that the NS/NNS dichotomy does not capture the evolving nature and changing face of English in both post-colonial as well as non-colonial contexts, where English has also been acculturated and is used by some as first or only language in their daily language practices. Therefore, new theoretical concepts should be developed or old ones, such as *English as a first language*, should be revisited to include individuals in post-colonial contexts who, just like their counterparts in the Inner Circle, also use English as 'a first language' or 'only language'. The last section discusses the pluricentricity and the related issue of the ownership of English. As I will argue later, this issue is intrinsically linked to the question of how one describes users of English in the Outer Circle communities such as Singapore and South Africa. I argue that speakers of English in these communities own the language, and I provide data from English usage in the African context in support of the advanced argument, showing that the language has been acculturated to suit the communication needs of its speakers in this non-traditional English context.

2 The new Englishes paradigm and the "world Englishes paradigm"

The 'new Englishes' paradigm and the 'world Englishes' paradigm have their roots in the pioneering work of my late mentor, Braj Kachru, who introduced them in the 1980s to model the pluricentricity of English around the world (Kachru 1983, 1986, 1987). The new Englishes paradigm is mainly concerned with the study of institutionalized varieties of English, that is, varieties that are used as second languages in former British colonies in Asia (e.g., Indian English, Singapore English) and Africa (e.g., Nigerian English, South African English). It is explained that the new varieties of English used in these regions are a by-product of prolonged contacts between English and indigenous languages; consequently, they have distinctive features (to be discussed later) at all levels of linguistic structure (lexis, syntax, semantics, discourse, phonetics and phonology) distinguishing them from the varieties of English spoken in Britain or the United States. Therefore, Kachru (1983: 10) argues that institutionalized varieties of English cannot be characterized in terms of 'acquisitional inadequacy' or be judged by the norms of 'Inner Circle' Englishes, such as British English or American English. Romaine (1992: 254) concurs, noting that "new Englishes have their own structural norms, their own characteristic features and even their own communicative styles" distinguishing them from the varieties of English spoken in traditional English settings. Accordingly, Kachru (1992) argues, these institutionalized new Englishes must be treated in terms of the range and depth they have in the host community. Range refers to the function the language performs in the community, and depth refers to the degree to which the language has become acculturated to reflect the community's norms and traditions. It is noted that, in terms of the range, new Englishes serve a wide range of functions in the post-colonies, among them instrumental, interpersonal, regulative, and creative/imaginative function (Kachru 1992). The interpersonal function refers to the use of English both as a symbol of eliteness and modernity, and as a link language – the linguistic glue that bonds speakers in ethnically and linguistically diverse and complex societies (Silva 1998: 76). The instrumental function refers to the use of English in a country's educational system. The regulative function concerns the use of English for the regulation of conduct in such domains as the legal system and the administration. And the imaginative/innovative function entails the use of English in various literary genres (Kachru 1983). In terms of the 'depth', institutionalized varieties of English are characterized by linguistic features not found in Inner Circle varieties. These features are evident at all levels of linguistic structure, as will be illustrated in Section 6, in which I discuss **"Ownership of English."** One of the features to be highlighted in that section is idiomatic expressions such as I *wrote it down in my head* (i.e. I made a mental note of it) (Tsitsi Dangarembga, 1988: 64), which is a literal translation of an African idiom into English. 'Ownership of English' is one of the two key questions addressed in this chapter, the first being a critique of the usefulness of the NS/NNS dichotomy, especially in light of the spread and consequent diversity of English around the globe.

Associated with the *New Englishes paradigm* is the *World Englishes paradigm*. In Kachru's words, the term *World Englishes* does not entail any divisiveness nor the *us* vs *them* in the English-using communities. Rather, it is intended to recognize the functions of the language in linguistically and culturally diverse pluralistic contexts (Kachru 1997: 67); to indicate distinct and/or multi-identities of the language and literature; to stress the *we-ness* among the users; and to symbolize variation in form and function as well as a range of variety in literary creativity (Kachru 1996b: 135). In particular, the term *World Englishes* entails that English has become pluricentric; that is, the language has many centers from which norms and innovations are created. Among other things, these centers recognize convergence of English with local languages as a natural process of convergence and acculturation; they consider the formal processes of nativization as an integral part of the linguistic variety; and acknowledge that regional varieties of English, 'native' or 'non-native', have primarily local, regional, and interregional context of use (Kachru 1997). In recognition of these centers and the spread of English around the globe, Kachru (1992) has proposed that users of English be divided into three groups, or what he calls "Three Concentric Circles of English": the Inner Circle, the Outer Circle, and the "Expanding Circle". The *Inner Circle* includes countries where English is used as a native language, among them Australia, Canada, New Zealand, the United Kingdom, the United States of America, and a segment of South Africa's white population, as explained in Kamwangamalu (2002) and later in this chapter. The Outer Circle includes countries where English is an institutionalized variety or second language. Former British colonies, such as South Africa, India, Nigeria, Zambia, to list a few, belong in this category. The *Expanding Circle* consists of countries where English is used as a performance variety, that is, a foreign language. Some such countries include Japan, China, Argentina, Korea, Rwanda, Senegal, Germany, Austria, etc.

The framework of "Three Concentric Circles of English" has been welcomed by some (Bolton 2005; Bhatt 2019; Chisanga and Kamwangamalu 1997; Zhiming 2001), but it also has been criticised by others (Bruthiaux 2003; Pennycook 2003; Saraceni 2015). In praises for the framework, Zhiming (2001: 357), for instance, notes that "the notion of the three circles . . . provides us with a useful tool to conceptualize the status of the English language in the world today." Bolton (2005) adds that the Kachruvian studies, including the 'Three Circles of English' framework, aim at promoting and legitimizing an inclusive, pluricentric approach to world Englishes, highlighting both the sociolinguistic realities and bilingual creativity of Outer Circle societies in particular. Put differently, rather than being an exclusive exponent of Judeo-Christian traditions, English now represents diverse sociolinguistic histories, multi-cultural identities, multiple norms of use and acquisition, and distinct contexts of function (Bhatt 2019). It follows that the 'three circles' classification of Inner, Outer, and Expanding Circle of English speaks to the propensity that English has for acquiring new identities, for adapting to decolonization as a language, and for being a flexible medium for literary and other types of creativity across languages and cultures (Kachru 1987: 222). Along these lines, Hino and Oda (2019) remark that the concept of world Englishes, with the three circle paradigm as its central tenet, has dramatically deconstructed the prevalent belief in the supremacy of conventional native speaker English, a point to which I shall return in Section 3, where I question the validity and usefulness of the NS/NNS dichotomy.

The Kachruvian studies, including the 'new Englishes' paradigm and the 'world Englishes' paradigm, along with the "Three Concentric Circles" model, have, indeed, received support in the literature, as discussed above; however, they have also had their critics (e.g., Bruthiaux 2003; Kobayashi 2018; Pennycook 1994; Saraceni 2015; Tan 2014). The main criticism stems from the changing face of English particularly in the 'Outer Circle' nations. Citing Singapore and the Philippines as examples, Kobayashi (2018: 561) notes that, in the former, a growing number of locals now use English as 'a new mother tongue' in the private and public sphere (Tan 2014); whereas in the latter, the three circles model is said to exist among the country's nationals who live in different socio-economic and linguistic environs (low income families who have no access to English, upper-class citizens residing in English-speaking communities) (Martin

2014). Accordingly, Kobayashi argues, the three circles model is no longer an optimal approach to accounting for the dynamics and complexity of English use in the ever changing world. In agreement, Deshors (2018) highlights the increasing diversity of Englishes in today's globalized world and calls for new theoretical models to comprehend more fully the changes that English is undergoing in the 21st century. According to Deshors, new models are needed because current models, including Kachru's circle model, apparently do not take into account the dynamism and such neglected aspects as attitudes toward English and language policies (Röthlisberger 2019). As a reviewer notes pointedly, Deshors appears to be concerned with the changes in the use of English that are linked to several sociolinguistic questions, but one could also argue that Kachru's work might not be sufficient to explain specific questions on the microsociolinguistic spectrum. Similarly, Pennycook (2003: 519–521) questions the Kachruvan model on, among other things, the following aspects: the descriptive (in)adequacy of the three circles, the focus on 'national' varieties of English, and an 'exclusionary' tendency "to shut out 'other Englishes'" (Bolton 2005:75). Bolton (2005) has addressed these charges at length, noting that Kachru's work speaks for itself. In particular, Bolton (2005: 78) points out that "the strength of the world Englishes paradigm has lain and continues to lie in its consistent pluralism and inclusivity," both of which constitute the pillars of Kachru's writings on the spread of English around the world. In his writings, Kachru has consistently called for a shift from the monolingual paradigms, which characterize English studies in general, to paradigms relevant and appropriate to multilingual and multicultural societies, which characterize world Englishes studies. Also, as Bolton (2005: 78) notes further, "the Kachruvian model of the three circles was never intended to be monolithic and unchanging." Rather, the circles were intended to account for the geographical spread of English around the world. They help not only to locate new Englishes but also to describe their usages, functions and relationships. Kachru's work describes the formal characteristics and functional roles of the new Englishes, demonstrates their systematicity, and explains them in terms of the linguistic, social, and cultural forces that shape their norms (Bhatt 2019; Bolton 2005). Another criticism levelled against the Kachruvian work, especially the three circles model, is that the distinction between the "Inner Circle" Englishes and the "Outer Circle" Englishes, which the literature has misleadingly equated, as I argue in Section 3, with the distinction between native vs non-native Englishes, presents some varieties as peripheral or marginal (Mufwene 2001). Hino and Oda (2019) make a similar point, though their focus is on the Expanding Circle, arguing for an eclectic and integrative approach toward egalitarianism among all users of world Englishes. It must be noted, though, that egalitarianism and inclusive plurality have been the hallmark of the Kachruvian studies. As Hilgendorf

(2019) remarks, and this is the view in this chapter, the very goal of Kachru's work, including the circles model, has been to recognize the plurality of English around the world; to argue against the paradigm of marginalization; and to call for greater inclusivity of the Englishes that have emerged in communities where the language historically had been a foreign code. In the next section, I take up this issue of the distinction between native and non-native Englishes, which, critics contend, is apparently rooted in the distinction Kachru (1992) makes between the 'Inner Circle' and 'Outer Circle' of English.

3 Native vs non-native speakers (NS/NNS) of English

Kachru (1996b) remarks that the success story of English, its alchemy, and the resultant ecstasy, have unleashed a variety of issues related to identity, elitism, power and ideology and attitudes toward and perceptions of its users, who are traditionally divided into three groups: English as native language (ENL), English as Second Language (ESL), and English as a foreign language (EFL) users. The concept of English as a native language (ENL) has been challenged (Kachru 1997), for, as Kachru remarks, it elevates a particular type of 'native speaker' – the Inner Circle speaker – to a position of 'cultural superiority', and cultivates specific attitudes toward the Caucasian race in general. The literature on world Englishes has tended to conflate *English as a native language* (ENL) and *English as a first language*, which I spell out to avoid confusion with English as a foreign language (EFL)'. I argue that the two concepts may seem to be synonymous, but they are not, as will be explained below. Therefore, the concept of *English as a first language* does not, arguably, run into the same problem – clean-looking, monolithic view of English – just as *English as a native language* does. *English as a first language* has more to do with the order in which the language has been acquired, whereas ENL, traditionally, refers to individuals who are born into and raised in one of the Inner Circle countries (Giri 2014). Viewed from this perspective, ENL is not inclusive, for it marginalizes individuals in the Outer Circle who may also have been born into the language. In contrast, *English as a first language* appears to be more inclusive than ENL, for it is intended to apply to anyone who uses English as a primary language to carry out their personal, social and/or professional activities (Shariffian 2010, cited in Giri 2014: 193). Also, since it refers to the order in which the language is acquired, *English as first language* presupposes that the speaker may have other languages in his or her linguistic repertoire, which he/she uses depending on the context of situation. Furthermore, unlike *English as a native language*, *English as a first language* does not entail a power hierarchy according to which one variety of English – the one spoken in the Inner Circle – is more privileged than another: the one spoken in the Outer Circle. Thus, it seems to me that the NS/NNS dichotomy, which mirrors the traditional ENL/ESL dichotomy, is flawed on several counts.

First, let us consider the claim to **'native-ness'**. Indeed, every language, including English, has individuals who speak or claim it as a native language. However, as Mufwene (2001: 138) remarks, the NS/NNS distinction may have contributed more to marginalizing the so called 'non-native Englishes' rather than to helping us understand why they are legitimate offspring of English in their own right. The very fact that Outer Circle varieties have been spoken successfully for so long in their respective communities, Mufwene argues, is evidence that 'native speakers' are not needed for new linguistic systems to normalize. (Also, see Paikeday 1985's aptly titled book, *The native speaker is dead!*).

The second challenge to the NS/NNS dichotomy is **language ownership or appropriation**, a topic to which I will return in Section 6. As Mufwene (1994) notes further, the dichotomy between NS/NNS fails to shed light on what happens when English is acquired by people in a non-Anglo-Saxon setting. In such a context, as we will see in Section 6, English has been restructured and acculturated to meet the communicative needs of its new speakers. The acculturation of English is evident at all levels of linguistic structure, the most noticeable being phonetic/phonology, marked by segmental and suprasegmental features not found in Inner Circle Englishes (Zhiming 2001). For example, in their report on Namibian English, Kautzsch, Schroeder, and Zahres (2017) describe several vowel mergers and splits, which seem to be specific to Namibian English since they are, apparently, unattested in other African Englishes. Furthermore, the authors remark that the pronunciation of English vowels in Namibia differs by ethnic group, which in turn suggests that Namibian English cannot be seen as a monolithic whole but rather as a bundle of local sub-varieties. In a similar study into the stress and rhythm in Educated Nigeria English, Essien (2017) observes that Nigerian English stress and rhythmic patterns are significantly different from the British English stress and rhythmic patterns; consequently, Educated Nigerian English features more stressed syllables than those found in Inner Circle varieties of English. (For additional examples, see Kamwangamalu 2019: 124.)

The third challenge to the NS/NNS dichotomy is **the norms** on which the dichotomy is based. As Bokhorst-Heng, Alsagoff, Mackay, and Rubdy (2007) point out, the NS/NNS dichotomy describes Outer Circle speakers' English on the basis of Inner Circle speaker norms. They point to studies by a number of scholars (e.g., Kandiah 1998: 5–10; Pennycook, 1994: 176) arguing that such categorization not only "suggests negative assumptions regarding their [i.e., Outer Circle speakers'] general proficiency level, the credibility of their intuitive judgments, and their overall authority over the language in terms of their confidence and sophistication in using it," but it also "does not take into account how the speakers themselves feel about their sense of ownership, belonging, or identity towards English" (Bokhorst-Heng et al. 2007: 426). The authors note further that the NS/NNS dichotomy assumes a single uncontested linguistic norm within which English operates in Outer Circle countries. They point out, however, that the debates around Singapore English (Singlish) and English in Singapore, for example, indicate that some Singaporeans prefer exonormative standard of English, while others embrace the development of indigenous endonormative standards. In a related study titled 'Language ideology and native English speaker privilege in academia', Saenkhum and Duran (2019) report on the findings highlighting two major professional components: teaching that leads to students' perceptions of non-native-English-speaking instructors, and publications that involve peer-review processes, including comments about non-native features in writing from reviewers and editors. The study demonstrates that English language norms generated by Inner Circle speakers of English are commonly privileged, and that such practices continue to create negative attitudes toward Outer Circle users of English, although these users are equipped with academic knowledge and skills. Additionally, the authors note, Outer Circle usage, or 'non-nativeness' of English remains stigmatized and is considered unacceptable. These findings suggest that the NS/NNS dichotomy still exists even in the diversified multilingual-multicultural world.

Fourth, the NS/NNS distinction entails ***a hierarchical relationship*** between Inner Circle speakers and Outer Circle speakers, with the varieties used in the former being perceived as superior to and more prestigious than the varieties spoken in the latter. As Zhiming (2001: 359) points out, the distinction "favours the maintenance of the status-quo: high prestige for the 'Inner Circle Englishes', and low prestige for the 'Outer Circle Englishes'". In agreement, Bhatt (2019) comments that maintaining the status-quo is in line with the politics of conformity to Inner Circle (or 'native') norms (Prator 1967; Quirk 1988), which world Englishes literature opposes, especially since the English language has acquired multiple centers from which norms and innovations are created, as noted earlier. Indeed, because of their assumed 'superiority', Inner Circle varieties tend to be perceived as the target for language learning (Schreiber and Janz 2019). Holliday (2006: 385) refers to this phenomenon as native-speakerism, an ideology that favors a monolithic vision of English, presents differences as deficit, innovations as errors, change and variation as the product of fossilization (Bhatt 2019), and "is characterized by the belief that 'native speaker' teachers represent a 'Western culture' from which spring the ideals both of the English language and of English language teaching methodology" (Kobayashi 2018: 558). This monolithic vision of English, however, does not hold in Outer Circle communities (Holliday 2006). These communities' post-colonial Englishes have, at all levels of linguistic structure, their own norms and standards according to which they are used, as noted above with regard to Namibian English and Nigerian English. The fact that there are so many varieties of English around the world, say Ugandan English, Singapore English, South African English, Indian English, etc., is a clear indication that Inner Circle varieties are not a model for language learning in the communities associated with the named Outer Circle varieties of English. On the contrary, as will be shown in Section 6, speakers of English in these communities have taken ownership of the variety of English they speak, and consider it not peripheral but a center and norm-providing in its own right (Watanabe 2019). Meierkord (2019) concurs in her discussion of 'center and periphery' with reference to Uganda and Rwanda. In particular, Meierkord notes that 'centrality' has often been associated with the Inner Circle countries, and periphery with such nations as Uganda, a former British colony (and Rwanda, a former Belgian colony). However, Uganda may be viewed as 'central' for Rwanda. The author explains that during the civil war from 1990–1994, many Rwandans sought refuge in Uganda, where they learned English in Ugandan schools. Today, Rwandans who can afford it and who prefer for their children to be educated through the medium of English continue to send their offspring to Uganda for secondary and/or tertiary education. To these individuals, Meierkord notes further, the model of English they have acquired and are using in their language practices has nothing to do with 'native-speakerism'; instead, it is Ugandan English, a variety central rather than peripheric to meeting their communication needs. This means, in response to a reviewer, that in Rwanda different varieties of English are spoken that model Ugandan English for it is perceived as being more prestigious.

Finally, the asymmetrical relationship between NS/NNS is of little or no value at all to understanding the changing face of English in post-colonial settings, where some children are either born into and so use English as a first language, or are using English as their only medium of communication as a result of marked, parents-driven language shift from the indigenous languages to English (Fishman 2004; Kamwangamalu 2003). Also, there is the case of countries around the world, such as Nepal in Asia and Namibia and Rwanda in Africa, that have no colonial ties to Britain or the United States; yet, they have adopted and use English as the official language of the state. Clearly, due to financial constraints, not every citizen in these nations has access to English. However, those who do, especially highly educated families in urban centers, also use English in the same way the language is used in comparable families in the 'Outer

Circle' – as first or only language. This raises the question of how to model users of English not only in post-colonial but also non-colonial contexts. As a reviewer asks, are users of English in these contexts native or non-native speakers of English? Can they also claim ownership of English? These and related issues are as yet to be investigated. I must note, in passing, that individuals who are born into the language, irrespective of the circle (Inner, Outer, Expanding), and use English as their first or only language are native speakers of the variety of English they speak and can claim ownership of the variety, as will be explained in Section 6. For now, I would like to return, in the next two sections, to the central focus of this paper, the NS/NNS dichotomy, which the foregoing discussion has shown to be problematic. The intent is to suggest, again, that the concept of *English as a first language* be revisited to accommodate the users of English in the Outer Circle who have been born into the language. I will use, as a case study, users of English in Singapore and South Africa, two polities that I know well, having taught there for a while and so have first-hand knowledge of their linguistic landscape and language practices. I will first consider *English as first language* in South Africa, with a focus on South African Indian English, and will then turn to *English as a first language* in the island state of Singapore, where the younger generation of the country's population is increasingly becoming monolingual in English.

4 English as a first language in South Africa: focus on South African Indian English (SAIE)

South Africa is a multiracial and multilingual country, with at least 25 languages being spoken within its borders. Of these languages, eleven have been recognized as official languages of the state. They include English and Afrikaans, English's historical arch-rival, and nine African languages, namely Zulu, Xhosa, Swati, Pende, Ndebele, Swana, Sotho, Tsonga, and Venda, all of them newcomers onto post-apartheid South Africa's official languages map (Kamwangamalu 2002). According to the 1996 census statistics, English is spoken as home language by 3,457,467 (9%) of the people, including 1,711,603 (39%) Whites; 974,654 (94.4%) Asians; 584,101 (16.4%) Coloreds (people of mixed blood); and 113,132 (0.4%) Africans. The percentages refer to the number of people in each community (e.g., Whites, Asians, etc.) who speak English as home language. For example, 94.4% of Asians speak English as home language, while only 0.4% of the entire African community speak it as home language. Kamwangamalu (2002: 3) reports that English has a wider distribution than most official languages, but the majority of its speakers are concentrated in metropolitan and urban areas. English is the most dominant language in South Africa, much as it is in other former British colonies in the African continent and elsewhere. It performs all the functions identified in Kachru (1992), including the interpersonal, instrumental, regulative, and imaginative function, as described earlier. South African English is not monolithic. The language has a wide range of varieties, much as it does in any English-speaking country in the world. Against the background of the apartheid system and the walls it built between communities, varieties of English in South Africa are distinguished along ethnic and racial lines: White South African English (SAE), Black SAE, Indian SAE, and Colored SAE. These varieties do each have their own standard and sub-varieties (Lanham 1986; Makalela 2004). Lanham (1986), for instance, distinguishes three varieties within White SAE: Conservative SAE, Respectable SAE, and Afrikaans English including its variant, Extreme SAE. The first is associated with whites of British descent; the second with whites of Jewish descent; and the third with whites of Dutch descent. Similarly, the literature shows that black language communities, such as the Zulu, the Xhosa, the Tswana, etc. each have their own variety of English with its distinct characteristics (Kasanga 2006; Makalela 2013). South Africa's Outer Circle varieties of English, such as Black, Colored, Indian, and Afrikaans SAE are heavily marked, at every level of linguistic structure, by the native languages of the speakers of these varieties: African languages for Black SAE, Afrikaans for the Colored and Afrikaans SAE, and Indian languages for Indian SAE. Concerning the latter, Lanham (1986: 326) remarks that, despite the fact that South African Indians have lost their languages and have shifted to English, their English is characterized by an accent carrying the hallmarks of Indian English elsewhere in the world.

In South Africa, English fits into two of Kachru's (1992) three concentric circles: the Inner-Circle and the Outer-Circle. English belongs in each of the two circles because it is used as a native language by some, with the term 'native' referring to whites of British descent; and as a second language by others, namely Afrikaans-speaking whites, that is, whites of Dutch origin, and a minority of the black population who have had the privilege to be educated at English-medium schools. There is, however, a significant segment of South Africa's population, including the younger generations of South African Indians (94.4%) and 'Coloreds' (16.4%), who are born into and speak English as a native language. However, the 'native vs non-native' discourse does not count the afore-named segments of the South African population as native speakers of the language, since 'nativeness', as it applies to English, is traditionally restricted to Inner Circle speakers, as noted earlier. This is where the concept of *English as a first language* is more appropriate than the concept of *English as a native language* (ENL), for it accommodates speakers of English in both the Inner Circle as well as the Outer Circle communities, including the South African Indian community.

Rajend Mesthrie, who has written extensively on South African Indian English, remarks that the existence of this social dialect, SAIE, is a consequence of the indentured immigration scheme instituted by Britain, which brought 152,185 Indians to South Africa, mainly as cheap labor for the cane fields of Natal between 1860 and 1911 (Mesthrie 1988: 5). SAIE is a product of language shift from the immigrants' languages to English, a process that must have started early into the twentieth century. Bughwan (1970, cited in Mesthrie 1988: 5) noted that a process of language shift in the direction of English was, in the late 1960s, nearing completion. It can be stated, unequivocally, that over 50 years later that process must be complete. Mesthrie (1988: 5) himself points out that in the South African Indian community, "English has taken over as the usual language of the home, though older persons use a vernacular Indian language in the home to varying degrees. A generation of children is growing up with little or no fluency in an Indian language, and with a variety of English that nevertheless owes a great deal to the substrate Indian languages." As a matter of fact, notes Chishimba (1991), Mesthrie's work testifies to the ethnolinguistic status of South African Indian English as a first language for most of its speakers, and to the fact that the Indian community in South Africa is an English-speaking community, using English as the primary means of communication. Prabhakaran (1998: 302) describes the shift from Indian languages to English as a conscious choice that Indian parents made for their children. She explains that parents forced their children to learn English and discouraged them from learning Telugu or any other Indian languages because, first, the social identity associated with English was more desirable than that associated with Indian languages and, second, the government's language policies did not assign the Indian languages any role in the South African society. Parent-driven language shift is not unique to South Africa. Parental ambitions for the children are also said to have contributed to what Crowley (1996) calls *pragmatic language shift* from Irish to English in Ireland; and to a shift from Tamil to English in Tamil communities in Singapore and Malaysia (Gupta 1997), a point to which I shall return in the next section, where I discuss *English as a first language* for the younger generations of Singaporeans. South African Indian parents forced their children to switch to English because, in South Africa, English is the language of job opportunities, interethnic and international communication and is the language most used for the conduct of the business of the state. It is seen by many as the language of power, prestige and status, and as an open sesame by means of which one can acquire unlimited vertical social mobility (Kamwangamalu 2002: 3). Since ENL (*English as native language*) is ideologically loaded and is traditionally used with reference to speakers of English in the

Inner Circle, I believe that *'English as a first language'* is the most appropriate cover term for describing not only Outer Circle users such as the younger generations of South African Indians and Singaporeans, but also Inner Circle users of the language as well. Using the same term 'English as a first language' for the Inner and Outer Circles does not entail blending the two circles; rather, the circles remain separate conceptually but the term is used to refer to speakers from both circles. One may be tempted, though, to use the term "native language" for all who speak English as home language. But we know too well that the term "native speaker" is attitudinally and ideologically loaded, as already noted. When a call is made on the Linguistlist for native speakers of English to participate in a research project, for example, it is unmistakeably directed solely to speakers of English in the Inner Circle, for their variety is perceived as superior to the varieties of English spoken in the Outer Circle, as Holliday (2006: 385) has noted with respect to *native-speakerism*. Also, using the term "native speaker" for all who speak English as a home language will take us back to the very concept the chapter is challenging – the *native speaker* – which the literature has used with reference only to Inner Circle speakers. I now turn to the changing face of English in the Island State of Singapore.

5 English as a first language in Singapore

Like South Africa, Singapore is a multi-ethnic, multi-racial and multilingual nation, with at least 20 different languages under the three major ethnic groups – Malay, Chinese, and Indian – and other minority groups (Kamwangamalu and Lee 1991). It has what Kuo and Jernudd (1988: 5) refer to as a policy of pragmatic multilingualism, prescribing four official languages including Malay (which is also designated as the national language), Mandarin Chinese, Tamil, and English. English is the only official language that is not directly related to any major ethnic group. Like English in South Africa, English in Singapore is not monolithic. On the contrary, the language has varieties that can be associated one each with the nation's three main ethnic groups that make up its population: Chinese, Malay, Tamil. Also, English has penetrated the Singapore society so much so that there has developed a unique brand of Singapore English known as 'Singlish' (Alsagoff 2007; Gupta 1994), which is the product of a prolonged contact between English and Singapore's ethnic languages and is perceived, by the government, as non-standard and so as bad English. As an institutionalized variety, English performs all the functions identified in Kachru (1992), namely instrumental, interpersonal, regulative, and creative/imaginative function as described earlier. The government promotes an expansion of proficient use of standard (British) English through campaigns such as the 'Speak Good English Campaign' (Bruthiaux 2010; Rubdy 2001), and has, since 1985, required the entire educational system, including primary, secondary and tertiary institutions to use English as the sole medium of instruction (Rubdy 2007). Singapore's government unwavering determination to promote English has resulted in language shift from the nation's ethnic languages to English, and many scholars call for English to be identified as the 'mother tongue' for the growing number of Singaporeans, who use English as a first, if not only, language in their daily language practices (Alsagoff 2010; Koyabashi 2018; Stroud and Wee 2007; Tan 2014; Wee 2002). Stroud and Wee (2007: 261), for example, found that "a significant number of Singaporeans in their mid-40s or younger are claiming to be monolingual in English, indicating that English language monolingualism might be an emerging trend rather than one that is passing . . . ". Bokhorst-Heng, Alsagoff, McKay and Rubdy (2007: 424) concur, noting that although some Singaporeans, I assume the older generations, do indeed learn English as a second language, others, especially the younger generations, "acquire it in the process of its use and interaction, much like first language speakers in Inner Circle countries." The authors state, emphatically, that "among other things, this makes these speakers native users of their variety of English" (2007: 424). In a related study, Tan (2014: 320) states that "the latest 2010 census reveals that over 30 per cent of Singaporeans report English to be the primary language used in the home, an increase from about 20 per cent in 2000." Therefore, Tan calls for "English in Singapore to be re-conceptualized as 'a new mother tongue'", at least for the younger generations of Singaporeans. It is worth noting that the literature has questioned the usefulness of the concept of 'mother tongue', describing it as misleading, essentialist, static and unitary (Canagarajah 2002: 107). It is argued that "much of the world's verbal communication takes place by means of languages that are not the users" 'mother tongue,' but their second, third, or nth language, acquired one way or another and used when appropriate (Ferguson (1992: xiii). Accordingly, Ferguson (1992: xiii) suggests that the whole mystique of 'mother tongue' should be dropped from the linguist's set of professional myths about language. However, unlike Ferguson, other scholars (e.g., Pennycook 2002) view 'mother tongue' as 'a strategically essentialist argument', one that, as Canagarajah (2002: 108) puts it, "has its uses in the exercise of power". Therein lies the dilemma for Tan's (2014) call for English in Singapore – Singlish – to be re-conceptualized as 'a new mother tongue.' Clearly, in terms of the power relationship between Singlish and standard (British) English, the latter wins over the former, especially since the government has been promoting it over the years, as noted earlier. It seems that Tan's call for Singlish to be re-conceptualized as 'a new mother tongue' has more to do not so much with the power relationship between the varieties of

English spoken in the island state, but rather with the issue of ownership, that is, the degree to which the younger generations of Singaporeans project themselves as legitimate speakers with authority over the language (Higgins 2003: 615). The question, as Higgins (2003) puts it, is whether Outer Circle speakers, such as the younger generations of Singaporeans, can be viewed as equivalent to speakers of English in the Inner Circle, with whom the concept of 'native speaker' or 'mother tongue' has traditionally been associated. I have argued that Outer Circle speakers of English own and so are native speakers of the variety of English they speak, much as their counterparts in the Inner Circle are of theirs. In the next and last section, I turn to this issue of 'ownership of English', for, as noted earlier, this issue is intrinsically linked to the question of how one describes users of English in the Outer Circle communities such as Singapore and South Africa. I argue that speakers of English in these communities own the language, and I provide data from English usage in the African context in support of the advanced argument. In conclusion, I raise the issue of how to model the users of English in Expanding Circle countries such as Namibia and Nepal, where a segment of the population uses *English as a first language*, or in similar countries such as Rwanda, where, in a generation or two, the country is likely to have citizens who use *English as a first language*.

6 Ownership of English

In this section, I present sample data from African Englishes as evidence that English has been appropriated in this part of the world, and I reiterate the argument made throughout this paper, that users of English in Africa who have been born into the language qualify as legitimate speakers of *English as a first language*. Unlike the concept of "*native speakers of English*," the term speakers of "*English as a first language*" entails not only the order in which the language was acquired, but it also means that in addition to English, the speakers are proficient in some other languages, in this case African languages. As I have pointed out elsewhere (Kamwangamalu 1997), the issue of "Who owns English?" has been brought about by the spread of the language around the world (Bokhorst-Heng et al. 2010, 2017; Crystal 1997; Norton 1997; Rubdy et al. 2008; Wardhaugh 1987; Widdowson 1994). This issue has received considerable attention in the literature, with some arguing for the ownership to be open to all who use the language, as natives or as non-natives (e.g., Kachru 1983, 1986); while others argue, explicitly or implicitly, that non-native Englishes are illegitimate varieties, deviations from and imperfect replications of the native norm, and that, therefore, only 'native speakers' can claim ownership of English (Prator 1968; Quirk 1988, 1990). Unlike Quirk and Prator, Widdowson (1994) remarks that 'to own' a language means to bend it to your will, to turn it to your advantage, to assert yourself through it rather than simply submit to the dictates of its form. Like Widdowson, Wee (2002: 283, cited in Tan 2014: 324) argues that to own a language is to "assert a specific relationship between the speaker of the language and the language itself" to the degree to which, as Higgins (2003: 615) noted earlier, speakers of English project themselves as legitimate speakers with authority over the variety of English they speak. Along these lines, since language is dynamic regardless of the context in which it is used, I support the position of Chinua Achebe that to claim ownership of English in the African context, for example, means to make English carry – as Achebe (1975: 62) puts it – "the weight of my African experience . . . " and make it become "a new English, still in communion with its ancestral home but altered to suit its new African surroundings." Users of English in the African continent have made English carry the weight of their cultural experiences by introducing features – lexical, semantic, syntactic, discoursal, phonetic and phonological – that distinguish African Englishes from the varieties of English spoken in the Inner Circle (Kachru 1992) and elsewhere in the world. There is a vast literature in which these features are discussed (Kasanga 2006; Kautzsch, Schroeder and Zahres 2017; Magura 1984; Makalela 2014; Schröder and Schulte 2019). In what follows, however, I draw on some of my own work (Kamwangamalu 2001 and 2019; Kamwangamalu and Chisanga 1996; Chisanga and Kamwangamalu 1997) to present a sample of some such features, with a focus on the lexicon, syntax, and semantics. The intent in presenting these features is to support the discussion of the acculturation and ownership of English in Outer Circle communities, where English is spoken by some as first or only language, as already noted with respect to Singapore and South Africa. In these contexts, then, the term *English as a first language* is more inclusive and so more appropriate than *English as a native language* and the related distinction between NS/NNS of the language.

6.1 Features marking ownership of English in the African context

In this section, I present some of the features that attest to the ownership of English in Africa, with the focus on lexical transfer, lexical creativity, tag questions, and idiomatic expressions.

6.1.1 Lexical features

At the lexical level, the evidence for the ownership of English in former British colonies in Africa can be seen in *the transfer of vocabulary items* from the indigenous languages into English, as in examples (1)-(4), or in what I call *internal lexical creativity*, resulting in compound nouns such as those in example (5). Some of the areas most prone to such transfer include local foods, garments, cultural ceremonies, socio-political discourse, and kinship terms (Kamwangamalu 2019). The lexical items drawn from these areas are usually not translated into English, irrespective of the discourse, verbal or written, in which the items are used. This is because the translation does not convey all the shades of meanings that these items have in the indigenous languages. Consider, for instance, the word *lobola*, which is widely used in the Southern African diaspora of English.

(1) Away with this *lobola*. Why do they have to be so demanding for their daughters? (*The times of Swaziland*, November 6, 1992)

(2) Abolish *lobola*, bring freedom to women and liberation to men. (*DOME* no. 6, University of Natal [South Africa], September 1994)

(3) Those who say *lobola* is outdated must think twice (*DOME* NO. 6).

As noted elsewhere (Chisanga and Kamwangamalu 1997: 92–93; Kamwangamalu 2019: 119–120), *lobola* translates loosely as *dowry* or *brideprice* in English. *The Concise Oxford Dictionary of Current English* (1990: 353) defines *dowry* as 'property or money brought by a bride to her husband'; and *brideprice* as 'money or goods given to a bride's family *especially in primitive societies*' (my emphasis) (1990: 138). Both definitions fail on several counts to convey the socio-cultural meanings of *lobola* in the Southern African context. Some of these meanings were first highlighted in Chisanga and Kamwangamalu (1997: 93). To begin with, in Southern Africa (and in sub-Saharan Africa in general) it is the bridegroom, and not the bride, who must bring the money and other property (e.g. cattle, clothes, etc.); this money and property is not given to the bride but to the bride's parents. On this count, and notwithstanding its attitudinally loaded dictionary meaning, the word *brideprice*, but not *dowry*, closely matches only one socio-cultural aspect of the word *lobola*: the money goes from the bridegroom to the bride's family, but not the other way round. However, both words, *dowry* and *brideprice*, fail to convey other cultural aspects of *lobola*, including the following: First, the money and property brought in to the bride's parents officialize and thereby legitimize the agreement of marriage between the bride and the bridegroom. Second, in most cases, if the marriage fails, the bridegroom can claim the *lobola* given to the bride's parents. Third, it is traditionally tacitly agreed that, should the bridegroom die, the bride will be 'inherited' by the bridegroom's brother or any designated member within the bridegroom's family. Fourth, in some cultures, if the marriage fails, the bride is not, by tradition, allowed to re-marry while the bridegroom is alive. Fifth, if the bride proves to be barren, the bridegroom can claim one of the bride's sisters to become his wife and bear him children. All of these cultural practices are encapsulated in the term lobola. Users of English in Southern Africa are subconsciously sensitive to the cultural content of the word *lobola* and, therefore, they tend to use this word instead of its apparent English equivalents, *dowry* and *brideprice*.

This sensitivity also explains why in the following example, for instance, the highlighted indigenous lexical items, which are names of traditional medicines, are not translated into English. In this example, which is one of the many advertisements that appear regularly in local newspapers, a traditional healer, Doctor Akuchanga, lists traditional medicines that he uses to 'cure' a wide range of social ills, including love or business-related problems, issues or dissatisfaction with one's sex life, etc.

(4) Advertisement by a traditional healer, Dr. Akuchanga (*Daily News*, February 27, 1998)

All you need is the right healer. I solve almost all your problems.
Eg: voodoo to calm abusive husband/wife; calling back your lost lover in a few hours by using **bwera-bwera** and **chikundi** for your lover to love you for ever; ladies vagina to be small and dry; penis enlargement for life from medium to extra large; lover's proposal powder; help in any kind of financial problems; special **Kapeta** to win in the casino and **Chanana** for lotto; revenge on enemies; help with any business to grow and be busy all the time. Old and unfinished jobs are welcome.
For full info contact: 078-175-1000. We deliver in 24 hours and we travel anywhere.

6.1.2 Internal lexical creativity

By internal lexical creativity, I mean the lexical changes that are taking place within the language itself. In other words, these changes do not seem to be caused by the contacts between English and the indigenous languages (Kamwangamalu 2019). Rather, as new situations develop, such as the end of apartheid in South

Africa, new expressions are created to accommodate or reflect these situations. In the context of South Africa, the compound *rainbow-X* (where *X* stands for an English noun), is a case in point. It refers either to the coming together of people from previously racially segregated groups; or to something that affects or benefits these people. The term *rainbow* can combine with any English noun. This results in compound nouns such as the following: *rainbow nation, rainbow complacency, rainbow swimming pool, rainbow blanket, rainbow circle, rainbow gathering, rainbow-nation school, rainbow alienation, rainbow hand, rainbow warrior*, etc., each of which is used to reflect the multiracial and multi-ethnic nature of the South African society. The same process of compound noun formation is evident in expressions such as *Madiba magic, Madiba shuffle (dance), Madiba blanket, Madiba shirt, etc.*, which consist of an English noun preceded by South Africa's late President Nelson Mandela's nickname – Madiba.

(5) ... We have all got to happily traipse into the future, hand in *rainbow hand*, embracing African Renaissance ... (*Daily News*, 27 August 1999)

(6) Mrs van Reenen has taken her two older children .. to the *rainbow-nation school* across the road, where she teaches Standard 2. (*Sunday Times*, July 1996)

(7) *Rainbow-gathering* mourns IFP man–R. Haripersaad–who was killed in a helicopter crash (*Daily News*, December 30, 1998)

(8) And the pool, in Newlands West, has already been named *rainbow-pool*, because it brings everyone together (*Daily News*, January 11, 1999)

(9) Afraid to shock the nation out of its *rainbow complacency*, the SABC warned that the programme contained a highly critical view of the new South Africa (*Sunday Times*, February 14, 1999).

(10) The SABC is run by a cabal where afternoon drinks with the right people will get you commissions. If you dare question the status quo or your proposal falls outside *the rainbow circle*, you might as well forget it. (*Sunday Times*, February 14, 1999).

6.1.3 Syntax: The tag Question 'is it?'

The tag question *is it?* is pan-southern African, that is, it is found in all varieties of English spoken in the Southern African diaspora of English, including South

African 'White' English. This expression is so widespread that it recurs in virtually all conversations involving Southern Africans, who use it as a discourse marker. It is not surprising, thus, that the conversation presented below is similar to the one presented in Chisanga and Kamwangamalu (1997: 97), where the tag question '*is it?*' is also used. Clearly, the expression *is it* in (11) appears to be a sentence in its own right, for it does not follow the traditional tag, which usually appears in sentence (or utterance) final position, as in in (12)-(15). Here, however, I am analysing both types under the same category functionally. The expression *is it* appears to have displaced the traditional tag forms in Inner Circle Englishes, which take into account gender, number and person. As Chisanga and Kamwangamalu (1997: 97) observe, one seldom comes across forms such as *Did/didn't you? Has/hasn't she? Was/wasn't he? Have/haven't they?* etc, even if an interaction involves a Southern African and a foreigner. Instead, the speakers tend to use the tag question *is it?*, irrespective of the number, gender and person in given utterances, as illustrated in (11). Also, it seems that the negative counterpart of *is it?*, namely, *isn't it?* seldom occurs in everyday interaction. However, I have come across this form in creative writings, as illustrated in the structures in (12)-(16), taken from the Zimbabwean writer Tsitsi Dangarembga's (1988) novel, *Nervous Conditions*. The structures show that *isn't it?* is also used in the region, except that it is certainly not as widespread as its positive counterpart, "*is it?*".

(11) Conversation between the author (B) and a South African female colleague (A).
A: How is your family?
B: Everyone is doing fine.
A: *Is it?* I have not seen your son lately.
B: Oh, he is fine too. He is still studying at the University.
A: *Is it?* What is he studying at the varsity?
B: He is studying psychology.
A: *Is it?* So he wants to become a psychologist eh?
B: Yah. That's what he has chosen to do.
A: Is it?
Etc.

(12) I came to look after my sister, **isn't it**? (Dangarembga, 1988: 157)

(13) You must be joking, **isn't it**? (op. cit., p. 157)

(14) And now we both have what we wanted, **isn't it**? (op. cit., p. 160)

(15) So we make it good, **isn't it**? (op. cit., p. 163)

(16) But there are still mad people in the world, **isn't it?** (op. cit., p. 170).

6.1.4 Idiomatic expressions

All of the expressions presented below, except (22), are also taken from Dangarembga's (1988) novel, *Nervous Conditions*. For most of these expressions, e.g. (17)-(23), the speakers refer to the various parts of the body to convey personal feelings. This practice, which Magura (1984: 154) calls 'body symbolism', has its roots in the indigenous languages and has been carried over into English. The remaining expressions, (24)-(25), are translations of lexical structures from the indigenous languages into English. On the surface, all these expressions look English. Underlyingly, however, they are what Chantal Zabus (1991:v) calls *palimpsests* or *calques/loan translation* (Arndt 1998) beneath whose scriptural surface can be traced imperfectly erased remnants of the indigenous languages.

(17) I *wrote it down in my head* (i.e. I made a mental note of it) (Tsitsi Dangarembga, 1988:64)

(18) She looked at him *with murder in her eyes* (i.e, She was extremely angry) (1988: 114)

(19) Snakes started *playing mini soccer in my spine* (I became very excited).

(20) People should give us *a hand that visits the head*
 (People should give us something to eat).

(21) He *entered in my mouth* (i.e., He interrupted me)

(22) He *is in my chest* (i.e., He is my close friend)
 (Magura 1984:154)

(23) They never *squeeze their bowels* in that family. (i.e. They never go hungry)

(24) Don't *take it in you* (i.e. Don't take it personally).

(25) *To see once is to see twice* (i.e. Once bitten twice shy).

As noted earlier, my goal in presenting the features highlighted in this section is to support the fact, attested to in the literature (Achebe 1975; Chisanga and Kamwangamalu 1997; Dangarembga 1988; Magura 1984) that the English language has been appropriated in Outer Circle contexts, in this case the African diaspora of English. Some members of this diaspora speak English as first or only language. This raises the question whether such speakers qualify as native speakers of English, just like their counterparts in Inner Circle communities. The term 'native speaker', however, has traditionally been used with reference to Inner Circle speakers of English, as reflected in the NS/NNS dichotomy, which I have challenged throughout and in the conclusion to this chapter.

7 Conclusion

This chapter has addressed the issue of the pluricentricity and ownership of English, with a focus on the native speaker/non-native speaker dichotomy. It has argued that though Inner Circle Englishes tend to be perceived as norm-providing, the literature on world Englishes, including my own work, argues that the English language has become *pluricentric*, for, besides the Inner Circle, the language has other centers from which norms and innovations are created, namely, the Outer Circle and, arguably, the Expanding Circle. These norms are context-bound; that is, they do not transgress the boundaries of local contexts. This is evident from the discussion of the ownership of English, where I have shown that features such as lexical transfer and idiomatic expressions, for example, reflect the morphosyntactic structure of the indigenous languages. Focusing on the Outer Circle communities, I have argued, like others (Alsagoff 2007; Bokhorst-Heng et al. 2007; Chishimba 1991; Essien 2017), that the users of English in these communities have owned the language. In particular, they have introduced into their respective varieties of English a wide range of features not found in Inner Circle varieties. The features, which can be seen at all levels of linguistic structure, including the lexicon, syntax, semantics, discourse, phonetic and phonology, are intended to make each Outer Circle variety meet the communication needs of its users. Among these users, some, being born into the language, use *English as first language*; while others, as a result of language shift from their ancestral languages to English, use it as an only language. Such speakers are, in my view, native speakers of the variety of English they speak, just like Inner Circle speakers of English claim to be native speakers of their respective varieties. Therefore, I have argued that the native speakers/non-native speakers dichotomy should be expanded to include speakers of English in traditionally non-Anglo-Saxon contexts, where the language has been appropriated, as explained earlier. Alternatively, new theoretical concepts should be developed or old ones, such as *English as a first language*, should be revisited and adopted to accommodate users of English in the Outer Circle, especially the afore-described two types – users born into the language and those using English as a result of language shift. The field of world Englishes is better served by revisiting the concept of *English as a first language* not only for the types of Outer Circle users just described, but also for users in the Expanding Circle nations, such as Nepal in Asia (Giri 2014) or Namibia (Kautzsch et al. 2017) in Africa. Expanding Circle nations, by definition, do not have colonial ties to Britain or the United States; yet, some of the citizens in nations such as Nepal and Namibia use *English as a first language* or as only language. Also, there is the case of Rwanda, which, like Nepal and Namibia, has no colonial ties to Inner Circle nations; yet, again, this French-speaking former Belgian colony has, due to political imperatives (Samuelson and Freedman 2010), replaced French with English as its official language. In a generation or two, Rwanda is likely to have citizens who use *English as a first language*. If the native speaker/non-native speaker dichotomy is not expanded, let alone challenged, and the concept of *English as a first language* is not revisited and adopted as suggested here, then the field of world Englishes should be prepared to develop new theoretical concepts to model new users of English in this Expanding Circle nation – Rwanda – and potentially others around the globe. In conclusion, there is no question that the face of the native speaker of English is changing and will continue to change as the language penetrates the territories (e.g. Ruanda) it was never expected to penetrate before. Therefore, it may be that as this happens, the concept of native speaker may become irrelevant, especially since speakers, whether in the Inner Circle, Outer Circle, or Expanding Circle will claim ownership of the variety of English they speak. Also, how useful, if it is at all, is the distinction between native speakers and non-native speakers of English and related concepts such as mother tongue? How does the distinction benefit or advance the field? I have briefly attempted to address these questions, but more research is needed to contribute to this ongoing debate over the changing face of 'the native speakers of English' around the world.

Author's Positionality

Nkonko M. Kamwangamalu was born and bred in the Democratic Republic of the Congo (former Zaire) and is currently a Full Professor of Linguistics and English at Howard University, Washington, DC., USA. He holds a PhD in Linguistics from the University of Illinois at Urbana-Champaign, Illinois, where he was trained under his late mentor, Professor Braj B. Kachru, the founder of the field of World Englishes. That training laid the foundation for Kamwangamalu's research interests in this field and exposed him to the debates over a wide range of issues concerning the spread of English around the world, including the issue of the wanting dichotomy between native speaker (NS) vs non-native speakers (NNS) of the language. He expressed his views regarding the NS vs NNS dichotomy in an interview with Anna Wu of NNEST (Non-Native English Speaker Teacher) in 2008, when he was asked the following question:

> Sridhar and Sridhar (cited in Coetze-Van Roy, 2006) argue that the existing Second Language Acquisition theories have lost their explanatory power because they do not take the contexts of world Englishes learners into consideration. As an expert in multilingualism, language and identity, and sociolinguistics, what issues do you think need further research? What topics can NNES professionals better contribute with their background as resources?

In response, Kamwangamalu argued, as he does in his contribution to this volume, that the emergence of new varieties of English in former British and American colonies indicates clearly that English has become pluricentric, that is, the United Kingdom and the United States no longer have the monopoly over norm creation and innovations in the language. Accordingly, Kamwangamalu remarks, NNES professionals should begin by problematizing rather than subscribing to the very concept of NNES itself. This concept, which seems to be entrenched in the literature, is the flip side of an old, value-laden dichotomy of native vs non-native speakers of English. The dichotomy raises a number of questions that Kamwangamalu believes should be of interest to professionals in the field. Some of these, such as 'who owns English?,' have been the object of inquiry over the years (Chisanga and Kamwangamalu 1997, Hayhoe and Parker 1994, Kachru 1992, Kamwangamalu 2001, Prator 1968). Others, however, are as yet to be investigated. For instance, what do we call the children who, due to language shift–as is the case for the younger generations of Singaporeans (Bokhorst-Heng, Alsagoff, McKay, and Rubdy 2007) and of South African Indians (Prabakaran 1998)–speak no other language but English? Are these children "native speakers" of English, of at least the variety spoken in their communities? As he has argued elsewhere (Kamwangamalu 2019), if we are to legitimize the varieties of English that have emerged in postcolonial countries in Asia and Africa, it must be acknowledged that there are children in those countries who speak English as first language, and, in some cases, as the only medium of communication available in their linguistic repertoire, just as is the case for the children in the former metropole – the Inner Circle (Kachru 1986). Investigating such questions might, Kamwangamalu notes, generate a new research paradigm for new Englishes, one that does away with or, at the very least, interrogates the current dichotomy of native vs non-native speakers of English.

Kamwangamalu believes, in agreement with Kachru (1986), that English belongs to all who speak it, regardless of how the literature describes them, as "native" or "non-native." Because he lives and works in an English-speaking environment, he has, like Nadja Kerschhofer-Puhalo (this volume) and many other speakers of English as a foreign language, been asked the question "Where do you come from?" or "Where is home?" and the related subsequent question, "Where do you really come from?" or "Where is your real home?" These questions are legitimate, but they point to the variation and changing faces of speakers of English around the world.

Kamwangamalu came to English well beyond the critical period for language acquisition, when he was in high school, where he was taught English, in French, for three hours per week. Therefore, he cannot nor need he pass for or pretend to be a "native speaker" of English.

However, like Nikolay Slavkov (this volume), English has become, for Kamwangamalu, his "strongest tool of written expression" while his other languages, among them French, Ciluba, Swahili, and Lingala, have largely remained underused as tools for written expression. His current research interests include topics not only in the field of World Englishes, but also in language policy and planning for minoritized languages in the global south, with the focus on the role of English in the educational systems and its impact on the development of indigenous languages. He has written extensively on such topics, arguing that English has become a naturalized African language in Anglophone Africa (Kamwangamalu 2019) and, therefore, it should no longer be considered a foreign language. Rather, he proposes that for the indigenous languages to develop and also become a viable medium of instruction in the educational systems, they must be accorded some of the privileges and perquisites that English has, which motivate language consumers (parents, students, policy makers, etc.) to embrace English-medium education at the expense of an education through the medium of their own indigenous languages. Further, Kamwangamalu (2016) argues that it is not enough to simply give official recognition to selected indigenous languages, as happened in South Africa after the end of apartheid and elsewhere in the African continent and beyond; language consumers need to know what, compared with English-medium education, an education through the medium of an indigenous language will do for them in terms of upward social mobility. This question should become the focus of research and policy-making in Africa and other English-speaking postcolonies around the world if we are to develop and make the indigenous languages attractive to their own speakers as a viable medium of instruction in the educational systems.

References

Achebe, Chinua. 1975. English and the African writer [Reprinted from *Transition* (Kampala) 4, 18 (1965)]. In Ali A. Mazrui (ed.), *The Political Sociology of the English Language: An African Perspective*, 217–223. The Hague: Mouton.
Alsagoff, Lubna. 2010. English in Singapore: Culture, capital and identity in linguistic variation. *World Englishes* 29(3). 336–348.
Alsagoff, Lubna. 2007. Singlish: Negotiating culture, capital and identity. In Viniti Vaish, S. Gopinathan and Yongbing Liu (eds.), *Language, capital, culture: Critical studies of language and education in Singapore*, 25–46. Rotterdam: Sense Publications.
Arndt, Susan. 1998. *African Women's Literature. Orature and Intertextuality. Igbo Oral Narratives as Nigerian Women Writers' Models and Objects of Writing Back*. Bayreuth: Bayreuth African Studies Breitinger.
Bhatt, Rakesh M. 2019. The poetics and politics of Englishes in late modernity. *World Englishes* 1–12. https://doi.org/t0.tttt/weng.12392
Bhatt, Rakesh. 2001. Language economy, standardization, and world Englishes. In Edwin Thumboo (ed.), *The three circles of English*, 401–422. Singapore: UniPress.
Bokhorst-Heng, Wendy; Rani Rubdy, Sandra McKay and Lubna Alsagoff. 2010. Whose English? Language ownership in Singapore's English language debates. In Lisa Lim, Anne Pakir and Lionel Wee (eds.), *English in Singapore: Modernity and management*, 133–157. Hong Kong: Hong Kong University Press.

Bokhorst-Heng, Wendy; Lubna Alsagoff, Sandra McKay and Rani Rubdy. 2007. English language ownership among Singaporean Malays: going beyond the NS/NNS dichotomy. *World Englishes* 26 (4), 424–445.

Bolton, Kingsley. 2005. Where WE stands: Approaches, issues, and debate in world Englishes. *World Englishes* 24 (1), 69–83.

Bruthiaux, Paul 2010. *The Speak Good English Movement:* A web-user's perspective. In Lisa Lim, Anne Pakir and Lionel Wee (eds.), *English in Singapore: Modernity and management*, 91–108. Hong Kong: Hong Kong University Press.

Bruthiaux, Paul. 2003. Squaring the circles: Issues in modeling English worldwide. *International Journal of Applied Linguistics* 13 (2), 159–178.

Bughwan, Devamonie. 1970. *An investigation into the use of English by the Indians in South Africa, with special reference to Natal*. Unpublished Ph.D. dissertation, Department of English, University of South Africa.

Buschfeld, Sarah and Alexander Kautzsch. 2017. Towards an integrated approach to postcolonial and non-postcolonial Englishes. *World Englishes* 38 (1–2), 104–126.

Canagarajah, Suresh. 2002. A review of Teaching the Mother Tongue in Multilingual Europe (edited by Witold Tulasiewicz and Anthony Adams 1998. London and New York: Cassell). *International Journal of the Sociology of Language* 154, 106–112.

Chisanga, Teresa and Nkonko M. Kamwangamalu. 1997. Owning the other tongue: The English language in Southern Africa. *Journal of Multilingual and Multicultural Development* 18 (2), 89–99.

Chishimba, Maurice. 1991. Southern Africa. In Jenny Cheshire (ed.), *English around the World: Sociolinguistic Perspectives*, 435–45. Cambridge: Cambridge University Press.

Crowley, Tony. 1996. *Language in History: Theories and Texts*. London: Longman.

Crystal, David. 1999. The future of English: A Welsh perspective. *TESOL '99 preliminary program*, pp. 4–5.

Crystal, David. 1997. *English as a Global Language*. Cambridge: Cambridge University Press.

Dangaremgba, Tsitsi. 1988. *Nervous conditions*. Harare: Zimbabwe Publishing House.

Deshors, Sandra C. 2018. *Modeling World Englishes: Assessing the interplay of emancipation and globalization of ESL varieties*. Amsterdam: John Benjamins.

Doerr, Neriko M. 2009. ed. *The native speaker concept: ethnographic investigation of native speaker effects*. The Hague: Mouton de Gruyter.

Essien, Nkereke M. 2017. Stress and rhythm in the educated Nigerian accent of English. Paper presented at the *18th IAWE Conference*, Syracuse, New York, July 2017.

Ferguson, Charles. A. 1992. Foreword to the First Edition. In Braj B. Kachru (ed.) *The Other Tongue: English Across Cultures* (2nd ed.), xiii–xvii. Delhi: Oxford University Press.

Fishman, Joshua A. 2004. Language maintenance, language shift, and reversing language shift. In Tej Bhatia and C. Ritchie William (eds.), *The Handbook of Bilingualism*, 406–436. Oxford: Blackwell Publishers.

Giri, Ram 2014. Changing faces of English: why English is not a foreign language in Nepal. *Journal of World Languages* 1(3),192–209.

Gupta, Anthea F. 1997. When mother-tongue education is not preferred. *Journal of Multilingual and Multicultural Development* 18 (6), 496–506.

Gupta, Anthea F. 1994. *The step-tongue: Children's English in Singapore*. Clevedon: Multilingual Matters.

Hayhoe, M. and Parker, S. (eds). 1994. *Who Owns English?* Buckingham: Open University Press.

Higgins, Christina 2003. 'Ownership' of English in the outer circle: An alternative to the NS-NSS dichotomy. *TESOL Quarterly* 37(4),615–644.
Hilgendorf, Suzanne. 2019. Peripheries and centers, or plurality with inclusivity? Paper presented at the 24th International Association for World Englishes. Limerick, Ireland, 20–22, June 2019.
Hino, Nobuyuki and Setsuko Oda. 2019. Struggling with the peripherality of the Expanding Circle toward equality. Paper presented at the 24th International Association for World Englishes. Limerick, Ireland, 20–22, June 2019.
Holliday, Adrian. 2006. Native-speakerism. *ELT Journal*, 60 (4), 385–387.
Kachru, Braj B. 1998. English as an Asian language. *Links & Letters* 5, 89–108.
Kachru, Braj B. 1997. World Englishes and English-using communities. *Annual Review of Applied Linguistics* 17, 66–87.
Kachru, Braj B. 1996a. English as lingua franca. In Hans Goebl, Peter H. Nelde, Zdenek Stary, and Wolfgang Wolck (eds.), *Contact Linguistics* 1: 906–913. Berlin – New York: Walter de Gruyter.
Kachru, Braj B. 1996b. World Englishes: Agony and Ecstasy. *Journal of Aesthetic Education* 30 (2), 135–155.
Kachru, Braj B. 1996c. Models for non-native Englishes. In Braj B. Kachru (Ed.), *The other tongue: English across cultures* (2nd ed.), 48–74. Delhi: Oxford University Press.
Kachru, Braj B. 1992. The second diaspora of English. In Tim W. Machan and Charles T. Scott (eds.), *English in its social context: Essays in historical sociolinguistics*, 230–252. New York: Oxford University Press.
Kachru, Braj B. 1986. *The Alchemy of English: The Spread, Functions, and Models of Non-native Englishes*. Oxford: Pergamon Press.
Kachru, Braj B. 1983. Models for non-native Englishes. In Braj B. Kachru (ed.), *The other tongue: English across cultures*, 31–57. Oxford: Pergamon Press.
Kachru, Braj B. 1976. Models of English for the Third World: White man's linguistic burden or language pragmatics? *TESOL Quarterly* 10, 221–39.
Kamwangamalu, Nkonko M. 2019. English as a naturalized African language. *World Englishes* 38:114–127. https://doi.org/10.1111/weng.12395.
Kamwangamalu, Nkonko M. 2016. *Language Policy and Economics: The Language Question in Africa*. London & New York: Palgrave Macmillan.
Kamwangamalu, Nkonko M. 2007. One language, multilayered identities: English in a society in transition, South Africa. *World Englishes* 26(3), 263–275.
Kamwangamalu, Nkonko M. 2006. South African Englishes. In Braj B. Kachru, Yamuna Kachru, and Cecil Nelson (eds.), *The handbook of world Englishes*, 158–171. Malden, MA: Blackwell Publishing.
Kamwangamalu,Nkonko M. 2003. Social change and language shift: South Africa. *Annual Review of Applied Linguistics* 23, 225–242.
Kamwangamalu, Nkonko M. (Ed.). 2002. The social history of English in South Africa. *World Englishes* 21 (1), 1–8.
Kamwangamalu, Nkonko M. 2001. Linguistic and cultural reincarnation of English: A case from Southern Africa. In Edwin Thumbo (Ed.), *The Three Circles of English: Language specialists talk about the English language*, 45–66. Singapore: UniPress.
Kamwangamalu, Nkonko M., and Chisanga, Teresa. 1996. English in Swaziland: Form and function. In Vivian de Klerk (Ed.), *English around the world: Focus on South Africa*, 285–300. Amsterdam: John Benjamins.

Kamwangamalu, Nkonko M. and Cher Leng Lee. 1991. Chinese-English codemixing: A case of matrix language assignment. *World Englishes* 10 (3), 247–261.

Kandiah, Thiru. 1987. New varieties of English: The creation of the paradigm and its radicalization. *Navasilu* 10: 31–41.

Kasanga, Luanga A. 2006. Requests in a South African variety of English. *World Englishes* 25 (1), 65–89.

Kautzsch, Alexander; Anne Schroeder, Frederic Zahres. 2017. The phonetics of Namibian English: Investigating local features in a global context. Paper presented at *the 18th conference of the IAWE*, Syracuse, New York, July 2017.

Kobayashi, Yoko. 2018. East Asian English learners crossing Outer and Inner Circle boundaries. *World Englishes* 37:558–569.

Kuo, Eddie C. Y. and Bjorn Jernudd. 1988. Language management in a multilingual state: the case of planningin Singapore. Working Papers, 95. Department of Sociology, National University of Singapore.

Lanham, Len W. 1986. English in South Africa. In: Richard W. Bailey and Manfred Gorlach (eds.), *English as a world language*, 324–352. Ann Arbor: The University of Michigan Press.

Magura, Benjamin. 1984. *Style and meaning in African English: A sociolinguistic analysis of South African and Zimbabwean English* (PhD thesis). USA: University of Illinois at Urbana-Champaign.

Makalela, Leketi. 2013. Black South African English on the radio. *World Englishes* 12 (1), 93–107.

Makalela, Leketi. 2004. Making sense of BSAE for linguistic democracy in South Africa. *World Englishes* 23(3),355–366.

Martin, Isabel P. 2014. Philippine English revisited. *World Englishes* 33(1),50–59.

McArthur, Tom. 1987. The English languages? *English Today* 3 (3), 9–13.

Meierkord, Christiane. 2019. Perceptions of 'central' and 'peripheral' in Uganda and Rwanda. Paper presented at the 24th International Association for World Englishes. Limerick, Ireland, 20–22, June 2019.

Mesthrie, Rajend. 1988. Toward a lexicon for South African Indian English. *World Englishes* 7 (1), 4–14.

Mufwene, Salikoko. 2001. New Englishes and norm-setting: How critical is the native speaker in linguistics? In Edwin Thumboo (ed.), *The Three Circles of English*, 133–141. Singapore: UniPress.

Mufwene, Salikoko. 1994. New Englishes and criteria for naming them. *World Englishes* 13, 21–31.

Norton, Bonny. 1997. Language, identity, and the ownership of English. *TESOL Quarterly* 31, 409–29.

Onysko, Alexander. 2019. Centers and peripheries? A view from the language contact typology of world Englishes. Paper presented at the 24th International Association for World Englishes. Limerick, Ireland, 20–22, June 2019.

Paikeday, Thomas M. 1985. *The Native Speaker is Dead!* Toronto: Paikeday.

Pennycook, Alastair. 2003. Global Englishes, Rip Slyme and performativity. *Journal of Sociolinguistics* 7, 513–533.

Pennycook, Alastair. 2002. Mother tongue, governmentality, and protectionism. *International Journal of the Sociology of language* 154, 11–28.

Pennycook, Alastair. 1994. *The cultural politics of English as an international language*. Harlow: Pearson Education.
Prabhakaran, Varija. 1998. Multilingualism and language shift in South Africa: The case of Telugu, an Indian language. *Multilingua*, 17 (2-3), 297-319.
Prator, Clifford. 1968. The British heresy in TESL. In Joshua A. Fishman et al. (eds), *Language Problems in Developing Nations*, 459-7. New York: John Wiley and Sons, Inc.
Quirk, Rosenbaum. 1988. The question of standards in the international use of English. In Peter Lowenberg (ed.), *Language Spread and Language Policy: Issues, Implications and Case Studies*, 229-41. Washington, D.C.: Georgetown University Press.
Quirk, Rosenbaum 1990. Language varieties and the language standard. *English Today* 6(1), 3-10.
Romaine, Susan. 1992. English: From Village to Global Village. In Tim W. Machan and Charles T. Scott (eds.), *English in its Social Context*, 253-260. New York: Oxford University Press.
Röthlisberger, Melanie. 2019. A review of *Modeling World Englishes: Assessing the interplay of emancipation and globalization of ESL varieties* (Edited by Sandra Deshors). *LINGUIST List*: Vol-30-2826. Fri Jul 19 2019.
Rubdy, Rani. 2007. Singlish in the school: An impediment or a resource? *Journal of Multilingual and Multicultural Development* 28 (4), 308-17.
Rubdy, Rani. 2001. Creative destruction: Singapore's Speak Good English Movement. *World Englishes* 20(3),341-355.
Rubdy, Rani; Sandra McKay, Lubna Alsagoff and Wendy Borkhost-Heng. 2008. Enacting English language ownership in the Outer Circle: A study of Singaporean Indians' orientation to English norms. *World Englishes* 27 (1), 40-67.
Saenkhum, Tanita and Chatwara Duran. 2019. Language ideology and native English speaker privilege in academia. Paper presented at the 24th International Association for World Englishes. Limerick, Ireland, 20-22, June 2019.
Samuelson, Beth Lewis and Sarah W. Freedman. 2010. Language policy, multilingual education, and power in Rwanda. *Language Policy* 9 (3), 191-215.
Saraceni, Mario. 2015. *World Englishes: A critical analysis*. London: Bloomsbury Academic.
Schreiber, Brooke and Mihiri Jansz. 2019. Breaking down nativespeakerism through online intercultural collaborations. Paper presented at the 24th International Association for World Englishes. Limerick, Ireland, 20-22, June 2019.
Schröder, Anne and Marion Schulte. 2019. Namibia's linguistic landscapes in Windhoek and Swakopmund. Paper presented at the 24th International Association for World Englishes. Limerick, Ireland, 20-22, June 2019.
Sharifian, Farzad. 2010. Cultural Conceptualisations in Intercultural Communication: A Study of Aboriginal and Non-Aboriginal Australians. *Journal of Pragmatics* 42: 3367-3376. doi:10.1016/j.pragma.2010.05.006.
Silva, Penny. 1998. South African English: Oppressor or liberator? In Hans Linquist, Staffan Klintborg, Magnus Levi, and Maria Estling (eds.), *The major varieties of English: Papers fromMAVEN 97*, 69-92. Vaxjo: Vaxjo University Press.
Stroud, Christopher and Lionel Wee. 2007. Consuming identities: Language policy and planning in Singaporean late modernity. *Language Policy* 6 (2), 253-279.
Tan, Ying-Ying. 2014. English as a 'mother tongue' in Singapore. *World Englishes* 33 (3), 319-339.
Wardhaugh, Ronald. 1987. *Languages in Competition: Dominance, Diversity, and Decline*. Oxford: Basil Blackwell Ltd.

Watanabe, Yutai. 2019. Perfectionism: A Japanese ideology towards a native-like accent in the EIL paradigm. Paper presented at the 24th International Association for World Englishes. Limerick, Ireland, 20–22, June 2019.

Wee, Lionel. 2002. When English is not a mother tongue: Linguistic ownership and the Eurasian community in Singapore. *Journal of Multilingual and Multicultural Development* 23 (4), 282–295.

Widdowson, Henry. 1994. The ownership of English. *TESOL Quarterly* 28, 377–89.

Zabus, Chantal. 1991. *The African palimpsest: Indigenization of language in the West African Europhone novel*. Amsterdam: Editions Rodopi B. V.

Zähres, Frederic. 2019. Namibian English(es) on YouTube. Paper presented at the 24th International Association for World Englishes. Limerick, Ireland, 20–22, June 2019.

Zhiming, Bao. 2001. Grammatical stability and the nativized English. In Edwin Thumboo (ed.), *The three circles of English*, 357–368. Singapore: UniPress.

Wendy D. Bokhorst-Heng, Kelle L. Marshall
Chapter 11
"I want to be bilingual!" Contested imaginings of bilingualism in New Brunswick, Canada

Abstract: This chapter concerns Anglophones' efforts in New Brunswick, Canada to define their subject position vis-à-vis French language education within the province's dichotomous framework of official bilingualism. New Brunswick's bilingual policy is that of siloed institutional bilingualism, originally developed to establish linguistic rights for the province's Francophone minority. Anglophones' positioning within this framework is less clear, and due to this ambiguity, ideologies circulate regarding who may become bilingual, who should have access to bilingualism – often conceived of as native speaker-like proficiency in two languages – and by which means bilingualism might be attained. Through analysis of one historical episode surrounding the government's proposal to eliminate Early French Immersion education, we consider how Anglophone parents confronted these challenges as they sought to position themselves and their children within the imagined provincial bilingual community. Of significance is their (Anglophone majority) use of an Acadian (Francophone minority) cultural tradition to establish their language rights and identity. We discuss how the construct of imagined linguistic identity contributes to a nuanced understanding of parents' and students' imagined identities regarding their target language. We suggest ways that language education programs could foster students' imagined bi/multilingual language identities vis-à-vis their country's official languages in local and transnational spaces.

Keywords: French immersion, language ideology, language ideological debates, imagined communities, semiotic processes, native speaker, identity, discourse

---

Wendy D. Bokhorst-Heng, Crandall University, e-mail: wendy.bokhorstheng@crandallu.ca
Kelle L. Marshall, Pepperdine University, e-mail: kelle.marshall@pepperdine.edu

https://doi.org/10.1515/9781501512353-012

(Government of New Brunswick, Official Languages Act,1969/2011)
An Act Recognizing the Equality of the Two Official Linguistic Communities in New Brunswick.
Chapter Outline
(1) Recognition of English linguistic community and French linguistic community and affirmation of equality of status and equal rights of each
(2) Protection of the equality of status and equal rights and privileges of official linguistic communities
(3) Promotion of cultural, economic, educational and social development

(Canadian Charter of Rights and Freedoms, 1982)
16.1 (1) The English linguistic community and the French linguistic community in New Brunswick have equality of status and equal rights and privileges, including the right to distinct educational institutions and such distinct cultural institutions as are necessary for the preservation and promotion of those communities.
16. (2) English and French are the official languages of New Brunswick and have equality of status and equal rights and privileges as to their use in all institutions of the legislature and government of New Brunswick.

1 Introduction

On July 15, 2016, a member of the Order of Canada welcomed new citizens to Canada at a swearing-in ceremony held in New Brunswick (NB), a small, rural province on the Eastern coast of Canada. "We are very pleased to welcome 18 candidates including 17 minors to receive citizenship," Arsenault said, "candidates who come from 32 different countries and whose numbers include 73 Anglophones and 13 Francophones" (Arsenault 2016). Her reductive comment is indicative of local language ideologies resulting from the province's official English-French bilingual policy, including erasure of linguistic diversity in alignment with the province's official English-French bilingual policy framework. But of particular relevance to this volume, her comment also reflects ideologies of who can be counted a native speaker of French. While anyone who does not speak French is apparently considered Anglophone, Francophones are more narrowly defined. There is no officially established definition of Francophone in Canada, although the national census does attempt to develop a composite measure: A Francophone (Statistics Canada 2015) is defined by "mother tongue" and/or by "first official language spoken". That is, if someone whose mother tongue is neither French nor English nevertheless uses French as their primary official language, they would be considered Francophone. Given the very small percentage of immigrants in NB (4.6% of the population, Statistics Canada 2016), it is the former category that dominates the local definition of Francophone – as we see in Arsenault's speech above. These definitions have implications for the meanings of bilingualism in the province. Because the official definition of Francophone is based on a native-speaker model, bilingualism has often been interpreted as native-like proficiency in two languages (Dewaele, Bak and Ortega, this volume; Roy and Galiev 2011), what Grosjean (1989: 4) describes as "two monolinguals in one person". And so, following the definition's logic, for bilingual Anglophone speakers of French, this political construct (Jessner, Hofer, and Malzer-Papp, this volume) means that they can never legally be considered native speakers of French, even at high levels of competency, as English is their "first official language spoken". This definition thus presents challenges for bilingual education, for who has access to bilingualism, and for who can be considered bilingual.

The focus of our discussion in this chapter is on Anglophones' efforts to define their subject position within NB's dichotomous framework of official bilingualism vis-à-vis French language education. New Brunswick's population of 747,100 comprises two primary language groups:[1] 31.6% Francophones (primarily Acadian), of whom 72.5% are bilingual in French and English; and 67.1% Anglophones, of whom 16.2% report being bilingual. The overall provincial French-English bilingualism rate is 34% (Statistics Canada 2016). These linguistic communities are unevenly distributed throughout the province: some regions are predominantly Francophone (Northeastern NB); some primarily Anglophone (e.g. Fredericton, the capital); and Southeastern NB, including NB's largest metropolitan area, bilingual. What Heller (1999: 143) says of Canada at large also applies to NB:

> On the one hand, we can think of Canada as two monolingual societies somehow fated to share the same territory. On the other, there is the reality of having to live together, which has somehow been possible for the last two centuries or so, albeit all the while separate (even ignorant of) each other, although there is evidence that cohabitation has been paradoxically both harmonious and fraught with strife.

New Brunswick's Official Languages Act (OLA) (Government of NB 1968/2011) was put in place to primarily protect its minority Francophone population's language and cultural rights. However, while individual bilingualism never was the goal of the OLA, the policy has nonetheless become the impetus for province-wide promotion of French Second Language (FSL) education (Haque 2012; Hayday 2015). Under the auspices of the provincial Official Languages Act, NB has a dual education system, with separate schools for Anglophone and Francophone

---

[1] As well, 4% self-identify as Aboriginal, and 1.3% declare other languages as mother tongue.

children under the direction of two Assistant Deputy Ministers. Within Anglophone schools, there is mandated French Second Language (FSL) instruction until Grade 10, with French Immersion – French medium of instruction for FSL learners – being one option. In 2016–2017, 86% of eligible students were enrolled in FSL (Canadian Parents for French 2018).

This complex framework of linguistic and cultural duality raises questions regarding the meaning of bilingualism, who defines it, and who has access to bilingualism. It is useful here to think of Heller's (2007: 2) "social approach" to bilingualism – capital "B" Bilingualism – which considers the "social relations, social meanings and relations of power" involved. NB's two official linguistic communities and the provincial government have, at times, taken up this definition differently. For example, embedded in the Canadian Virtual Museum's resources for teachers is an obscure document published in both French and English by the Heritage Branch of NB's provincial government (2006) entitled: *J'ai un rêve: les droits linguistiques au Nouveau-Brunswick* ('I have a dream: Language rights in New Brunswick'). The document is fronted with a painting, *Chemin à parcourir* ('Miles to go'), described as reflecting "the effectiveness of the Official Languages Act of 1969" with respect to the Acadian people. Its thirteen sections detail various aspects of the Official Languages Act's historical development and the heroes involved. In this imagining (Anderson 1991), official bilingualism embodies the story of the Acadian people's determination for equal rights. "I have a dream," the clear evocation of the powerful words of American civil rights leader Martin Luther King and his clarion call for social justice. This imagining of Bilingualism is couched within the discourse of minority language loss (Jaffe 2007: 53) and, of significance to this discussion, not linked to a bilingual community of practice but rather ideologies of language rights.

A different definition of Bilingualism has been presented by the New Brunswick Commissioner of Official Languages (Office of the Commissioner of Official Languages, NB 2013: 3), whose mandate is to promote the province's bilingual identity. The Commissioner describes the Official Languages Act as "touch[ing] the very core of New Brunswick's identity;" and later (2015: 22) declares: "the equality of New Brunswick's two official languages and two official communities has been a fundamental value in this province". Indeed, bilingualism is visibly dominant throughout the province. English-French bilingual signs are mandated (see Figure 11.1), service in English or French is guaranteed in all public service offices and hospitals, there are English and French newspapers and radio stations, and New Brunswick's (NB) unique bilingual status is featured prominently on all provincial descriptors.

Figure 11.1: Bilingualism in New Brunswick (photos by Author).

The visibility of bilingualism supports several significant components identified in the Commissioner's interpretation of official bilingualism. First, bilingualism is represented as a "value," a moral principle integral to provincial identity. Bilingualism is also presented as a neutral space within which the imagining of this provincial identity occurs. The Commissioner (2005) defines the policy of bilingualism through a discourse of individual rights regarding choice of official linguistic code (Figure 11.2); this "choice" is "what makes New Brunswick so great". Bilingualism is thus presented as equally accessible to all.

The focus of our discussion in this chapter is on yet a third perspective of Bilingualism. Within the Anglophone community there is a significant group who, perceiving themselves as a disenfranchised majority, also regard the province's official bilingualism as a "right," as a primary means by which to access the assumed related economic and political capital that come with bilingualism (Hayday 2015: 150). Their imaginings are also not linked to a bilingual community of practice, but rather to ideologies of the "right" to access Bilingualism. Furthermore, these Anglophones regard *Early* French immersion (EFI) as the primary embodiment of that right, even though there is nothing in FSL policy that specifically guarantees EFI.

To understand the meanings of Bilingualism from the perspective of these Anglophones, we consider one "historical episode" (Blommaert 1999: 9) of language ideological debate: An Anglophone parent-led protest held in 2008 in the village of Sackville as part of a province-wide movement against the provincial government's decision to eliminate EFI. This is one of the most salient moments in NB's recent history when Anglophone language ideologies were visible through public action. We first present an overview of the theoretical constructs informing our analysis:

Figure 11.2: Choice (Ad produced by the OCOL-NB, 2005. Reproduced with the permission of the Office of the Commissioner of Official Languages, NB).

language ideologies (Blackledge 2000; Kroskrity 2000), *language ideological debates* (Blommaert 1999), and *imagined communities* (Anderson 1991). We then identify key aspects of NB's language ideological debates (LIDs) within NB's educational duality and French immersion (FI) education. This overview frames our analysis of the Sackville historical episode, extending Irvine and Gal's (2000) three semiotic processes of *erasure, iconization,* and *fractal recursivity* as analytical tools. Finally, we discuss how the complexities of the LIDs concerning bilingualism in NB, evident in this historical episode, present ambiguities for Anglophone learners of French regarding their linguistic identity positioning within the province. We suggest ways that language education programs could foster student's imagined linguistic identities within local and global contexts. In so doing, we bring the discussion of 'who is a native speaker' into the global contexts of transnationalism, and the development of bilingual and multilingual identity.

2 Analytical framework

Scholarship has increasingly recognized the "social positioning, partiality, contestability, instability and mutability" (Blackledge 2000: 26) of language ideologies. Kroskrity (2000: 8), for example, defines language ideologies as "represent[ing] the perception of language and discourse that is constructed in the interest of a specific social or cultural group". Language ideologies are embedded in social relationships, comprising the beliefs, affect, and conceptions about language that are shared by a group. For instance, social groups may draw on language ideologies (usually power-based) in order to distinguish one from the other, or to create in-group solidarity. Kroskrity (2000) sees language ideologies as also informing – and being informed by – decisions related to language use. It is important to note with Kroskrity that individuals may display varying degrees of awareness of language ideologies: sometimes individuals may explicitly describe language ideologies, other times their language ideologies are only observable through social practice (see also Kerschhofer-Puhalo and Slavkov, this volume).

While Kroskrity's (2000) construct of ideology is useful in describing the language ideological underpinnings of social relationships and interactions, it is also important to consider how such ideologies are formed and promoted. Because language ideologies are "(re)constructed and negotiated in debates," Blommaert (1999: 1) suggests the notion of language ideological debates as one way that ideology formation can be observed. He defines LIDs as "debates in which language is central as a topic, a motif, a target, and in which language ideologies are being articulated, formed, amended, enforced". These LIDs are "historical episodes" that "develop against a wide socio-political and historical horizon of relationships of power, forms of discrimination, social engineering, nation-building and so forth" (Blommaert 1999: 2). Current language ideologies and practices can thus only be understood when we first make sense of their historicity. At their core, LIDs involve competing visions of what language – and the meanings of that language within a community or nation – should be. They can involve such interrelated issues as the quality or value of a language/variety, power relations between speakers of different languages/varieties, or the promotion of a language/variety for national, community, and cultural identity – all of which are related to national/community/group identity, or, using Anderson's (1991) term, *imagined communities*.

For Anderson (1991), imagined communities, such as nation-states, highlight the sense of community that members experience by imagining their connection with others across time and space, even though they may never meet them. The concept of imagining and imagined communities is relevant to our discussion of LIDs because, like Pavlenko (2003: 253), we "consider imagination not as a personal attribute but as a terrain of struggle between different and often incompatible ideologies of language and identity in particular sociohistoric contexts". As a social process, imagination emphasizes the power dynamic in LIDs, how certain ideological constructs "win" while others are deemed "unimaginable". At the same time, imagination emphasizes the dynamic nature of identity, as a site of struggle, multiple and contradictory (Norton 2013). These constructs of ideology, LIDs, and imagination together frame our analysis of one language debate in NB.

3 French language education in New Brunswick

The history of French immersion education in NB needs to be understood within the broader context of the provision of French language education (Edwards 1986) and the socio-political history of the Acadians (Boudreau 2016). NB was originally part of the French colony *Acadie* (Acadia) founded in the seventeenth century and has one of the lengthiest provincial histories of contact between Francophones and Anglophones. Colonial conflict between the British and the French (later the Acadians) peaked with the Acadian expulsion (1755 – 1763, a period known as the *Grand Dérangement,* or 'Great Upheaval.') during the Seven Years' War. Following the Treaty of Paris (1763), Acadians were permitted to resettle; however only in remotely dispersed communities in the British colony of Nova Scotia, relegating them to the margins of the colony's political and economic spheres, with British settlers assuming positions of power. Schooling for the Acadians was provided ad hoc by the Catholic Church, and, even when later supplied through the provincial Common School Act in 1871, was substandard (Laxer 2007). By 1920, the rate of illiteracy among Acadians was significantly higher than that of their Anglophone counterparts (Laxer 2007).

The 1960s saw significant changes in the socio-economic and political conditions for Acadians in NB. Encouraged by Francophone mobilization in Québec, NB Acadians advocated for equal rights and status to those of Anglophones. Acadian activists increasingly re-imagined their role in political and economic affairs through the medium of official bilingualism (Boudreau 2016) and education became the catalyst for much of their struggle. NB's Premier Louis Robichaud, himself a bilingual Acadian, led the movement with his platform of "equal opportunity" in all areas, including language. With full support from both Conservative and Liberal parties (Stanley 1984), Robichaud's government instituted NB's 1969 Official Languages Act thereby making French and English NB's "equal" official languages.

The parameters of bilingualism were outlined in Robichaud's *Statement on Language Equality and Opportunity* (a precursor to NB's 1969 Official Languages Act), which he presented to the NB Legislative Assembly on December 4, 1968:

> On an individual basis it is the right of New Brunswickers to be and remain unilingual, or to speak two or more languages. The Government does not expect that as a result of its action to promote linguistic and cultural equality of opportunity, that all New Brunswickers will become fluent in the two official languages . . . [the] the objective is to ensure that no unilingual New Brunswicker finds himself at a disadvantage in participating in the public life of our Province. (Government of NB 1968: 7)

The Official Languages Act is thus premised on a model of institutional linguistic co-existence, without any expectation of individual bilingualism. Furthermore, given the context of Robichaud's social reform agenda, NB's bilingual policy was essentially designed to protect minority language rights (as is seen later in the Charter, Canada's constitution), premised on minority language unilingualism.

Yet, while no unilingual New Brunswicker should be "disadvantaged," Robichaud's conception of official bilingualism with provincial linguistic duality in all public sectors suggested very real advantages to English/French bilingualism – and disadvantages to unilingualism (Edwards 1986; Hayday 2015; Stanley 1984). Few Anglophones were bilingual, and the move to provide government services in both official languages created new tensions in the province. These perceived disadvantages spurred heated debate concerning the provision of FSL education for Anglophone children. Edwards (1986: 41) quotes J. Rice, president of the NB Federation of Home and School, writing in 1963: "If we deny our New Brunswick English children their right to bilingualism, we deprive them of a cultural enrichment, a social, intellectual, perhaps an economic advantage, and risk, by our own ineptitude, the sorrow of their looking back in anger". It appears in Rice's comments that the "right to bilingualism" was really about the right to access full participation in the province which Anglophones felt was being denied them because of the bilingual policy. Some Anglophone parents began sending their children to local French schools; however, the French schools, which had been admitting Anglophone children, responded by tightening enrolment requirements to only Francophones, worried about the assimilationist impact Anglophone enrolment would have on Acadian children's culture and language (Edwards 1986: 47–50). School districts began to increase FSL opportunities in Anglophone schools. In the early 1970s, Anglophone School District 15 (Moncton) established the first official French immersion (FI) program (Edwards 1986: 50). And by 1977, NB instituted the first provincial policy (Policy 501) on immersion, giving Anglophone schools the option to offer FI education. In 1981, Policy 501 was revised, making the provision of FI mandatory where there was sufficient demand and resources. Thus, unlike elsewhere in Canada where FI programs began as a result of pressure from parents (Hayday 2015) and where FI is regarded a totem of class status (Heller 1990: 72), in NB, the school districts initiated its inception and mandated it through law, making FI a provincial right for Anglophone children.

Today, NB's independent French and English educational sectors have strict admission policies designed to protect each official linguistic community. Policy 321 states that only children who are "proficient in French" or who has at least one parent "proficient in French" can attend Francophone schools and only children who are "proficient in English" can attend Anglophone schools; children who are "proficient in neither official language" can choose which school to attend. The policy also explicitly states that "the superintendent shall not admit a French-speaking student or bilingual student to the French Immersion Program in English language schools". Education Policy 309 (French Language Programs, which replaced Policy 501 in 2009) requires FSL instruction in all Anglophone schools and FI programming where there is sufficient demand and resources. There are currently three FSL program options (See Figure 11.3): English Prime (Grades 4–10), where students learn French as a subject – expect for Grade 5 when the majority of their day is taught in French except for Math, Music and Physical Education; EFI (Grade 1 entry, with 70–90% of the curriculum taught in French in Grades 1–8, 50% in Grades 9–10, and 25% in Grades 11–12); and Late French Immersion (Grade 6 entry). In addition, the province has launched FLORA (French Learning Opportunities in Rural Areas), a blended program combining teacher instruction and personalized digital learning to increase access to FSL in rural areas.

French immersion has historically been the subject of intense controversy and perpetual scrutiny by government, academics, and members of the private sector, including debates about access, entry point, curriculum, assessment, levels of proficiency, and program effectiveness in meeting expected targets and levels of bilingualism (Edwards 1986; Hayday 2015; Rehorick, Dicks, Kristmanson, and Cogswell 2006). Every few years there are government-commissioned reports which become the basis for subsequent amendments to policy or practice. In the discussion that follows, we focus on one such historical episode. While the controversy was province-wide, our analysis centres on the centre of the controversy in Sackville, NB – a village of 5,500 residents located in the southern Tantramar region. This region was first settled by Acadians in the early 1700s; however, largely a result of deportation and resettlement, today 92% of Sackville's residents report English-only as their mother tongue, with only 3.8% French (and 4.2% other); 20.1% of all residents report being bilingual (Statistics Canada 2016).

Chapter 11 "I want to be bilingual!" Contested imaginings of bilingualism — 295

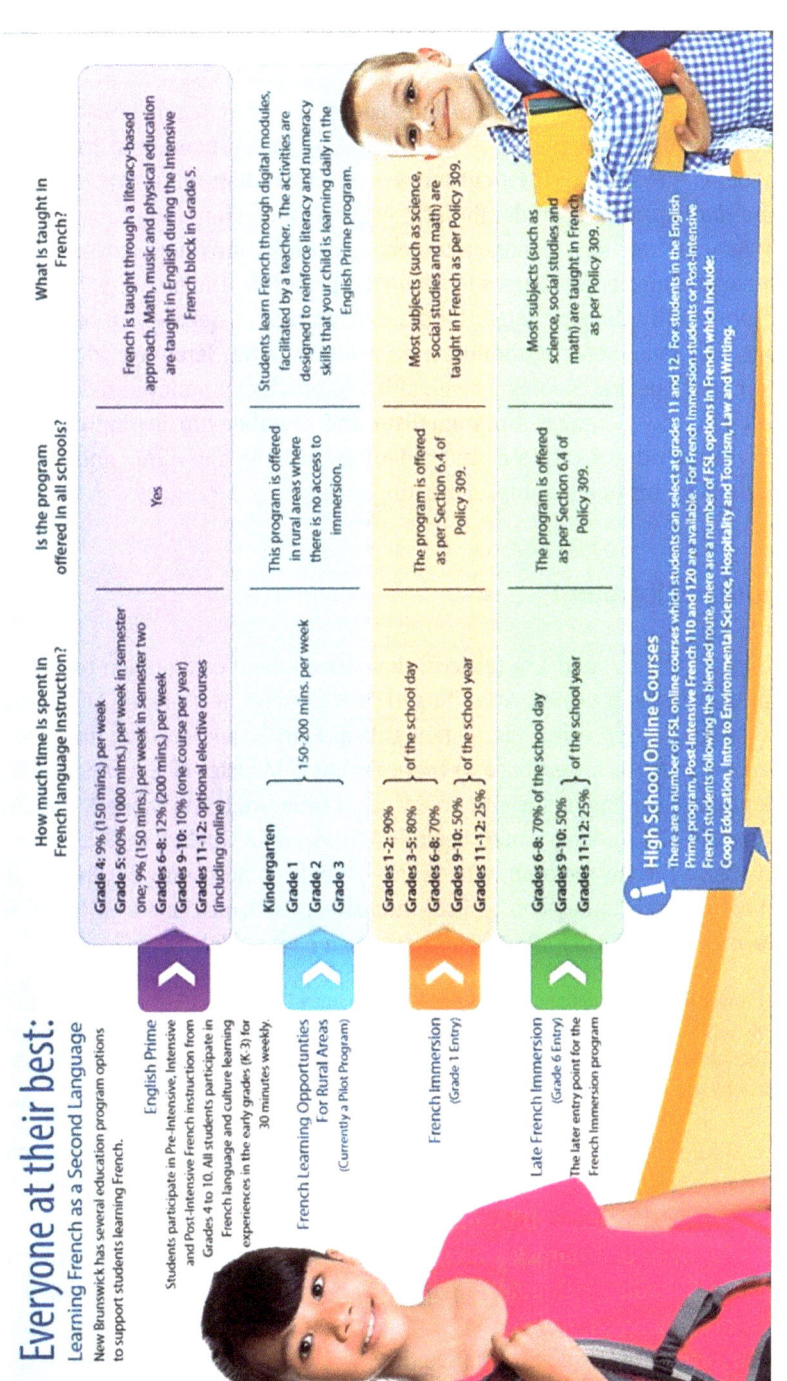

Figure 11.3: FSL Options in New Brunswick, Government of NB (2019).

4 The tintamarre: one "historical episode"

The significance of the historical episode discussed here concerns how Anglophone (majority) parents played at ethnic and linguistic borders in their language debates – evident in their curious use of an Acadian (minority) tradition called the *tintamarre* in a predominantly Anglophone community located in a formerly Acadian territory to stage a protest against the provincial government, and the use of minority discourses to frame the protest by the majority. Furthermore, it powerfully demonstrates the dialogic impact of debates on language ideologies and imagined communities: on the one hand, language ideologies based on native speaker ideologies embedded in provincial policy and designed to protect minority language unilingualism and membership in that community; and on the other hand, a counter-ideology of language rights and access to that language through ideologies of bilingualism.

4.1 Some background

In February 2008, Croll and Lee released their government-commission report on the status of FI in the province. According to their findings, few Grade 12 FI graduates met the graduation competency standards in French, and attrition from FI in high school was high. In response to these findings, Minister of Education Kelly Lamrock proposed changing the entry point for FI from Grade 1 to Grade 5, thereby eliminating EFI. All students would begin FSL learning in Grade 5 through a universal Intensive French program, after which parents could choose for their children either a French Immersion or Post Intensive French placement in Grade 6. The Government of NB's (2008) news release stated Lamrock's rationale:

> The French Second Language program improvements will allow us to increase the number of New Brunswick children who graduate reaching the proficiency targets for speaking French as second language. They will also improve our scores in literacy, math and science by giving all children an equal chance at a positive classroom environment.

However, while the proposed changes were perhaps good intentioned, parents and activists throughout the province interpreted the proposed changes as a threat to their right to access Bilingualism.

Within a week of Lamrock's announcement, thousands signed up on the "Save EFI in Canada's Bilingual Province" Facebook page, which was instrumental in organizing protests on the legislation (Cooke 2010). An Open Letter by the Consortium of Canadian Universities Advising the Canadian Association of Immersion Teachers (2008) asserted that Lamrock's recommendations would be a "gigantic mistake and a huge step backwards for New Brunswick" and an affront to NB's unique status as Canada's only officially bilingual province and leadership in FI education. Anglophone parents staged demonstrations, held public debates (Dicks 2008), and newspapers were flooded with letters from all sectors (e.g., Canadian Broadcasting Corporation, March 26, 2008). Sackville was the epicentre, with Canadians for Educational Choice (CEC) participating in a decisive legal battle against the government (*Small and Ryan v. New Brunswick (Minister of Education)*).[2] Mount Allison University professors and CEC members Diana Hamilton and Matthew Litvak created a blog (http://hamlit2008.blogspot.ca/) to consolidate communication related to the legal battle and the protests.

This brings us to the 2008 Sackville historical episode. To understand the significance of the Sackville protesters' use of a *tintamarre*, a brief historical overview of the practice and its current meanings as a cultural practice is useful. Cooke's (2010: 49) account of the event describes the *tintamarre* as an "*ancient* Acadian tradition" (emphasis added). However, the "tradition" in its current rendition is quite recent, only dating back to 1979 (Labelle 2007). Chiasson (2004: 150) observes that, "By a strange twist, this event has been turned into a tradition and people are disappointed that they are unable to find any historical basis for it, *but that will come*" (translated; emphasis added), suggesting its contemporary history. The first mention in *Acadie* of a *tintamarre* occurred in 1955 when the Catholic Church organized celebrations commemorating the bicentennial anniversary of the Acadian deportation (Labelle 2007). According to Labelle (personal communication, June 15, 2016), the Church was then the established power in *Acadie*, and therefore would have been reluctant to use the more established term *charivari*. The *charivari* was a (noisy) form of social coercion used by communities to enforce their standards regarding marriage, spousal relationships and so forth. While it could be a form of public celebration, it was principally associated with community censure. The Church therefore used the less contentious term *tintamarre* to highlight the term's celebratory nature: "Once the prayer is finished," the communiqué read, "there will be a joyful *tintamarre* lasting for several minutes, featuring anything, everything and everyone that can make noise, shout and ring: mill whistles, car horns, bicycle bells, squawking objects, toys, etc." (cited in Labelle 2007: 3).

There is no mention of any *tintamarre* again until 1979, the 375th anniversary of *Acadie*'s founding when the *Société des Acadiens du Nouveau-Brunswick* of Caraquet organized a *tintamarre* as a "joyful celebration of Acadian presence" (Labelle, personal communication, June 15, 2016). This version of the *tintamarre* has since

---

[2] Small and Ryan's children were registered to begin EFI in Grade 1. Their lawyers argued that because the children were already registered, cancelling the program was a breach of contract.

become a central feature of National Acadian Day holiday celebrations and of the imagined unified Acadian community in diaspora. Every 15th of August, festivities are held in Acadian communities throughout NB featuring Acadian music, clothing, and *tintamarres* with participants marching through their communities to the sound of bells, horns, pots, wooden spoons, whistles and other noisy devices. By creating a tradition, drawing elements of a *charivari* into a new context (Labelle 2007), the Acadian community has thus established the *tintamarre* as an icon of Acadian identity. Notably, the uptake of this form of iconization is not uniform throughout the Acadian community. Labelle (2007: 6) observes that the practice is less common in areas where the Acadians are a distinct minority: "It seems to be more difficult to introduce the custom of holding an annual *tintamarre* in the south of the province [including predominantly Anglophone Sackville], where the majority of the population is English-speaking and Acadians are still reluctant to display their identity". This is deeply ironic, as it was the Anglophone community that brought the *tintamarre* to Sackville, where the Acadians themselves could not.

Returning, then, to the Sackville *tintamarre* protest, about 185 Anglophone parents and members of the CEC in Sackville organized a *tintamarre* on March 19, 2008 as part of their multi-layered protest against Lamrock's decision to eliminate EFI. The choice of a *tintamarre* was made by about 75 organizing members (Tower 2008). The *tintamarre* began with an introductory speech (in English) made by the event chair and Mount Allison University professor Bruce Robertson. The protesters then marched through the town, banging pots, pans, and aluminum garbage can lids and blowing horns. Many carried placards bearing messages such as "Save EFI," and "I want to be bilingual" (see Figure 11.4). The *tintamarre* was captured on video by Diana Hamilton and Matthew Litvak, uploaded onto *YouTube* (*Sackville march to save early French immersion*, 2008) and linked to the CEC's blog. Our analysis is premised on this 2008 historical episode.

4.2 Methodology

The data from which our analysis were drawn come from a larger multimodal discourse analysis surrounding this historical episode. Newspaper opinion articles and letters to the editor were collected in Southeastern NB's two primary newspapers, *The Times and Transcript* and *The Telegraph Journal*, covering the period from the release of the Croll and Lee report (February 27, 2008) until mid-April 2008 when the public furor related to this episode began to diminish. Articles posted on the CEC blog were downloaded, including the Croll and Lee report and activists' responses to the report, and the *YouTube* video of the CEC's *tintamarre* which was subsequently transcribed for analysis. Finally, in fall 2015

Figure 11.4: "I want to be bilingual".

and spring 2016, we interviewed various actors involved in the protests, including Diana Hamilton and Berkeley Fleming. This analysis focuses particularly on the video's transcript and interviews.

This historical episode requires at least two layers of analysis. The first is the parents' choice of a *tintamarre* to stage their protest, a Discursive (using Gee's [2014] big "D") framing of the event. The second is the discourse (Gee's [2014] small "d") of the speech as documented in Hamilton and Litvak's *YouTube* video. These layers align with Blackledge's (2005: 20) distinction between the contents of a discourse that involve textual analyses for emergent themes, and analyses of the historical, political and social contexts within which the text was produced. Following Irvine and Gal (2000), we suggest that the discourses within LIDs involve a number of semiotic processes, in particular, iconization, fractal recursivity, and erasure (see also Kerschhofer-Puhalo and Slavkov, this volume) – but expand upon these constructs within the context of this analysis. In this multimodal analysis, we propose that iconization involves the transformation of linguistic and cultural practices to become iconic representations of cultural and group identity, bringing them together in ways that appear to be inherent. We interpret fractal recursivity more broadly than used by Irvine and Gal (2000), proposing that the term may also describe processes that involve the reinterpretation/

translation and projection of discourses from one social context onto another.[3] And we regard erasure as the process whereby some persons, activities, perspectives, experiences are made invisible in the discursive construction of ideology. These semiotic processes allow us to examine the dynamic processes of LIDs involved in the imagining of linguistic communities, and the Anglophone parents' positioning within that imagining.

4.3 Analysis

4.3.1 Discursive framing of the *tintamarre*

When asked why the CEC members chose a *tintamarre* to stage their protest, Diana Hamilton (personal communication, June 16, 2016) recollected, "I think it was sort of a duality thing. I think we are a province with two languages and two heritages, and we're about to become the only province in Canada that doesn't have French Immersion and we're the only bilingual province in Canada". The *tintamarre* was thus a discursive means used by members of the Anglophone community to position themselves within NB's imagined bilingual community. Through fractal recursivity, the Anglophone parents appropriated a practice that has become symbolic of Acadian identity – "the sound of the heartbeat of French-speaking Acadia" (Levésque, in Labelle 2007: 3) and reverted its meaning to its original significance – "as a form of social coercion to enforce their [community] standards" – but with a twist. First, rather than against a community member, the demands were against the government. Second, rather than enforcing standards, the parents demanded rights. And third, rather than asserting community-defined standards, the parents aimed to hold the government accountable to the provincial standard – its educational policy concerning FI and the provincial bilingual policy. At the same time, they played on the *tintamarre*'s iconic meanings. The contemporary *tintamarre* gives the aura of saying 'we, too, are not going anywhere.' It was a way for Anglophone parents to manifest their imagining of the rightful place of bilingualism in New Brunswickers' identities and their rightful place within that imagining.

Hamilton's claim that NB was soon to become the "only province in Canada that doesn't have French Immersion" is also significant. For, in fact, it was EFI that was at stake, not FI. It could be argued that this was merely a slip. However,

---

[3] This is akin to a sound-editing technique, *remixing*. The Oxford English Dictionary (2018) describes remixing as: "To create a new version of (a recording) by rebalancing or recombining the separate instrumental or vocal tracks; (now also) to reinterpret or rework (an existing music recording), typically by altering the rhythm or instrumentation, often in a radical way."

as we will discuss below, her conflation of EFI and FI is consistent with the discourse of the protest. Hamilton's argument also includes erasure. The contemporary significance of a *tintamarre* is to solidify Acadian presence in the province against of history of marginalization. This significance is erased in the Anglophone parents' *tintamarre* and is subsumed by the discourse of "duality". This not only erases the power dynamics of minority/majority inequality within this identity, but also carves out space for the majority to demand its "rights". The erasure is even more significant when we remember that Sackville is near Fort Beauséjour, the very place where the British took definitive control of Acadian territory.

The *tintamarre* is thus layered in complexity – a practice that bears the aura of ancient custom yet is only a recent tradition; one that is primarily associated with Acadian identity and community, yet has been redefined by one Anglophone community; one that has an uneasy presence in Anglophone areas, yet was appropriated by Anglophones; one that celebrates Acadian identity and minority cultural revitalization, and one that was misappropriated by the majority to demand majority rights. It is an example of how indexicality is not just context-sensitive, but also context creating (Jaffe 2016). On the one hand, prior histories of indexicalization are presupposed by the *tintamarre* protest – indexing Acadian tradition. Protesters assumed that it constituted a shared ground for the interpretation of the protest (Jaffe 2016), as a bridge to Acadian culture – a way to demonstrate that they were not protesting against "the other" (the Acadians), but rather aligning *with* them, assuming a shared struggle for language rights. But in this alignment, the parents were not evoking the rights of a minority; rather, their own rights to bilingualism. Peritz (2008) articulated this alignment in her coverage of the protests: "These New Brunswickers are the children of Pierre Trudeau's vision of a bilingual and bicultural Canada. And the focus of their protest is the ticket they think gets them there: early French immersion".

Notably, nowhere in this historical event were Acadian or Francophone language rights mentioned, suggesting an alignment through erasure and an act of legitimation. To be fair, it is possible that many of the participants in the *tintamarre* protest were not aware of its provincial and cultural significance. We do not suggest there was a purposeful attempt at erasure or fractal recursivity regarding Acadian historical struggles – which is why more traditional arguments of appropriation cannot apply in this analysis. However, we argue that the choice of the *tintamarre* for their protest does in fact play into the significance of how the parents' protests fit into the provincial LIDs.

In addition to the discursive framing of the event, micro level discursive practices are significant in the Anglophone community's imagining of NB's bilingual community.

4.3.2 Discursive practices of the *tintamarre*

Diana Hamilton and Matthew Litvak's video of the *tintamarre* (lasting 5:44 minutes) begins with Bruce Robertson's speech outlining the key issues (*Sackville march to save early French immersion* 2008):

> . . . exciting outcome of the meeting from two nights ago where we *all* felt that we needed to do something – not in a couple of weeks' time, because we *sure* do need to do something in a couple of weeks' time, not in a *month's* time – but that we *also* want to do something *right away* to express our dissatisfaction about this situation. And so I am delighted to have you all here today. I want to begin though, by thanking Matt Litvak and Diana Hamilton for their *excellent* report [holds up the report; loud clapping and noise-making]. This report shows that the decision of our government is based on bad counting, not good governance and that we should desire to have EFI based on *good thinking* and to *stop* the *lie* and give us our EFI. [loud clapping and noise-making].
>
> Let me tell you we are not alone in feeling this way. I have a letter here [waves letter] from Mike Olscamp, our MLA [Member of the Legislative Assembly] . . . He apologises for not being here, marching with us today, but he has a committee meeting. He wants the crowd to know that he supports our efforts, and he wants us to continue in them. He opposes the government's decision to deny parents and kids the *choice* to start French immersion in Grade 1. [loud clapping, noise-making] . . . He finally says, and this is the most exciting thing, he looks forward to working with Tantramar people over the coming days to *oppose what the government is doing*. [loud clapping and noise-making]. And so a big thanks to Mike Olscamp for that.
>
> [Video stopped; continues with protesters walking through the community, banging pots and pans and other noise-makers, and carrying placards – e.g., "Save EFI;" "I want to be bilingual"]
>
> [Parade ends; Robertson speaks again]. We also know how many of us care about this issue, and I am hoping you will also continue to support it. Because this is really us getting together for the first time in a long battle that will be continuing. And the next step in that battle, the next important step, is the march at the legislature, March 27, at the legislature in Fredericton. And they would like to see not only adults but also children whose lives have been so positively affected by Early French immersion there to join their parents in protesting this unhappy turn of events. I do want to thank you all for coming.

Parents' positioning of themselves and their children (Davies and Harré 1990) within the imagined bilingual community is discursively achieved through a number of semiotic processes. First, iconicity is established through the parents' evocation of a heightened sense of urgency and crisis, a rallying of the troops that solidified their cause and identity: "We *all* felt that we needed to do something – not in a couple of weeks' time, because we *sure* do need to do something in a couple of weeks' time, not in a *month's* time – but that we *also* want to do something *right away* to express our dissatisfaction about this situation". The urgency intensifies with a sense of crisis created by the use of "*save* EFI" on the placards and references to battle. The right to EFI is presented as a *fundamental* right of children, adding potency to the crisis. For example, a placard declaring "I want to be bilingual" is strategically propped on a baby stroller (see Figure 11.3), and children are described as victims: "children *whose lives have been so positively affected by Early French immersion* there to join their parents in protesting this unhappy turn of events". Second, iconicity is established through the definition of group boundaries through the selective use of pronouns, which play a key role in the discursive construction of identity, creating alignments between speakers and their topics and their hearers (Malone 1997). Goffman (1967) uses the notion of "footings" to describe how pronouns are used by speakers to position themselves as a means of polarizing representations of in-groups and outgroups. In the video transcript, the pronoun "we" is used four times in the opening sentence and 8 times throughout; "our" four times in just the first paragraph; and "us" six times throughout. The frequency of in-group referencing stands in stark contrast to outgroup: "The Government" is used only four times in the text. Fourth, iconicity is reinforced through establishing external legitimacy of the cause, and by extension, the Anglophone protesters' identity. Robertson first brings in the voice of MLA Olscamp, who is also a retired French teacher. "We are not alone", he says. And he references a letter from Olscamp: "He [Olscamp] opposes the government's decision to deny parents and kids the *choice* to start French immersion in Grade 1". He then brings in professors Hamilton's and Litvak's (2008) critique of the report on which the government based its decision. The critique "show[ed] that the decision of our government is based on bad counting, not good governance and that we should desire to have EFI based on *good thinking* and to *stop* the *lie* and give us our EFI". Finally, Robertson establishes a moral basis for the group's cause and identity within the language ideological debate by creating oppositions that organize and structure binaries around "good" and "bad", and "good thinking" and "lie".

Processes of erasure are evident in how the assumption of bilingualism's value silences the intense debates that had been and continue to be active in the province regarding the place of bilingualism in provincial imagining (Boudreau, 2016). Blackledge (2005) identifies three options with respect to identity: some identity options are negotiable; others are either imposed (and thus non-negotiable) or assumed (and thus not negotiated). In the identity imagined through the *tintamarre*, bilingual identity – as institutionalized through the public education system – is assumed, as the parents have adopted the rights-based provincial rhetoric of linguistic choice. It suggests they believed that the government alone was responsible for their children's acquisition of French, however, this produced an uncomfortable alliance with the government against whom they protested. For, the government's position was not the elimination of bilingualism from provincial identity, but rather (in its view) the elimination of EFI to ensure bilingualism's success. As such, a second layer of erasure was necessary – a slippage between the terms "bilingualism" and "Early French Immersion," presenting the two terms as synonymous. The CEC blog title overtly states this position: "Immersion delayed is immersion denied". Other references made earlier regarding the denial of children's rights similarly suggest a view that the elimination of EFI would negate the chance for child to be bilingual. Their processes of erasure thus "[simplified] the sociolinguistic field" (Irvine and Gal 2000: 38). Via erasure, facts seen as inconsistent with the ideological positioning taken are filtered and silenced.

Postscript: A final response to the 2008 LID came through the judge's decision on the *Small and Ryan v. New Brunswick (Minister of Education)* (2008) case which came to epitomize many of the protesters' concerns. The presiding Justice McLellan concluded that, "Early French Immersion for Anglophones in New Brunswick, the linguistic majority in this province, is not protected by the *Charter* provision for Minority Language Educational Rights". His statement thus denied the Anglophone *tintamarre* protesters access to minority discourses in their LID. He also discounted the assumed synonymous relationship between EFI and bilingualism: "I am not convinced that the general words regarding bilingualism and linguistic communities in section 16 and 16.1 of the *Charter* provide any legal basis to challenge the decision of Minister of Education regarding Early French Immersion". However, McLellan also issued the government a "speeding fine" – ruling that the Minister of Education did not give adequate time to "allow for a full debate" regarding its decision (Canadian Broadcasting Corporation, 11 June 2008). Ultimately, a compromise between Anglophone parents and the Minister of Education was found: In fall of 2010, entry to EFI was moved to Grade 3.[4]

5 Discussion

In our analysis, we have discussed how the complexity of NB's language ideological context originates from its bilingual sociocultural history and its linguistic majority-minority struggles with competing ideologies linked to linguistic identity. Its complexity further emerges from the perception of disenfranchisement by some members of the province's majority. And, in the *tintamarre* episode, its

---

4 In September 2017, EFI was moved again to Grade 1 under the Liberal government.

complexity results from the parents' appropriation of minority discourses and cultural icons as a means to access the linguistic and material capital enshrined in the bilingual policy designed to protect the minority. At issue is the subject position that NB French immersion parents imagine they and their children occupy as a result of participation in French immersion education (Norton and Toohey 2011). All of these complexities confirm the need for analyses that go beyond mere minority/majority dynamics to one of imagined linguistic identities within LIDs, with an emphasis on historicity and ideological (re)production. For, as we discussed, while the government's response was a reinforcement of the policy-driven, top-down ideologies, these language ideologies were, ironically, once bottom-up ideologies among the Francophones (cf. Haque 2012; Boudreau 2016). The government's response effectively stifled the Anglophone parents' play at new bottom-up language ideologies of bilingualism. While the parents used the *tintamarre* to negotiate that position within the parameters of the OLA policy, they ultimately found that the French immersion policy did not enable them to transcend the distinct boundaries framing the two linguistic communities framed by the OLA. The overall impact of this historical episode was thus the reification of the top-down ideology of provincial bilingualism strictly as defined in and instituted by NB's OLA.

This analysis demonstrates how the (re)production of ideology within LIDs were made visible through analyses of semiotic processes. The two layers of analyses used to interpret this historical episode demonstrate the significance of the socio-historical and political embeddedness of language ideology and the power relationships framing that embeddedness. Processes of erasure stripped the *tintamarre* of its significance as a symbolic act of Acadian identity and of their collective response to oppression and marginalization, enabling the Anglophone parents to use it as their mode of protest. Erasure also intensified the debate by enabling a conflation of EFI and bilingualism, suggesting that the elimination of EFI (a policy) was tantamount to the elimination of bilingualism (a right). Through fractal recursivity, the *tintamarre* was reinterpreted as a form of protest, rather than celebration of identity; it was a protest against the government, rather than local community; and it captured the voice of the majority, rather than the marginalized minority. And processes of iconicity enabled Anglophone parents to imagine their identity within a bilingual province, accessed through EFI. These semiotic processes thus allow us to examine the processes of the language ideological debate, embedded in the power dynamics that frame its socio-political context, shaping this historical moment.

As we distill the primary themes from our analysis, we follow Norton and Toohey (2011: 418) by drawing on Davies and Harré's (1990) notion of the "position" of language learners. The concept of position has to do with how identities are partial and fluid, and how they are often context-dependent in that "while identities or positions are often given by social structures or ascribed by others, they can also be negotiated by agents who wish to position themselves" (Norton and Toohey 2011: 418). While the parents used the *tintamarre* to negotiate that position within the parameters of the Official Languages Act, they ultimately found that the French immersion policy did not enable them to ideologically transcend the distinct boundaries framing the two linguistic communities by the Official Languages Act. Within this context, two primary themes emerge.

First, our analysis contributes to discussions concerning the imagined (linguistic) communities that parents envision for their children (Dagenais 2003; Norton 2013). In his *tintamarre* speech, Robertson called for more children's participation in the protests – essentially calling them to enact the imagining instituted by their parents. As the Douglas Fir Group (2016: 35) notes, language ideologies "influence people's choices for approaching language learning, their investments in their target languages". It is thus especially important in the conception of educational policy to examine such historical moments of the public manifestation of LIDs in relation to language education and the impact they ultimately have on language educational pathways.

Second, our analysis aligns with others outside of NB (Roy and Galiev 2011) who have noted that, due to language ideologies, FI programs may ambiguously position their students' identities as language learners. For instance, in the province of Alberta, Roy and Galiev (2011) found that Anglophone students of FI considered themselves neither Francophone nor bilingual. Instead, they classified themselves as failures for not achieving balanced siloed L1+L1 bilingualism (Grosjean 1989; Roy and Galiev 2011). Yet, in the globalized, transnational world, bilingual, or even multilingual competence in French and another/other language(s) enables learners of French to speak the language in a variety of countries, professional sectors, and among a diversity of peoples. Explicit conversation about the different imaginings of French multilingual identity available in local, national, and global contexts would be an important step: first, in developing mutual understanding with Francophones in Canada and, second, in paving the way for Anglophone children's development of an imagined cosmopolitan identity (Norton and Toohey 2011) associated with French fixed in the global community of practice available to *all* speakers of French, whether as a mother tongue or as an additional language. The FI curriculum documents in NB do suggest possibilities for such a focus, through repeated reference to the advantage FI students will have in communicating with Francophones throughout Canada and around the world; however, these objectives are not fully developed nor linked to intercultural competencies (Keating Marshall and Bokhorst-Heng 2018).

One way forward is to consider Norton's (2013) work which demonstrated that learners' target-language identities vary greatly, depending on their investment in the target language and participation in target language communities of practice. As Darvin and Norton (2015: 41) observe, the "asymmetric distribution of power no longer rests on the simple dichotomy of native speaker and language learner. Beyond inclusion in a target community of speakers or the acquisition of material and symbolic resources, learners are able to participate in a greater variety of spaces in both face-to-face and virtual worlds and assert themselves to varying degrees as legitimate speakers". It is therefore important that parents and teachers help children develop metacognition to consider their different investments in the language practices of their communities and in the global community, to understand the range of possibilities – and the constraints – for their imagined identities (Norton and Toohey 2011).

6 Conclusion

As we consider some of the practical implications of our analysis, we note the significance of not so much who is a native speaker, but rather, within global contexts of transnationalism, the development of bilingual and multilingual identity (see also Bono, this volume; Kerschhofer-Puhalo and Slavkov, this volume). Our analysis may be especially informative in countries where learning one of the official languages is inherently linked with local and/or national language ideologies. One might think of Cameroon, with French and English as official languages, or Switzerland, with its four official languages, or Singapore, with its four official languages. In these countries, too, learners may or may not develop an identity attached directly to the target language(s). As others have before us (Risager 2006; Norton and Toohey 2011; Darvin and Norton 2015), we suggest that language educational programs seek to deliberately foster students' imagined identities first as intercultural citizens of their own countries and as multilinguals with a transnational perspective (Byram 2008; Risager 2006). Work by Byram and colleagues (e.g., Byram, Gribkova, and Starkey 2002; Wagner, Perugini, and Byram 2017) using the Common European Framework of Reference for Languages (Council of Europe 2001) to develop intercultural competences, and by Scarino and Liddicoat (2009) in the Australian national curriculum, provide practical suggestions for teachers to intentionally incorporate the development of students' bilingual identity and intercultural citizenship into FI instruction. The revised FSL curriculum in Ontario (Government of Ontario 2013) includes specific outcomes and curricular guidelines related to intercultural competence and global competencies. And in the United States, Can-Do Statements on Intercultural Communication jointly published by the National Council of State Supervisors for Languages and American Council on the Teaching of Foreign Languages provide a tangible description of the sorts of intercultural knowledge and behaviors which might be developed at each level of linguistic competency (NCSSL/ACTFL 2017). NB's current emphasis on Self Evaluation Learning Folios (SELFs) encourages students' development of metacognition, and when applied to French language learning, involves identifying meeting language skills outcomes but also the socio-cultural aspects of language learning that would link to their development as bilingual selves. Through such strategies, identity development may be prioritized in societal expectations of language education, conversations with parents, pedagogical practice, classroom discourse, and most importantly, in student learning – in a model that transcends the native speaker model aiming instead for plurilingual, global citizens (Byram 2008).

Authors' Positionalities

Wendy Bokhorst-Heng is first generation Canadian, the daughter of Dutch immigrants. She grew up in a tight community of similar Dutch immigrant families and remembers vividly her shock the first time she heard an elderly person speak English "well" – she was not aware that proficiency in English was possible for people her grandparents' age! Characteristic of the Dutch community in general (Ganzevoort 1998) her parents were intent on full and rapid assimilation, with minimal commitment to language retention. Her parents did not want their children to enter school sounding as non-native speakers of English. However, she became an unintentional bilingual; that is, although her parents declared the deliberate home language policy to be English only (although they themselves had only begun to learn English upon their arrival to Canada), over the years she picked up enough Dutch to eventually be able to communicate with her Dutch extended family in The Netherlands.

Years later, through her academic journey, Bokhorst-Heng became increasingly interested in linguistic diversity, how governments perceived and managed that diversity, the language ideologies that are constructed discursively to support that management, particularly in relation to education. When she moved to Singapore, she was fascinated by the hyper-linguistic diversity of the country (not just in terms of language varieties but also in terms of how people used language), and by the engineering of the "mother tongue" – an allocation based on one's father's ethnicity and through the dismantling of Chinese dialects within the populace's repertoire. Added intrigue came from the existence of varieties of native-speaker English in Singapore. She was intrigued by the writing of scholars such as Kachru (1983), Crystal (1997) and Pennycook (1993), and considered the twin dynamics of colonialism and globalization at play in the development of English diversity. She saw socio-linguistic and power dynamics embedded in the relationships between these varieties play out when her Singaporean colleague's son was required to attend remedial English classes while attending an international school in China, and again when her own child was recommended for speech pathology when her family was stationed in the USA for a few years – both on account of their othered native variety of English. Her current location in New Brunswick, in a community that is rapidly diversifying with increasing numbers of immigrants in an officially bilingual province, has again brought conversations of native speaker to the fore. While all children in the province are required to study French, local definitions of French based on native speaker standards and aligned with francophone identity have kept at arms-length any claim to bilingual identity, often resulting in a permanent linguistic identity tied to the status of learner (e.g., I am a French immersion student) and linguistic insecurity (Roy and Galiev 2011). She has seen her own children even resist the notion that French could claim an everyday presence in their lives outside of school. All of these reflections on native speaker norms in World English, in French immersion, and in bilingualism have been guided by Bourdieu's "thinking tools" (Rawolle and Lingard 2013) of fields, capital, and habitus (e.g., Bourdieu and Wacquant 1992) that together inform the ideologies, practices and identities embedded in language education policies and language ideological debates.

Kelle L. Marshall was raised as a monolingual English speaker in the border states of Texas and Arizona in the United States. Growing up in these two states, the first language she recalls hearing besides English was Spanish, the minority language in the Southwestern U.S. Due to neoliberal language ideologies (e.g. Bernstein et al. 2015), many people, particularly in the Southwest, consider Spanish competency as it is the "practical" language to learn for conducting business in the region. Her older brother studied Spanish in secondary school and she remembers hearing he was quite good at speaking it – with a "native accent," as it was said, in accordance with ideologies of bilingual competence in the United States favoring the L1 + L1 conception of balanced bilingualism (Grosjean 1989; Kearney 2015).

Despite this ideological context, Marshall was drawn to the French language, partly thanks to a song by her favorite musical group, The Manhattan Transfer. Though she had no family ties to the language, no Francophone friends, and no "practical" reason for doing so, she began to study French at the age of eighteen, originally to fulfill her university language requirement. Later as a French major and so-called "late learner" of French, her goal, driven by ideologies of balanced bilingualism, was to be mistakenly identified as a 'native speaker' of French. Yet, after having spent time in France and Belgium and then after having studied and conducted research in *Québec* and in *Acadie*, it became clear to her that 'native speaker' could not be a monolithic concept, nor could the notion 'Francophone.' She questioned these notions further when a speaker of French L1 told her that her French was better than theirs. This interaction gave her first-hand insight to how the ideology of "Standard French" (e.g. Lodge 1993) creates a hierarchy, regimenting linguistic marketplaces in Francophone societies (e.g. Boudreau 2016).

Subsequent dialogue with Canadian Francophone colleagues led Marshall to apply Bourdieu's constructs of linguistic marketplaces, linguistic capital, language ideologies, and language identity to language use in minority Francophone spaces and in Acadian artistic productions. She then investigated these same Bourdieusian notions in relationship to French language education, involving both university students of French in the United States and French immersion students in Canada. Now of particular interest to her are the notions of legitimacy and authenticity in Francophone communities of practice and the development of intercultural competence (e.g. Byram 2021) in learners of French, equipping them to navigate diverse Francophone spaces. She favors intercultural orientations to language teaching as a means by which to challenge neoliberal language ideologies of linguistic commodification through the promotion of social and cultural capital. She considers these approaches as effective for fostering curiosity in students on cultural and linguistic diversity. Finally, she views these approaches as means to counteract essentializing effects of language ideologies, particularly through guided reflection on students' bi/multilingual identities (e.g. Melo-Pfeifer 2017). She no longer considers the mythical 'native speaker' as her ideal, aspiring instead to be a multilingual subject (Kramsch 2009) who practices intercultural mediation (Kohler 2015).

References

Anderson, Benedict. 1991. *Imagined communities*. London and New York: Verso.
Arsenault, Rita. 2016. Speech given at the Swearing in Ceremony for new Canadian citizens at Capital Theatre, Moncton, NB, 15 July 2016.
Bernstein, Katie, Emily Hellmich, Noah Katznelson, Jaren Shin & Kimberly Vinall. 2015. Critical perspectives on neoliberalism in second/foreign language education. *L2 Journal* 7, 3–14.
Blackledge, Adrian. 2000. Monolingual ideologies in multilingual states: Language, hegemony and social justice in western liberal democracies. *Estudios de Sociolingüística* 1(2), 25–45. Doi.org/10.1558/sols.vli2.25
Blackledge, Adrian. 2005. *Discourse and power in a multilingual world*. Amsterdam/ Philadelphia: John Benjamins Publishing.
Blommaert, Jan. 1999. The debate is open. In Jan Blommaert (ed.), *Language ideological debates*, 1–38. Berlin: Mouton de Gruyter.
Bourdieu, Pierre & Wacquant, Loic. 1992. *An invitation to reflexive sociology*. Chicago: University of Chicago Press.
Boudreau, Annette. 2016. *À l'ombre de la langue légitime: L'Acadie dans la Francophonie*. Paris: Classiques Garnier.
Byram, Michael. 1997/2021. *Teaching and assessing intercultural communicative competence: Revisited*. Bristol, UK: Multilingual Matters.
Byram, Michael. 2008. *From foreign language education to education for intercultural citizenship: Essays and reflections*. Clevedon: Multilingual Matters.
Byram, Michael, Bella Gribkova, and Hugh Starkey. 2002. *Developing the intercultural dimension in language teaching: A practical introduction for teachers*. Strasbourg: Council of Europe. https://rm.coe.int/16802fc1c3
Canadian Broadcasting Corporation. March 26, 2008. *Moncton supporters rally to save French immersion*. http://www.cbc.ca/news/canada/new-brunswick/moncton-supporters-rally-to-save-french-immersion-1.714746
Canadian Broadcasting Corporation. June 11, 2008. *N.B. Early French Immersion cuts 'unfair and unreasonable': Judge*. http://www.cbc.ca/news/canada/new-brunswick/n-b-early-french-immersion-cuts-unfair-and-unreasonable-judge-1.695845
Canadian Charter of Rights and Freedoms, s 7, Part I of the Constitution Act, 1982, being Schedule B to the Canada Act 1982 (UK), 1982, c11.
Canadian Parents for French. 2018. French as a second language enrolment statistics 2012–2013 to 2016–2017. http://www.cpf.ca

Chiasson, Herménégilde. 2004. Oublier Évangéline, in Simon Langlois and Jocelyn Létourneau, *Aspects de la nouvelle francophonie canadienne*, 147–163. Québec: Les presses de L'Université Laval.
Consortium of Canadian Universities advising the Canadian Association of Immersion Teachers. 2008. *Open Letter to the Honourable Kelly Lamrock, Minister of Education, Province of New Brunswick*. http://www.unb.ca/fredericton/second-language/_resources/pdf/fsleview/letterlamrock.pdf
Cooke, Max. 2010. A collision of culture, values, and education policy: Scrapping early French immersion in New Brunswick. *Education Canada* 49(2), http://www.cea-ace.ca
Council of Europe. 2001. *Common European framework of reference for languages: Learning, teaching, assessment*. Cambridge: Cambridge University Press. https://rm.coe.int/1680459f97
Croll, James & Patricia Lee. 2008. *Report of the French Second Language Commission*. Fredericton, NB: Department of Education.
Crystal, David. 1997. *English as a global language*. Cambridge: Cambridge University Press.
Dagenais, Diane. 2003. Accessing imagined communities through multilingualism and immersion education. *Journal of Language, Identity, and Education* 2(4), 269–283. http://dx.doi.org/10.1207/S15327701JLIE0204_3
Darvin, Ron & Bonny Norton. 2015. Identity and a model of investment in applied linguistics. *Annual Review of Applied Linguistics* 35, 36–56.
Davies, Bronwyn & Ron Harré. 1990. Positioning: The discursive production of selves. *Journal for the Theory of Social Behavior* 20(1), 43–63.
Dicks, Joseph. 2008. *The case for early French immersion: A response to J. Douglas Willms*. http://www.unb.ca/fredericton/second-language/_resources/pdf/lricnotes/spring2008.pdf
Douglas Fir Group. 2016. A transdisciplinary framework for SLA in a multilingual world. *The Modern Language Journal* 100, 19–47. http://dx.doi.org/10.1111/modl.12301
Edwards, Viviane. 1986. *French immersion in New Brunswick: The early years (1969–1985)*. Unpublished master's thesis), the University of New Brunswick, Fredericton, New Brunswick.
Ganzevoort, Herman. 1998. The Dutch in Canada. In Leen d'Haenens (ed.). *Images of Canadianness: Visions on Canada's politics, culture, and economics*, 91–108. Ottawa: University of Ottawa Press. https://doi.org/10.2307/j.ctt1cn6s1m.8
Gee, James P. 2014. *An introduction to discourse analysis: Theory and method*. [4th edition]. London: Routledge.
Goffman, Erving. 1967. *Interaction ritual*. New York: Doubleday.
Government of New Brunswick. 1968. Statement on language equality and opportunity. Tabled in the legislative assembly Province of New Brunswick, December 4, 1968. Honourable Louis. J. Robichaud, P.C., Q.C., Premier. http://leg-horizon.gnb.ca/e-repository/monographs/31000000049161/31000000049161.pdf
Government of New Brunswick. 2008. *Improvements being made to French second-language programs and services (Anglophone sector)*. http://www2.gnb.ca/content/gnb/en/news/news_release.2008.03.0310.html
Government of New Brunswick. 2011. An act recognizing the equality of the two official linguistic communities in New Brunswick, RSNB 2011, c 198. http://canlii.ca/t/lcj4

Government of New Brunswick. Heritage Branch. 2006. J'ai un rêve: les droits linguistiques au Nouveau-Brunswick. http://www.virtualmuseum.ca/edu/ViewLoitCollection.do;jsessionid=81C93D6BC6442C1C963F12D6181F59D4?method=previewImageandlang=FRandid=11

Government of New Brunswick. Education and Early Childhood Development. 2019. *Everyone at their best: Learning French as a second language.* Brochure. Available at https://www2.gnb.ca/content/dam/gnb/Departments/ed/pdf/promo/EveryoneAtTheirBest.pdf

Government of Ontario. 2013. The Ontario curriculum: French as a second language. http://www.edu.gov.on.ca/eng/curriculum/elementary/fsl18-2013curr.pdf

Grosjean, François. 1989. Neurolinguists, Beware! The bilingual is not two monolinguals in one person. *Brain and Language* 36, 3–15.

Hamilton, Diane & Matthew Litvak. 2008. Response to the Croll and Lee comprehensive review of second language programs and services within the Anglophone sector of the NB Department of Education. https://sites.google.com/site/hamlit2008/

Haque, Eve. 2012. *Multiculturalism within a bilingual framework.* Toronto: University of Toronto Press.

Hayday, Matthew. 2015. *So they want us to learn French. Promoting and opposing bilingualism in English-speaking Canada.* Vancouver and Toronto: UBC Press.

Heller, Monica. 1990. French immersion in Canada: A model for Switzerland? *Multilingua* 9(1), 67–85.

Heller, Monica. 1999. Heated language in a cold climate. In Jan Blommaert (ed.), *Language ideological debates*, 143–170. Berlin: Mouton de Gruyter.

Heller, Monica. 2007. Bilingualism as ideology and practice. In Monica Heller (ed.). *Bilingualism: A social approach*, 1–22. New York, NY: Palgrave Macmillan.

Irvine, Judith & Susan Gal. 2000. Language ideology and linguistic differentiation. In Paul Kroskrity (ed.), *Regimes of language: Ideologies, polities, and identities*, 35–84. Santa Fe, NM: School of American Research Press.

Jaffe, Alexandra. 2007. Minority language movements. In Monica Heller (ed.), *Bilingualism: A social approach*, 50–70. New York, NY: Palgrave Macmillan.

Jaffe, Alexandra. 2016. Indexicality, stance and fields in sociolinguistics. In Nikolas Coupland (ed.), *Sociolinguistics: Theoretical debates*, 86–112. Cambridge: Cambridge University Press.

Kachru, Braj, B. 1983. *The other tongue: English across cultures.* Oxford: Perfamon Press.

Kearney, Erin. 2015. *Intercultural learning in modern language education: Expanding meaning-making potentials.* Bristol, UK: Multilingual Matters.

Keating Marshall, Kelle & Wendy D. Bokhorst-Heng. 2018. "I wouldn't want to impose!" Intercultural mediation in French immersion. *Foreign Language Annals* 51, 290–312 doi: 10.1111/flan.12340

Kohler, Michelle. 2015. *Teachers as mediators in the foreign language classroom.* Bristol, UK: Multilingual Matters.

Kramsch, Claire. 2009. *The multilingual subject: What foreign language learners say about their experience and why it matters.* Oxford: Oxford University Press.

Kroskrity, Paul. 2000. Regimenting languages. In Paul Kroskrity (ed.), *Regimes of language: Ideologies, polities, and identities*, 1–34. Santa Fe, NM: School of American Research Press.

Labelle, Rondald. 2007. *Tintamarre*: A new Acadian 'tradition'. *Encyclopedia of French cultural heritage in North America*. http://www.ameriquefrancaise.org/en/article-319/Tintamarre:__a_New_Acadian_%E2%80%9CTradition%E2%80%9D__.html

Laxer, James. 2007. *The Acadians in search of a homeland*. Toronto: Anchor Canada.

Lodge, Anthony. 1993. *French: From dialect to standard*. London: Routledge.

Malone, Martin. 1997. *Worlds of talk: The presentation of self in everyday conversations*. Malden, MA/Cambridge: Polity Press.

Melo-Pfeifer, Sílvia. 2017. Drawing the plurilingual self: How children portray their plurilingual resources. *International Review of Applied Linguistics in Language Teaching* 55(1), 1–20. doi: 10.1515/iral-2017-0006

NCSSFL and ACTFL. 2017. *NCSSFL-ACTFL Can-Do Statements*. Retrieved May 27, 2019, from https://www.actfl.org/sites/default/files/CanDos/Intercultural%20Can-Do_Statements.pdf

Norton, Bonny. 2013. *Identity and language learning: Extending the conversation*. [2nd edition]. Bristol: Multilingual Matters.

Norton, Bonny & Kelleen Toohey. 2011. Identity, language learning, and social change. *Language Teaching* 44(4), 412–446.

Office of the Commissioner of Official Languages (NB). 2005. Choice. It's mine. http://officiallanguages.nb.ca/sites/default/files/imce/pdfs/choicechoixadseng.pdf

Office of the Commissioner of Official Languages (NB). 2013. Living with two languages. Fredericton: Office of the Commissioner of Official Languages for New Brunswick. http://www.officiallanguages.nb.ca

Office of the Commissioner of Official Languages (NB). 2015. *2014–2015 Annual Report*. Fredericton: Office of the Commissioner of Official Languages for New Brunswick.

Pavlenko, Aneta. 2003. "I never knew I was a bilingual": Reimagining teacher identities in TESOL. *Journal of Language, Identity, and Education* 2(4), 251–268. http://dx.doi.org/10.1207/S15327701JLIE0204_2

Pennycook, Alastair. 1994. *The cultural politics of English as an international language*. London: Longman.

Peritz, Ingrid. 2008, March 31. "We want to be bilingual!" "We love French!" *The Globe and Mail*. https://www.theglobeandmail.com/news/national/we-want-to-be-bilingual-we-love-french/article17982750/

Rawolle, Shaun & Bob Lingard. 2013. Bourdieu and educational research: Thinking tools, relational thinking, beyond epistemological innocence. In Mark Murphy (Ed)., *Social theory and education research: Understanding Foucault, Habermas, Bourdieu and Derrida* (pp. 117–137). Routledge.

Rehorick, Sally, Joseph Dicks, Paula Kristmanson & Fiona Cogswell. 2006. Quality learning in French Second Language in New Brunswick: A brief to the Department of Education. Second Language Education Centre, University of New Brunswick. http://www.unb.ca/fredericton/second-language/_resources/pdf/fslstudy.pdf

Remixing [Def. 2]. 2018. *Oxford English Dictionary*. Oxford: Oxford University Press.

Risager, Karen. 2006. *Language and culture: Global flows and local complexity*. Clevedon: Multilingual Matters.

Roy, Sylvie & Albert Galiev. 2011. Discourses on bilingualism in Canadian French immersion programs. *The Canadian Modern Language Review* 67(3), 351–376.

Sackville march to save early French immersion in NB, Canada. 2008. YouTube. https://www.youtube.com/watch?v=rJa7AJn4sDE

Scarino, Angela & Anthony Liddicoat. 2009. Teacher and learning languages: A guide. Australian Government. Department of Education, Employment and Workplace Relations. http://www.tllg.unisa.edu.au

Small and Ryan v. New Brunswick (Minister of Education). Court of Queen's Bench of New Brunswick, Trial Division, Judicial District of Saint John. 2008.

Stanley, Della. 1984. *Louis Robichaud: A decade of power*. Halifax: Nimbus Publishing.

Statistics Canada. 2015. Portrait of official language minorities in Canada – Francophones in New Brunswick. https://www150.statcan.gc.ca/n1/pub/89-642-x/2011005/article/section1-eng.htm

Statistics Canada. 2016. *Census of population*, Statistics Canada Catalogue no. 98-400-X2016056. http://www12.statcan.gc.ca/census-recensement/2016/dp-pd/dt-td/Lp-eng.cfm?LANG=EandAPATH=3andDETAIL=0andDIM=0andFL=VandFREE=0andGC=0andGID=0andGK=0andGRP=1andPID=0andPRID=0andPTYPE=109445andS=0andSHOWALL=0andSUB=0andTemporal=2016andTHEME=118andVID=0andVNAMEE=andVNAMEF=

Tower, Katie. 2008, March 19. Parents fight government's decision to eliminate EFI. *Sackville Tribune Post*, pp. 1,3.

Wagner, Manuela, Dorie C. Perugini & Michael Byram (ed.). 2017. *Teaching intercultural competence across the age range: From theory to practice*. Bristol: Multilingual Matters.

Nadja Kerschhofer-Puhalo, Nikolay Slavkov
Chapter 12
Questioning the questions: Institutional and individual perspectives on children's language repertoires

Abstract: This chapter discusses institutional practices of asking questions about children's "native" or "home" language(s) as well as individual perspectives of children describing their own multi/plurilingual repertoires. Data from two separate studies – one on school registration forms in Canadian elementary schools and the other on children's verbal and visual representations of their plurilingual repertoires – show difficulties and incompatibilities between the experiences of children living in transnational and multilingual families and educational practices of language profiling and institutional categorization, which are strongly oriented towards monolingualism and singleness rather than plurality. The Canadian study illustrates school language background profiling that asks parents to identify their children's "first language", "home language", and "other" languages and discusses the underlying ideologies that these categories imply. This top-down institutional perspective is contrasted with bottom-up qualitative data from a corpus of Austrian migrant children's verbal and visual representations. The bottom-up approach reveals how children position themselves towards various criteria, such as origin, affiliation, language use, or proficiency, to qualify as a "native speaker". We discuss the ideological dimensions and practical limitations of questions about the "first", "home", or "dominant" language as well as some dilemmas that children face in finding answers to questions about their complex and dynamic language repertoires.

Keywords: language background profiling, ideology, repertoire, school registration forms, plurilingual self(-concept), elementary/primary school

---

Acknowledgments: The project *My Literacies* was financed by the funding program Sparkling Science of the Austrian Federal Ministry of Education, Science and Research. The project *Reimagining Language Background Profiling at Canadian Elementary Schools: Towards Bilingual and Multilingual Norms* was financed by the Social Sciences and Humanities Research Council of Canada (Insight Development Grant 430-2017-00558).

Nadja Kerschhofer-Puhalo, University of Vienna, e-mail: nadja.kerschhofer@univie.ac.at
Nikolay Slavkov, University of Ottawa, e-mail: nikolay.slavkov@uottawa.ca

https://doi.org/10.1515/9781501512353-013

1 Introduction

Linguistic diversity in contexts of schooling can be viewed as a fact, a problem, an opportunity, a challenge, a right, capital, or commodity. The ways in which plurilingual individuals (cf. Coste, Moore, and Zarate 1997, 2009a/b) talk about their experiences with multilingualism[1] and their language repertoires (Blommaert and Backus 2011, 2013; Busch 2012) as well as the way educational institutions communicate about the linguistic background of their "clients", that is, students and their families, can be revealing about underlying assumptions, orientations and ideologies regarding language and ethnicity. In school contexts, various orientations and ideologies may be propagated by artefacts such as curricula, textbooks or school registration forms. They are shaped by educational practices and in turn influence educators, policy makers, administrators, parents, and ultimately students. Therefore, the way incoming students and their families are asked questions about "their languages" is not a trivial issue; to answer these questions is not an easy matter, either. We believe that a closer look at the ways individuals speak about their languages as well as the questions that institutions and their agents (school administrations, teachers) ask about children's first/native/family or heritage languages provides valuable insights into societal discourses and underlying ideologies on language and society in general, evoking notions of family, competence, identity, origin or belonging.

Based on a comparison of qualitative and quantitative data and of top-down vs. bottom-up perspectives, we will discuss the implications of terms like "first language", "native language", "home language", "main language spoken", etc., and will examine the impact that the notion of the "native speaker" – with its underlying implications and ideological orientation – has on the ways institutional questions are formulated and individual answers are given. We will be guided by the following research questions:

(1) How do institutions profile children's language background by categorizing and labeling them?
(2) How do children think and talk about their language repertoires and about their "native" and "non-native" languages in particular? How do children position themselves towards practices of labeling, categorizing, profiling, or

---

[1] In this chapter we alternate between the terms multilingualism and plurilingualism in an attempt to be terminologically faithful to the literature we cite; this mixed usage also reflects our own view of certain overlap of the two notions in the literature. We do not understand multilingualism on the individual level as separate and equal linguistic proficiency or parallel multilingualism within a single person (see also the introduction to the volume for further clarification of our terminological position as both authors and editors).

diagnosing in monolingually-oriented educational settings while experiencing multilingualism on a daily basis?
(3) What do the qualitative and quantitative data presented here show in terms of individual and societal understandings of a child's "native language(s)" or his/her language repertoire? What are the underlying assumptions and ideologies that contribute to particular forms of *questions* about children's "language background" and to the *answers* that children or their parents would give?

Our central interest is to argue that in times of globalization, transnational mobility and translocal communication the notion of a "native speaker" may be too reductionist or insufficient to describe children's complex repertoires. We will show that different methods of investigating a child's language repertoire may yield different results. We will argue that the methods themselves reflect individual, societal and institutional understandings that potentially cause both clashes and overlaps of opposing ideologies about plurilingual individuals. We offer data from two different studies, one in Canada and another one in Austria. The Canadian study focuses on language background profiling in a primary education context, investigating language-related questions used in school registration forms; it offers a (descriptive) quantitative analysis of a sample of 126 forms from five provinces in Canada. We then juxtapose this approach with data from another study in Vienna, Austria, where children themselves paint a holistic picture of their language repertoires. Our goal is not to draw a comparison between the two countries or use comparable sets of data from the two contexts but rather to use the insights of the two studies in order to look at two different perspectives: institutional versus individual, or top-down versus bottom-up. Such views may be revealing about the situation in many contexts around the world affected by migration, multilingualism and globalization. After discussing our findings, we end the chapter with a general conclusion advocating for further deconstruction of monolingually-oriented views of plurilingual children and their families, and by questioning underlying ideas of essence, unity and singleness.

2 Theoretical background and methodological considerations

Discussing multilingualism as an abstract and context-free phenomenon reduces linguistic diversity and language use to a few aspects related to demographics or language proficiency without considering social relationships or embeddings that are so relevant in sociolinguistic research. Rather than seeing multilingualism as a combination of serial or parallel monolingualisms, we focus on the great diversity of "multilingualisms" (Piller 2016: 26) and the many variables such as language status, speaker status, national histories and policies, and the interaction of individual proficiencies and identities in socio-historic, political and institutional contexts. In order to acknowledge the social nature of processes that link people with particular languages and to avoid difficulties that arise when emphasizing biological over social aspects of the problem, Rampton (1990) proposed three alternative concepts: *expertise, inheritance* and *affiliation*. However, as we will see in section 4, even these notions refer to a range of individual interpretations. We will therefore refer here to another crucial sociolinguistic concept: the repertoire.

2.1 Repertoires

The origin of the concept of the linguistic repertoire is commonly traced back to the early 1960s and the work of John Gumperz, who originally used the term "verbal repertoire" (Gumperz 1964: 137–138). In his work, the repertoire was related to and constrained by the speech community, a central analytical unit. That is, a speaker's repertoire is viewed within the speech community as the full set of acceptable ways of communicating messages. Individuals choose how to express a message based on the acceptable grammatical norms as well as the socially mandated rules of style and register within the particular community.

Over time, a number of other scholars have used and modified the concept of the linguistic repertoire. Some recent work drawing on the concept of superdiversity (Vertovec 2007) has proposed a rethinking of the linguistic repertoire consistent with contemporary phenomena related to migration and globalization. Blommaert and Backus (2011, 2013) reposition the concept from the outside perspective of the speech community to the internal perspective of the *individual*. They argue that in the current context of multiple exposures to various languages through personal trajectories influenced by migration or frequent travel in a globalized world, this *perspective from within* is more appropriate. Busch (2012) notes that such re-conceptualizations of the repertoire "mark a shift away from structure, system, and regularity toward approaches that acknowledge fluidity and creativity in linguistic practices" (2012: 506). Another important aspect of such new reflections is the emphasis on complexity, invoking the notion of complex multilingual repertoires not in the sense of polyglots who are equally proficient in all their languages, but in the sense of multiple languages spoken with different proficiency, at different times, for different purposes, at different locations, and so on. This idea is advanced by the plurilingualism framework (Coste, Moore, and Zarate 1997, 2009a, b and subsequent work).

The complexity of the linguistic repertoire is discussed by Blommaert and Backus (2013) who take Blommaert's personal trajectory as an example and list 38 languages as part of his repertoire. These are divided in four categories, including "maximum competence" (i.e. languages in which the speaker has fully developed both oral and literacy skills), "partial competence" (i.e. languages that the individual may be able to read and speak but not write, for example), "minimal competence" (i.e. languages in which the speaker has only restricted functionality to only a few contexts or domains, such as shopping, having a simple conversation, etc.), and "recognizing competence" (i.e. languages that the speaker has been exposed to in some capacity in the past and can thus recognize and name upon encounter). This example underscores the complex and layered nature of repertoires; furthermore, the authors argue that people might have such complex repertoires without even realizing it (until they start reflecting on this). This internal bottom-up perspective of the language repertoire is important as it provides valuable insights and is different from a top-down, external and linear view referring to concepts such as a person's "native language" or "dominant language" or from the dichotomy of native vs. non-native speakers.

Another important point about the language repertoire in its modern-day conceptualization with a focus on individuals and on complexity is that it lends itself to new methodologies.

2.2 Methodological aspects

While questionnaires and large survey research are suited for quantitative and large-scale analysis, they may lack the capacity to obtain individual in-depth information or answers to more complex questions. However, question formulations, categories and response options in questionnaires or censuses can never be neutral: they are closely intertwined with policies and ideologies. The ideological dimension of language questions and their socio-political impact has been discussed in various recent studies (e.g. Duchêne, Humbert and Coray 2018; Leeman 2018; Slavkov 2016, 2018, 2020) and will also be exemplified by the study of Canadian primary school registration forms described in Section 3 of this chapter.

In contrast to questionnaires, interviews provide opportunities to collect extended declarative data and participants' personal accounts; they can also be studied as speech samples and interactional events, subject to conversation analysis as well as linguistic and content analysis (Codó 2008). In recent years visual and creative methods have been increasingly used in applied linguistics research (e.g. Busch 2010, 2012, 2016; Prasad 2014; Chik, Markose, and Alperstein 2018; Kalaja and Melo-Pfeifer 2019). One of these tools is the so-called *language portrait* (for a comprehensive discussion, see Busch 2018), a research arrangement where participants are asked to draw their languages on a body silhouette, having freedom to use different colours, images, and symbols associated with languages and placed on different parts of their own body. Participants are also asked to add captions or give comments in written or spoken form. Initially used as a language awareness exercise in educational contexts (e.g. Neumann 1991; Krumm and Jenkins 2001; for a review see Gogolin 2015), the tool has become an established research instrument to approach questions about experiential perspectives and subject positioning as well as emotions and biographical aspects of multilingualism. Most of these studies are based on a socio-constructivist rather than an essentialist notion of speakers' language(s) and identities. Many studies relate to the exploration of language repertoires and provide insights into ideologically inferred ideas about language(s) and multilingualism (e.g. Busch 2010, 2012). Using language portraits in studies on multilingualism is therefore a way of combining visual and verbal elements in order to gain insights into individual perspectives and subject positioning that are closely intertwined with societal views and discourse at large. This will be illustrated by the Austrian study with primary school children in Section 4.

2.3 Discourse and ideologies

From a discourse perspective, thinking about people as "native speakers" of a specific "language", as having one "mother tongue" that they are "born into" and therefore possess "native" ultimate proficiency, while skills in all other languages are compared to this proficiency level and are expected to be less developed or deficient, will be considered here as an ideologically based view. This view seems to be "common ground" and is naturalized as "the normal case". In our understanding of ideology, or rather ideologies, people refer to such assumptions and beliefs about what generally seems to be "common sense" or "normal", to what is "usually" done, thought, or said (and what is not done, thought, or said). These common ground views are not produced by specific single actors (e.g. a political party or a government), but are products of discourses penetrating people's lives in general, their reflections, decisions, preferences and daily practices in private as well as in institutional contexts. Our understanding of the term ideology refers to the view "that it penetrates the whole fabric of societies or communities and results in normalised, naturalised patterns of thought and behaviour"

(Blommaert 2005: 159). Ideologies operate simultaneously in discourse on differing layers of sharedness, coherence and historicity (Blommaert 2005: 160).

We are interested in processes of ideological practice as ongoing "ideological work" (Irvine 2019: 68) that is invested when people project, imagine, interpret and construe their actions and rely on specific assumptions and categorizations influenced by the individual's social position. Educational or administrative practices are such forms of action. In this sense, we consider ideologies not only as sets of beliefs or ideas in our minds, but as having a material substance (texts, utterances, classroom practices). We therefore see the necessity to consider the social, material, political and institutional environments where ideologies operate and the social practices by which they are constructed, organized, mediated, reproduced, and recontextualized. In these environments, ideologies and their *semiotic substance* are institutionalized with the effect of being "socially embedded and persistent, outlasting individuals and the particulars of the moment" (Irvine 2019: 71). Schools are perhaps the most prototypical example for such institutional environments.

Institutions also establish unities and instruments to categorize and measure individuals in order to enable comparisons and typifications (Gal 2016), such as language tests, questionnaires, census data, registration or application forms, etc. These involve several forms of regimentation, that is, processes of "organizing something, reducing variation, and excluding what doesn't fit" (Irvine 2019: 71). Such processes and actions may have the effect that the underlying unities and prototypes are perceived as existing entities, as "properties of the natural world, existing outside of human interests or social perspectives" (Irvine 2019: 70).

Irvine and Gal (2000) identify three central semiotic processes of ideological representations: *iconization*, *recursivity* and *erasure*. Iconization refers to processes of "picking out qualities supposedly shared by the social image and the linguistic image, the ideological representation–itself a sign–binds them together in a linkage that appears to be inherent" (2000: 38). Recursivity describes a form of ideological regimentation that projects a conceptual contrast or deletion/ignorance of contrast that is reproduced on some other scale, in other words occurring recursively on different levels of individual and social action (Irvine and Gal 2000: 38, Irvine 2019: 69). Erasure refers to processes of ignoring specific forms of language use, variation, multilingualism or speakers associated with these linguistic characteristics, for instance by not mentioning them or subsuming them under a more general label: "Facts that are inconsistent with the ideological scheme either go unnoticed or get explained away. (...) Because a linguistic ideology is a totalizing vision, elements that do not fit its interpretive structure – that cannot be seen to fit – must be either ignored or transformed" (Irvine and Gal 2000: 38). Through erasure, ideological elements function as simplification of the sociolinguistic field.

By implementing these processes and actions together through underlying ideologically-based common ground views and assumptions, notions such as a homogeneous standard language, the monolingual nation state, the monolingual classroom, or the idea that individuals or families have one single dominant or "native" language are established as normal or natural (in contrast to having more than one family language) and are normalized. Such institutionalized ideas, concepts and practices are established on multiple layers of routines and by several actors operating on different hierarchical levels so that their "subjection-effects are 'combined' in each subject's own acts, which are inscribed in practices, regulated by rituals, and so on." (Althusser [1971] 2014: 199). As specific ideas and ideologies become institutionalized, they create expectations on the one side and potential dissonances and dilemmas on the other. In this sense, we argue that the idea of the "native speaker" together with concepts of bi- or multilingualism, origin, affiliation, and proficiency have become institutionalized and are reproduced on several discourse levels and domains, in educational settings, private environments and language policy, in families, classrooms, school statistics or registration forms.

As ideologies are ubiquitous, individual *subjects* are their products. From their early years on children are confronted with several ideologized views about the status of specific communicative means, about differing forms of belonging to social groups (family, peers, communities), about their selves and others, about imagined identities and imagined communities. Here, the issues around *naming, labeling, categorizing*, but also *not mentioning* and *avoiding* specific terms become relevant. Using (or not using) a specific term or label for a language, an ethnic group or any other kind of social group and its individuals is not only a way of referring to something assumed to "exist in the real world", but also a way of creating social meaning and constructing social reality, which has in itself an impact on social structures. The same holds for asking or labelling a particular language in a child's repertoire as first, second, primary, native, or home language, as will become evident in the description of the two studies below.

3 Study 1: School registration forms in Canada

3.1 The Canadian context and language background profiling at elementary schools

Canada's current population is approximately 47 million. The country has traditionally had high immigration rates and close to one million new immigrants were estimated to arrive in the two-year period between 2018 and 2020 (Citizenship and Immigration Canada 2018). Canada has two official languages, English and French; however, due to a high level of diversity, over 20% of the population reports another language as a mother tongue,[2] in addition to speaking English and/or French (Statistics Canada 2017a). This is in fact a higher percentage than that of people who are able to carry on a conversation in both official languages (Statistics Canada 2017b).

Diversity is particularly high in urban centres, where schools may have highly multilingual student populations. School boards typically survey parents or legal guardians with regard to the languages of their children upon school entry. This process is done through specific questions included in *school registration forms*. The forms' primary purpose is to collect personal details needed for school entry, but a small section is usually dedicated to the child's language background. The number, type, and wording of language related questions, however, vary vastly from one district school board to another within a given province, and also from one province to another.[3] For example, in the province of Ontario, most forms ask between one and three questions related to language, but a school board in a metropolitan area was found to ask eleven questions regarding incoming students' language profiles.

The purposes of language background profiling are not overtly stated on the registration forms or in other publicly accessible documents; in general, information from these forms may be used by school boards and subsequently by provinces to report demographic data about incoming students (e.g. regarding linguistic diversity), and to potentially offer linguistic support to students whose languages are other than the main language of schooling.

3.2 The data

The data reported in this section come from six English-speaking provinces spread across Canada: British Columbia (BC), Alberta (AL), Manitoba (MA), Ontario (ON), Prince Edward Island (PEI) and Nova Scotia (NS). The methodology involved collecting samples of publicly available elementary school registration forms from various school boards across these provinces and then extracting,

---

[2] 'Mother tongue' is the official term used by Statistics Canada in census data.
[3] A district school board is a cluster of schools in a given city or region; the term district school board itself may vary across provinces; this chapter focuses only on publicly funded English school boards or schools.

coding, and analysing the language related questions. Complete methodological details and more thorough presentation of most of these data, except for NS, have been included in previous work by Slavkov (2016, 2018, 2020). Here we offer a summary of this work based on 126 school registration forms and then we move on to the Austrian study and to the central issues of discussion identified in the beginning of this chapter.

The sample of registration forms analysed was not balanced in the sense of trying to collect an equal number of different registration forms from each province. This is due to issues related to access to the forms and to the fact that Canadian provinces vary by size and population to a large degree. Thus, a large province like Ontario has over 70 public school boards and it was possible to obtain a sample of 44 different school registration forms from them (over 50%); for smaller provinces, a lower number of registration forms was available (e.g. three forms for NS, which has a total of eight school boards, and one form for PEI which has only two school boards). The total number of registration forms collected from each of the six provinces is summarized in Table 12.1.

Table 12.1: Number of registration forms collected per province.

Ontario	Alberta	British Columbia	Manitoba	Nova Scotia	Prince Edward Island	TOTAL
44	28	24	26	3	1	126

The objective of the series of previous registration form studies by Slavkov (2016, 2018, 2020) was to determine the level of variation in the number, type, wording/formulation, combination patterns and detail of language related questions within and across provinces, thus obtaining an overall picture of how language background profiling of incoming students in elementary schools across Canada is done. This in turn was related to the general goal of using language background profiling as a window into institutional and societal understanding of the dynamics and complexities of multilingualism and related underlying ideologies.

As already indicated, a large degree of variation was attested in terms of the number of questions asked per form. Furthermore a high level of variation was also established with regard to the wording of the questions and the types of questions, among others. For this reason, in analyzing the data, the questions were placed into different categories referring to specific general notions. In this chapter the focus is on the following five categories: 1) first language, 2) home language, 3) primary language at home, 4) language spoken most often or most fluently, and 5) other languages. These five categories capture the overall picture of the questions related to a child's language background that emerged from the sample forms collected. Within each category, individual question formulations differed. For example, questions that fell within category 1 included wordings such as *first language, first language spoken, my child's first language learned (specify), birth language*, etc.; questions in category 2 included formulations such as *home language(s), language spoken at home, language at home, language student speaks at home, student is a bilingual learner (e.g. speaks both English and another language in the home)*, etc.; questions in category 3 included formulations such as *main language spoken by the student at home, primary language spoken most often at home, what language is mainly spoken at home?*, etc.; questions in category 4 included formulations such as *language spoken most often, primary language in which student is most fluent, language most used*, etc.; and questions in category 5 included formulations such as *other language(s) spoken, 2nd language spoken, languages known/spoken*, etc. Close to 150 distinct question formulations falling within the various general categories were identified in the sample of registration forms obtained from the six provinces. On the one hand, the variation with regard to the wording of questions suggests some fluidity and flexibility across district school board boundaries. On the other hand, this variation is problematic if the centralized educational institutions (provincial agencies or ministries of education) want to achieve a reliable language background profiling mechanism for all incoming students in their jurisdiction.

Turning to the categories of questions found most frequently in the sample, Table 12.2 offers a summary of these data.

Table 12.2: Number and percentage of questions per category (all six provinces).

Category	1. First language	2. Home language	3. Primary language at home	4. Language spoken most often/fluently	5. Other languages
Number of tokens (%)	59/126 (47%)	71/126 (56%)	38/126 (30%)	10/126 (8%)	14/126 (11%)

As indicated, the highest number of questions relate to the home language category, asked in 56% of the forms collected across the six provinces. The second most frequent type of question that appeared in the sample was from category 1, related to the first language. The distribution of these data among the six provinces is outlined in Figure 12.1.

As the data indicate, the most commonly asked question in the sample of registration forms in Ontario is from category 1, first language (included in 86% of the forms collected for the sample for this province) while in British Columbia

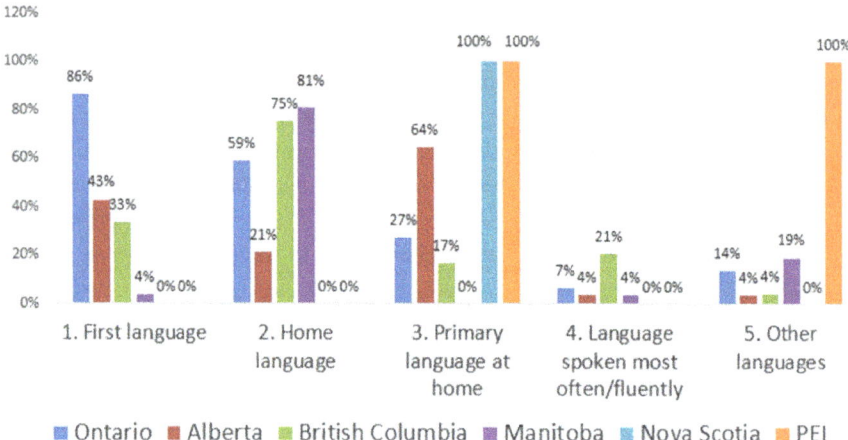

Figure 12.1: Question categories for the six provinces.

and Manitoba the most commonly asked questions come from category two, home language (75% and 81%, respectively, of the forms collected as samples for these two provinces). In Alberta, Nova Scotia, and Prince Edward Island the most frequently asked questions on the forms were from category three, primary language at home (64%, 100%, and 100%, respectively).

3.3 Discussion: A top-down perspective

As a whole, the picture that emerges from these data is one of a very high variability in the language background profiling orientations across the different provinces. In terms of societal understanding of issues related to multilingualism, we see that in some provinces more nativist conceptualizations may underlie the questions asked (category 1) while in other provinces conceptualizations based on a child's home or primary language (category 2 or 3) may prevail.[4] It is interesting to observe that category 4 which relates to the strongest language in a child's repertoire seems to be the least frequently invoked one in the sample. It could be argued that this category is in a sense more useful and less centred

---

[4] It should be noted that many forms in the sample ask questions from more than one category (e.g. first language and home language, or home language and other language(s), etc.). An analysis of the combination patterns of the different categories found on individual forms within different provinces is beyond the scope of this chapter, but is available in Slavkov (2020).

on a native-speaker based ideology than the other categories. That is, from a practical point of view, school administrators may want to know what the child's most fully developed language is, rather than asking questions about their native language, for example. Overall, a question about the first language is more essentialising, may target information about immigrant background or ethnicity, and shows a preoccupation with a nativist ideological orientation. Such a question may not necessarily be the most useful one in case a child was born in another country and exposed to a certain first language but subsequently migrated to Canada and become more proficient in English, for example. In that case declaring the first language would not be as useful as declaring the current most developed language in the child's repertoire.

Similarly, the category of home language may not be as accurate or useful because, once again, a child's home language may not be the most developed language in that child's repertoire. Furthermore, questions about home language may sometimes be interpreted as the language of the household in general, and such an interpretation may be biased towards the languages spoken by the parents or other adults in the home. Children in migrant situations, however, may not be as strong in that language necessarily, as they are often exposed to the majority language outside of the home and tend to shift to that language overtime.

A final consideration relates to the conceptualisation of language as a singular or a plural entity. Two of the question categories described in Figure 12.1 (first language and home language) are particularly relevant in this regard. An additional analysis of the data indicates that over 97% of the forms that include a question about a child's first language use the concept in the singular and permit only a single answer to that question. In other words, the possibility of an incoming student already being a simultaneous bilingual or multilingual (i.e. with two or more native/first languages) is largely not recognized.[5] With regard to home language, over 61% of the forms collected from the six provinces use the concept in the singular (i.e. home language rather than home languages), which again points to a predominantly monolingual orientation.

Overall, the data in this section are an illustration of a top-down approach to language background profiling. They relate to seemingly mundane, everyday practical issues such as taking stock of the diverse array of languages spoken

---

[5] It should be noted that since the original data collection and analysis, a number of forms used in Ontario have changed to allow three answer slots in the first language category (i.e. parents can list up to three first languages for a given child). This is evidence of an evolution in the thinking and practices that requires further investigation in future work.

by incoming students. Two obvious and generally well-intentioned objectives of such profiling may be for educational administrations to know their student populations better and to offer linguistic support as necessary. However, such mundane and normalized as well-intentioned objectives are affected by societal discourses, nation-state traditions, and political views that are ideologically grounded. In general, the data show a monolingual bias in various ways. For instance, the widespread underlying assumption that a child has only one first language is a prime example of a monolingual norm, and a surprising finding in a country that embraces bilingualism (i.e. legislation recognizing two official languages at the federal level). This is reminiscent of the well-known metaphor of the *two solitudes* (Cummins 2008; MacLennan 1945) representing separate monolingualisms rather than bilingualism. A preoccupation with the idea of a first language may be conditioned by a specific ideology that conceives of those who are not "first language speakers" of the language of schooling or the dominant language of society as different or deficient. As already indicated, category 1, which relates to children's first language, is the second most frequently occurring category in the data, and as such this preoccupation is significant (especially in the province of Ontario). This focus on a single first language further reveals a pervasive orientation towards native language and native speaker status as an important and indeed defining characteristic of a human being, reminiscent of the processes of iconization and erasure (Irvine and Gal 2000) mentioned in Section 2.

From an equity and post-colonial point of view, and in the context of globalization, migration, and superdiversity, the languages we were born with need not define who we are. To deconstruct or denaturalize normalized society discourses, it is important to reflect on whether it is truly necessary for the school as an institution to know what students' first or native languages are. Perhaps alternative ways of asking parents or even children themselves about their language profiles, without highlighting categories such as first or even home language, may offer a picture that is less focused on a person's ethnicity and belonging and more neutrally on a child's complex linguistic repertoire.

Another interesting observation in the data was that certain provinces seemed more interested in knowing the student's home language while the first language question was more present in the registration forms of others. This indicates that the ideological dimensions of conceptualizing language background profiling vary across the country. Thus, we are perhaps witnessing unstable and changing ideologies that may evolve and transform (for example, there may be a general trend towards eliminating first language questions and focusing on home language questions that may take over the entire country over time).

To conclude this section, the data collected in this study indicate that educational institutions across Canada are interested in creating language background profiles of incoming students, and are clearly aware of the linguistic diversity that these students bring with them. However, this institutional profiling, due to a high degree of variation in formulations, number of questions, and question categories raises certain questions of accuracy and reliability, in addition to questions about the ideological orientation of the content. In many cases it may not be easy for parents or children themselves to answer such questions as their profiles may simply not fit easily within these top-down, predefined, and reductionist question categories. To illustrate this point further, in the next section we chose a bottom-up approach focusing on children's own perspectives in describing their complex language repertoires through a research project implemented at Austrian primary schools. It is important to point out once again that by drawing on these two different studies we do not attempt a direct comparison between Canada and Austria as countries or contexts, or a direct comparison of the data. Our goal is to illustrate and compare two different approaches that yield different results and illustrate different perspectives on approaching sociolinguistic and societal issues which we then revisit in the general discussion and conclusion.

4 Study 2: Primary school children in Austria talking about their language repertoires

4.1 The Austrian context

In 2019 Austria had 8.9 million residents. 1.4 million were foreign nationals (16%). Around 2 million (23%) were residents with a so-called migration background (i.e. both parents born abroad) who lived in Austria, of which 1.49 million (17%) belong to the so-called first generation (i.e. they were born abroad and then moved to Austria later in their young lives). 530 000 (6%) were born in Austria as children of foreign-born parents (second generation) (Statistik Austria 2019).

In the school year 2017–18, 15.5% of all Austrian pupils were foreign nationals, and in the capital Vienna 35% of all primary school pupils were of foreign nationality. Based on the framework for school statistics according to the Education Documentation Act (BilDokG) data are available about children's "language(s) spoken on a daily basis" ("im Alltag gebrauchte Sprache(n)"). In 2018–19, 31% of all Austrian and 59% of Viennese primary school children used a language other than German on a daily basis (Statistik Austria, no year), a number that is interpreted in statistical reports as the proportion of children for whom German is not the primary language in everyday life (The Expert Council for Integration 2019; Breit et al.

2019). It is, however, necessary to consider whether the available statistical data is directly indicative for the pupils' language use and competence. These numbers could also be interpreted as a bias in school registration procedures to label students as "having another first language" than German, even if they have a good command of German; the data could also be interpreted as children's and parents' higher commitment to plurilingualism and family/heritage languages. Indicating a language other than German as the first answer to the question "language(s) used in everyday life" does not mean that a child is not also proficient in German.

4.2 Children's multilingual and multiliteracy repertoires

Children's repertoires and language practices are often too complex to fit into a "one answer says it all" format. In most cases not very much is known about children's out-of-school language practices or literacy experiences in languages other than the school language (family or heritage languages, or a global language like English) and even less is known about children's understanding of everyday literacy practices and their perspectives on multilingualism. The project *My Literacies*, carried out by the Literacies and Multilingualism research group at the University of Vienna (Kerschhofer-Puhalo and Mayer 2020; Kerschhofer-Puhalo, Schreger, and Mayer 2020) set out to gain insights into plurilingual children's language and literacy practices in daily life, in school and out-of-school contexts, with a special focus on the children's perspectives. The central aim of the research program was to investigate the diversity of everyday literacy practices in the language of schooling as well as in other languages (family or heritage languages). With a theoretical background in the New Literacy Studies (Barton and Hamilton 2000; Street 2016), the Pedagogy of Multiliteracies (Kalantzis and Cope 2012) and principles of a Critical Literacy education (Freire and Macedo 1987; Gee 2000; Luke 2012), the project focuses on children's attitudes and emotions about language and literacy practices in plurilingual families and communities in contexts of largely monolingual education systems.

In a participatory research design, more than 90 children in grades 3 and 4 (age 8–11, 80–90% of so-called "migration background") in three primary schools in Vienna (Austria) were encouraged to explore as co-researchers their experiences with written language in everyday life and to record literacy practices in school and out-of-school contexts within their families and communities, in media, and in public spaces. The research team regularly visited the classes over a period of two school years to organize several thematic campaigns around topics of special interest. Creative methods and structured activities were used to collect data about literacy events and practices. Children were encouraged to produce visual materials (such as drawings, photographs, or collages) and to share them along with their ideas in a conversation with a member of the research team (two core members and research assistants).

The corpus is organized in six sub-corpora that correspond to the thematic campaigns and the structured activities that were carried out: (1) language portraits, i.e. individual self-portraits (drawings) that include all languages that have a role in the child's life, (2) drawings and photos of the classroom with a specific focus on written artefacts and literacy practices, (3) photos of written things in daily life, (4) photos of multilingual literacy events and artefacts, (5) a corpus on advertising, and (6) visual "learning biographies," a collage about learning experiences from birth until the last week of the 4th school year. Digital cameras were used to collect a corpus of over 1,500 photos. We moreover collected a corpus of 90 language portraits, 64 classroom drawings, 57 collages, and various additional materials. The children presented their photos and drawings in a one-on-one conversation with a member of the research team. These conversations were video-recorded, transcribed and annotated. The total corpus consists of over 500 video recordings (107 hours of footage) and more than 2,000 visual artefacts (photos, scans).

4.3 Examples from the My Literacies project

The data presented here are taken from two of the project's campaigns, the language portraits and the visual learning biographies. In both activities, visuals served as a starting point for a conversation with the children who were encouraged to present their visual products, their experiences, opinions and perspectives. By combining the interpretation of visual and verbal data, we explored how the children selected, represented, and explained their experiences and views on their plurilingual selves. In the first campaign, we asked children to draw visual self-representations, where they represented "languages that have a role in your life" by coloring different parts of the visual image and adding captions. In the last campaign (June, grade 4) we asked children to create a visual learning biography to illustrate important learning experiences and achievements.

The examples presented here are selected to illustrate some of the ambivalences, difficulties and dilemmas of children when asked about their "first language" or "mother tongue", about their family languages or most dominant languages and about their relative proficiency in these languages in oral and written communication. For reasons of space, we will present only extracts of longer conversations and only a few examples of the large corpus. For ethical reasons and to protect the privacy of children and their families, we will not present all information about their lives and their families that are available to us. The children's names are anonymized and only an initial letter for the pseudonym will be indicated.

The visual and verbal data are considered as the result of individual processes of selection and attention that are co-constructed in the conversation between the child and the investigator in the context of the ongoing project. Therefore our analysis of the data does not focus on what the researchers see in the visuals or consider as relevant or correct, but rather what the child wanted to show and communicate to us.

4.3.1 Example 1 'first language' or 'mother tongue'?

The first example is an extract of a conversation with Y taking place in the last week of grade 4. At the end of the conversation about his "learning biography collage", Y is asked by the interviewer IN_A one final question: "*What was your first language?*"

Transcript 1: "What was your first language" (Y)

IN_A	Kurze Frage noch, weil ich's, weil du's nicht erwähnt hast ahm
	One more short question, because I, because you did not mention it ahm
	Was war deine erste Sprache?
	What was your first language?
Y	((looking upwards)) Ooow
	Meine Muttersprache . . . ((kneift die Augen zusammen))
	My mother tongue . . . ((slightly squinting his eyes))
	Griechisch ((Kopfschütteln)) oder Englisch
	Greek ((shaking his head)) or English
	Ich weiß nicht ganz genau
	I don't know exactly
	Meine Mutter spricht G . . . Griechisch, aber
	My mother speaks G.Greek, but
	((Einatmen, Kopfschütteln))
	((Breathing in, shaking his head))

> für mich ist es Englisch
> ((crosses his arms and looks down to the table))
> for me it's English

IN_A Ok, ja
      Ok, yes

The investigator's question about L's "first language" is immediately reformulated by Y as "my mother tongue" and is followed by a short sequence of deliberating which answer might be most appropriate. Y finally decides for English and not Greek as his "mother tongue", though English is not the "first language" of his mother. We know from previous conversations with Y that his family uses English as the dominant language at home and that they have lived in several countries since he was born. His mother migrated to the United States as a teenager, where she met her husband, who had also lived in several countries. Her "mother tongue" Greek is not the language the mother mostly speaks with her children, which makes it difficult for Y to answer the question about his "first language" or "mother tongue". Y told us that Greek is only used for saying Good Night at home, but that his visits in Greece and the contact with the great-grandparents are opportunities to practice Greek. As Y stated several times during this study, his feelings about his proficiency in Greek are ambivalent and he often states that he should become better in Greek than he is at the moment.

This example shows us a typical dilemma of many children of mixed couples or families with multiple migration history. We observe ambivalent relations between conceptions of language of origin, language use and language proficiency. This ambivalence might also be related to the unequal status of the languages involved: The language predominantly used at home seems to be English for all family members, even though they had been living in German speaking countries for several years. Greek, Y's mother's language or his father's language of origin (that Y even does not seem to know about) or other languages of countries, where the family had lived before, concur with the strong hyper-central language English. In our conversations with Y throughout the project, we observed processes of continuous re-negotiation of issues around his own and his mother's Greek origin on the one hand and his proficiency or deficiency in this language. We moreover observe erasure along the 'global language hierarchy' (de Swaan 2001) with respect to the language background of his father: While Y knows that his father is proficient in English and French, he says that he does not know about any other languages his father speaks, e.g. of the country his father was born in. The example also shows processes of recursivity in the narrative construction of the family members' origin and affiliation that is based on plurality rather than singleness as a result of the family's multiple migration history. This explains Y's difficulties to answer questions about "*the* first/mother/native language", as these concepts are mostly rooted in the basic assumption of singleness.

4.3.2 Example 2 "my language"

In the next example, we also observe processes of erasure that become only evident when we combine the information obtained from the child with external information. The excerpt is part of a recording where M describes her language portrait. In the drawing, M's body is colored in three horizontal stripes: Bulgarian (purple), German (green) and English (red). She wrote Portuguese (blue) on the right leg and Serbian on the left leg.

Transcript 2: "My language is Bulgarian" (M)

(. . .)
M	Das ist Bulgarisch, weil ich Bulgarisch SPREche,
	This is Bulgarian, because I speak Bulgarian
	Das ist DEUTSCH – ich kann auch/ n auch Deutsch,
	This is German – I also/ n also know German
IN_B	Mhm. Mhm.
M	Das is Englisch, kann ich auch ein bisschen,
	This is English, I know also a little
IN_B	Mhm
M	Serbisch kann ich auch,
	I also know Serbian
	Mhm
	Und Portugelisch (sic!)kann ich auch.
	And Portugalish ('Portuguese') I also know
IN_B	Kannst du mir erklären, mit weem duu/?
	Could you explain to me, with whoom youu/?
	Dass du Deutsch in der Schule sprichst, ist • klar?
	That you speak German in school is clear?
	Mit mein Bruder.
	With my brother.
	Mit wem • noch • sprichst du Deutsch?
	With whom else do you speak German?
IN_B	Mhm.
(. . .)	
IN_B	Aalso, gut, das ist das Deutsch. Das Bulgarisch? ((zeigt auf Zeichnung))
	Ok, good, so this is German. This Bulgarian? ((pointing to the drawing))
M	Ich/ rede mit mein Papa • auch manchmal • Deutsch und meiner Mutter,
	I speak with my dad • also sometimes • German and with my mother,
IN_B	Mhm.

M	Und ((2.0s	)) d/ MEIne Sch/ Sprache ist Bulgarisch.
	And ((2.0s	*)) d/ MY la/ language is Bulgarian.*
	(. . .)	
IN_B	Und, weenn du jetzt sagst, • welche Sprache glaubst du kannst du am besten.	
	And iif you say now, . . . which language do you think you know best	
M	Deutsch, • Serbisch und Bulgarisch.	
	German, . . . Serbian and Bulgarian.	
IN_B		Deutsch, Serbisch und Bulgarisch.
		German, . . . Serbian and Bulgarian.
	Gibt es/ aahm • • Sachen, wo du sagst, wenn ich darüber spreche, dann geht es in der einen Sprache viel besser als in der anderen	
	Are there aahm • • things that you would say, if I talk about them, then it is in one language better than in the other	
M	Nein. ((leiser))	
	No. ((lower voice))	
	(. . .)	
IN_B	Und wenn du groß bist? Welche Sprache, glaubst du, kannst du am besten sprechen?	
	And when you are grown up – which language do you think you will speak best?	
	Deutsch und Bulgarisch.	
	German and Bulgarian.	
IN_B		Deutsch und Bulgarisch.
		German and Bulgarian. ((repeating in lower voice))
	(. . .)	

Before coming to Austria, M's family had lived in Bulgaria, Serbia and Portugal, which explains the Serbian and Portuguese (she calls it *Portugelisch*) in her language portrait. In several conversations, M repeated that her language is Bulgarian and that she speaks Bulgarian with her mother and her father. German is another home language that she uses with her cousin or her brother. However, we do have recordings of her speaking with a classmate, who also told us that he spoke only Bulgarian with his family. An analysis of this recording shows that the language M speaks and labels as Bulgarian is not what others would consider to be Bulgarian, nor any other Slavic language, but a different language with some Slavic words, presumably a Romani variety. In all our conversations, neither M nor her classmate would ever mention another name than Bulgarian for the language they speak with each other. We can interpret this as a form of *erasure* of a language that she does speak but that is, just as the group it is associated with, socially marginalized and therefore subject to *erasure*. Moreover, the example shows an ideologically based notion of language that is strongly influenced by a territorial or nation-based definition of language: Living or being born in Bulgaria is set as equivalent to speaking "Bulgarian". "Bulgarisch" is the language spoken in Bulgaria and "Portugelisch" is the language of Portugal.

Another interesting aspect is found in M's answers to the investigator's questions about "the language she knows best": M names three languages – German, Serbian and Bulgarian as best languages – and when asked for "the language she will know best" as an adult, she also names two languages, German and Bulgarian. Her answers show a pluralistic orientation, even if the investigator's questions are implying an underlying orientation towards singleness with respect to current or future proficiency in a specific language. While the investigator IN_B seems caught in normalized and naturalized notions of singleness about language use and proficiency in questions about "the language known best", for M plurality seems to be more natural.

4.4 Discussion: A bottom-up perspective

The bottom-up perspective illustrated in the Austrian study is in sharp contrast with the top-down perspective illustrated in the Canadian study, where a seemingly straightforward question with a seemingly straightforward answer about a child's first language was included in a large number of school registration forms. Children in the Austrian sample name a range of "languages" and "varieties" that have a role in their everyday life. Many but not all of the languages mentioned are closely associated with their family. They may include languages of their peers or languages they have learned in school or during their holidays that were added into their repertoires. The overall picture shows that the knowledge of many languages is a desired value for all children. Therefore, they show different strategies to position themselves as plurilingual.

However, the data also illustrate how children express quite ambivalent emotions concerning their proficiency in those languages that – from an outside view – are considered as their "native languages" or "family languages". This ambivalence is expressed in verbal, non-verbal and visual ways. The data also indicate the differential status of languages in a child's repertoire which is connected with different forms of investment in these languages, such as taking part in so-called "mother tongue classes" (Muttersprachlicher Unterricht) organized in school or in extra-curricular language courses in complementary schools (Kerschhofer-Puhalo and Mayer 2020).

It is important to emphasize that the central focus in the interpretation of these data was the child's perspective and the child's story in the version he or she wanted to tell us. This relates to ethical considerations that we had to take into account in doing research with younger children. Of course, we collected additional information in conversations with teachers or school administrators or parents as part of our ethnographic material, but in several cases, external information from school administrators, teachers or parents differed from the version that the child presented to us. In several cases we received slightly differing information in conversations with the same child at different points in time, but also contradicting information from children and adults. The examples showcased here are typical examples where the child's story differs from external evidence: In some cases, like the case of Y, the teacher gave us information that differed from what the child told us or knew. And in other cases, we had external information that the child explicitly did not give us, e.g. about the language that M is calling Bulgarian. Different versions and descriptions of the "same" situation are due to several reasons: Children are not told everything by their parents, or they are told not to tell everything (e.g. that they belong to an ethnic or religious minority or another social group), or they lack some background knowledge about socio-historic or political conditions (e.g. about the situation of minorities in the countries of origin) to understand potential tensions, conflicts and contradictory opinions or actions of adults.

Languages come and go, they gain or lose importance, when families move from one country to the other or when new constellations develop (e.g. after displacement or divorce, etc.). Children have to create their personal accounts of these dynamics and have to accommodate their personal experiences with the family's narratives or the ways they are positioned by others, such as teachers, peers, etc.

From a socio-constructivist view, we must acknowledge that our conversations with the children, the visuals they create, e.g. the language portraits, and the stories they tell us are products "of the moment", embedded in discourses and results of personally experienced actions and narratives. They are co-constructed products formed by children engaging in a conversation with the investigator at a particular point in time, in the particular setting of the classroom during the ongoing project. These visual and verbal data are a small part of a child's ongoing identity construction, a process that is strongly influenced by the discourses and ideological positions the child is confronted with. In the data, we find traces of the discourses children are exposed to: discourses on controversial topics such as migration, multilingualism, education, integration or success. Regarding societal multilingualism or their individual language repertoire, children find themselves in a field of partly overlapping, either convergent or contradicting discourse positions. In our conversations with children and in their visual products, we see traces of underlying, often contradicting ideologies, practices, and discourse positions. These include monolingual classroom practices contradicting with children's plurilingual repertoires or the idea of a monolingual nation state that does not fit with the situation of minorities in the family's country of origin, host country, and so on.

5 General discussion – comparing top-down and bottom-up perspectives

In this chapter we approached the notion of the native speaker from two perspectives: the perspective of institutional language background profiling and the individual conversations with children about their language repertoires. Looking at the overall picture of the two very different sets of data, we find difficulties and dilemmas on both sides.

Turning to the first research question about institutional practices of profiling children's language background through categories and labels, our data drew on the study of school registration forms carried out in Canada. We saw a top-down, reductionist, essentializing, and simplicity-based, nativist perspective on the repertoire because children are often framed as speakers of a first language (rarely given the chance in the forms of being described as speakers of two or more "first languages", despite Canada often being discursively portrayed as bilingual). Alternatively, children are framed as speakers of a home language (again mostly in the singular). Sometimes a first language and a home language are used as separate categories on the forms, corresponding to discrete rather than intertwined entities, where limited space allows little practical or conceptual room for a complex answer. Answers are expected to be linear, single, static and concise: for example, First Language: French; Home Language: English, or First Language: Mandarin; Language most often spoken: English. The complex and multi-layered reality of speaking different languages with different family members, or mixing different languages and varieties at home or at school simply cannot be conveyed in such a manner; the forms are blind to it.

This top-down approach clearly obviates and indeed erases potentially very complex processes and practices related to a multifaceted repertoire influenced by mixed parenthood and patchwork families, migration, travel, flight, expatriate work, and so on. An ideologically-construed simplistic view of a child's repertoire is indeed enforced and perpetuated by the artefact of the registration form, which must be filled out in order for a child to begin schooling. From that point on, this uncritical characterization is naturalized and the children are set to carry this "baggage" with ideological nuances of a reduced, native-speaker-centered view of languages throughout their educational career and perhaps throughout their lives; this may potentially erase the true richness and complexity that their personal history may have given them, and they may potentially internalize this simplistic view as they grow up to be members of society.

When focusing on the ways in which children respond to practices of profiling, categorizing, and labeling, the *My Literacies* study with migrant children in

Austria shows us "the other side of the story," a view from the bottom up. While from the institutional perspective, clear-cut boundaries are assumed between children's first/native/home languages on the one hand and the language of schooling and foreign languages on the other, many children struggle with practices of classifying only *one* language as their "first" or "native" or "main" or "strongest" language. This is the case because this type of conceptualization does not seem adequate for their complex language repertoires and the plurality of languages they use in out-of-school settings. At the same time, labelling such children as not being "first language" or "native" speakers of the school language may also create a sense of deficiency that they or their families may internalize. The data suggest that children do have an understanding of the "criteria" for a native speaker and that they refer not only to aspects of origin or belonging, but also to questions about language use, proficiency and expertise. Many children do not feel as proficient or literate in the language that others would call "their native language" as they would feel in the language of schooling. Relative differences in proficiency in oral versus written forms of a given language make the situation even more complex. Some data also show that many children have a lower self-esteem in their L1s, especially when it comes to literacy in these languages, in which they do not receive sufficient schooling or even no support at all (Kerschhofer-Puhalo and Mayer 2020).

Overall, the top-down practices in education and administration favour a reductionist and monolingually-oriented view and often require the choice of one particular language over others. Here children experience dilemmas and conflicts between school practices and their lived experiences of multilingualism. Moreover, children have to weigh and compare different aspects of qualifying as a "native speaker", referring to notions of origin and belonging on the one side and competence and proficiency on the other.

Reflecting on the underlying assumptions and ideologies that contribute to these contrasts and contradictions between the top-down and the bottom-up perspective, we observe that educational institutions are on the one hand clearly aware of the linguistic and cultural diversity of incoming students that they try to account for by taking a "snapshot" of it (i.e. brief language background sections on registration form); on the other hand, these institutions seem conceptually and methodologically not sufficiently well equipped to deal with the level of complexity and diversity at hand. Even if institutions seem to be aware of the complexity at least to a certain degree, the institutional tools and practices used to "handle" it (registration forms or databases) reveal a dominance of monolingually-based orientations that implicitly rely on the notion of the "native speaker" and consider "languages" as static, separate and fixed. We see how school boards struggle with this diversity and complexity that conflicts with traditional practices and procedures largely due to dominant language ideologies associated with "the monolingual habitus" (Gogolin 1994) in institutions and modern nation states at large.

6 Conclusion

Back in the 1990s, Leung, Harris, and Rampton (1997: 557) thought that the binary "native-speaker-versus-other" distinction was increasingly redundant and that critical questioning and open analysis together with working with new ideas in the classroom and a sharper awareness for the learners' different needs may ultimately lead to more responsive pedagogies. What actually should count in the classroom is a more holistic approach to the learners' language repertoires, expertise and identities.

"Questioning the questions", as used in the title of our chapter means that we must be aware of the fact that in many cases there is no correct or single clear-cut answer to questions about a child's native language(s). From the perspective of children with daily multilingual experiences through their families, peers, and communities we saw that such questions often cannot be answered straightforwardly and that children do have difficulties finding themselves in fixed categories such as a "native speaker" or a "proficient user" of family languages. We also identified the need to consider children's full range of communicative resources seen as a complex repertoire, instead of "downsizing" their repertoire to a single "native language" or "mother tongue".

Moreover, "questioning the questions" means that we must consider the reasons and motivation behind "questions about language": Why do we actually ask about the "the native language" of a child? What exactly do we want to know? How are the answers in registration forms or questionnaires further processed? What impact do they have on the image and further career of a child? Which institutional practices and underlying ideological "common ground" assumptions stand behind these processes of asking and classifying children as "native" or "non-native" in a particular language? Do these questions and normalized institutional practices contribute to problematic naturalized discourses and assumptions about linguistic origin, affiliation, ethnicity or race that may re-inforce educational and societal discrimination? This is just a small sample of the series of questions that we as critical researchers have with regard to the questions asked by institutions about children's languages.

"Questioning the questions" also refers to a research practice that is guided by a continuous monitoring of the researchers' positionalities as they influence procedures in data collection (e.g. when asking questions in an interview) or in data interpretation. We are well aware of the reality of most research practices, including our own, where different forms of including and excluding and of reducing complexity and individuality takes place in order to make the model, the theory, the system, the conversation, or the classroom work.

To improve pedagogical as well as research practices we should consider how questions about children's language identities could be formulated in ways that encourage them to tell us their "whole story" from their point of view. For pedagogical reasons, it is also important to ask further questions such as: What does the teacher really need to know about the *languages* present in the classroom, e.g. about their structural characteristics and different forms of use? How can one foster inclusion and representation of multiple languages in the classroom, even if one does not speak these languages and if they do not constitute the main language of schooling? And finally, in order to make a multicultural and multilingual classroom "work", we may also want to ask teachers or school administrators which languages they know and use, and encourage them to familiarize themselves with children's repertoires from the bottom-up, by letting children talk about their languages.[6]

To conclude, there are several problems with aspects of essence, unity and singleness of identity inherent to the notion of the "native speaker". We do not want to posit here that there is necessarily a single monolithic native speaker ideology, but rather that the concept of "the native speaker", just as the criticisms of it, is informed by different competing, overlapping, or conflicting language ideologies that put plurilingual children and their families as well as educational institutions in a dilemma. Living in a globalised world with its many forms of transnational mobility, multilingual and globally acting enterprises, plurilingual family patchworks and a range of possibilities for translocal communication allows individuals to be affiliated with several social groups and identities at the same time. Therefore, the idea of being "a native", i.e. being born into *one* language associated with *one* territory – corresponding to a monolingual nation state – or belonging to *one* ethnic or language group appears as a simplistic monolingually-oriented position, even if it seems so "natural" and "common ground". We saw that such an ideological position is not appropriate to account for many family constellations. An alternative view of speakers or language users with individual complex repertoires of various communicative resources and non-static and multifaceted, or multiple identities might fit better current research in sociolinguistics and applied linguistics. We must, of course, be aware that this view is also based on specific

---

[6] We are, of course, aware that this may already be done by some teachers and administrators.

underlying ideological orientations. The ideological assumption that language users have complex repertoires and dynamic linguistic identities might be less easily captured in numbers and causes more "problems" in streamlining demographics and statistics, but it might be more suitable to describe the situation of individuals who are *"natives"* of plurilingual families, a multilingual society, and a globalised world.

Authors' Positionalities

Please see the introduction of the volume.

References

Althusser, Louis. [1971] 2014. *On the Reproduction of Capitalism: Ideology and Ideological State Apparatuses*. London et al.: Verso.

Barton, David and Mary Hamilton. 2000. Literacy practices. In David Barton, Mary Hamilton and Roz Ivanič (eds.), *Situated Literacies: reading and writing in context*, 7–15. London: Routledge.

Blommaert, Jan. 2005. *Discourse: A Critical Introduction*. Cambridge: Cambridge University Press.

Blommaert, Jan and Ad Backus. 2011. Repertoires revisited: „Knowing language" in superdiversity. *Working Papers in Urban Language and Literacies* 67. https://www.academia.edu/6365319/WP67_Blommaert_and_Backus_2011._Repertoires_revisited_Knowing_language_in_superdiversity (accessed 30 december 2020)

Blommaert, Jan & Ad Backus. 2013. Superdiverse Repertoires and the Individual. In Ingrid de Saint-Georges & Jean-Jacques Weber (eds.), *Multilingualism and Multimodality: Current Challenges for Educational Studies*, 11–32. Rotterdam, Boston, Taipei: Sense Publishers. https://doi.org/10.1007/978-94-6209-266-2_2 (accessed 30 December 2020)

Breit, Simone, Barbara Herzog-Punzenberger, Silvia Salchegger & Philipp Schnell. 2019. Mehrsprachige Schüler/innen am Ende der 8. Schulstufe: Kompetenzen und familiäres Sprachumfeld. In Ann Cathrice George, Claudia Schreiner, Christian Wiesner, Martin Pointinger & Katrin Pacher (eds.), *Kompetenzmessungen im österreichischen Schulsystem: Analysen, Methoden und Perspektiven*, 179–198. Münster, New York: Waxmann. http://nbn-resolving.de/urn:nbn:de:0111-pedocs-178084 (accessed 30 December 2020)

Busch, Brigitta. 2010. School language profiles: valorizing linguistic resources in heteroglossic situations in South Africa. *Language and Education* 24 (4), 283–294.

Busch, Brigitta. 2012. The Linguistic Repertoire Revisited. *Applied Linguistics* 33 (5), 503–523. https://doi.org/10.1093/applin/ams056 (accessed 30 December 2020)

Busch, Brigitta. 2018. The language portrait in multilingualism research: Theoretical and methodological considerations. *Working Papers in Urban Language and Literacies* 236. https://www.academia.edu/35988562/WP236_Busch_2018_The_language_portrait_in_multilingualism_research_Theoretical_and_methodological_considerations (accessed 30 December 2020)

Chik, Alice, Susan Markose & Diane Alperstein (eds.), 2018. *Languages of Sydney:
   The People and the Passion*. Hong Kong: Candlin and Mynard ePublishing.
Citizenship and Immigration Canada. 2018. International migration to Canada reached record
   levels in second quarter of 2018. *Canada Immigration Newsletter*, Sept 2018, https://
   www.cicnews.com/2018/09/international-migration-to-canada-reached-record-levels-in-
   second-quarter-of-2018-0911230.html#gs.aecztj (5 July, 2019.)
Codó, Eva. 2008. Interviews and questionnaires. In Li Wei & Melissa G. Moyer (eds.),
   The Blackwell Guide to Research Methods in Bilingualism and Multilingualism, 158–177.
   Blackwell Publishing.
Cope, Bill & Mary Kalantzis (eds.) 2000. *Multiliteracies. Literacy learning and the design of
   social futures*. London: Routledge.
Cope, Bill & Mary Kalantzis. 2009. Multiliteracies: New Literacies, New Learning. *Pedagogies:
   An International Journal* 4, 164–195.
Cope, Bill & Mary Kalantzis. 2015. The things you do to know: An introduction to the pedagogy
   of multiliteracies. In Bill Cope & Mary Kalantzis (eds.), *A Pedagogy of multiliteracies:
   Learning by design*, 1–36. London: Palgrave.
Coste, Daniel, Danièle Moore & Geneviève Zarate. 1997. *Compétence plurilingue et
   pluriculturelle. Vers un cadre européen commun de référence pour l'enseignement et
   l'apprentissage des langues vivantes: Études préparatoires*. Strasbourg: Éditions du
   Conseil de l'Europe.
Coste, Daniel, Danièle Moore & Geneviève Zarate. 2009a. *Competence plurilingue et
   pluriculturelle*. Division des Politiques Linguistiques, Strasbourg. https://rm.coe.int/
   090000168069d29c (accessed 30 December 2020).
Coste, Daniel, Danièle Moore & Geneviève Zarate. 2009b. *Plurilingual and pluricultural
   competence*. Strasbourg: Council of Europe, Language Policy Division. https://rm.coe.int/
   090000168069d29b (accessed 30 December 2020).
Cummins Jim. 2008. Teaching for Transfer: Challenging the two solitudes assumption in
   bilingual education. In Nancy H. Hornberger (ed.), *Encyclopedia of Language and
   Education*, 1528–1538. Boston, MA: Springer. https://doi.org/10.1007/978-0-387-30424-
   3_116.
de Swaan, Abram. 2001. *Words of the world. The global language system*. Cambridge, UK: Polity.
Duchêne, Alexandre, Philippe N. Humbert & Renata Coray. 2018. How to ask questions on
   language? Ideological struggles in the making of a state survey. *International Journal of
   the Sociology of Language* 252, 45–72.
Freire, Paulo & Donaldo Macedo. 1987. *Literacy. Reading the word and the world*. London:
   Routledge.
Gal, Susan. 2016. Scale-making: comparison and perspective as ideological projects. In
   E. Summerson Carr and Michael Lempert (eds.), *Scale: Discourse and Dimensions of
   Social Life*, 91–111. Berkeley: University of California Press.
Gee, James. 2000. The new literacy studies: From 'socially situated' to the work of the social.
   In David Barton, Mary Hamilton & Roz Ivanic (eds.), *Situated Literacies: Theorizing
   Reading and Writing in Context*, 180–196. London: Routledge.
Gogolin, Ingrid 1994. *Der monolinguale Habitus der multilingualen Schule*. Münster: Waxmann.
Gogolin, Ingrid. 2015. Die Karriere einer Kontur – Sprachenportraits. In İnci Dirim, Ingrid
   Gogolin, Dagmar Knorr, Marianne Krüger-Potratz, Drorit Lengyel, Hans H. Reich & Wolfram
   Weiße (eds.), *Impulse für die Migrationsgesellschaft. Bildung, Politik und Religion*,
   294–304. Münster, New York: Waxmann.

Gumperz, John J. 1964. Linguistic and social interaction in two communities. *American Anthropologist* 66 (6), 137–153.

Irvine, Judith & Susan Gal. 2000. Language ideology and linguistic differentiation. In Kroskrity, Paul (ed.), *Regimes of language. Ideologies, polities, and identities*, 35–84. Santa Fe: School of American Research Press.

Irvine, Judith. 2019. Regimenting ideologies. *Language and Communication* 66, 67–71. https://doi.org/10.1016/j.langcom.2018.10.005 (accessed 30 December 2020)

Kalaja, Paula & Sílvia Melo-Pfeifer (eds.) 2019. *Visualizing Multilingual Lives: More than words*. Bristol, Multilingual Matters.

Kalantzis, Mary & Bill Cope. 2012. *Literacies*. New York, Melbourne: Cambridge University Press.

Kerschhofer-Puhalo, Nadja & Werner Mayer. 2020. Pluriliterale Identitäten und Selbstkonzepte von Grundschulkindern im Spannungsfeld zwischen Schule, Familie und Communities. In Mirjam Egli Cuenat, Giuseppe Manno, Giuseppe & Magalie Desgrippes (eds.), Mehrschriftlichkeit und Mehrsprachenerwerb im schulischen und ausserschulischen Umfeld / Plurilittératie et apprentissages plurilingues à l'intérieur et hors du contexte scolair [Special Issue]. *Bulletin Suisse de Linguistique Appliquée* 2020, 259–277. https://doc.rero.ch/record/11876/files/bulletin_vals_asla_2020_special.pdf (accessed 30 December 2020)

Kerschhofer-Puhalo, Nadja, Christian Schreger & Werner Mayer. 2020. My Literacies. Insights into children's extracurricular literacy experiences. *Proceedings of the 3rd International Conference Literacy and Contemporary Society: Identities, Texts, Institutions*, 674–686. Nicosia: Pedagogical Institute Cyprus. http://www.pi.ac.cy/pi/files/epimorfosi/synedria/literacy/2019/3rd_Lit_Con_Proceedings.pdf (accessed 30 December 2020)

Krumm, Hans-Jürgen & Eva-Maria Jenkins. 2001. *Kinder und ihre Sprachen – lebendige Mehrsprachigkeit: Sprachenportraits*. Wien: Eviva.

Leeman, Jennifer. 2018. It's all about English: The interplay of monolingual ideologies, language policies and the U.S. Census Bureau's statistics on multilingualism. *International Journal of the Sociology of Language* 252, 21–43. https://doi.org/10.1515/ijsl-2018-0013

Leung, Constant, Roxy Harris & Ben Rampton. 1997. The idealised native speaker, Reified ethnicities, and classroom realities. *TESOL Quarterly* 31 (3), 543–560.

Luke, Allan. 2012. Critical Literacy: Foundational Notes. *Theory Into Practice* 51 (1), 4–11, https://doi.org/10.1080/00405841.2012.636324 (accessed 30 December 2020)

MacLennan, Hugh. 1945. *Two solitudes*. Macmillan Canada.

Neumann, Ursula. 1991. Ideenkiste: Ich spreche viele Sprachen. *Die Grundschulzeitschrift* 43, 59.

Piller, Ingrid. 2016. Monolingual ways of seeing multilingualism. *Journal of Multicultural Discourses* 11 (1), 25–33. https://doi.org/10.1080/17447143.2015.1102921

Prasad, Gail. 2014. Portraits of plurilingualism in a French international school in Toronto: Exploring the role of visual methods to access students' representations of their linguistically diverse identities. *The Canadian Journal of Applied Linguistics* 17 (1), 51–77.

Rampton, Ben. 1990. Displacing the "native speaker": Expertise, affiliation, and inheritance. *ELT Journal* 44 (2), 97–101.

Slavkov, Nikolay. 2020. Language background profiling at Canadian elementary schools and dominant language constellations. In Larissa Aronin and Joseph Lo Bianco (Eds.), *Dominant language constellations*, 117–138. NY: Springer.

Slavkov, Nikolay. 2018. What is your 'first' language in bilingual Canada? A study of language background profiling at publicly-funded elementary schools across three provinces, *International Journal of Bilingual Education and Bilingualism* 21(1), 20–37.

Slavkov, Nikolay. 2016. In search of the right questions: Language background profiling at Ontario public schools, *Canadian Journal of Applied Linguistics* 19(1),22–45.

Statistics Canada. 2017a. *Census in brief: Linguistic diversity and multilingualism in Canadian homes*. Retrieved from http://www12.statcan.gc.ca/census-recensement/2016/as-sa/98-200-x/2016010/98-200-x2016010-eng.cfm (15 September, 2017.)

Statistics Canada. 2017b. *Census in brief: English-French bilingualism reaches new heights*. Retrieved from http://www12.statcan.gc.ca/census-recensement/2016/as-sa/98-200-x/2016009/98-200-x2016009-eng.cfm (15 September, 2017.)

Statistik Austria. 2019. *migration and integration. zahlen.daten.indikatoren 2019*. Wien: Statistik Austria. https://www.statistik.at/web_de/services/publikationen/2/index.html?includePage=detailedViewandsectionName=Bev%C3%B6lkerungandpubId=579 (accessed 30 December 2020)

Statistik Austria. no year. Schülerinnen und Schüler 2018/19, für die Deutsch nicht die erstgenannte im Alltag gebrauchte Sprache ist. https://www.statistik.at/wcm/idc/idcplg?IdcService=GET_PDF_FILEandRevisionSelectionMethod=LatestReleasedanddDocName=029650 (accessed 30 December 2020)

Street, Brian. 1984. *Literacy in Theory and Practice*. Cambridge: Cambridge University Press.

Street, Brian. 2016. Learning to read from a social practice view: Ethnography, schooling and adult learning. *Prospects* 46 (3–4), 335–344. https://doi.org/10.1007/s11125-017-9411-z (accessed 30 December 2020)

The Expert Council for Integration. 2019. *Integration Report 2019. Integration in Austria – Statistics, developments, priorities*. Vienna: Federal Minister for Europe, Integration and Foreign Affairs. https://www.bmeia.gv.at/fileadmin/user_upload/Zentrale/Integration/Integrationsbericht_2019/IB2019_EN_web.pdf (accessed 30 December 2020).

Vertovec, Steven. 2007. Super-diversity and its implications. *Ethnic and Racial Studies* 30 (6), 1024–1054.

Jim Cummins
Afterword

A recurring thought kept jumping into my mind as I read through the 12 chapters of this wonderful book: "Why am I enjoying this so much?" "Why do I find this so engaging?" Academic books focusing on linguistic terminology are not supposed to be fun. I found myself flitting through its pages rather than trudging from cover to cover.

As I thought about it, I realized that the themes taken up by the authors are universal and of direct import to people around the world, whether ordinary citizens completing census forms, or multiple other forms, parents deciding on which language(s) to speak to their children or which school they should attend, teachers facing a mini-United Nations in their classrooms, university professors wondering what accommodations in grading should be afforded to students whose academic writing falls short of their expectations for grammatical accuracy or word choice, policymakers and politicians instituting language tests as gatekeepers to immigration and possibly later citizenship. We are all implicated on a regular basis in the hierarchical structuring of relationships and opportunities that are mediated by our language use and performance. Some of us have the power to dictate the shape of these hierarchies in a way that positions our experiences, privileges, and status in their upper echelons; some of us experience exclusion from those upper echelons by virtue of country of birth, language usage, gaps in educational opportunities, racism and other forms of discrimination. Starting from those five innocent-looking letters – NS/NNS – the contributors to this volume have woven an intriguing and complex tapestry of human experience and the societal and interpersonal power relations within which everyday interactions are embedded.

The universal relevance of this volume is reflected in the experiences and memories it will likely trigger in many readers. To illustrate, for me, the following thoughts and recollections (among many others) came to mind during the course of my reading:

- The organizer of a conference on International Schools in Vienna at which I presented in the mid-1980s told me after my talk that soon after I had started speaking, a woman seated next to him asked: "Where's he from?" The organizer replied: "He's Irish", to which the woman responded: "Oh, I thought he had a speech defect."

Jim Cummins, University of Toronto, e-mail: james.cummins@utoronto.ca

https://doi.org/10.1515/9781501512353-014

- A good friend of mine in Toronto who is of Portuguese background was doing substitute teaching, standing in for an English-as-a-second-language (ESL) teacher who was sick. During the morning recess, José got talking to several regular teachers at the school who asked him what he was teaching. He responded that he was teaching ESL. One of them burst out in disbelief: "**YOU'RE** teaching ESL!!??" Her reaction was based on the fact that José had an identifiable Portuguese accent and, in her mind, this translated into lower levels of proficiency in English, which, in turn, should have disqualified him from teaching English. What the teacher didn't know was that José had fluent knowledge of five European languages and partial knowledge of several others, and was in the process of writing his Ph.D. dissertation on comparative literature (in English) at the University of Toronto. On any measure of English reading comprehension or vocabulary knowledge, José would have far outperformed this teacher since he had access to most of the low-frequency words in English that have Latin (and Greek) roots. Furthermore, his spoken English was fluent and error-free.
- A friend who grew up in Romania but whose English and French were 'native-like' (if I may be permitted to use the word . . .) recounted an interaction she had with one of her long-time friends who was Canadian-born and whose first-learned language was English. My friend used the word *dingy* to describe a place she had been and her friend (a lawyer by training) responded: "There's no such word in the English language!" Obviously the word *does* exist (meaning *gloomy* or *drab*) but the power of the 'native-speaker' meant that this incorrect correction went unchallenged.

So-called 'native speakers' don't have it all their own way, however. A report in *The Guardian* newspaper (8 August, 2017) entitled *Computer says no: Irish vet fails oral English test needed to stay in Australia* recounted how Louise Kennedy, an Irish veterinarian with degrees in history and politics obtained in English (and presumably also veterinarian medicine qualifications), failed a computer-based machine-scored English test that indicated she was unable to speak English fluently enough to function in that language in Australia. The test, developed and administered by the multinational Pearson company, uses voice recognition technology to test speaking ability. If the scoring engine for this test rejected the fluent English of a highly educated middle-class 'native speaker', there would presumably be very little prospect of Australian settlement for 'native speakers' of English from the inner cities of Glasgow, London, Belfast or Dublin, let alone the English-speaking Caribbean.

This example illustrates how linguistic biases are being systematically (albeit unintentionally for the most part) built into the algorithms that increasingly shape our lives. These unintentional biases, however, were exerting pernicious effects on the life chances of minoritized and racialized youth long before the advent of the new technologies of the past 40 years. McCollum's (1999) research among middle school students from both language groups in a Spanish-English dual language program documented the systematic devaluation by the teacher of the linguistic variety of Spanish spoken by the 'native' Spanish-speaking students in the program. Spanish-speaking students came to prefer English over their home variety of Spanish as a result of the ways in which the (well-intentioned) teacher, who was from their own community, constantly corrected their speech and made negative comments about their 'nonstandard' Spanish or use of 'vernacular' constructions. At the same time as the fluent Spanish of the Spanish-speaking students was being undermined by the teacher, she was praising the English home language students for their efforts to produce a few incomplete phrases in Spanish.

So what do these examples tell us about the changing face of the native-speaker? First, they suggest that an individual's perceived status as either a 'native speaker' or a 'non-native speaker' is one among many categorizations related to class, 'race', gender, economic status, etc. through which interpersonal and structural societal power relations operate. The 'native-speaker' status of the Spanish-speaking students in McCollum's (1999) study did not prevent them from systematic devaluation of their identity in a dual language program where they might have expected to excel. Thus, researchers must move from an analytic focus on the 'native speaker' construct in isolation to an exploration of how this construct intersects with other forms of 'othering' to reinforce coercive patterns of societal power relations.

A second consideration is that the operation of these power relations will vary according to the context. Native speaker privilege will typically play out unproblematically for the native speakers in contexts where they represent the dominant group. But even here, complexities abound. In countries such as Brazil, Japan, and many others, economic imperatives fueled by the linguistic imperialism of English (Philipson 1992) dictate that so-called 'native speakers' of English (with the possible exception of Irish veterinarians . . .) are preferred as teachers of English over so-called non-native speakers, despite the total absence of empirical support for these policies with respect to student outcomes. In these contexts, native speakers of English are far from the dominant group, but they are favoured over competent 'non-native' teachers from the dominant group as a result of a range of discredited misconceptions that are documented in the preceding chapters.

A third consideration is that the terminological challenges faced by the native speaker construct are by no means unique. They parallel ongoing debates about what to call or how to label (a) school-age (K-12) students who are learning the language(s) of schooling (e.g., minority language students, immigrant students, *allophones* [in French], etc.), (b) immigrant-background individuals and communities (e.g., migrants, New Canadians, visible minorities, etc.) and (c) languages other than the official, national, or official languages in a country (heritage languages, community languages, ancestral languages, international languages, *langues d'origines*, etc.). All of these terminological options position minoritized individuals and communities in relation to the dominant societal group(s) and are consequently entangled in patterns of societal power relations. Terminological fashion is dynamic and constantly changing as a result of the fact that these relative positionings are contested by groups and individuals. The definitions of particular constructs suggested by researchers (and frequently reflected in dictionary definitions) do not stay still – they migrate across discourse communities, absorb connotations through varied use in different contexts, and frequently collapse as coherent constructs under the weight of excess baggage.

Thus, I see nothing *inherently* problematic for me to say that I am a native speaker of English, meaning that English is the first language I learned in my home in my early years. This statement says nothing about my current competence in various aspects of English as compared to other languages, my identity affiliation to English as compared to other languages, or my relative competence to teach English as compared to so-called non-native speakers of English. But as pointed out by the editors of this book in their Introductory chapter and by the authors of other chapters, these connotations of the term are all in the public realm and far beyond the capacity of researchers to control. When the use of the term 'native speaker' is extended into discourse realms where it is used as a contrast to 'non-native speaker', the likelihood of a hierarchical relationship between these constructs increases dramatically (as in the case of the hiring of teachers of English in many contexts).

So where do we go from here? As I mentioned, researchers can't directly control how terms are used in the world outside of scholarly discourse or the ideological baggage that these terms accumulate. However, we can at least try to get our own house in order by agreeing on the contexts where a term like 'native speaker' might be potentially acceptable and innocent of pushing the diminished construct of 'non-native speaker' to the base of social hierarchies. We can also explore alternatives that might avoid or shed the extraneous baggage that has accrued to the native speaker construct (as discussed by Dewaele, Bak and Ortega, this volume).

This process can be illustrated by the terminological migration over the past 50 years of labels employed to categorize students from immigrant backgrounds who are learning the language of instruction. Terms commonly used in official policies to refer to students such as 'English-as-a-second-language' (ESL), 'English-as-an-additional-language' (EAL), 'English-as-a-new-language' (ENL), 'English language learners' (ELL), and 'long-term English learners' (LTEL), are often seen as problematic because they define students only in terms of what they lack, namely adequate proficiency in English to achieve academically without additional instructional support. The term 'non-native speaker' similarly defines teachers or students by what they lack in comparison to 'native speakers'. To counter this connotation, some scholars (e.g. García, 2009) have used terms such as 'emergent bilingual' to highlight the linguistic accomplishments of students rather than their presumed linguistic limitations. The terms 'bilingual' and 'multilingual' embody the same intention.

None of these terms is completely accurate in all contexts. For example, 'emergent bilingual' does not account for the fact that in many contexts students who arrive at school largely monolingual in their home language lose much of their fluency in that language over the course of schooling and often leave school with much less fluency in their home language than in the dominant school language. Similarly, the terms 'bilingual' and 'multilingual' do not capture the reality of many language learners in the very early stages of learning the school language when they may be largely monolingual in their home language. It is also important to note that many children growing up in multilingual social contexts around the world come to school essentially as simultaneous bi/multilinguals with knowledge of two or more languages differentiated by their domains of acquisition (e.g. home, neighborhood/playground, daycare/preschool, etc.). The seemingly straightforward term 'home language' also embodies multiple complexities depending on how many languages are spoken in the home and the dynamic patterns of interactions among family members. Thus, no one term or set of terms captures the complex reality of the diverse array of acquisition contexts experienced by multilingual children and students.

However, despite these challenges, progress has been made. For example, the term *multilingual language learner* (MLL) is currently used in the state of Connecticut to refer to students who are speakers of various languages in their homes and are learning the language of instruction (English) in school. This term is accurate, asset-based, and avoids most of the problematic connotations of previous labels. If we were to extend the scope of this terminological initiative to the NS/NNS debate, we might come up with a number of contextually specific variants that go some way to providing labels for phenomena that we need to talk about while avoiding the implicit devaluation inherent in terms such as non-native speaker.

For example, in the context of schooling we might distinguish *native speakers of the school language* (NSSL) from *multilingual learners of the school language*

(MLSL). The rationale for making this distinction would be to identify students who may benefit from additional instructional support in order to succeed academically. The distinction would also serve to highlight the linguistic accomplishments of students who may speak multiple languages.

For any other distinctions that parallel the NS/NNS dichotomy, it would be necessary to advance a coherent rationale for making the distinction. For example, in the context of teaching in an English language school in Brazil, Japan, or some other country, is there any rationale for distinguishing between *native speaking teachers of the school language* and *multilingual teachers of the school language*? I don't think so; furthermore, to make such a distinction automatically implies that there is some difference in the quality of instruction that these two 'types' of speakers are capable of delivering, with 'native speakers' presumed to be superior. In a more general societal context, there may be some rationale (e.g., census purposes) for distinguishing between *monolingual speakers of the societal language* (MoSSL) and *multilingual speakers of the societal language* (MuSSL). However, in this case, the valorization is clearly weighted towards citizens who are more linguistically accomplished in comparison to their monolingual compatriots.

In conclusion, I believe that applied linguists can take the lead initially in getting our own house in order so that the distinctions we make are asset-based and do not contribute to social inequality and devaluation of identities in the way that the NS/NNS dichotomy has done. This process involves articulating a clear and coherent rationale for the distinctions that are proposed and also carefully considering any potential 'collateral damage' that might be generated unintentionally by these distinctions. When we have our own house in order, then we can pursue the more daunting task of identifying and challenging inequitable social hierarchies associated with language use in the wider society. This book represents a major step in that direction.

References

García, Ofelia. 2009. *Bilingual education in the 21st century. A global perspective*. Boston: Basil Blackwell.
Phillipson, Robert. 1992. *Linguistic Imperialism*. Oxford: Oxford University Press.
The Guardian. 8 August, 2017. Computer says no: Irish vet fails oral English test needed to stay in Australia. https://www.theguardian.com/australia-news/2017/aug/08/computer-says-no-irish-vet-fails-oral-english-test-needed-to-stay-in-australia#:~:text=An (accessed 25 May 2021).

Index

adoption, international adoption 28–29, 134
agency 16, 32, 133, 136, 140, 217
attrition, language attrition 36, 163, 296
assimilation 29, 90, 138, 143, 149, 234–235, 237–238
authenticity 15, 26, 72, 79, 180, 238, 244

benchmark 36, 48, 54, 62
bilingual, bilingualism 6, 11, 35–36, 122, 149, 159–160, 211–212, 237, 285–293, 328
– bilingual infidelity 237

codeswitching 83, 84, 211–214
colonial, colonialist, colonialism 9, 72–76, 81, 93, 247, 253, 276, 292
cultural chauvinism 53

decolonial 33
deficit view 25, 34
discourse 133, 210, 285, 320
discrimination, discriminatory 6, 16, 25, 31–32, 149, 291, 340, 347
dominant language constellation 6, 59
dynamic and complex systems theory, DSCT 9, 47
dynamic model of multilingualism (see multilingualism)

enunciative space 179, 190
equity, equality, equitable 2, 10, 25, 32, 39, 107, 113, 181, 247, 286, 293, 328, 352
erasure 247, 286, 290, 299–304
ethnocentrism 104, 106
exolingual, exolingual situation 109–112,

globalization 1, 156, 242, 317, 328
glotopolitical hierarchies 248

heritage
– language (see also home language) 28, 58, 142, 156 (all the chapter)
– speaker 156 (all the chapter), 235

hybrid, hybridization, hybridity 6, 49, 74, 94, 136, 219, 245, 247

iconization 290, 298, 299, 321, 328
ideology 25, 31, 49, 55, 146, 149, 187, 259, 291, 296, 305, 315, 320, 327
– language ideology (see also language representations) 14, 237, 261, 287
– linguistic ideology 321
– monolingual ideology 201, 238
– native-speaker ideology 1, 341
– racist ideology 25
identity 179, 285
– identity construction 141–148
imagined communities 136, 285, 290–291, 296, 322
immersion 56, 80, 185, 290 (all the chapter)
individual multilingualism (see multilingualism)
inequality, injustice (see also equity, equality, equitable) 38, 124
intercomprehension 209 (all the chapter)
interpretative framework 1

L1/LX user 26 (all the chapter), 60
language
– dominant language 28, 55, 59, 80, 156, 157, 201, 212, 240, 246, 264, 319, 328
– first language 3, 6, 29, 35, 50, 73, 83, 106, 115, 117, 124, 134, 144, 155, 182, 239, 241, 254, 256, 266, 316, 324, 327–328, 338, 350
– foreign language 9, 26, 57, 75, 144, 156, 171, 182, 210, 216, 243, 246, 253, 259, 339
– home language (see also heritage language) 4, 14, 156, 188–189, 202, 243, 263, 316, 322–328, 338, 351
– minority language 30, 55–56, 71, 77–80, 93, 146, 200, 288, 293, 350
– mother language 28, 134
– named languages 149, 222, 226
– preferred language 4, 194

https://doi.org/10.1515/9781501512353-015

- reference language 215
- second language 31, 35, 37, 52, 57, 206, 259, 287, 236
- strongest language 326, 339
- target language 37, 56, 61, 216, 222, 285, 306–307
language background profiling 314–342
language domains 56, 233
language family 210 (all the chapter)
language ideological debates 285
language portraits, self-portraits 320, 331
language user 25, 33, 36, 38
language representations (see also language ideology) 103, 189
language transmission 156
lingua franca 26, 53
languaging 49, 109, 213, 233, 236, 239, 241, 247
linguistic
- linguistic appropriation 84
- linguistic border(s) 209, 210, 218, 222, 225, 296
- linguistic / language biography 107, 123, 179, 183, 215, 223
- linguistic construct 9, 50
- linguistic identity 86, 199, 224, 285, 290, 304
- linguistic resources 7, 49, 64, 183, 212, 227
literacy 155 (all the chapter), 203, 296, 319, 330–331

migration 29, 58, 74, 80, 92, 109, 124, 156, 188, 191, 201, 238, 317, 318
modernity 73, 80, 256
monoglossic 11, 59, 217, 226
monolingual, monolingualism
- paralel monolingualisms 209
mother tongue 9, 27–30, 74, 106, 114–115, 133–137, 158, 171, 181, 218, 220, 233 (all the chapter), 254, 267–268, 286, 320, 323, 332
muda, linguistic mudes 84
multicompetence 2, 34, 55, 62, 184
- multicompetent language user 47, 58, 63
- multicompetent speaker 171, 211

multilingual
- multilingual communication 209 (all the chapter)
- multilingual interaction 209 (all the chapter)
- multilingual repertoire 211, 318
- multilingual turn 1, 3, 4, 11, 39
multilingualism 1, 6, 35, 52, 89, 134, 183, 238, 244, 248, 316–318
- dynamic model of multilingualism 51, 60
- individual multilingualism 1, 182
- societal multilingualism 1, 266, 337
myth, native speaker myth 49, 180

nation, nation-state 3, 49, 89, 136, 233 (all the chapter), 291, 328
nationalist, nationalism 9, 73–74, 8, 90, 136, 237
national identity construction 133 (all the chapter)
native
- digital natives 63–65
- native language 6, 28, 30, 50, 106, 136, 156, 195, 240, 254, 259–260, 316
- native speaker particularly: Introduction and chapters 1, 2, 4, 5
- native speaker norm 52–53, 162
- new native speaker 63–64
- non-native speaker 3, 7, 33–37, 50, 71 (all the chapter), 111, 124, 126, 180, 214, 254, 259–263, 319, 349
nativeness 9, 47, 50, 55, 60, 62–64, 117, 124, 160, 243, 264
native-speakerism 11, 30–33, 54–58, 261
naturalize, naturalization 147, 240
(neo)racism 32, 33, 55, 75, 347
- (neo)racist ideology (see ideology)
new speakers 71 (all the chapter)
norm, language norm 37, 49, 52–53, 58, 106–107, 202, 262, 268, 275, 328

other, otherness 12, 50, 75, 77, 92, 201
ownership 218, 253, 256, 260, 268

parents 139, 158–159, 189, 234, 240, 262, 265, 296, 300–307

personal narratives 233 (and all the chapter)
pluralistic approaches to languages 104, 125
pluricentricity, pluricentric 156, 253
plurilingualism 1, 6, 10, 108, 117, 118, 125, 181, 183, 184, 188–189, 182, 211
plurilingual
– being plurilingual 211–214
– plurilingual identity 183–184, 192–195
– plurilingual self 212, 214, 315
– plurilingual strategies 218
policy makers 249, 316
post-colonial, non-colonial 11, 13, 245, 253, 255, 262, 328
postmodern 32–33
power 4, 27, 32, 39, 49, 53, 73, 75, 106, 114, 124, 182, 287, 198–200, 246, 259, 267, 288, 291–292, 247, 249
practice-proof concepts 209 (all the chapter)
privilege 5, 26, 50, 203, 220, 233, 235, 240, 261, 348, 349
proficiency 4, 34, 36, 50, 52, 54, 56–57, 60–62, 160–161, 182, 185, 211, 220, 261, 287, 294, 316, 318, 322, 339, 351

racism, (neo)racism 32, 33, 55, 75, 347
rap 120–121
recursivity 290, 299, 321
repertoire 208, 315, 318
– individual repertoire 216
– linguistic repertoire 1, 38, 59, 109, 201, 201, 211–217, 259, 318–319

– plurilingual repertoire 194, 196, 211–212, 214, 237
– semiotic repertoire 211, 215, 224
representation
– language representation 188
– social representation 179, 184

school registration forms 315
social construct 50–51, 183, 226–227
societal multilingualism (see multilingualism)
sociolinguistic reality 113, 126
stereotypes 15, 91, 188, 191, 220
subject, subjectivity 75, 88, 233

teacher
– multilingual teacher 352
– teacher as native speaker 4, 26, 29, 55–57, 251–252, 349
– teacher as non–native 4, 30–33, 55–57, 75, 347, 349
– teacher education/ training 2, 209, 215
theorethical perspectives 6
tintamarre 296, 300, 302
trademark 53–54
translanguaging 6, 59, 109, 111, 113, 124, 184, 209 (all the chapter), 245
transnational, transnationalism, translocal 235, 241, 290, 307, 317, 341
two solitudes 2, 328

Volksstimme 26

www.ingramcontent.com/pod-product-compliance
Lightning Source LLC
Chambersburg PA
CBHW071734150426
43191CB00010B/1572